what was the
nature of the
choice

Peters
Weikler

SPIRIT-WORD-COMMUNITY

Spirit-Word-Community:
Theological Hermeneutics
in Trinitarian Perspective

AMOS YONG

Wipf & Stock
PUBLISHERS
Eugene, Oregon

SPIRIT-WORD-COMMUNITY: THEOLOGICAL HERMENEUTICS
IN TRINITARIAN PERSPECTIVE

ISBN:1-59752-550-2

Manufactured in the U.S.A.

To

Robert Cummings Neville,

doktorvater and friend

Contents

Preface ix

Acknowledgements xiii

Introduction: On Theological Hermeneutics 1
and Theological Method

Part I: Foundational Pneumatology: Toward a 25
Trinitarian Theology and Metaphysics

1   Beginning with the Spirit: Biblical Motifs for a 27
    Foundational Pneumatology

2   Pneumatology and Trinitarian Theology 49

3   Toward a Foundational Pneumatology: 83
    Metaphysics and Ontology

Part II: The Pneumatological Imagination: 119
Epistemology in Triadic Perspective

4   The Imagination as Pneumatic Activity 123

5   The Pneumatological Imagination and 151
    Truthful Discernment

6   The Pneumatological Imagination and 185
    Normative Engagement

Part III: Theological Interpretation: The Trialectic 219
of Spirit-Word-Community

7   The Acts of Interpretation: Spirit 221

8   The Objects of Interpretation: Word 245

9   The Contexts of Interpretation: Community 275

Provisional Conclusions 311

Bibliography 317

Scripture Index 339

Name Index 343

Subject Index 349

Preface

My journey has taken me from the Pentecostalism of my upbringing to Evangelicalism to Orthodoxy, from charismaticism to biblicism to community, from the Spirit to the Son to the triune God. While my arrival to Orthodoxy is not (at least, not yet) in the formal ecclesial sense, yet I have begun to deeply appreciate its theological intuitions. It is certainly the case, however, that the third moment does not leave behind but includes the other two with much of their particularities. As such, my Orthodox orientation needs to be understood not over-and-against but alongside both my evangelical commitments and my pentecostal affections and experiences. The same thing should be said of my communal vision and my trinitarian theology, that they do not presume to sublate either the Spirit or the Word. In one sense, then, the theological method in this book may be interpreted as a "homecoming" (of sorts) to Orthodox faith. On the other hand, sensitive readers will notice that its deep structures and guiding motifs, as pneumatologically driven, are profoundly pentecostal. Does this volume therefore present what might be called a pentecostal theological hermeneutic and method? What about the evangelical convictions, and the Orthodox leaven? The title, *Spirit-Word-Community*, signifies the indispensability of all three moments to the theological task, not the dominance of the first, nor the triumph of the third.

The influence of my *doktorvater*, Robert Cummings Neville, can be clearly seen in the pages of this book. His architectonic mind has challenged me to think things through systematically. The inspiration for the arrangement of this book comes in part from the splendor of his own project in systematic philosophy, the three volumed *Axiology of Thinking*, even as specific elements of his metaphysical vision seem to me to make eminent sense. However, his attraction to a quadratic framework, derived from Plato's "Divided Line" (in the *Republic*, Book 6), has been "reduced" one notch in this volume to a triadic structure. I am certainly not suggesting that triads have greater explanatory power than quads. Perhaps the difference may stem from his thinking philosophically (and therefore with Plato, since, as Whitehead remarked, the history of Western philosophy may consist of nothing more than footnotes to Plato), and my working theologically (and therefore within a trinitarian framework). Alternatively, the difference may also reflect my being overwhelmed at the prospect of thinking systematically in quads instead of triads since the former move involves not simply the "addition" of any one thing to the existing framework, but rather the (exponential) multiplication of ideas and their implications across a four-trajectoried system. My dedicating this book to Dean Neville therefore means only that this student continues to learn from his mentor, and aspires to one day do theology as he does both theology and philosophy: in a global context.

During this time of completing my doctoral program (1996–1998), the community of Christians with whom I worked and worshipped, New Beginnings Christian Fellowship in Mansfield, Massachusetts, supported and encouraged me in every way, thus enabling me to chew on and enjoy the intellectual feast of graduate study. The mission of the congregation was and remains, "Transforming Lives by Word and Spirit in Christian Community." It was during my sojourn in Mansfield that I first conceived of the title for this book.

My dissertation, now published as *Discerning the Spirit(s): A Pentecostal-Charismatic Contribution to Christian Theology of Religions* (Sheffield Academic Press, 2000), made some preliminary forays into the question of theological method. These ideas have also been developed over the years in published essays and conference presentations. Frank Macchia encouraged me to turn these various pieces into a book. Jim Shelton helped me to see through the problem of both christological or pneumatological subordination, and gave me the language of "mutual subordination" regarding Christ and the Spirit, thus opening up toward a "trinitarian subordination of mutuality." Stanley Grenz provided encouragement in the early stages of this project, and recommended publication of my proposal to Ashgate. His writings have also pushed me "towards the center."

Rev. Dr. Dennis W. Cheek, also pastor of New Beginnings in Mansfield, has been supportive of my work since we met in 1996, and provided feedback and comments on portions of the manuscript. Clark Pinnock has encouraged me over the years as well, and has done so again with this book. I am grateful to Dale Coulter for reading the section on Richard of St. Victor. Simon Chan and James K. A. Smith read my original introductory chapter; both then turned around and gave me feedback on various sections of the manuscript: Simon on Part One, and Jamie especially on the introductory chapter (again), and on Part Two. I am especially indebted to Bradford Hinze who did yeoman's labor in reading through and commenting in detail on the manuscript as a whole, as well as pointing me to important sources relevant to aspects of my argument. His willingness to help me improve my argument is an example of selfless Christian collegiality since his own project dovetails in part with my own, and the appearance of this book no doubt preempts his contribution. The book is vastly superior to what it would have been without all of this input. If theological work is accomplished communally, then I have been providentially blessed with these friends and colleagues (and many others who are not named here, while some of you will see your work referenced in the pages which follow), and any contribution this volume makes to advancing its topic is as much a credit to them as to my own efforts. Nevertheless, as stubborn and fallible as I am, errors of fact and interpretation remain for which I am solely responsible.

Thanks to the Administration of Bethel College for encouraging scholarship and for providing the necessary funding to finish this project. I am also grateful to Betty Bond and her interlibrary loan staff at Bethel College for all of their assistance in feeding my sometimes voracious appetite for books. The Bethel Alumni Association provided a research grant during the summer of 2001 for assistance with this book. Special thanks are due to Chelsea DeArmond for her painstaking work of copy editing the manuscript and typesetting it in camera-ready form for Ashgate. Sarah Lloyd's professionalism eased the technical process of publication. Her response halfway through this project that I was already way over the word limits for volumes in this New Critical Thinking in Theology and Biblical Studies series meant that I had to cut out two chapters from the originally proposed volume. One of them would have been a proposed test case of the method prescribed in this volume with regard to Christian theology of religions. Those interested in the details of that chapter can consult my forthcoming *Beyond the Impasse: Toward a Pneumatological Theology of Religions* (Baker Academic, 2002).

My wife, Alma, has been a continual source of encouragement, inspiration, and support. In bearing patiently with my reading and writing, she is also partially responsible for the birth of this book. Words cannot express my gratitude for her love. She has been the quintessential wife and mother. The community of children that she has nurtured in the Word through the Spirit have been a constant source of joy and reminder that theological reflection proceeds not in an ivory tower but in a real world. Aizaiah, perhaps dad can now return to the basketball court with you and, in the process, cheer you on to fulfilling all of your life's dreams as you are led by the Spirit. Alyssa, may the Spirit continue blow her creative winds upon your literary and artistic imagination. Annalisa, your deferring attitude anticipates those great accomplishments which follow those who by the power of the Spirit always seek the best for others.

Crystal, Minnesota
Epiphany 2002

Acknowledgments

Portions of chapter three appeared in another form in "On Divine Presence and Divine Agency: Toward a Foundational Pneumatology," *Asian Journal of Pentecostal Studies* 3, 2 (July 2000): 167–88. Section one of chapter five was previously published in part one of "The Demise of Foundationalism and the Retention of Truth: What Evangelicals Can Learn from C. S. Peirce," *Christian Scholar's Review* 29, 3 (Spring 2000): 563–88. Segments of my reviews of Daniel Albrecht, *Rites of the Spirit: A Ritual Approach to Pentecostal-Charismatic Spirituality*, in *The Pneuma Review*, 4, 1 (2001): 60–62, Matthias Wenk, *Community-Forming Power: The Socio-Ethical Role of the Spirit in Luke-Acts*, in *The Pneuma Review*, 4, 2 (2001): 70–73, and Stanley Grenz and John Franke, *Beyond Foundationalism: Shaping Theology in a Postmodern Context*, in *Evangelical Review of Theology*, 26, 2 (2002): 181–84, have been incorporated into the book. My thanks go to the editors and publishers of these journals for permission to use and revise previously published material. Unless otherwise noted, the scriptural quotations contained herein are from The New Revised Standard Version Bible, copyright © 1989 by the Division of Christian Education of the National Council of the Churches of Christ in the U.S.A., and are used by permission. All rights reserved.

Introduction:
On Theological Hermeneutics
and Theological Method

It is arguable that Christian theology as an academic discipline is as vigorous and vibrant now at the beginning of the twenty-first century as it has ever been. Theology is now a global conversation that is rethinking old questions even while engaging new ones. One of the more ancient notions currently experiencing revival and renaissance is trinitarian theology. Another which is re-emerging, albeit along wholly uncharted directions, is the whole topic of pneumatology. And, in recent decades, somewhat new questions regarding theological method and theological hermeneutics have begun to permeate Christian theological discourse and reflection.

This said, one wonders about the need for another book on any of these topics. Stephen Sykes' comment that "there has never been one, single, universally agreed methodology for solving the inherent conflicts of Christianity, and we have every reason to suppose that there never will be" (1984, 264) applies just as well to theological hermeneutics and theological method. I am encouraged to believe, however, that the ideas present here contribute to each of these areas of theological inquiry. While my aim, succinctly stated, is to develop a trinitarian theological hermeneutic and method from a pneumatological starting point, I anticipate that the result will be less an altogether novel contribution and more of what might be called a mediating or "consensual hermeneutic" (cf. Kärkkäinen 2001, 152). Consensuality is important and sought precisely because of the innumerable and continuously multiplying proposals in each of these areas. One of the tasks envisioned here, then, is the bringing together of diverse voices into a more or less unified but yet exploratory framework. For these reasons, the following is offered in the form of an essay in mediating theology that attempts to draw from across the spectrum of Christian traditions. More important, in contrast to a thesis that argues toward a solution, an essay is a more open-ended means of inquiry into a topic in the hopes of being suggestive for resolving at least some of the problems therein. These pages propose just such an approach, but do so by way of a speculative hypothesis that engages, complements, and perhaps even sup- plements the existing theological reflections on these topics. It is driven by the conviction that consensus can be found only through engaging the particular- ities and differences which underwrite the beliefs and practices of the wide variety of Christian communities, and not apart from them.

As such, three interrelated theses are involved which together serve as an attempt to bring together the latest theological developments. First, with re- gard to the overarching objective, I will exhibit the convergence of theological method and theological hermeneutics insofar as the latter is reconceived in a robustly trinitarian sense. Second, I suggest that this task of reconception is best accomplished through the categories inspired by pneumatology. This in- volves showing, third, how the pneumatological categories are inherently tri- adic, at once being metaphysical, epistemological, and hermeneutical, thus undergirding both a trinitarian theological method and a hermeneutical the- ology that are mutually informing. The following introduces each of these elements which are then developed in the remainder of this theological essay.

Theological Hermeneutics and Theological Method

I advance in this book a theological hermeneutic sufficiently wide-ranging so as to be indistinguishable from a viable theological method. The former con- cerns the activity of interpretation for explicitly theological purposes, while the latter concerns the fundamental question of how one goes about doing theology. While clearly and traditionally distinct in theological literature and understanding, as developed here, hermeneutics involves methodology and vice versa: one cannot interpret theologically without going about doing the- ology, and one cannot query about how to do theology without interpreta- tion. This, however, begs the former question, namely, What is theology?

Theology is one of any number of subjects that human minds ruminate or speculate on. As a product of reflection on the human situation, it is a strictly second-order affair that proceeds in abstraction from first-hand experience. Recognizing the ambiguity around the notion of experience, I am here simply distinguishing between theology as a cognitive enterprise from lived and per- ceived reality. It is crucial not to confuse to two, even if it is often difficult to demarcate where experience stops and where reflection begins. This said, a further distinction is important. On the one hand, the content of theology narrowly construed concerns the topics of divinity and of ultimate reality. On the other hand, theology broadly understood concerns the totality of God and God's relationship to human selves and the world understood from the perspective of faith.[1] Depending on which sense of theology is meant, a more or less appropriate hermeneutic and methodology recommends itself. In this book, I work with the wider notion of theology, one that assumes God is real as the creator and sustainer of this world, and that human selves perceive and experience such a God who is related to themselves and the world. Given this framework, I argue that only a robustly trinitarian hermeneutic and methodology suffices to engage the theological task.

But, to continue the process of clarification, what is a theological hermeneutic? Let me spell this out by clarifying what it is not. First, theological hermeneutics is not equivalent to either biblical or canonical hermeneutics. Biblical hermeneutics focuses explicitly on the rules and methods for interpreting Christian scripture. Its goal is exegesis—understanding the biblical text in its original contexts in order to render accurately its original meaning to the reader and reading community. Canonical hermeneutics focuses on interpreting the scriptures as Christian texts, gathered together by the Church and for the Church. Insofar as biblical scholars like Francis Watson (1993; 1994; 1997), hermeneuticians like Charles Scalise (1994; 1996) and narrative theologians like Hans Frei (1986; 1993) have re-emphasized the importance of biblical and canonical hermeneutics for the theological task, they have called attention to the ways which theological reflection has and should engage Scripture as text *and* as canon. My focus, however, lies explicitly on the hermeneutics of the divine (theological hermeneutics) rather than only on the hermeneutics of scripture (whether biblical or canonical). Contra Watson—who suggests that theological hermeneutics "exists only *within* the sphere of biblical theology" (1997, 13; italics orig.)—I argue that theological interpretation is not limited to Scripture in the former task, even if scriptural exegesis remains a necessary element. While I anticipate theorizing about biblical and canonical hermeneutics and applying both, my goals include neither commenting explicitly on

---

[1] What "faith" means could itself be debated. For the purposes of this book, doing Christian theology from a faith perspective simply means that I proceed as a believing Christian. This does not deny that one's faith perspective could be different—e.g., as a Muslim, or a Jew—or perhaps even not present with regard to the faith tradition in question. Examples of the latter might include the reflections of an agnostic on the God-question or that of Maimonides on Allah. Inevitably, however, such reflections would engage God or Allah as alleged to be phenomenologically expressed in the concrete rituals, doctrines, scriptures, practices, etc., of the world's religious traditions. In that sense, then, faith perspectives are rarely, if ever, completely absent from theological reflection.

the principles or science of biblical interpretation, nor developing theory of textual or canonical interpretation in general. In fact, I will argue that a hermeneutics of the divine that fails to properly account for the interpretation of the extra-Scriptural world will ultimately sabotage the theological task regardless of how polished one's biblical or canonical hermeneutics is. In short, biblical and canonical hermeneutics are only two aspects of theological hermeneutics, and perhaps not obviously the most important ones at that.

Second, theological hermeneutics is distinct from spiritual hermeneutics—the hermeneutics of the spiritual life—although they come close in a number of ways. The focus of a spiritual hermeneutics is on interpreting and understanding the spiritual quest. Its motivating questions are how one lives as a spiritual being, what spiritual exercises are, what are the goals of spiritual practice, how one undergoes spiritual formation and transformation, and so forth (cf. Chan 1998; Palmer, Sherrard, and Ware 1979–). The difference between theological hermeneutics and spiritual hermeneutics may be analogous to that between fundamental, systematic and practical theology. In the latter case, all three are distinct fields of theological inquiry, yet clearly interrelated. I will contend that one's theological hermeneutic will be proportionately viable or anemic to the same extent that one's spiritual hermeneutic is perspicacious or dull. In a word, a robust theological hermeneutics includes a penetrating spiritual hermeneutic, and developing the latter is crucial for the theological task.

Third, it is valid to ask at this point about how theological hermeneutics differs from hermeneutics in general. On my account, the difference is a material one in that a theological hermeneutic includes God in an explicitly intentional sense. Certainly it should be recognized that a general or philosophical hermeneutic may or may not offer an account of engaging, interpreting or understanding divinity insofar as it is neither motivated first and foremost by the God-question nor committed in an a priori sense to the "existence" or reality of God. On the other side, it is also the case that philosophy raises metaphysical and ontological questions in such a way so as to often tread in the waters of theology. It is important here to acknowledge the legitimate autonomy of both disciplines even while recognizing their interdependence. Only in this way can we steer a via media between either subordinating theology to philosophy or vice-versa. Those guilty of the former—perhaps philosophers like Heidegger and Gadamer—struggle mightily to overcome the constrictions which the traditions of philosophical discourse impose on theological reflection. Those guilty of the latter (subordinating philosophy to theology) suffer from the reverse problem. Kevin Vanhoozer's claim that all hermeneutics is theological (1997, 160), for example, builds on the conviction that all interpretation assumes theological notions like human fallenness and the resulting epistemic dissonance; it requires theological virtues like faith, hope, and love in order to fulfill its task; it brings the "other" (of the text) closer to the interpreter in an empathetic or reconciling sense, etc. This is all true. But to say that all hermeneutics is theological in this sense makes it difficult to maintain any distinction between implicit and explicit theological intentionality. Further, if all hermeneutics is theological, then no hermeneutics is theological since hermeneutics itself is trivialized and swallowed up by theology without remainder. In this case one might as well cease talking about hermeneutics and talk only about theology.

My focus, then, is intentionally on theological hermeneutics. Yet despite what has already been said about hermeneutics in general and biblical hermeneutics in particular, the notion of theological hermeneutics is still somewhat difficult to define. Perhaps this is because traditionally, even theologians (in contrast to biblical scholars) who have discussed theological hermeneutics have understood it as indistinct from biblical hermeneutics, with the additional goal of doctrinal formulation or theological understanding. Thus, the discussion of theological hermeneutics has inevitably focused, at least until recently, on bridging the gap between the sources of theology—Scripture, the biblical and interpretive traditions, etc.—and the context wherein theology is done (e.g., Jeanrond 1988; 1991). Certainly, the predominantly textual focus of theological hermeneutics cannot be denied. Charles Wood makes the point clearly: "theological hermeneutics is…a reflection upon the aims and conditions of what may be called the 'Christian understanding' of Christian scripture and tradition" (1993, 21). As such, theological hermeneuticians have assumed—or at least implied to the reader—that the problem lies primarily on the side of the text or object of interpretation. But in reality, the side of the reader or interpreter is equally problematic. However, since formulation of latter problem has been obscured, theological hermeneuticians have generally neglected questions that concern interpreting both the interpreter and the world of the interpreter. Those who have inquired into these latter issues have had other considerations that are not strictly theological in mind, whether that be about the hermeneutical dilemma in general or homiletic concerns more specifically.[2]

---

[2] With regard to the hermeneutical in general, the English philosopher of history, R. G. Collingwood, recognized the need for what he called "historical imagination" in "re-enacting" a historical text or object of study for contemporary understanding and relevance. John P. Hogan (1989) has inquired about the theological implications of Collingwood's hermeneutical project,

I will argue that a hermeneutic that is theological in the broadest sense of that term is much more comprehensive than the kind of "science of interpretation" normally discussed in books devoted to the subject of theological hermeneutics. These latter have focused on reading and interpreting texts—in most cases, for Christians, the Bible. Recalling the definition of theology presented earlier, I submit that a robustly theological hermeneutic is one that aims at interpreting the totality of human experience—and that includes God and God's relationships with human selves and the world as a whole—from a perspective that is specifically and explicitly informed by faith. Thus even Werner Jeanrond, who focused his own project in theological hermeneutics on the problematic of the text, concludes that

> hermeneutical thinking may be able to make the theologian more sensitive towards the need to engage in a world-wide conversation on all aspects of the human search for meaning in this universe….Thus a proper hermeneutical training may very well be an appropriate starting-point for any journey towards a more adequate understanding of God, the human self and the mystery of our being in this world. (1991, 182)

Jeanrond's conclusion is my starting-point. This includes not only hermeneutics specifically defined as interpreting a text or object at some historical distance, but also epistemology and metaphysics—defined as interpreting both interpreters themselves and the realities that interpreted objects and interpreters find themselves in. This broad inquiry is crucial for a proper and holistic theological vision. Theologians need to be adept at interpreting texts, reading signs of various sorts, and discerning the *sign*-ificance of experiences and events in the world. Thus theological interpretation includes semiotics, broadly understood as the science and theory of signs, signification, meaning and communication. So far, however, much of the theological literature on semiotics has focused on biblical interpretation in order to uncover the structural codes between the text and the world of the text (e.g., Entrevernes Group, 1978). Theological semiotics, however, requires that the codes between text and the world of the text be correlated with the codes of the reader and the world of reader vis-à-vis the God-question. This is because theological meaning derives from the interpretation of the conjunction of all three "worlds": the text's, the reader's,

but his emphasis on the historical problematic to the neglect of the present and his focus on the interpretation of texts rather than reality itself means that he falls short of the robust theological hermeneutics I am attempting here.

and God's. The theological hermeneutic aimed for in this book therefore can be understood as proceeding from the perspective of faith toward a hermeneutics of reality as a whole.

At this point, one begins to see how theological hermeneutics verges with theological method. The latter concerns the scope, aims and sources of theological inquiry, and how theological inquiry commences and is sustained. Insofar as the theological hermeneutic here aims at interpreting and understanding from the perspective of faith not only the biblical text but also life and reality—the totality of God-self-world—it's scope is equivalent to that of a comprehensive theological method. I propose in what follows that the continuous interplay of Spirit, Word, and Community serves not only to clarify the hermeneutical activity of theological interpretation, but also to locate the sources of theological inquiry. For those like Gordon Kaufman who want to emphasize not the starting-point of theological method but its sustained movement "from preliminary to ultimate, from creatures to God" (1995, 2), I will argue that this trinitarian relationship of Spirit, Word and Community is also a movement—call it a hermeneutical trialectic—and that such movement is sustained insofar as it proceeds from a pneumatological starting-point. In order to see how this is the case, more needs to be said explicitly about the method and argument of this book.

A Pneumatological Starting-Point

My argument is situated within a pneumatological framework that might be said to derive from a *pneumatic* intuition. Pneumatological and pneumatic are not synonymous. As with the concept theology, it is important also to be clear that pneumatology is itself a second-order discourse about what Christians experience as the Holy Spirit. This experience can be understood in terms of a (perhaps ongoing) series of pneumatic encounters. In one sense, it is appropriate to say that this project proceeds from such pre-theoretical encounters with and experiences of the Spirit of God. Experience, however, is necessarily thematized for purposes of theological reflection and communication. I will therefore eschew, for the most part, references to "pneumatic" unless clearly discussing the experiential rather than theological aspect of "spirit."

This distinction itself serves as a point of entry to the ferment currently taking place in pneumatology (e.g., Lampe 1977; McIntyre 1997; Bloesch 2000). To be clear, this book is not strictly a biblical pneumatology, nor is it properly a discussion of pneumatology proper, especially as the latter has traditionally been delineated according to the categories of the person and work of the Holy Spirit. Certainly, I do interact with the recent work done in some of these areas. But my biblical exegesis and pneumatological reflections are structured toward the development of a systematic or holistic vision of interpretation. More specifically, I am interested in how pneumatology informs and relates to the "object" of theological knowledge, broadly considered, i.e., God-self-world. (God is certainly not an object, but our experience of God is thematized and in that sense, objectivized, for purposes of reflection, understanding, and communication.) Correlatively, the pneumatological inquiry to be conducted includes not only theological, but also epistemological (related to the self) and metaphysical (related to the world) trajectories. I wish to explore how pneumatology structures and relates to the world, to the knowing process, and, ultimately, to theological hermeneutics and method. Taken together, the wide-ranging and multifaceted character of this project means that it may be better understood as a thought experiment in hermeneutics and method from a pneumatological perspective. As such, it might be called a "pneumatology of quest."

The strategy adopted here therefore resonates in part with the recent revolution in theological method that commences the theological quest with the third article of the Creed rather than the second (e.g., Van Dusen 1958; Freyer 1982; Pinnock 1996; Dabney 1996). Certainly, this move is to be commended since the theological enterprise has been dominated traditionally by the symbol of the Word (or the Logos), resulting in part with a textually constructed theology (*theo-logia*) whereby emphasis is placed on the internal coherence of the Christian scheme of understanding rather than on the full correlation of the biblical text with the realities which the text reflects or points to. The former way of doing theology validates meaning via an intratextual method that cites agreed-upon authorities (cf. Farley 1982), but does not require the pursuit of the further question of truth in the extratextual sense. By way of contrast, I will maintain that a pneumatologically inspired research program cannot avoid taking the world into account theologically. This is because, as the title of this volume insists, a pneumatologically driven agenda does not—and indeed cannot—neglect the second theological moment of the Word, even if this second moment is neither the be-all nor end-all of the theological task. More specifically, whereas traditionally Spirit has been subsumed under Word, and whereas some might be led to believe that the recent turn to pneumatology in theological method frees the theological task from the constraints imposed by the particularity of the Word (in incarnation and the biblical canon, for example),

I hope to show that the pneumatological impulse includes the christological one and vice versa, with neither defining the other in a circular or exhaustive sense precisely because of the nature of pneumatology itself.

Why this is the case and how the case can be successfully argued relates to the trinitarian motif that permeates this work. I propose that a pneumatological approach to theology (in general and theological hermeneutics in particular) opens up toward a trinitarianism that is much more robust than that which has emerged to date from a christological starting point (cf. Buckley and Yeago 2001). The latter, especially as developed in the West, has resulted in pneumatology being not much more than an afterthought—an appendix regarding the "shy member of the Trinity," as it were—to christology and patrology. A pneumatological starting point, however, is both christological and patrological—the Spirit being the Spirit of Christ and the Spirit of the Father simultaneously—but in different respects. This difference stems from the fact that while the Spirit is related to the Son and to the Father, it is a dual relationship with different theological implications. Pneumatology therefore insists on a vigorous trinitarianism in a way that christology which draws attention to the Father-Son relationship does not.   *The Spirit of the Fall - a theological view of Sin and its Consequence*

The centrality of the trinitarian motif to this book should not be underestimated. Of course, others have attempted various formulations of a trinitarian hermeneutics. James A. Sanders' *triangle* hermeneutic (1984, 77–78; 1987, 87–105) is a textual-canonical model of interpretation that includes three interrelated moments of discernment: that of the text and the interpreter's context (at the two corner bases of the triangle), and that of the hermeneutical strategies employed by the interpreter and his or her community on the text (at the top of the triangle). Sanders project is parallel in many ways to my own, except that I provide a metaphysics and epistemology to match the hermeneutical vision. Charles Dickinson (1999) proposes a "triple dialectic" between constructive theology and scriptural exegesis; between biblical study and the arts and humanities; and, finally, between constructive theology and the full range of academic disciplines including the sciences. Francis Watson discusses a trinitarian hermeneutic in the context of the early church's christological confessions (1994, 241–64, esp. 255), and R. W. L. Moberly proposes the principle of interpreting the Bible theologically according to a "trinitarian rule of faith" (2000, 232–37). However, what Watson describes is how a proper reading of the Christ-event arrives at a trinitarian theology. He does not discuss how the doctrine of the Trinity either structures or informs hermeneutical reflection. Moberly begins to do the latter, but his discussion is only programmatic.

Anthony Thiselton mentions the "triadic relation between the Other, the self, and a content that emerges from the dialogue and from the self-transformation or self-transcendence that results from it" (1999, 133), but does not develop this point further. Mention should also be made of Francis Schüssler Fiorenza's (1984) foundational hermeneutics that includes the three distinct and yet essentially interrelated elements of hermeneutical reconstruction, retroductive warrants, and background theories[3]; Ormond Rush's (1997) hermeneutical triad, formulated in dialogue with Hans Robert Jauss' reception aesthetics, featuring understanding (the experience of faith), interpretation (of the Scriptural and traditional questions and answers, themselves interpretations) and application (of originary faith to new contexts); and James Callahan's (2001) argument for a triadic notion of Scripture which includes its contextuality (the text in its original context), intertextuality (the canonical shape of the text), and intratextuality (the text in relationship to readers across space-time).

What is missing from each of these otherwise valuable contributions is a robust pneumatology to sustain the triadic movement. This is precisely the lacuna that is detected in the recent triadic methodologies proposed by Kevin Vanhoozer and by Stanley Grenz and John Franke. The former's *Is There a Meaning in This Text? The Bible, the Reader, and the Morality of Literary Knowledge* (Vanhoozer 1998) displays a fairly substantive triadic structure involving an interrelated complex of motifs: author–text–reader; metaphysics–epistemology–ethics; hermeneutic realism–hermeneutic rationality–hermeneutic responsibility; locution–illocution–perlocution; creation–incarnation/revelation–sanctification; Father–Son–Spirit. Yet the framework of Vanhoozer's trinitarian hermeneutic is constrained by his arguments against post-structuralism and deconstructionism. Since his goal is to develop a chastened hermeneutic that nevertheless takes seriously the normative claims that texts—specifically the biblical text—lay on readers, his energies are therefore directed toward establishing the reality of textual meaning as intentionally delivered through the communicative actions of their authors (cf. Iseminger 1992). The ethical reading of any text is therefore measured by how well it preserves the integrity of the author's communicative intent. So far, all is well and good. But to secure the claim that the meaning of any text is grounded in the author's intentional communicative act is only part of the problem in theological method. The other part includes, at least, accessing that meaning, and determining the ongoing significance(s) of that meaning for later times. Insofar as Vanhoozer's focus is on the author and the product

[3] In a later work, Fiorenza adds a fourth element: that of the ecclesial community (1991, 70–84).

via the Spirit,

[handwritten: What's wrong w/ that. The author had the initial insight? /a jump - conclusory?]

of the author's communicative activity (the text), he only belatedly speaks about the reader's role (1998, ch. 7) and other related aspects of the theological task. Doing so privileges the author over the reader, and the interpretation of texts over the interpretation of the totality of God-self-world. The result makes possible good biblical exegesis, certainly central but by no means the end of the theological endeavor. If I am correct to say that theological hermeneutics is, at least in part, an interpretation of the revelation of God for the interpreter's situation, then it is always and already at least a triad of readers- and doers-of-texts-within-communities. In that case, rather than diminishing Vanhoozer's accomplishment, the present volume aims to supplement his emphasis on the Logos (the objectivity of the text) with emphases on Spirit (the subjectivity of the readers and doers) and Community (the contextuality of theological reflection), with the hopeful result of sustaining a robustly trinitarian theological hermeneutic and theological method.

In the case of Grenz and Franke's *Beyond Foundationalism* (2001), there are, in fact, two triads central to doing theology in the postmodern world: that of Scripture (as norming norm), tradition (the interpretive trajectory), and culture (the embedded context); and, that of Trinity (the structural motif), community (the integrative motif), and eschatology (the orienting motif). They are finally unclear, however, about the role of the Holy Spirit in theological method. Yes, the Spirit does appear at key places throughout their discussion of theology's sources, whether that be as the formative power of the world through the Scriptures, as the authority behind both Scripture and tradition, or as the power through whom culturally embedded Christians live faithfully in but not of the world. But if in fact, as Grenz and Franke maintain, the Bible is never read in a vacuum, and that it both comes already culturally embedded and is engaged by readers and communities who are similarly culturally located; if in fact gospel and culture are always already interacting rather than two terms which need to be correlated a la Niebuhr or Tillich; and if in fact the Spirit speaks through Scripture, tradition, and culture; then how does the Spirit enable the truthful and critical reading of the Scriptures in such a way so that discernment of the ideological forces which are at work in all cultural constructions can occur? At the practical level, what gives one Christian community the right to say that its reading of the Scriptures is inspired of the Spirit over and against that of other Christian communities with whom they disagree? While the trinitarian vision is impressive, the pneumatological component needs development.

[handwritten: Consensus - pray + fast.]

Similar questions can be posed regarding the most promising methodologies

[handwritten: bk of Original Monotheism and its implications ⇒ There are cultural pieces to the picture which God through which God reveals himself.]

in the current theological landscape, and this because they proceed from the dialectical tension intrinsic to dualistic (dyadic rather than triadic) assumptions. Gordon Kaufman's theological method, for example, explicitly consists of three logical (rather than chronological) moments: the first which moves from experience to constructing a concept of the world; the second which moves to relativize the world-concept through a generation of a God-concept; and the third which returns to re-engage the world in light of the God-concept (Kaufman 1995, 51–86). Yet Kaufman himself admits in the new Preface to his book that the real engine that drives the method he proposes is the dialectic between faith and the imagination, a dialectic that inheres throughout the various moments. His dialectical movement thus resembles Tillich's method of correlation between the situation and revelation, Rahner's neo-Thomistic account of nature and grace and transcendental method, and Pannenberg's historico-eschatological hermeneutic and anthropological-theological method. Yet in each of these cases, however, two recurrent questions threaten to undermine the viability of the proposed method. On the one hand, at various moments, one side of the dialectic imposes its authority over the other side resulting in the subordination of the latter and the breakdown of the dialectic. Kaufman privileges the imagination in his proposal, thus inevitably overpowering the dictates of faith, while Rahner, as another example, consistently retains the logical priority of grace within an a priori dogmatic framework. On the other side, whether it be philosophy and theology, nature and grace, or from-below and from-above, the question will always persist of how to bridge the two insofar as the tension that stretches the dialectic finds no suitable mediation. Pannenberg's movement from a hermeneutic of history to a hermeneutic of science, both of which are strenuous efforts to discern the presence of the divine in the world, has not answered critics' questions about how his from-below, *a posteriori* method, is able to properly account for revelation.

In Tillich's case, while the correlation between theology and philosophy stands out, the method itself is focused on correlation in its broadest terms: between religion and culture, between question and answer, and between form and content (cf. Clayton 1980). However, Tillich's attempt to protect the autonomy of Christian faith led him to exempt the content of Christian theology from cultural assimilation. The result was the lack of a genuine reciprocity between the two terms to be correlated. Therefore, a truly dialectical encounter between religion and culture was prevented from occurring in Tillich's system. Tillich himself recognized this while writing volume three of the *Systematic Theology*, and lamented that "…the system crumbles…" (qtd. in Lai 1994, 116).

One senses that he recognized the movement to pneumatology in volume three of his *Systematic Theology* pointed a way forward from his method of correlation, but various factors mitigated against his rethinking these implications from the ground up.[4]

This criticism pertains also to those who have built on the work of Tillich and Pannenberg, and precisely for the same reason. David Tracy's (1975 and 1981) revision of Tillich's method of correlation in a genuinely two-way direction—the situation and revelation both questioning and providing answers—remains, in the end, dialectical. Similarly, Pannenberg's historical-theological method has been further developed by F. LeRon Shults (1999) in conversation with the science-religion dialogue and the postfoundational method of inquiry advocated by J. Wentzel van Huyssteen (1999). Yet, on close inspection, Shults' efforts to negotiate what he calls the "couplets" of theological method—beliefs and experience, the objectivity of truth and the subjectivity of knowledge, self and community, universal understanding and contextual explanation—show that he has inherited Pannenberg's less than robust dialectical assumptions rather than reconstructed the framework of theological method altogether. The result is that the dualistic hermeneutical framework that saddles Pannenberg himself (on this point, see Loder 1998, 30–31) is not overcome.

I suggest that in every one of these cases, it is the dyadic framework within which the problem of method is framed that prevents a fully satisfactory resolution. Now granted that dyadic structures are by no means inherently problematic. Yet insofar as intractable dualisms are at the heart of the current debate in theological method, the question arises as to how a sustained response can be forthcoming if, in these cases, the problem itself is underwritten by dualistic presuppositions?[5] The stage is therefore set for a more robustly mediating theology to emerge, one that not only truly correlates religion and culture such that both religion and culture asks questions even while both provide answers, but also that dynamically motivates the ongoing engagement between religion and culture such that the provisionality of all questions and

[4] I would further note that insofar as Tillich stands in the mainstream of the Reformation tradition in general and in the Lutheran tradition, more specifically, the unavoidable conclusion to be drawn is that Protestant correlational method, straddled as it is within the framework of Luther's subordination of law to gospel, has failed to be truly dialectical and dialogical. For a lucid argument about the continuity between Tillich's correlation of existence and revelation and Luther's between law and gospel, see Wayne G. Johnson (1981).

[5] Other versions of a correlational and dialectical methodology that emphasize a hermeneutical approach with similar weaknesses are by Werner Jeanrond (1988) and Claude Geffré (1987). A survey of theological methodologies through the early 1980s (e.g., Mueller 1984) will confirm my basic point.

answers are embraced. Central to the argument in this book is that a pneumatological starting point reconfigures altogether the methodological problematic framed by dialectic precisely because it opens up toward a trinitarian conception. Previous theological methodologies either fail to sustain the dialectical movement or collapse the dialectic altogether because they lack a pneumatological "engine."[6] I will endeavor to show that a vital pneumatology is indispensable for a truly healthy dialectic in that it drives the to-and-fro movement necessary to sustain both poles. In this sense, pneumatology is what guarantees the rigor of the dialectic so as to prevent it from "shutting down" (i.e., collapsing toward either pole). More than that, however, I will argue that pneumatology also leads to a vigorous "trinitarian rhythm" with regard to hermeneutics and theological method in the same way as it leads to a robust trinitarianism with regard to the doctrine of God. Thus, a trinitarian—what I call *trialectical*—relationality emerges from the pneumatologically propelled dialectic. This results in a transformation at the core of the hermeneutical and methodological framework itself. The back-and-forth movement underwriting the dialectical problematic now opens up toward a trinitarian configuration of Spirit, Word and Community. In short, pneumatology sublates dialectics, transforming them into the service of a genuine trialectical movement.

A Trinitarian Vision

As will be clear in the course of this book, the notion of a hermeneutical trialectic functions at distinct and yet interrelated levels. Let me expand on how the trialectic both underwrites and yet is informed by the trinitarian vision that guides this project by commenting further about its theological, philosophical, and hermeneutical aspects.

The trialectic to be developed in these pages is *theological* insofar as it revolves around the three theological concepts of Spirit, Word, and Community and the realities to which they point. My central thesis is that theological hermeneutics—the activity of reading or interpreting things related to the divine—is a continuous interplay of Spirit, Word, and Community. Let us look briefly at each in turn.

The distinction between "Spirit" and "spirit" needs to be noted up front.

6 A similar failure can be seen in the neo-Barthianism of Donald Bloesch. While beginning with the intention of developing a theological method of Word and Spirit, when confronted with the "Wesleyan quadrilateral" Bloesch ultimately collapses the dialectic in favor of what he calls the "unilateral authority" of the biblical revelation (1992, 208–11).

The former is a biblical and theological reference, and when used without qualification in this book, always refers to the Holy Spirit. The latter, however, has rhetorical, anthropological, and metaphysical connotations. Rhetorically, "spirit" is a metaphor that calls attention to ethos, atmosphere, and perhaps tradition (i.e., somber spirit, exuberant spirit, spirit of an institution, neighborhood, or organization) and characterizes animated intentionality (i.e., school spirit; cf. Smith 1988). This leads, however, to spirit as an anthropological category which in turn dovetails into theological anthropology in that the "spirit" of any person or thing is its *élan vital* that is God-given and God-related. Uncapitalized, spirit is what explains the commonality of our human experiences; it is that which underlies our common rationality; it is the stuff of our common humanness. In short, spirit is the relationality that provides the contexts of our human life and interactions in the world. I will elaborate later on these aspects of the human spirit, and there address the issue of diversity and difference that some say vitiates the notion of commonality or even universality.

But the rhetorical and anthropological uses of "spirit" in this book beg for metaphysical analysis. The metaphysics of spirit can be outlined under three broad categories. First, spirit at the metaphysical level points to that which sustains commonality—both human and cosmic. Our common human experience points to our mutually shared and publicly owned world. At the same time, our discrete experiences in and of this world point beyond themselves and is suggestive of a common relational context. Second, spirit points to the energetic or field dimension that sustains the concrete or phenomenological aspects of things in the world. The important qualification here is that "thing" is also a technical metaphysical term and should not be understood as referring only to material objects. Lastly, spirit points to the dynamic aspect of things, the same qualification holding. Dynamism can and will be understood in other metaphysical terms: generals, laws, habits, dispositions, vectors, trajectories, and so forth. Each of these three metaphysical categories of spirit—metaphysical commonality, the energetic or field dimensions of things, the dynamic aspect of reality—will be developed in detail in Part One, but all are operative in the concept at some level throughout this work.

When it appears in this volume, "Word" will always have a theological reference, whether that be to the incarnation—the living Word—or to the Christian canonical Scriptures. However, "Word" in the title is much more inclusive than its appearance would suggest. As "spirit" is to be understood metaphysically, so also does "Word" have its metaphysical connotations. To distinguish "Word" in its theological senses from "word" metaphysically understood,

I will use "Logos," especially in philosophical discussion.

The metaphysics of Logos can be briefly sketched along two lines. First, Logos has historically been taken to refer to the rational structure or form of things (things, again, metaphysically understood). The *logoi* (plural) in the philosophical tradition has therefore been understood as the essential structures of things. As a thing, the human mind also has its own Logos—its own essential form and structure. Rationality or intelligibility, then, can be seen as the correlation between the forms of things and the structures of the mind: this issues forth in knowledge. If we move from the substance–accident metaphysics of Aristotelianism, however, then Logos needs to be understood not so much as pointing to the substantive essence or structure—the what—of things, but to the dynamic interrelationships—the how—by which things confront, oppose, engage, and resist other things. I will develop these ideas later, and there pay heed to the structuralist and post-structuralist challenge to the whole onto-theological project traditionally associated with the Logos, whether that be regarding metaphysical inquiry in general or about notions such as ontological essentialism and epistemic realism.

Secondly, Logos as used metaphysically serves as the conceptual counterpart to spirit understood as the field aspect of things. Logos therefore names the concrete, manifest aspect of things. Metaphysically, this follows from the Logos as framing a thing's reality: its phenomenological manifestation reveals the forms and dynamics by which its interactions with other realities are structured. Theologically, this follows from the fact that the Word was spoken concretely (resulting in the creation of the world) and enfleshed (incarnation). The former results not only in a "what," but reveals the "how" of God's activity. The latter further discloses the how of God's interaction with the world. "Word" in the title of this book thus has not only theological significance but also metaphysical underpinnings.

Finally, "Community" is correlated with the first trinitarian person. The Father, understood in the theological sense as the aboriginal source of which Word and Spirit are the two hands, is reconceived for this hermeneutical project according to the category of Community. This is because the Christian deity, while affirmed in a robustly monotheistic sense, is nevertheless not equivalent to Jewish or Islamic versions of the same. Rather, the Christian God is always God the Father who is always paternally related to the Son; further, the relationship of Father and Son is inseparable from, if not constitutive of the "communion of the Holy Spirit" (2 Cor. 13:13). While all this will be elaborated on in detail later, note that in the same way as the Father symbolizes the divine community, so Community symbolizes the communal contexts of hermeneutical inquiry, interpretation, and discernment. At this theological level, Community refers to the believing faithful. This will be explicated at three levels: the immediate community of faith (i.e., a local church, a local community of churches, a denomination of churches), the larger community of faith (i.e., the Christian community, the Catholic Church, the communion of Orthodox churches), and the historic Christian tradition itself (whether understood dogmatically as Catholics and the Orthodox do, or taken purely descriptively as referring to the history of Christianity as a whole). Communities, however, even theological ones, have to be understood as complex networks of relationships interacting with and including others beyond their normally defined boundaries.

Yet as with the Spirit and Word, Community also admits of other than strictly theological connotations. Considered epistemologically, Community denotes the cooperative public domain of inquirers. Inquiry should never be taken in an entirely individualistic sense, but should always be understood as communally situated. Theological inquiry, following the delineation of the ecclesiological community developed above, takes place most immediately within the community of faith one is affiliated with, even if such a community of inquirers is located within the larger Christian community and the Christian tradition as a whole. Yet, while human knowledge is shaped by these communities and their motivations, concerns, questions, intentions, and so forth, it is still possible for inquiry to transcend these contexts.

Such transcendence occurs in part because of the dialogical aspect of Community. A gathering of as few as two or three persons in relational conversation is sufficient to constitute a community. Theologians rarely ever limit their conversations to those within their immediate faith communities, and often conference and consult with voices from "outside" their faith tradition as a whole. They have neighbors and friends who are non-Christians, secularists, humanists, agnostics, and atheists. Are they not open to conversation with these persons and groups of people? I will argue that a community of inquiry is a dialogical community, one that should be open to engaging with any and all who are interested in the subject matter. This is especially crucial for theological inquiry and the fulfillment of the theological task.

It is important at this juncture to emphasize what will be periodically repeated: Spirit, Word, and Community should not be understood hierarchically with reference to each other. In fact, this volume was initially titled *Word and Spirit in Community*, reflecting then our habit as Western Christians of pairing the terms in this order, and signaling our inclination to accept the sequential implications of the *filioque*. However, it is precisely for this reason that I resolved to follow the lead of Henry Pitt van Dusen (1958) who more than a generation ago spoke about Spirit before Word. It is time for the West to consciously resist the subordination of the former to the latter, and such resistance needs to occur rhetorically, programmatically, and theologically. Further, this reversal also highlights the pneumatological starting point of this project. Yet, at the same time, beginning with Spirit does not mean switching priorities and subordinating the Word instead. Rather, as I hope to show, it leads to a robust trinitarianism wherein Spirit and Word mutually interpenetrate and coinhere in Community without losing their distinctness. Therefore, all three should be understood as moments in the one hermeneutical and methodological movement. The dialectical relationship between Spirit and Word is played out in the context of Community. The dialectical relationship between Word and Community is mediated by Spirit. The dialectical relationship between Spirit and Community is anchored in Word. Spirit implicates Word and Community; Word implicates Spirit and Community; Community implicates Spirit and Word. None of the three are subordinate to either of the other, and all assume and require each other. And this is as it should be given that the trinitarian structure of the book's argument seeks to emulate the perichoretic model of the Christian doctrine of the Trinity. While I do engage in trinitarian theology proper, my focus is primarily to re-construe Spirit, Son, and Father as (at least) hermeneutical categories. And, I suggest, the success of this reconstruction rides on the dialectical movement from pneumatology to Trinity and vice-versa since it is precisely this dialectic of pneumatology and Trinity that preserves the integrity of the trinitarian framework. Additionally, however, the potency of a pneumatological trinitarianism is not exhausted in theology proper—the doctrine of God—at least not insofar as theology concerns not only God but also human selves and the world. The pneumatological trinitarianism developed here is thus theological in the broadest sense because it is also philosophical and hermeneutical.

The trialectic in these pages is *philosophical* insofar as it blends and combines trinitarian theology, epistemology and metaphysics. It is, at one and the same time, theological, epistemological and metaphysical, each of these vis-à-vis the divine reality, the human reality created in the *imago Dei*, and the created order considered altogether—and this precisely because of the pneumatological point of departure adopted herein. And, far from being inconsequential to my argument, epistemology and metaphysics are central to the endeavor here since what is attempted is not only a textual hermeneutic but a theological hermeneutic that engages life and reality in its complexity. In one sense, what I attempt here could be considered a pneumatological–trinitarian hermeneutic. In another sense, what follows is also a pneumatological–trinitarian epistemology as well as a pneumatological–trinitarian metaphysics.[7]

At the same time, I make no claims to originality in any of these areas on inquiry considered on their own. This book falls far short of a comprehensive discussion of either metaphysics or epistemology proper. Certainly, if my metaphysical and epistemological intuitions are correct, the reader uninitiated in these areas should go away from this book with an adequate theory both of reality itself and of what it is to know. My objective, however, is not to engage these subjects in and of themselves, but to build from a metaphysic and an epistemology informed by trinitarian ontology toward a comprehensive theological hermeneutics and methodology. Insofar as the focus in this book is on *theological* hermeneutics, my conviction is that theological presuppositions and categories are to be followed out rather than subordinated to philosophical ones. For this reason, the trinitarian starting point adopted here should not be under-appreciated.

Having said that, it also needs to be said that the conjunction between trinitarian theology, metaphysics and epistemology derives from my conviction that the goal of a theological hermeneutics cannot be accomplished by subordinating metaphysical and epistemological considerations in a simplistic sense to theological ones. This is because a theological hermeneutics includes and, it may be said, is sustained by a philosophical hermeneutics—what is means to *interpret* the reality of the self and the world, and how we actually do interpretation itself, both descriptively and normatively. It cannot be denied that in the wake of Heidegger and Gadamer, theology not only involves hermeneutics, but theology is inherently hermeneutical as well. Thus, while the trinitarian vision here translates into a hermeneutical theory—a theological hermeneutics, more specifically—this hermeneutical framework itself also in turn constrains and informs the trinitarian vision. Herein arises what some consider to be a dilemma of interpretation: how a given object (theologically and metaphysically understood) presents or reveals itself for interpretation and how the spectacles (framework of interpretation) through which one looks at the object shapes the way one understands it. To put it another way, this is the

---

[7] For previous developments of a pneumatological epistemology, see McDonnell (1982; 1985), and Abraham (1990); for a trinitarian epistemology, see van Beeck (1999). Various approaches toward a trinitarian metaphysics include those of Boyd (1992), Gunton (1993), Milbank (1995), Schwobel (1995), and Bracken and Suchocki (1997).

problem of how the objects of knowledge inform the knower and how the processes of knowing itself influences what is known. A subsidiary aim of this book is to demonstrate why this is the case, how it cannot (and should not) be avoided, and how a trialectical notion of interpretation alleviates the felt dilemma by setting it within an altogether different (triadic) frame of reference.

In short, the trialectic developed in these pages is not only theological and philosophical but also *hermeneutical*. By this, I refer to more than just the book's hermeneutical content, but to its method, structure, and dynamic. This book in theological hermeneutics may just as well be a book in hermeneutical theology. I will argue that theology is essentially hermeneutical and that hermeneutical reflection is part and parcel of theology itself, and not only a preliminary starting-point or even subordinated aspect of it (see, e.g., Geffré 1974, 43–46 and 1987, Part I; Lawrence 1981). Method cannot be artificially separated from material, form from content, hermeneutics from theology. Rather, there is always a dialectical relationship between the former and the latter. Parallel notions include Von Balthasar's (1982, 126) claim that fundamental theology (concerned with the epistemology, perception and reception of revelation) and dogmatic theology (the content of revelation) are inseparable, and Moltmann's discovery that his theological method arose in and through the process of writing his systematic contributions to theology—"The road emerged only as I walked on it" (2000, xv).

What this means is that this is a book on theological philosophy—where both the method and material of theology informs the doing of philosophy, in this case, metaphysics and epistemology—as well as a book on philosophical theology—where the form and content of metaphysics and epistemology informs the doing of theology, the God-self-world relationships considered as a whole. My project will attempt to resist the temptation to either overwhelm the philosophical argument via recourse to theological categories or subsume the theological to the philosophical. Rather, as I hope to show, philosophy will serve to exemplify and clarify theology and vice versa. It will be important to allow both sides to mutually inform, shape, and transform the other without confusion or the creation of a *tertium quid*. And, this dual qualification is robustly dialectical precisely because of the trialectic of interpretation that takes place amidst a community of inquirers such that theology inspires and fills in philosophy and vice versa—such 'filling in' emerging out of the interpretive process itself. For this reason, this book is not ultimately *either* theological or philosophical, nor is it *either* theological or hermeneutical; but it is *both* theological and philosophical, and *both* theological and hermeneutical. In this way

I hope to follow, at least in part, Huston Smith's warning that "we always know more than we know how we know it, from which it follows that to channel our knowing through methods we are explicitly aware of restricts our field of vision" (2000, 174). Therefore, the best approach to issues of method is by doing what one's methodology is striving to engage: in this case, doing theology itself, and not just speculating about theological method.

If the major arguments of this book are successful, then this project is better seen as attempt in constructive trinitarianism rather than dogmatic trinitarianism. Implications of the former for the latter will be recognized, but exploration of dogmatics will be kept to a minimum. Instead, I will, in keeping with the spirit of this pneumatology of quest, follow out the pneumatological starting point wherever that may lead beyond the loci of theology proper as traditionally conceived, as well as beyond the confines of the institutional *ecclesia*. Specifically, a trinitarian vision of the world and of knowledge will be pursued. Finding and developing such a triadic construct of reality, of knowledge, and, ultimately, of the processes of interpretation itself means that this is best conceived as a trinitarian *Weltanschauung*. As such, trinitarianism is deeply embedded in this project, intrinsic to the categories employed, the aesthetic structure, the theological content and the overall vision. Insofar as the vision of this book is successfully communicated, it joins in the chorus celebrated by the renaissance in trinitarian theology in recent decades.

The following overview trace out the main lines of the argument. Part One begins the "pneumatology of quest" in earnest by laying out how pneumatology opens up toward a trinitarian framework, and suggesting that analogously, foundational pneumatology informs as well as is itself shaped by a trinitarian metaphysics and ontology. Such an account is important not only theologically and philosophically in exemplifying the basic features of reality, but also hermeneutically in exemplifying the triadic activity of interpretation. In other words, theological hermeneutics involves the subjectivity of an interpreter, the objectivity of what is engaged or encountered, and an interpretive process or context. Therefore, if in fact interpretation is understood not merely as a purely subjective enterprise, but rather as an objective engagement with an objective reality, then at some point theological hermeneutics requires an account of this external (to the interpreter) otherness. A foundational pneumatology, it will be argued, sustains not only the process of inquiry after such an account, but also offers clues as to how this account correlates with the task of theological interpretation. Pneumatology thus opens up to christology and patrology—in short, to the doctrines of God and of the Trinity; and, trinitarian reflection will in turn bear fruit with regard to reconceptualizing the categories of metaphysics, epistemology, and interpretation. The goal here is thus both to show how a pneumatological reorientation to these topics culminates in a trinitarian hermeneutical construct that connects meaning and reality, the knower and the known, and the knower and the unknown, and to understand the nature of the reality that is interpreted from within the framework of a foundational pneumatology.

Part Two continues the pneumatology of quest by moving from foundational pneumatology—metaphysics and ontology, the objectively known—to the process of knowing—epistemology, the subjectivity of knowing—by way of what I call the "pneumatological imagination." Whereas knowledge and rationality have traditionally been connected to the Logos, I show that there is a pneumatological dimension to knowing without which rationality is itself undermined. Such an imagination is thereby at once theological and philosophical—at once pneumatic and trinitarian. It is pneumatic in terms of the experiences of the Spirit and the categories drawn from foundational pneumatology. It is trinitarian in the way it structures the processes of knowing itself, of truth and error, and of normative living. This means that pneumatology provides the proper interpretive key to understanding both the structures and the processes of knowledge and the failure of the knowing process to adequately and correctly grasp its object. I argue that truth and error are possible precisely because knowledge emerges from an interpreter's encounter with reality as mediated by interpretants (signs of various kinds). Yet at the same time, such interpretants do not exist on their own but are intimately connected both with the objects they represent and the interpreting subjects. I suggest that a pneumatological imagination is capable of negotiating this trialectical interplay so as to provide for an epistemology adequate not only for the human engagement with the world in general and with others in particular, but also for the human quest for theological understanding more specifically.

How the pneumatological imagination and trinitarian epistemology give way toward a specifically theological hermeneutics or methodology is the topic of Part Three. Theological interpretation, I will argue, is a trialectical process of Spirit, Word, and Community. It is an imaginative engagement with and in the world (understood as a context or a community) that aims at knowing the totality of God, self and the world. Here, the acts, objects, and contexts of interpretation are delineated in light of the theological task. The possibilities of theological knowledge are constrained by the trialectic of interpretation. The trialectic of Spirit, Word and Community means that the dualistic chasms between object and subject, text and context, interpreter and community/communities of interpretation are surmounted by mediation, such mediation itself being the third, relational term symbolized by the "and" between each pair. In other words, theological interpretation is relational through and through: Spirit, Word and Community all coinhere and inform each other within a robust and thoroughgoing trialectical framework. None are seen to operate apart from the other, and each informs the other such that what emerges is knowledge of the divine and of divine things that is always *in via*. Within this matrix, the pneumatology of quest is provisionally complete.

The final chapter concludes with some thoughts on the nature of inquiry, of interpretation, and of theological knowledge itself. The motivating query here is: Whither the hermeneutical trialectic?

The argument of this book therefore develops in what could be called a trialectical spiral. The initial triad of chapters one through three are given more precise focus in the second triad of chapters four through six and the third triad of chapters seven through nine. In each case, I proceed in both pneumatological and trinitarian fashion from Spirit to Word to Community. This trialectical spiral can also be traced within the sections and sub-sections of each chapter and, analogously, across the chapters. Themes and motifs developed in earlier sections and sub-sections reappear in later sections and sub-sections in different contexts and with regard to different purposes. Throughout, however, the pneumatological and trinitarian structure of the book holds. The pneumatological categories, whether metaphysically, epistemologically or hermeneutically specified, are meant to demonstrate and illuminate the explanatory power of a pneumatological starting point. But, being pneumatological means being trinitarian rather than simply related to the third article of the Creed. Thus the starting point gives way toward a trialectic— whether such be considered theologically, philosophically, or hermeneutically— since they lead out (or in, depending on which metaphor is employed) to the trinitarian categories, and do so in a consistently theological manner.

In turn, the trinitarian categories themselves are suggestive of the fact that each aspect of the argument is necessary for the meaning of the whole rather than being of either primary, secondary or tertiary (hierarchical) importance. The traditional doctrine of the coinherence of trinitarian persons bears this out. This means that while there is a progression in the argument, this progression is to be understood as a spiral rather than in linear terms. This also means that the ideas presented need to be intuited aesthetically as much as grasped argumentatively. As develop in what follows, the triadic sequence of the argument in each chapter does proceed from Spirit to Word and then to Community. But since the argument networks and overlaps symmetrically, the sections of each chapter and (especially) subsections within each section are reversible or re-arrangeable without doing damage to the argument. The pneumatological starting point means not that the order of the argument is sacrosanct, but that the central categories of the argument are intrinsic, coinhering and mutually defining. The trialectical spiral is therefore at once biblical, theological and philosophical; at once pneumatological, christological, and trinitarian (communitarian); at once metaphysical, epistemological, and hermeneutical.

The book's overall thesis is therefore strengthened precisely because of the intertwining of themes throughout the trialectical argument. Spirit, Word and Community are the central motifs that together spiral toward a theological hermeneutic in successive chapters as strands in a cumulative argument. Yet the trinitarian framework underlying this book also demands that at each juncture, the other two aspects not be neglected with respect to the argument that is made. The hermeneutic is trialectical precisely because no matter where one finds oneself in the argument, there is always the interplay of Spirit, Word and Community.

This method proceeds from my overall conviction that while arguments are important, so are the media through which they are made. And because my goal here is both to convince and to impart a vision, the trialectical spiral is employed. It will allow the main ideas of the argument to be revisited successively from various perspectives and with different intentions. While this not only keeps such revisitation from being repetitive, the different perspectives and respects gained from spiraling further into the topic also generate, hopefully, deeper and deeper insights. The image of three spirals zeroing into a target from three distinct but interconnected starting points perhaps serves to illustrate both how the structure of this book sustains its primary arguments, and the theological vision that motivates it. The increasing spiral should therefore be understood as an effort both to complexify the book's thesis and to provide rational argument (argumentation, as Peirce calls it): one should therefore be gripped not only by the rationality, intelligibility, and explanatory power of the argument but also by its aesthetic vision! Enthusiasts, rationalists, and communitarians are all invited to come along for the ride. Welcome to the journey...

PART ONE

Foundational Pneumatology: Toward a Trinitarian Theology and Metaphysics

It has already been suggested that theological method cannot be divorced from theology in both its broad and its narrow senses. Methodological convictions proceed from basic theological intuitions and even while theological conclusions are framed by faithfully following out a methodology. This means that one never begins from no-where, but takes up one's theological task amidst the hermeneutical circle. It may also mean that one can approach either the methodological question from the "starting point" of theology or vice-versa. In other words, perhaps beginning with Part Three of this book, the one devoted explicitly to defending the "trialectical method," would be equally legitimate. However, I begin with the basic theological and metaphysical issues and work toward the methodological because my focus in this volume is on the latter. I would suggest that the alternative procedure would be more conducive and is usually adopted if one's goal was theology rather than methodology. In short, it seems eminently reasonable to me to say that one's objectives in part guide where one enters into the hermeneutical circle.

In this part of the book, then, I will lay out the theological, ontological and metaphysical framework within which the epistemological and methodological questions will be considered. However, since method cannot be divorced from theology, in itself, chapters one through three will reflect the methodological assumptions and movements which will not be made explicit until Part Three. The Spirit-Word-Community trialectic explicated later can be seen in germinal form here. The objective in Part One, however, is to set forth and defend a trinitarian metaphysics that is relational, realistic, and communal. To accomplish this task, I develop the idea of "foundational pneumatology" and explicate its biblical, theological and metaphysical aspects. The movement is therefore from a biblical pneumatology to a pneumatological and foundational theology, and concluding toward a theological metaphysics. The underlying and overarching framework throughout, I hope to show, will be trinitarian through and through, and that precisely because of the pneumatological motif which guides the argument.

1 Beginning with the Spirit: Biblical Motifs for a Foundational Pneumatology

Certainly, the argument can proceed in the reverse direction: from the abstract metaphysics through the foundational theology to the biblical pneumatology. Yet I begin with pneumatology in part for pedagogical reasons which prefer argument from the concrete to the abstract, and in part because of my own theological background, locatedness, orientation and intuitions. And, I propose not just pneumatology in general—although what follows will certainly be abstract enough for many readers—but a Christian, and, more specifically, biblical pneumatology. The idea, simply, is to build from the biblical bases toward the metaphysics and, finally, the method.

But, of course, the biblical text is never read apart from some interpretive grid or other. One always hopes that one's interpretive lenses do not so obfuscate one's vision that one loses sight of the distinctive and particular message one is interpreting and its demands on oneself as a reader. So, one attempts to be as cognizant as possible about the lenses one wears so as to be doubly armed with regard to discerning just how one's presuppositions are influencing one's engagement with the text. In what follows, then, I propose to read the pneumatological narratives in Scripture through three basic categories: that of relationality, rationality, and *dunamis* or power of life and community. I will argue that these are legitimately pneumatological categories which emerge out of engagement with the text.[1] Whether or not I am successful, the reader will have to judge. In the process, I hope to lay out a biblical basis for the foundational theology and metaphysics that undergirds the methodological vision to be detailed later.

One preliminary word about categories, categorial construction and categorial thinking before proceeding. I cannot say whether or not the categories to be used in this essay are a priori since I do not have a transcendental

---

[1] On method and Christian pneumatology, see Robert Louis Wilken's (2000) illuminating paper about the early Church Fathers' pneumatological methodology: from experience and liturgy to Scripture and back to experience, liturgy and Scripture again, and so on, in an ongoing hermeneutical spiral; I am in basic agreement with Wilken's remarks.

perspective from which to make that pronouncement. I can say that they are at least a posteriori insofar as they have arisen from experience understood broadly. I will also affirm that they are not necessary or essential categories in the sense that they are neither exclusive nor definitive. Finally, I do not claim any of the categorial sets in this essay to be exhaustive. Categories are simply heuristic tools for thinking which is a process of abstracting from experience. In that sense, theology cannot avoid categorial construction. Theology does not, however, have to claim a priori essentiality, infallibility, or exhaustiveness simply because it trades on the necessity of operating with some set of categories or other. Whether or not the categories utilized in what follows are valid will need to be determined along the way and, especially, at the end. We will return periodically to this question as we proceed.

1.1 The Spirit and Relationality

The recent appearance of a variety of pneumatologies from biblical, theological, and other perspectives is a testimony to the fact that the once "silent" and "shy" member of the Trinity is silent and shy no longer. The following discussion makes no pretense to develop either a comprehensive biblical or theological discussion. I do, however, hope to connect with important strands of the ongoing discussion in pneumatology which concern the Spirit who through incarnation and Pentecost relates God and the world, and who establishes in relationship the manyness of the world, each to and with the other (cf. Taylor 1973).

1.1.1 The first aspect to be explored is the relational role of the Spirit in and to the incarnation. I begin with the gospel narratives because they are stories, not just propositional statements, about God's relationship to the world. This relationship is centered, of course, on the person at the heart of Christian identity, Jesus of Nazareth. But notice the equally important role of the Spirit in the life and work of Jesus. For the sake of narrative coherence, I focus in what follows on the Lukan account, and supplement it as appropriate from the other evangelists.[2]

The infancy narratives themselves announce the coming of the Son of God through the agency of the Holy Spirit who descends upon Mary (Luke 1:35; cp.

[2] The following is an extremely brief sketch of Second Testament christology which follows from the Lukan depiction of Jesus as a man anointed with the Holy Spirit and power, otherwise known as Spirit christology. On recent Spirit christologies, see, e.g., David Coffey (1979), Gerald F. Hawthorne (1991), and Ralph Del Colle (1994). Paul W. Newman's (1987) is another proposal, but one which is perhaps finally adoptionistic, working outsides the lines of Nicene and Chalcedonian trinitarianism rather than within it.

Matt. 1:20), and who inspires the prophecies of the Son's mission (Luke 1:67–79 and 2:25–32). The Spirit's presence, in turn, is sufficient cause of the experience of a central motif in the Lukan accounts, that of being filled with the Holy Spirit (1:41–44). The child's development signals the ongoing gracious presence and activity of the Spirit. He is described as growing strong in spirit (1:80), and increasing "in wisdom and in years, and in divine and human favor" (2:52). The Spirit's presence is made remarkably manifest in the bodily form of a dove at the baptism of Jesus. The Father's voice followed, saying, "You are my Son, the Beloved; with you I am well pleased" (3:22).

Jesus' ensuing public ministry is no less superintended by the Spirit. Being full of and led by the Spirit (4:1), Jesus overcomes the temptations of the devil in the wilderness and returns to Galilee in the power of the Spirit to begin his ministry (4:14). As he himself declares from the prophet Isaiah, Jesus clearly understands his mission to be conducted under the anointing of the Spirit of God:

> The Spirit of the Lord is upon me,
>> because he has anointed me
>> to bring good news to the poor.
> He has sent me to proclaim release to the captives
>> and recovery of sight to the blind,
>> to let the oppressed go free,
>> to proclaim the year of the Lord's favor. (4:18–19; cp. Isa. 61:1)

The implications are unmistakable: Jesus' teaching, preaching, healing, exorcising, liberating, delivering, and saving words and deeds are the result of the Spirit's anointing. As recorded in Luke's gospel, the public ministry of Jesus is intended to display this empowering presence and activity of the Spirit which fulfills the Isaianic prophecy. For this and other reasons, Luke is later able to refer to Jesus as "a man attested to you by God with deeds of power, wonders, and signs" (Acts 2:22). Further, Luke recalls "how God anointed Jesus of Nazareth with the Holy Spirit and with power; how he went about doing good and healing all who were oppressed by the devil, for God was with him" (Acts 10:38).

The Spirit's work was not complete, however, with the public ministry of Jesus. Arguably, it is in the paschal mystery that the intimate relationships of the divine life are most fully manifest (cf. Durrwell 1986). One is given a glimpse of the triune mystery in Jesus' baptism, as well as in the self-awareness of Jesus as doing his Father's business (Luke 2:49, 22:42, etc.). Further, Jesus' relationship with the Father—exemplified most profoundly in the "abba" addresses—captures a sense of the deep union of purpose and identity especially when he says, "The Father and I are one" (John 10:30). But the triune mystery is also clearly depicted in the death and resurrection of Jesus (cf. Dabney 1997 and 2000). Jesus' willing deliverance of himself to death—saying "Father, into your hands I commend my spirit" (Luke 23:46; cf. John 19:30)—demonstrates the cross itself as a trinitarian event between Father, Son, and Spirit.[3] And, death was not, of course, the end of the story since Jesus was "made alive in the Spirit" (1 Pet. 3:18b). More emphatically, Jesus Christ the Lord "was declared to be the Son of God with power according to the spirit of holiness by resurrection from the dead" (Rom. 1:4). The resurrection and ascension of Jesus are, in turn, the prerequisites for his sending the Spirit in power upon those who believe in his name.

Before focusing on the pentecostal aspects of the relationality of Spirit, however, the point which needs to be emphasized from the preceding is the Spirit's role in the supremely revealing and redemptive work of God in the incarnation. If the "one mediator between God and humankind [is] Christ Jesus, himself human" (1 Tim. 2:5), then the means through which such mediation is brought about is the Holy Spirit. The Spirit enables the reconciliation between God and humankind; the Spirit empowers the new relationship established through Jesus Christ; the Spirit is the relational medium that makes possible the incarnational and paschal mysteries.

1.1.2 The story, of course, does not end with the gospel of Luke, but is extended in the book of Acts (volume two of the Lukan account) in the pentecostal outpouring of Spirit. Pentecost becomes the supreme symbol of the Spirit's relational power in bridging the gap between God and humanity as a whole. It is the baptism or filling with the Holy Spirit that was not only promised by Jesus (Luke 24:49; Acts 1:8, 2:33), but which also fulfills his mission as announced by John the Baptist and confirmed in each gospel account: "He [Jesus] will baptize you with the Holy Spirit and fire" (Luke 3:16; cf. Mark 1:8, Matt. 3:11, and John 1:33). Now this baptism in the Holy Spirit should be distinguished from the Spirit's agential work of baptizing believers into the body of Christ (1 Cor. 12:13). For the moment, however, the focus is on Jesus the baptizer, and the Spirit as the one in whom he baptizes. In a curious yet thoroughly relational manner, Jesus is who he is precisely because he is the man of the Spirit on the one hand; yet Jesus does what he does as savior precisely because he sends and baptizes with the Spirit on the other. "Baptism in the Holy Spirit,"

---

[3] See, e.g., John O'Donnell, SJ, (1989, 36) for the argument that the reference in John 19:30 (and, arguably, Luke 23:46) is to the Holy Spirit. The author of the Hebrews puts it this way: that Christ, "through the eternal Spirit offered himself unblemished to God" (Heb. 9:14).

clearly, is the metaphor preferred by the evangelists in talking about the saving act of God whereby estranged humanity is brought back into proper relationship with the creator (cf. Dabney 2001).

Salvation—understood as baptism in the Holy Spirit—is not, however, only a one time event in a forgone past, but is experienced as an ongoing and deepening relationship with God through Jesus Christ by the power of the Spirit. This gift of the Spirit is consequent upon repentance and baptism into Jesus' name for the forgiveness of sins, and is promised to all who believe and are called by God (Acts 2:38–39). It is this work of the Spirit that continues throughout the age of grace (without denying that grace itself can be resisted with stern consequences; cf. Heb. 10:29). More important, the pentecostal outpouring of the Spirit is the refreshing that anticipates the parousia of Jesus prior to the restoration of all things to God (Acts 3:19–21). For these reasons, Luke tells of the "acts of the Holy Spirit" by which the gospel is taken to those who are far off, not only toward the ends of the earth but also across the intervening centuries of time considered as "the last days" (cf. Acts 2:17). The pentecostal reality, in short, is the ongoing work of God by the Spirit to turn hearts back to the creator from whom they have been separated and alienated.

In Pauline terms, this is the truth of what has traditionally been called by the doctrines of justification, sanctification, and glorification. Each of these is brought about by the Spirit and has to be understood as distinct and yet entailing each other. To begin with, justification is the work of the Spirit that brings one into right standing with God (cf. Macchia 2000). Yet the justifying work of the Spirit is inherently connected with the Spirit's ongoing sanctifying work. As the Apostle Paul writes, "since we are justified by faith, we have peace with God through our Lord Jesus Christ" (Rom. 5:1). This peace is based on the grace of God in which we as believers now stand, and is accompanied by rejoicing in spite of the sufferings that are experienced, and the production from that suffering of perseverance, character, and hope, all because "God's love has been poured into our hearts through the Holy Spirit that has been given to us" (Rom. 5:5). The outpouring of love in the Spirit, however, is not just an emotional experience. Rather, it calls forth affective, cognitive, and materially embodied responses in dying to sin and living to Christ through the power of the Spirit (Rom. 6–8). These responses are, of course, both of believers and of the Spirit who empowers them in order to bring them to the fullness of redemption which is promised by God. This is because the same Spirit who justifies and sanctifies is the one who also glorifies the believer. The Spirit is the promised seal (Eph. 1:13 and 4:30), the "first fruits" (Rom. 8:23; cf.

2 Cor. 1:22) who guarantees the believer's glorious freedom to be accomplished eschatologically. The Spirit, in short, is the presence and activity of God which graces human life, reconciles humankind to God, and, finally, brings humanity into that eschatological reunion with its creator.

But how does the Spirit accomplish this saving work in the lives of human beings? The short answer is that by assimilating them into the life of God as revealed unsurpassably and gloriously in Jesus (cf. Gelpi 2001). This means, that the Spirit enables the believer to follow in the footsteps of Jesus, to bear the cross of Jesus, to endure persecutions and suffering for the sake of Jesus, to be endowed with the mind of Jesus—in short, to put on and "grow up in every way into him who is the head, into Christ" (Eph. 4:15). The Spirit therefore reconciles us to God precisely by uniting us with the life, death, and resurrection of Jesus so that we can go about doing the (even greater) works that Jesus did (cf. John 14:12).

So far, then, we have seen from the biblical narratives how the Spirit is the relational reality that makes possible incarnation and Pentecost as divine activities that bridge the (vertical) gap between God and the world, thus reconciling what was estranged by sin. In this light, the Spirit is central to the mediatorial function of the incarnation which unites both divinity and humanity in the person of Jesus on the one hand, and accomplishes the formal dimension of the reconciling work of God through the paschal mystery on the other. Further, the pentecostal outpouring of the Spirit is the fulfillment of the promised saving work of Jesus on the one hand, while yet being the means through which the Spirit herself becomes the agent of reconciliation in the world on the other. It is to this latter, horizontal, aspect of the Spirit's relational and reconciling work amidst the created order that I now turn.

1.1.3 The incarnational union of divine and human in Christ by the Spirit leads to the pentecostal creation of the body of Christ composed of many human members by that same Spirit. This one body features a diversity of gifts by the Spirit distributed to the different members. These gifts are orchestrated by the Spirit so that it is the members themselves who minister to, build up, and edify each other, all by, in and through the Spirit. According to the Pauline metaphor, each member's role in the body is absolutely crucial, serving particular functions necessary to the overall health and operation of the body. No member should look down on any other or say that his or her contributions are negligible. This is because each particular member drinks of the same Spirit (1 Cor. 12:13b) and is valued precisely for the distinctive contribution that he or she makes.

Yet in a peculiar way, this baptism by the Spirit into the body of Christ means that the differences which have formerly separated and divided human beings—differences of race and ethnicity, gender, and social class—have been overcome. It is not without reason that the baptism into the body of Christ reconciles human beings across racial, ethnic, gender, and social lines. In contrast to tendencies within charismatic movements to consider "having the Spirit" to be a sign of special status or of the possession of distinctive gifts that elevate one's spiritual standing, the outpouring of the Spirit in reality levels out just these kinds of differences which separate, divide, and serve as barriers to true relationship and fellowship (cf. Hordern and Bruner 1984, 65–108). The emergence of the ecclesial community from the pentecostal outpouring exhibited just these features. Included from the very beginning were God-fearing Jews "from every nation under heaven" as well as Gentile converts to Judaism (Acts 2:5–11). As the gospel progressed from Jerusalem to Judea to Samaria, and then, finally, to Rome, as symbolized by the "ends of the earth" (Acts 1:8), the complexity of those who were counted as Christians increased proportionately.

Gender barriers were also surmounted by the Spirit's reconciling work at Pentecost. Already in the life and ministry of Jesus, the discipleship of women, unheard of during the first century, was affirmed (Luke 8:1–3 and 10:38–42). The pentecostal outpouring sealed women for the work of the ministry. Peter, quoting the prophet Joel, proclaimed that as a result of this coming of the Spirit, "your sons and your daughters shall prophesy....Even upon my slaves, both men and women, in those days I [the Lord, appropriating the proclamation of Joel] will pour out my Spirit; and they shall prophesy" (Acts 2:17–18). Philip the evangelist's four daughters are among those through whom the spirit of prophesy was manifest (21:8–9). In addition, Luke records throughout his account of the early Church the important contributions of women: Dorcas (9:36); Lydia (16:14–15); Priscilla (always mentioned before her husband, Aquila; 18:18–26); Damaris (17:34a) and others who remain unnamed (1:14; 16:1; 17:4 and 17:34b).

Last but not least, social divides were crossed through the pentecostal outpouring. Widows were included among the ecclesial community (Acts 6:1–2). The unschooled and uneducated (4:13) worked and ministered alongside the learned. Included among the latter were other priests and synagogue leaders (6:7 and 18:8), Apollos, and Paul, identified as a disciple of Gamaliel, a leading Pharisee. Those who had shared with those who had not (2:44–45; 4:36–37; 5:1–2; 11:27–30). Followers of Jesus included public officials like Sergius Paulus of Salamis, Publius of Malta, Cornelius the centurian, the Philippian jailer, and the Ethiopian eunuch. This last mentioned individual provides especially pertinent commentary about the Spirit's reconciling work. Luke records Philip's ministry to the Ethiopian in the context of his discussing the extension of the gospel to the Samaritans (Acts 8). The overarching point is that Jesus' words about the gospel going beyond Jerusalem and Judea of the Jews toward Samaria and the ends of the gentile world were being fulfilled. But the eunuch's salvation signified that the gospel breaks down not only ethnic barriers, but socio-political ones as well, he being the treasurer in the court of Candace the queen of Ethiopia. Finally, however, as one who was emasculated, he was ritually excluded by Jewish law from the assembly of the Lord (cf. Deut. 23:1). That salvation had come to this Ethiopian eunuch was therefore an unmistakable sign of the *evangelion* as "good news" and a fulfillment of the prophecy given through Deutero-Isaiah that Yahweh would one day no longer exclude the foreigner and the eunuch from his solemn assembly (Isa. 56:3–8).

From the beginning of his account, it is clear that Luke is especially concerned that the gospel levels out the differences that are marginalizing. Mary's "Magnificat" announces the socio-political implications of the new work of Yahweh:

> He has brought down the powerful from their thrones,
>   and lifted up the lowly;
> he has filled the hungry with good things,
>   and sent the rich away empty. (Luke 1:51–52)

Jesus' ministry and teachings (cf. the beatitudes in the Sermon on the Plain in Luke 6:20–26) confirm the redeeming work of God. The pentecostal outpouring in turn unleashed the reconciling power of the relational Spirit. Truly, the coming of the Spirit reorders and transforms human relationships such that in Christ, there is no longer Jew nor Greek, male nor female, civilized nor barbarian, free nor slave (cf. Gal. 3:28 and Col. 3:11). Rather, each stands uniquely before God who does not show favoritism and accepts those from all nations under heaven (Acts 10:34–45).

The preceding has briefly explored the incarnational and pentecostal missions of the Godhead as depicted in the gospel narratives. Throughout, the motif of the Spirit as the supremely relational reality has been traced along both the vertical and horizontal axes. These narratives raise theological and ontological questions about the nature of the Spirit. We will return to these questions, however, after exploring some other categorial readings of the biblical portrait of the Spirit.

1.2 The Spirit and Rationality

A second fundamental pneumatological motif throughout the biblical traditions is that of the Spirit as rationality. I am not referring here to Enlightenment rationalism, but rather to the fundamental notion of intelligibility itself. I want to suggest that the Spirit is, on the one hand, the source of rationality and, on the other, the mediator or communicator of rationality. To further assess this proposal, we will proceed to examine the pertinent biblical data, explore the relationship between Spirit, Christ, and Scripture on this issue, and attempt to correlate our biblical findings with the beginnings of a theological anthropology.

1.2.1 The scriptural witness provides sufficient warrant to view the Spirit in general terms as rationality itself and the condition of intelligibility. More specifically, the Spirit serves at least functionally (if not ontologically) as the wisdom of God.[4] Synonymous notions include the Spirit as divine mind, understanding, and intelligence. In each case, the presumption seems to be that the Spirit as the divine mind, etc., is the condition for human mentality, wisdom, understanding, intelligence, and cognition. To build toward this conclusion, observe first the biblical testimony to the Spirit as rationality.

The biblical narrative begins by noting the *ruach* of God hovering over the formless darkness and empty void (Gen. 1:2). As will be discussed in greater detail below [1.3.1], the divine breath's presence and activity is the medium through which the creative word of God is uttered. From this Spirit-inspired utterance comes forth order out of chaos or nothingness. Needless to say, the robust monotheism of Israelite faith initially left little room for understanding pneumatology in a trinitarian framework. Clearly, however, the exilic and intertestamental periods provided fertile intellectual soil through which a distinctive notion of "holy Spirit" as personification of divine wisdom emerged from the concept of Yahweh (cf. Gaybba 1987, 10–11). Thus in the book of Proverbs, woman wisdom pre-exists the world and is the "craftswoman" alongside Yahweh as the world is formed (8:22–31). The world's features, boundaries, orders, and purposes are set in place through this process. In the sapiential tradition, woman wisdom now fully personalizes the creative activity of the divine breath (cf. Montague [1976] 1994, 91–110). This is the culmination of an extended passage wherein woman wisdom admonishes all who seek under-

---

[4] The literature on biblical wisdom is immense. Basic theological interpretations include Clements (1990; 1992), Hill (1996), Murphy (1990, 111–32), and, from a feminist perspective, Cole, Ronan, and Taussig (1996).

standing, justice and the knowledge of God to pursue after her (Prov. 1–9).

The later wisdom tradition proceeds to explicitly re-connect the Spirit and Word motifs to divine wisdom so that, as James Dunn says, "in pre-Christian Judaism Wisdom, Logos, and Spirit were all in very large measure synonymous" (1998, 337). God is said to have "made all things by your word, and of your wisdom have formed humankind," while it is at the same time asked of him, "Who has learned your counsel, unless you have given wisdom and sent your holy spirit from on high?" (Wis. 9:1b-2 and 17). Yet it is also this development which recovers and restores to centrality the pneumatological motif of the Spirit as divine rationality. Observe the significance of pneumatology in the following passage in the Wisdom of Solomon which is reproduced at length:

> There is in a spirit that is intelligent, holy,
>> unique, manifold, subtle,
>> mobile, clear, unpolluted,
>> distinct, invulnerable, loving the good, keen,
>> irresistible, beneficent, humane,
>> steadfast, sure, free from anxiety,
>> all-powerful, overseeing all,
>> and penetrating through all spirits
>> that are intelligent, pure, and altogether subtle.
> For wisdom is more mobile than any motion;
>> because of her pureness she pervades and penetrates all things.
> For she is a breath of the power of God,
>> and a pure emanation of the glory of the Almighty;
>> therefore nothing defiled gains entrance into her.
> For she is a reflection of eternal light,
>> a spotless mirror of the working of God,
>> and an image of his goodness.
> Though she is but one, she can do all things,
>> and while remaining in herself, she renews all things;
>> in every generation she passes into holy souls
>> and makes them friends of God, and prophets;
>> for God loves nothing so much as the person who lives with wisdom.
>> (Wis. 7:22b-28)

These are the twenty-one attributes of wisdom (cf. Winston 1976, 178–83). Pneumatological significance is granted to and associated with intelligence, purity, particularity, the good, omnipotence, omniscience, omnipresence, and divine glory, presence, and activity. Spirit-wisdom produces holiness of character, endows vital relationships, and enables vocational calling. She is the living breath which pervades and penetrates the creation, and gives it meaning, purpose and intelligibility relative to the creator.

As we shall see, this sapiential material provides the backdrop to the theological reflections of early Jewish Christianity. For the moment, however, the association between Spirit and rationality is what is being emphasized. The world is meaningful and intelligible because it, along with the human creatures who are its inhabitants, is the result of God's activity by his Spirit and his Word. Not surprisingly, identification of the Spirit with wisdom, creativity, and discernment can be found throughout the remainder of the scriptural tradition. The Spirit therefore is the source of ability and knowledge relevant to the creation and to the development of aesthetic beauty (Exod. 31:3–5). She is also the fount of wisdom, understanding, counsel, and the knowledge and fear of the Lord (Isa. 11:2; cf. Ecclus. 39:6). As she provides guidance and counsel for human vocation (1 Cor. 7:40) and brings direction out of confusion and perplexity (Acts 15:28), the Spirit thus is essential for right human living and relationship. Leo Perdue's summary of wisdom in his discussion of the cosmology of Israel's wisdom literature is pertinent to the present discussion:

> Wisdom is not only the imagination, skill, and talent of the artist and poet to create beauty, but it is also analytical and constructive reason that both observes and posits coherence and order, whether in reference to elements of nature or in the persuasive arguments of moral discourse. For the sages, divine wisdom creates and orders the world, originates and sustains all life, and, embodied in sapiential literature, teaches those who take up the path to sagehood. (1994, 332)

1.2.2 The question that now needs to be addressed, however, is the specific relationship between the Spirit and wisdom in light of christology. Whereas the sapiential tradition understood wisdom to encompass both the divine breath and the divine word, the earliest Christians seemed to favor christological rather than pneumatological associations with the wisdom of God. Thus Paul clearly equates "Christ the power of God and the wisdom of God" (1 Cor. 1:24 and 30), and the remainder of the Christian Testament does not seriously challenge this connection (cf. Luke 2:47, 52; 11:49; Matt. 11:19, passim). Yet at the same time, in an important section immediately following, Paul also clearly connects the Spirit with the divine mind:

> [T]hese things God has revealed to us through his Spirit; for the Spirit searches everything, even the depths of God. For what human being knows what is truly

human except the human spirit that is within? So also no one comprehends what is truly God's except the Spirit of God. Now we have received not the spirit of the world, but the Spirit that is from God, so that we may understand that gifts bestowed on us by. And we speak of these things in words not taught by human wisdom but taught by the Spirit, interpreting spiritual things to those who are spiritual. Those who are unspiritual do not receive the things of God's Spirit, for they are foolishness to them, and they are unable to understand them because they are spiritually discerned. Those who are spiritual discern all things, but they are themselves subject to no one else's scrutiny. "For who has known the mind of the Lord so as to instruct him?" But we have the mind of Christ. (1 Cor. 2:10–16)

How might these comments be understood in light of the preceding discussions both about Jesus as the wisdom of God and about the Spirit and rationality?

Any attempt to answer this question cannot avoid exegeting this motif in Paul's first letter to the Corinthians (cf. Davis 1984, Part One). In the initial few chapters, Paul seems preoccupied with distinguishing between the wisdom of the world from the wisdom of God. In the background, however, certain assumptions about wisdom seem to be operative. As previously noted, the intertestamental period saw a re-convergence of the conjunction of the divine breath and word in the wisdom tradition. This link led in a number of directions, such as the conjunction of wisdom and creation in the canonical Proverbs (8:22–31). Later, the deutero-canonical Ecclesiasticus, also known as the Wisdom of Jesus Son of Sirach, associates wisdom with the word of God. Specifically, the link between wisdom and the Mosaic Torah is argued for at length by Ben Sirach. This is elaborated upon in the writings of Philo of Alexandria (ca. 25 B.C.E.–50 C.E.) in terms of spiritual formation: wisdom derived from the word of God in general and the Torah particularly purifies the soul and enables it to make spiritual progress in its return to its creator. Following from this, as evident in communities like that of the Essenes at Qumran, leadership is recognized according to sapiential and pentecostal categories. The capable leader is spiritually mature, perfect in wisdom and understanding.

Many of these notions of wisdom appear to have been operative among and valued by the Corinthians. Paul's immediate concern is with the divisions among Christians at Corinth. Factions were formed following certain key personalities who had seized ecclesial position according to their displaying eloquence (1 Cor. 1:17 and 2:1) and wisdom (1:19–22 and 2:4). Further, these leaders appear to have been scribal authorities on the Torah (1:20b). Whether it be "the wisdom of this age [perhaps implicitly a reference to the wisdom of the Torah understood by Paul's opponents] or of the rulers of this age" (2:6) which opposed Jesus' living revelation of God (2:8), the result threatened not only to undermine Paul's ministry among the Corinthians, but also the gospel itself. The signs, eloquence, knowledge and wisdom which appear to have captivated the Corinthians had puffed them up (1:31 and 3:21), divided the body of Christ (1:10–13 and 3:3–9), and blinded them to the fact that worldly wisdom it no more than foolishness with God (1:18–20, 25–28, 2:14, 3:19).

Against these various forms of wisdom embraced by the Corinthians, Paul sets Jesus, the wisdom of God.[5] Contrary to the expectations of the Corinthians, this wisdom is most fully manifest in the cross (1:17, 30, and 2:2). Jesus as the wisdom of God is powerful for salvation not solely because he was an eloquent teacher of the law who confounded and awed his listeners with the authoritativeness with which he spoke. Rather, Jesus saves precisely in and through the event of the cross (1:18). This divinely appointed instrument of the cross is "wiser than human wisdom, and…stronger than human strength" (1:25). What is otherwise a scandalous affront to the world—being a stumbling block to Jews and foolishness to the wisdom of the Greeks and other gentiles nurtured in the hellenism of the first century—is precisely the means through which God's wisdom, "secret and hidden…decreed before the ages" (2:7), is unveiled.

But while Jesus is clearly the content of the wisdom of God, Paul also goes on to clearly identify the Spirit as the one who mediates and communicates the message of the cross (2:10ff.; cf. Orr and Walther 1976, 165–67). It is the Spirit who expresses and communicates the mind of God which is embodied and concretely manifest in Jesus (cf. Gelpi 1984, esp. 56–66; and MacDonald 1944, 106–25). There are at least three aspects of this communicating work of the Spirit which deserve brief comment here. First, apart from the Spirit, the true and deep things of God are unsearchable and unknowable (2:10–11). This means that any claims regarding the knowledge of God that are made in the flesh or according to worldly rather than truly spiritual standards are misguided. Second, it is only through the wisdom of God given by the Spirit that the spiritual or charismatic gifts are comprehensible (2:12, 14a). This is crucial to the Corinthian situation which featured a congregation enthralled with the gifts of the Spirit (cf. chs. 12–14). Finally, spiritual things, including (by implication) the things of God as revealed in the Torah, remain hidden unless communicated spiritually by the Spirit of God (2:14b–15). Torah cannot be understood solely according to human wisdom. Rather Torah can only be

[5] For a discussion of the connection between Christ and wisdom, see Barbour (1976), Balchin (1982), and Witherington (1995, ch. 7). But for an alternative reading of Paul's intentions in 1 Corinthians, see Fee (2000).

spiritually discerned through the divine breath. It is illuminated and made meaningful through the Spirit only in light of the cross of Jesus the wisdom of God. Apart from the Spirit, then, the divine wisdom remains incommunicable.[6] Thus does Paul also understand the distinctness and yet inseparability of Spirit and Word in the divine economy.

1.2.3 This togetherness of Spirit and Word is explicit in the early Church's understanding of the sacred writings. As divine and human come together in Jesus by the power of the Spirit, so do divine and human coalesce in the scriptures by the same power. Prophecy, while not of the human will, nevertheless comes about as "men and women moved by the Holy Spirit spoke from God" (2 Pet. 1:21). "All scripture is inspired by God" (2 Tim. 3:16), but yet needs to be "rightly explained" (2 Tim. 2:15). The letter of the law and of scripture on its own kills, "but the Spirit gives life" (2 Cor. 3:6; cf. John 6:63). Thus it is the Spirit who unveils and illumines even (especially!) the reading of the Torah of Moses rightly so important to the Corinthians then (2 Cor. 3:12–18) and to the Church since.

It is in this light that the meaning of Scripture has to be understood. The movement by Ben Sirach to identify the divine wisdom with the divine Word must be looked at within the broader canvas of the wisdom tradition which emphasizes the togetherness of Spirit and Word. The 119th Psalm, a wisdom Psalm, will only read in the fundamentalistic sense of sacred utterances possessing magical powers only if taken out of this broader context. This, I believe, points to the truth behind the insistence that all interpretation is by and of Spirit and Word, or, in the traditional order, of Word and Spirit—e.g., Augustine's *De Spiritu et littera* as a reading of the living, "spirited" Christian Testament over and against the "dead letter" of the Hebrew law (cf. Bloesch 1992, and Suurmond 1994). Against this background, however, the acknowledgment of the spiritual dimension of divinely communicated revelation and meaning is clearly suggested. Words in and of themselves are misunderstood, ineffectual, and ultimately, unintelligible. Meaning is finally borne in and by the Spirit through the medium of the Word, and never solely by either on its own apart from the other. Paul's statement that "the letter kills, but the Spirit gives life" (2 Cor. 3:6) therefore highlights the perennial tension which exists between the literal meaning of the biblical text and the living application of the Spirit (cf. Swartley 1984).

---

[6] This is a prevalent theme in the wisdom tradition. Even Philo's interpretation of Genesis 2:7, for example, shows his understanding of "the purpose, or function of the Spirit with regard to the soul, or mind: the Spirit makes possible the mind's knowledge of the divine" (cited in Davis 1984, 121).

Truth must also be understood to emerge out of this convergence of Spirit and Word. This is especially clear in the Johannine material (cf. Scott 1992, 162–65). Jesus is clearly *the* truth (John 14:6; cf. 1:14, 17) and teaches the truth (8:32). But the Spirit is the Spirit of truth (14:17, 15:26; 1 John 4:6, 5:6), of whom Jesus says "will teach you everything, and remind you of all that I have said to you" (14:26). But the truth the Spirit communicates is not strictly circumscribed by Jesus' teachings. Rather, the Spirit "will guide you into all the truth; for he will not speak on his own, but will speak whatever he hears, and he will declare to you the things that are to come" (16:13). Further, the anointing of the Spirit is the sufficient basis of *all* knowledge, teaching, and discernment of the truth over and against that which are lies (1 John 2:20, 27). In short, the Spirit will expand, illuminate, apply, and communicate the truth which is embodied in Jesus.

That divinely originated meaning and the mind of God can be grasped by human beings presupposes some sort of point of contact between the divine and the human. The mediating key, it should now be clear, is pneumatological. This explains the blurring of the boundaries between divine and human spirit throughout the Bible, especially in some places in the Second Testament where contextual considerations are the only clues that enable distinguishing—and even then, with great difficulty and without much certainty—between divine *pneuma* and human *pneuma* (e.g., Rom. 12:11 and 2 Cor. 6:6; cf. Moule 1978, 7–12). Of course, this should not be surprising by now given the previous discussions regarding the Spirit's role in creation and the relationality of Spirit considered both horizontally between human beings and vertically regarding human relationships with God. Human beings are rational precisely because they are spiritually created in the image of God. As such, the human spirit renders intelligibility itself as well as the human understanding and the interpretation of life. As Joseph Wong puts it summarizing the thinking of Rahner,

the human *pneuma* is also a created reality coming from the divine breath at the creation. It is the "organ of communication with the transcendent" [citing Paul Evdokimov, *L'Orthodoxie* (Paris: Delachaux et Niestlé, 1959), 64]. As receptivity for the divine Spirit, the human spirit is the peak of the human person through which he communicates with the beyond. As an expression of being the image of God, the *pneuma* reveals the celestial origin of human beings and renders them 'strangers and exiles on the earth' (cf. Heb. 11, 13), aspiring for the heavenly city. As *homo viator*, the human person is in a state of transit towards the future Passover; even more, he himself is this Passover. Thus, the human spirit coincides with his essential character of 'passing over,' i.e. with his innate longing towards the beyond. It is precisely this spirit which makes human beings capable of receiving the Spirit of God. (Wong 1992, 77; cf. Jones [1941] 1963)

In this way, it is clear that the Spirit not only communicates rationality to the created order and is the condition of human rationality, but also provides the guiding soteriological rationale for human existence vis-à-vis the purposes and intentions of the creator.[7] Thus is the category of "spirit" intimately related to the question of meaning and truth, and thus is it the case that when we speak of the contemporary postmodern "crisis of spirit," we are at the same time expressing our concerns regarding the "crisis of meaning" and the "crisis of truth." The recovery of both presumes and requires the recovery of Spirit, and the latter includes the recovery of the self as spiritual being, created to be in relationship with God and therefore to live meaningfully and truthfully.

In all of this, however, our concern is first and foremost theological even while recognizing that theology can be separated from soteriology only in an artificial sense, if at all. Yet my point has been to emphasize that the Spirit can be understood as the mind of God. She is the presupposition undergirding the intelligibility of divinity, our understanding the same, and the interpretation of the divine life, meant in the twofold sense of our interpreting theologically the divine life, and the divine life's interpreting itself and its activity—the created order. It is precisely for this reason that pneumatology cannot be isolated from the remainder of the theological loci since it is the Spirit who reveals the depths of the divine reality. This is evidenced in Paul's doxological exclamation:

> Oh, the depths of the riches and wisdom and knowledge of God! How unsearchable are his judgments, and how inscrutable his ways!
>
> "For who has known the mind of the Lord?
>   Or who has been his counselor?"
> "Or who has given a gift to him,
>   to receive a gift in return?"
>
> For from him and through him and to him are all things. To him be the glory forever. Amen. (Rom. 11:33–36)

I would suggest that the answers to Paul's rhetorical questions lie in

---

[7] This corresponds loosely to the tri-dimensional view of the Spirit's cosmic, anthropic, and regenerative work in Calvin's theology. For Calvin, the Spirit's work at the second level is primarily (if not only) preservative and restraining, while that at the third level is redemptive and sanctifying. For an overview of Calvin's pneumatology, see Bolt (1989).

pneumatology. It is only the Spirit who has known the mind of the Lord (1 Cor. 10–11). It is she who is his counselor (Isa. 11:2; Wis. 9:17). And, as we will see below [2.2.1], she is the gift of the Father who returns to him the love of the Son. Theological rationality and intelligibility is therefore pneumatological through and through. This does not, however, mean that theology is completely rationalizable in the sense of Enlightenment rationality. Rather, it means that there is a distinctively pneumatological rationality which informs theological method and hermeneutics—a pneumatological imagination, to be specific, which I will develop later.

1.3 The Spirit as the *Dunamis* of Life

The biblical pneumatology elaborated so far has been according to the categories of relationality and rationality. The third aspect to be discussed, pervasive throughout recent theological literature, is the Spirit as the dynamic power of life (cf. Moltmann 1992 and 1997; cf. Edwards 1999, 83–88). Life is our most treasured possession. At the same time, it is not ours by right, but by gift—the gracious gift of God. Life was initially given through the Spirit and the Word at the original creation of the world and its inhabitants, including human beings. Life continues to be given through the fall and the ambiguities of history in anticipation of the eschatological gift of eternal life. In what follows, I want to look at the Spirit as the power of life in creation in general, in humanity in particular, and in the dynamic movements of cosmic and historical existence directed toward the eschaton.

1.3.1 The Spirit is the power of life in creation. The creation account in Genesis includes the key statement in the prologue: "the earth was a formless void and darkness covered the face of the deep, while a wind [*ruach*] from God swept over face of the waters" (Gen. 1:2). This *ruach*, the divine breath which hovers or sweeps over the deep void and darkness, is the preparatory means through which the cosmos is created. Thus the Word of God that creates is carried by *ruach*: "Let there be light," is uttered through the divine breath of life.

The Hebrew Bible presents a consistent witness to the work of the Spirit in creation (cf. Murphy 1993). The Spirit of God fills the world and holds all things together (Ps. 139:6 and Wis. 1:7). The outpouring of the Spirit transforms deserts into fertile fields and forests (Isa. 32:15). All the creatures of creation—wild donkeys, birds, storks, goats, lions, the fish of the sea, etc.—are fed by Yahweh and nourished by his breath, apart from which "they die and return to their dust"; but, "When you send your Spirit, they are created; and you renew the face of the ground" (Ps. 104:29–30; cf. Judith 16:14). And, as with the creation narratives, God's creative work conjoins the Spirit and the Word: "By the word of the LORD the heavens were made, and all their host by the breath of his mouth" (Ps. 33:6).

It is therefore expected that the created order provides natural symbols of the divine Spirit who is her author and source. The Spirit is depicted throughout the Scriptures as wind, water, and even fire. True, these symbols are ambiguous, pointing to the destructive capacity of these elements as much as they are indicative of the life-giving and preserving power of that same Spirit. For the moment, however, observe how each of these symbols are typologically revealed in the cloud which sat over the people of Israel (Exod. 13:21ff.). Clouds, of course, are more or less condensed combinations of hydrogen oxide that are carried by the wind. In this case, the cloud by day became a pillar of fire each night to provide the traveling Israelites with light. This cloud/fire not only guided the Israelites in their journey across the wilderness, it also protected them from Pharaoh and his army of chariots (Exod. 14:19–20). Further, it was the means through which the glory of the Lord would be manifest to Israel (Exod. 16:10) and through which the provision of manna was delivered ("from heaven," Exod. 16:4). In short, the cloud/fire represented the glory, presence, and activity of God among the people of God. This is, expectedly so given the underlying Jewish character and Hebraic mentality of the earliest Christians, consistent with the affirmations of the Second Testament regarding the Spirit. Throughout the later canon, the Spirit is the Spirit of glory (1 Pet. 4:14) who is the life-giving presence and activity of God among the ecclesial community. As Gordon Fee summarizes, the Spirit is "God's way of being present, powerfully present, in our lives and communities as we await the consummation of the kingdom of God" (1994, xxi).

I will return later to the function of these natural symbols of the Spirit in the salvation of the people of God. For the moment, however, I simply want to note that the scriptural witness is unmistakable about the Spirit as the life-breath of God in and for creation. The God who is love (1 John 4:8, 16) is God who is Spirit (John 4:24). As such, God breathes out of himself an other—the created order—to cherish, nourish, and love. It is this created order which provides the environment for living creatures which in turn respond to their creator. And, it is the entirety of this living environment, the cosmos, which in turn serves as a habitat for the human species, the crown of God's creation (Ps. 8:5b, even if such needs to be understood non-anthropocentrically, as I will later argue), also caused to be by the life-giving Spirit of God.

1.3.2 The creation narrative is also clear that "the LORD God formed man from the dust of the ground, and breathed into his nostrils the breath of life; and the man became a living being" (Gen. 2:7). The parallelism between Spirit and Word in the biblical tradition (e.g., Ps. 33:6) and the connection between Spirit and wisdom come together in reflections on the formation of *homo sapien* in the Wisdom of Solomon where the author addresses God as the one who has "made all things by your word, and by your wisdom have formed humankind" (9:1–2). Having been given the breath of life, human beings are in turn able to breathe and utter words of life (Prov. 18:21). At the same time, the living person knows him or herself as alive, and that this is the gift of the breath of God (Job 33:4). The image of God in humankind consists, then, of at least the following characteristics: that human beings partake of the divine breath of life, and that they have conscious understanding of themselves, each other, and of their creator. As Gary Badcock puts it, "it is essential that our understanding of the work of the Holy Spirit should also be *humanizing* in its basic thrust" (1997, 264; italics orig.). In this way, the formation of the *homo sapien* from the dust of the ground brought about a living, rational and self-consciously relational creature (cf. Pannenberg 1970 and 1985).

Yet from the very beginning, all was not well. Humankind is "born to trouble," says Eliphaz the Temanite (Job 5:7), and with the creation of *ha adam* comes also the fall. This is a fall from life unto death, from a holy consciousness of God, self, others and the world to an unholy knowledge of both good and evil, from being intimately related to God and others to being separated from God, alienated from others and at odds with the very environment that sustains and nurtures life. The very capacity to know appears to bring about the possibility of knowing evil, and therefore of knowing (and experiencing) death (cf. Engnell 1955).

But the breath of life is not withdrawn and death is not given the final word. The gift of life is miraculously extended in and through the experience of death, the penultimate triumph of evil, and the experience of isolation, alienation, and loneliness. From these depths, experienced also by Jesus of Nazareth, the Spirit breathes forth anew, empowering resurrection life. That which is no more than dry bones in the valley of the shadow of death, is rescued through the life-giving breath of God. The bones are given flesh, skin, hope and new life (cf. Ezek. 37:1–14). This new life reaches to the depths of the human condition and constitution since it includes cleansing from impurities and idolatry as well as the endowment of the Spirit in a new heart (of flesh rather than of stone), symbolizing the total re-creation of what it means to be human (Ezek. 36:25–27; cf. Ps. 51:10–11). Thus could the Apostle Paul exclaim that "if anyone is in Christ, there is a new creation: everything old has passed away; see, everything has become new!" (2 Cor. 5:17). In the same way, "Death has been swallowed up in victory" (1 Cor. 15:54b).

In part because God loves the world without favoritism, the life-giving breath of God is poured out on all flesh. Not coincidentally, the Spirit is also characterized and imaged as a dove, an ancient symbol for love (Schroer 2000, 132–63). Yet the movements of the breath of God remain unpredictable (John 3:8). The Spirit's works, however, are to birth new life through water and fire. New life comes through the flood, a type of the baptism into the death and burial of Christ and raising from death with him (Rom. 6:1–14 and Col. 2:12), and of the baptism through water which saves because of Christ's resurrection from the dead (1 Pet. 3:20–21). New life also emerges from the purifying fire of the Spirit through whom Jesus baptizes (cp. Luke 3:16 and 1 Cor. 3:13–15; 2 Thess. 1:7; Heb. 12:29; 1 Pet. 1:7; 2 Pet. 3:7–12; Rev. 3:18). In both cases, the breath of God brings life out of death (cf. John 12:24) analogously to how water nourishes and sustains life, and how fire provides heat against the cold and serves as the means through which purification and renewal occur.

The form that life takes, however, is shaped by the Spirit of fellowship or communion (cf. 2 Cor. 13:13). Thus has the Spirit created *homo sapien* for community, and true community is to be experienced in the new body of Christ, the *ekklesia*. This is also the fellowship of the Spirit whereby human beings live in the mutual sociality of having all things in common, breaking and sharing bread, praying, and worshipping together (Acts 2:41–47). Such is the nature of life shared in the Spirit, that members of the body of Christ are of one mind, loving and giving to each other out of deference and humility, not looking for the interests of self but of the other (Phil. 2:1–4). It is this life in the Spirit which enables the fulfillment of the second commandment since it is the Spirit who frees human beings for each other by crucifying the flesh along with its passions and desires, and birthing, in their place, genuine expressions of love, joy, peace, patience, kindness, generosity, faithfulness, gentleness and self-control (Gal. 5:13–26). And, of course, loving one another by the power of the Spirit is, finally, a manifestation of the profound truth that one has been grasped and perfected by the love of God himself, thus being enabled to truly love God in return (1 John 4:7–21).

1.3.3 So far, we have been exploring the Spirit as the power and breath of life. The dynamism inherent in this biblical symbol points to the truth that the life given by the Spirit represents the Spirit's ongoing gift of herself to the world. Wind is characterized by vitality, energy, force, and movement. The vital, energetic, and dynamic *ruach* or *pneuma* of God is thus the wind that "infuses life, fertilizes matter, and engenders life" (Bobrinskoy 1999, 26). Creation can thereby be imaged as the product of the breath going forth and returning to the Godhead. History is the realm of this going forth and returning specifically vis-à-vis the affairs of humankind. Together, creation and history can be considered as the "playing field" on which the dramatic works of God are manifest. The Spirit as the power of life calls attention to the dynamic movements which constitute this drama. At various levels, the ongoing developments of this drama cannot be predicted in its entirety, and this precisely because of the unpredictability of the life-giving Spirit. Breath bestowed on the cosmic order endows it with its own autonomy, a differentiated autonomy appropriately pertinent to the diversity of creatures which constitute the creation.

What is perhaps in some sense predictable (and that only because it is received by faith and with hope as divinely revealed) is the ordained purposes for the creation. The Spirit who breathed life at the beginning is the same Spirit who continues to renews life in the world, and who will someday recreate it completely. In anticipation of that eschatological breath of life, the present work of the Spirit is to be the healing force and agent of what is concretely manifest in the life, death and resurrection of Jesus (cf. Johnson 1993a, 43). Thus Spirit's own mission is to heal the sick, the hurt, the wounded; to reconcile those who are alienated and estranged; to make whole that which is shattered, fragmented, and broken; to bring back into relationship those who are separated; to restore that which is lost; to provide meaning to the experience of the absurd, of apparently gratuitous evil and irredeemable suffering, of life in what might otherwise be a fortuitous universe; to complete that which is incomplete and longing for completion. Her work in Jesus the Christ is thus proleptic in that it anticipates the eschatological event consummating the purposes of God. In the meanwhile, however, the Spirit's anointing power is certainly not limited to the clearly identifiable people of God, as witnessed by her coming upon Balaam, a Mesopotamian soothsayer (Num. 24:2), and Cyrus, a Chaldean ruler (Isa. 45:1).

In any case, all of the teleologically directed movements of the Spirit pertain not only to the human sphere but to the world as a whole. The pentecostal outpouring was itself constituted by cosmic reverberations (Acts 2:19–21) signifying the universal implications and impact of the Spirit's work which correlate with the saving acts of God among human beings. Thus is divine salvation offered to and accomplished among human beings part of the larger redemptive work of God. This cosmic aspect of Pentecost is, in part, the response of the divine breath to the creation's longing for liberation and redemption. For this reason the Spirit leads us to pray "in accordance with God's will" for the revelation of that eschatological glory toward which the creation is directed, and for the working out of all things according to the divine purposes (Rom. 8:18–28). Toward these ends, the Spirit extends her invitation to those who have ears to hear (cf. Rev. 22:17).

Ruach/pneuma thus calls attention to the dynamism at the heart not only of the divine life but also of the natural and human spheres of the created order. If the Spirit is the dynamism or power of life, then reality is not other than differentiated dimensions of vitality, energy, and life, all sustained by the divine breath. Of course, the created order and historical time and existence are both characterized presently by sin, atrophy, and death as well. Yet it is precisely the ongoing and dynamic presence and activity of the Spirit which counters the effects of sin, reverses the atrophaic nature of fallen reality, and triumphs finally over death. This means that natural processes and existence in historical time do not have the final word. In fact, because of the dynamic nature of reality, there is no finality to cosmic perspectives, movements or events. The end can only be nothing other than the eschatological inbreaking (or, outbreaking, depending on which metaphor is preferred) of the kingdom of God wrought about in, by, and through the Spirit.

Meanwhile, the Spirit continues to lure creation toward its destiny even while she heals the fractures in its various orders. Of course, the activities of human beings—including the exercise of understanding, reason, and praxis directed toward the attainment and fulfillment of life—are mediated by and through the Spirit of God. This very fact in and of itself is further testimony to the penultimacy of all human thoughts, projects, and accomplishments, situated as they are within the horizon of the created order and of historical finitude. In short, the dynamic character of historical existence means that human thinking and acting attain finality only if, in a self-deceiving sense, human beings fail to recognize their provisional character and thereby claim for their thoughts and activities absolute ultimacy. Such beliefs and actions are idolatrous and demonic since they claim what belongs rightly only to God.

2 Pneumatology and Trinitarian Theology

Having now established from the biblical witness the central pneumatological categories employed in this essay, the objectives in this chapter are threefold. First, I wish to explore the properly theological implications of pneumatology for the doctrine of God. My argument here is that pneumatology is central to a robustly trinitarian vision of God. The following therefore builds from the pneumatological categories toward a fully pneumatological (read: trinitarian) theology. Because according to a fundamental principle of orthodox theology, *opera ad extra sunt indivisa*—the external works of God in the world are undivided, and belong to all three persons together—I propose to explore how the categories of relationality, rationality, and dynamic life illuminate both pneumatology and divinity. More important, I will also attempt to demonstrate that only a pneumatological theism is able to overcome binitarian conceptions of God and move toward a fully trinitarian theology. To accomplish this argument, two dominant trinitarian models, the social and the psychological, will be presented. The former emphasizes the divine mutuality and intratrinitarian relationality according (as I will suggest) to the way things are or the order of being (*ordo essendi*), while the latter focuses on the divine unity and causality (procession and spiration) as emergent from our epistemic perspectives or the order of knowing (*ordo cognoscendii*).[1] They will be discussed according to the two dominant metaphors which characterize the leading intuitions of each model: the Irenaean metaphor of the Word and Spirit as the "two hands of the Father," and the Augustinian metaphor of the Spirit as the "mutual love" between the Father and the Son.

Second, I wish to sketch a trinitarian framework that is sufficiently broad

---

[1] I introduce this nomenclature and distinction not in order to enter into debate with the medieval Schoolmen on this issue but because it serves as a convenient shorthand for specifying the problem of how human knowing corresponds to reality or the way things are. Epistemologically, Kant framed the question as that of how human knowledge as emergent from the interpretive categories of the mind could deliver truths about things in themselves. Theologically, the question is that of how knowledge that is always already hermeneutical (*ordo cognoscendii*) can deliver transcendental truths about God and God's relationship to the world (*ordo essendi*). This problematic is what drives our inquiry in parts one (devoted to metaphysics and ontology) and two (devoted to epistemology) of this book.

49

to situate the foundational pneumatology—ontology, metaphysics, and epistemology which underwrites the hermeneutic focus of this essay. My intention, therefore, is not to make primarily a dogmatic or historical argument regarding the doctrine of the Trinity, nor is it to explicate and defend another trinitarian formulation for its own sake. Rather, the motivation for what follows is to correlate the movement from pneumatology through theology to ontology and metaphysics, always with an eye toward epistemological, hermeneutical and methodological issues.

This leads, finally, to the goal of demonstrating throughout this and the next chapter on ontology and metaphysics how the pneumatological categories illuminate the hermeneutical circle. What I wish to inquire into is the logic of pneumatology that informs Christian faith. What kind of pneumatological rationality underwrites trinitarian belief and practice? The hypothesis to be tested is whether or not the pneumatological approach adopted here fulfills the promise of a robustly trinitarian and hermeneutical theology in anticipation of a trinitarian metaphysics that is more viable for our time, and if so, how so. If this hypothesis is confirmed, the result will take us some way toward a pneumatologically driven hermeneutical trialectic.

2.1 Spirit and Word as the "two hands of the Father"

Traditionally, the Church has understood the Word and the Spirit to represent the right and left hands (cf. Holl 1998) of God respectively. This no doubt followed the scriptural association of Jesus with the right hand of God (Acts 2:33, 7:55; Rom. 8:34; Eph. 1:20; Col. 3:1; 1 Pet. 3:22; Hebrews, passim), thus connecting the Son of God with what symbolizes strength and salvation throughout the Hebrew Bible. My reversing the order does not require a switching of the two hands. Rather, the reversal calls attention to the pneumatological emphasis being developed here even while it points metaphorically to the ambidexterity of God who does work *all* things according to his two hands. Accordingly, in what follows I will briefly trace the development of the "two hands" metaphor in the Church beginning with Irenaeus, specifically explore its logic in opening up toward a fully relational trinitarian theology among the fourth century Greek fathers, and make connections with recent proposals regarding relational models of the Trinity.

2.1.1 The clearest statement of the "two hands" metaphor by Irenaeus, bishop of Lyons (ca. 130–200), is in the Preface to Book IV of *Against Heresies* where he is discussing the human constitution: "Now man is a mixed organization of soul and flesh, who was formed after the likeness of God, and molded by His hands, that is, by the Son and Holy Spirit, to whom also He said, 'Let Us make man'" (IV.Pref.4; cf. V.1.3).[2] Later in the same book, in affirming the doctrine of creation as revelatory of God, he writes, "For with Him [God the Father] were always present the Word and Wisdom, the Son and the Spirit, by whom and in whom, freely and spontaneously, He made all things" (IV.20.1); and, "There is therefore one God, who by the Word and Wisdom created and arranged all things" (IV.20.4).

These remarks need to be understood in light of Irenaeus' usage of and repeated reference to the biblical metaphor of the handiwork of God (cf. Ps. 19:1; 102:25; Isa. 40:12). Given the clear scriptural data concerning the creative work of God through Spirit and Word, the "two hands of God" can be seen as an appropriate theological image emergent from the confluence of these two distinct strands of the biblical witness. As Irenaeus writes elsewhere,

> because God is rational [λογικός], he therefore created what is made by his Word [λογος], and, as God is Spirit, so he disposed everything by his Spirit....Therefore, since the Word establishes, that is, gives body and substance, but the Spirit disposes and shapes the variety of powers, the Son is rightly and properly called Word, while the Spirit is called the Wisdom of God. (*Demonstration of the Apostolic Preaching* 5, qtd. in Minns 1994, 50).

Throughout *Against Heresies*, then, Spirit/Wisdom and Word are thus understood as the two hands of God which formed the visible world, including its inhabitants, and accomplish the purposes of God (I.22.1; II.30.9; III.24.2; IV.7.4).

The significance of the two hands model for the purposes at hand should be made explicit. First, in looking beyond Irenaeus for the moment, credit needs to be given to the bishop of Lyons for developing a motif which has since proven to be a rich source for reflection in the Christian theological tradition. This is especially the case with regard to hermeneutics and the doctrine of Scripture. The magisterial Reformers retrieved this Irenaean metaphor for precisely this reason. Spirit and Word as the two hands of the Father were understood as inseparable, pointing to and revealed by and in Jesus through the Spirit, and signifying the togetherness of the Church and Scripture

---

[2] Unless otherwise noted, all quotations from the patristic fathers are from *The Ante-Nicene Fathers*, and the *Nicene and Post-Nicene Fathers*, First and Second Series, reprinted by Hendrickson Publishers, 1994. They will be referenced parenthetically in the text according to the book, chapter (where given), and (where given) paragraph divisions as found in this edition.

as illuminated by the Spirit. Thus, despite *sola scriptura*, for Protestants, "The Bible is the guide of preaching in the church and the church is the interpreter and proclaimer of the message in the Bible" (Prenter 1965, 6). This book proposes a fully trinitarian hermeneutical vision that builds on Irenaeus' insight concerning the relationship between the Spirit and the Word and argues for a more consistent re-appropriation of this motif suggested but not followed through by the Protestant Reformation.

Second, given the polemical intentions of *Against Heresies* against the threat of second and third century gnosticism, the two hands metaphor makes a number of emphatic statements. For one thing, Spirit and Word are not divine emanations from which emerge the created order, but the activity of divinity itself. Eternally co-existent with the Father, Spirit and Word are the Father's direct and immediate agents of creation. Further, as will be detailed below, incarnation and Pentecost continue the work of creation and are indicative of God's intrinsic and personal relationship to the world. Throughout, Irenaeus clearly intends to undermine the gnostic emphasis on the absolute transcendence of God, with regard not only to redemption but especially to creation (cf. Lawson 1948, 124–29). Thus in the incarnation and at Pentecost, God has not only revealed himself as radically immanent in the world, but in the process has also demonstrated that materiality is not impure and contaminated as asserted by gnostic dualism. The result, however, is that insofar as Spirit and Word are truly God's personal activity in creation, neither is subordinate to the Father ontologically. To put it crassly, without his hands, the Father is impotent and therefore neither creator nor divine; but it is precisely in and through the work of his two hands that the divinity of the Father is established as both creator and redeemer.

Last but certainly not least, the two hands metaphor connotes the interdependence of Spirit and Word in the work of creation and redemption. In this case, whether intentionally or not, this metaphor functions as one aspect of Irenaeus' overarching objective of countering the gnostic doctrine of hierarchical emanations. More important theologically, however, is that the two hands explicitly posits an intratrinitarian egalitarianism. Now insofar as this egalitarian relationality between Spirit and Word is connected to the headship and personhood of the Father, it feeds, albeit indirectly so far as Irenaeus himself is concerned, the third century debate on monarchianism. Yet at the same time, because of its non-subordinationist vision of Spirit and Word, it also contained the seeds for the radically relational trinitarianism developed by the fourth century Greek fathers. In this later vision, the mutuality of Spirit and Word as agents of the Father's creative and redemptive work are developed into a triune inter-relationality which the tradition has since conceptualized as the coinherence of the divine persons.

2.1.2 I want to suggest that the doctrine of coinherence logically follows from Irenaeus' two hands model and therefore presupposes it. This patristic doctrine—known later in Greek as *perichoresis* (mutuality of partners in a dance) and in Latin as either *circumincession* (to walk around) or *circuminsession* (to sit around) (cf. Durrwell 1986, 182 n 19)—builds on both aspects of Irenaeus' two hands model: that which envisions the interdependence and mutuality of the two hands, and that which emphasizes the unity of the two hands with the Father. In its basic form, to speak of trinitarian coinherence is to attempt to describe how Spirit, Son and Father can be one while each remains distinct from the other two. In order to examine my hypothesis, I propose to focus on the post-Nicene pneumatological considerations during the middle and latter half of the fourth century which finally confirmed trinitarian belief.

Not surprisingly, it is the champion of the *homoousios*, Athanasius of Alexandria, who first arrives at the notion of *trinitarian* coinherence in his *Letters Against Serapion*.[3] Building on his former anti-Arian polemics, Athanasius' pneumatological reflections proceed from the consubstantial relationship between Father and Son. "When mention is made of the Father, there is included also his Word, and the Spirit who is in the Son. If the Son is named, the Father is in the Son, and the Spirit is not outside the Word" (*Ag. Serapion* I.14). Going on from there, he discusses a number of natural triadic analogies such as that of the sun, its radiance, and its heat, and that of a fountain, its river, and its drink. With regard to the latter analogy, the Father is likened to the fountain, the Son to the river, and the Spirit to the one of whom we drink. Against this background, Athanasius queries:

> But if there is such co-ordination [συστοιχία] and unity within the holy Triad, who can separate either the Son from the Father, or the Spirit from the Son or from the Father himself?...How, when the Spirit is in us, the Son is said to be in us? How, when the Son is in us, the Father is said to be in us?...Or why, when the One is in us, the Triad is said to be in us?

His answer, of course, is that, "As the Son is in the Spirit as in his own image, so also the Father is in the Son" (*Ag. Serapion* I.20).

---

[3] For an overview of Athanasius' debate with Serapion and the Tropici (a different group than the Macedonians or "pneumatomachians" engaged by the Cappadocian fathers), see the "Introduction" in Shapland (1951, esp. 27–34). All quotations from Athanasius' letters *Against Serapion* will be from Shapland's translation.

Athanasius' response is illuminating given two crucial assumptions. First, he is convinced that an analogy pertains between the Son revealing the image of the Father and the Spirit revealing the image of the Son—i.e., in that the Spirit always calls attention to and glorifies the Son (cf. John 16:14). For this reason, knowledge of the Spirit is available to us only through the Son, although in a paradoxical way because of the reciprocity between Spirit and Son as the two hands of the Father, knowledge of the Son is also given through the Spirit. Second, and more important, is his insistence that the divine life is not dyadic, but rather triune. "For as the Son, who is in the Father and the Father in him, is not a creature but pertains to the essence of the Father...; so also it is not lawful to rank with the creatures the Spirit who is in the Son, and the Son in him, nor to divide him from the Word and reduce the Triad to imperfection" (*Ag. Serapion* I.21). More specifically, Athanasius' argues that, "if the Son is not a creature, because he is not in places assigned to him, but is in the Father, and because he is everywhere even while he is outside all things; it follows that the Spirit cannot be a creature, for he is not in places assigned to him, but fills all things and yet is outside all things" (*Ag. Serapion* III.4).

Now Athanasius' primary concern in his letters *Against Serapion* is as elsewhere in his polemical writings: to secure the Spirit's divinity and thereby preserve the Nicene formulation (cf. Torrance 1994, 7–20). Our interest, however, is what might be called the pneumatological logic or pneumatological rationality of trinitarian theology. Granting Irenaeus' equation of Spirit and Word as the two hands of the Father, and Nicea's affirmation of the latter as *homoousios* with the Father, the logical conclusion is that the Spirit cannot be understood as other than consubstantial with the Father in turn. To deny the Spirit's co-essential divinity with the Father's would be to either deny the Son's consubstantiality with the Father or to undermine the interdependence and mutuality of the two hands. Athanasius could not deny the former without compromising his entire mission of defending the *homoousion*, and the traditional consensus regarding the two hands motif rendered it severely problematic even for fourth century thinkers to articulate plausible objections to the latter notion.

But the post-Nicene fathers did not stop here. While historically the doctrine of coinherence emerged specifically from reflecting on the relationship between Father and Son (cf. John 1:18; 10:30, 38; 14:10–11; cp. Prestige [1952] 1985, 282–301), if in fact the Spirit is consubstantial with the Son and with the Father, then the result can be no less than a doctrine of *trinitarian* indwelling or coinherence. A host of patristic witnesses can be brought to bear on this point. The Cappadocians in the East explored various ways to formulate this idea in their works on pneumatology.[4] In the West, both Hilary, bishop of Poitiers, and Augustine clearly affirmed the notion of trinitarian coinherence. The former wrote, "For as the Father is Spirit, so is the Son Spirit; as the Father is God, so is the Son God; as the Father is Light, so is the Son Light….Thus mutually Each is in the Other, for as all is perfect in the Unbegotten Father, so all is perfect in the Only-begotten Son" (*On the Trinity*, III.1, 4), while the latter reflected extensively on "a trinity of persons mutually interrelated" (*On the Trinity* IX.1.1; cf. also V.5.6; VI.7.9; VI.9.10; VIII.10.14, passim). By the time of John of Damascus in the eighth century, the notion of coinherence (*perichoresis*) was thought to illuminate both to the mutual indwelling of the trinitarian persons and the distinctiveness yet togetherness of the divine and human natures of Christ (*Exposition of the Orthodox Faith* 18). It is as a trinitarian notion, however, that the concept has been most fruitful. To affirm the coinherence of the triune persons is to emphasize on the one side their mutuality, reciprocity, subsistence, interdependence and interrelationality, and to deny on the other any kind of ontological subordination, hierarchy, division, individualism or tritheism in the divine life. Certainly this did not mean that the fathers held to an undifferentiated monotheism. On the contrary, it was precisely the doctrine of coinherence which enabled them to affirm God as triune: three mutually indwelling persons, and one God expressed triunely.

Note, however, that considered in this way, the doctrine of trinitarian coinherence ultimately required the distinctions between the persons to be understood in terms of their relationships ad intra. Thus the theological tradition has insisted that everything—whether functionally or essentially—that is predicable of one is predicable of the other two except that the Father is unbegotten originator, the Son is the one begotten of the Father, and the Spirit has proceeded (by spiration) from the Father (and, perhaps, through the Son). Of course, in order to avoid subordination of either Son or Spirit to the Father, the Cappadocians insisted on the Father as originating source, albeit redefining the notion of causality such that this divine source was simultaneous with, rather than preceding, his effects. In this way, the mutuality and reciprocity of the trinitarian relationships could be maintained. The Father cannot be who he is apart from either the Son or the Spirit and vice-versa. The Spirit and the Son mutually constitute the other as the two hands of the Father. In short, the divine persons are understood not as individuals in the modern sense of

---

[4] See especially Basil's *Treatise on the Holy Spirit*; Gregory of Nazianzus's *Fifth Theological Oration on the Holy Spirit*; and Gregory of Nyssa's *On the Holy Spirit against Macedonius* and *On the Holy Trinity and of the Godhead of the Holy Spirit: To Eustathius*.

personhood, but as relationships in the perichoretic sense of the mutuality of partners in a dance. Father, Son, and Spirit are defined, finally, in terms of their mutual relationships each to the other.

2.1.3 I have suggested so far that Irenaeus' two hands model was filled out by the later Church fathers in the direction of a trinitarian and relational theology. In the contemporary theological landscape, the patristic notion of trinitarian coinherence and mutuality has been vigorously retrieved along two fronts: by those advocating social doctrines of the Trinity and by those advocating radically relational understandings of God. I will later return to comment on the former. For the moment, I want to focus on the latter especially insofar as these relational models enable us to see the centrality of pneumatology to the enterprise of trinitarian theology.

A more traditional restatement of the patristic synthesis recently is that by David Cunningham who challenges us to think, with Orthodoxy, of the triune reality in anti-individualistic terms as "relations without remainder" (1998, esp. 25–29, 55–74, and 165–94). Emphasis therefore lies on the divine relations rather than on a triad of persons, substances, or individuals. Language regarding "three individuals" is solely instrumental in providing stability for communication. Thus, "Father" and "Son" arise together in the filial relationship between Jesus and his divine source since neither precedes the other. But notice that their arising together is also a contrasting and constitutive relation that cannot be collapsed into either fatherhood or sonship; this third relation is Spirit. Cunningham's favorite metaphors are pregnancy and the musical orchestra, both of which call to mind participation, mutuality and perichoretic interconnectedness. The goal is to transcend individualistic conceptualizations of the Trinity prevalent historically, and to emphasize that God is "not three persons who 'have' relations, but rather, *three subsistent relations*" who are self-grounded precisely in their interrelationship. God, as Cunningham says, "*is* the relations that God has" (1998, 71).

This move frees up space to reconsider the notion of personhood from a trinitarian and perichoretic starting point rather than from a Cartesian one. The results may have implications not only our understanding of human personhood (cf. Lodahl 2001), but also for our pneumatology. I suggest that Cunningham's retrieval of the notion of "subsistent relations" from the theological tradition correlates with the pneumatological category of relationality in at least two ways. First, it provides theological specification for what otherwise remains a vague pneumatological notion. Explicitly stated, relationality at the heart of pneumatology turns out to be at the heart of trinitarian theology as well. In fact, the language of subsistent relations points precisely to the non-duality between personal individuality and personal relationality: the triune relations are the three persons even while the triune persons are constituted by their relationships with each other. My own references to the three divine persons, both in the preceding and the following, should therefore always be understood according to this notion of subsistent relationality. Second, subsistent relations completes the hermeneutical circle of the biblical data—interpretive category—pneumatological and theological concept. Is it the case that the category of relationality has only emerged out of prolonged engagement with the biblical data and is therefore removed (at least) at a second level from the lived experience of faith; or is it the case that it is clearly embedded in the self-consciousness of Jesus as preserved in the biblical data itself (especially the Johannine material)? Is relationality a category foreign to scripture and imported as a hermeneutical tool or is it ontologically emergent and theologically grounded in the biblical witness? Does my doctrine of the Trinity drive my exegesis (perhaps á la Barth) or the other way around? Which came first: the pneumatology of relationality or the Trinity of subsistent relations? Let the difficulty of answering these questions follow us as we continue our theological, epistemological and hermeneutical reflections.

In any case, it should be clear that the process of retrieving trinitarian theology in relational terms is congruent with the revival of pneumatological reflection as well. If, as is being suggested here, relationality, rationality, and dynamic life are constitutive features of pneumatology, it is not surprising to find these categories illuminating for trinitarian theology. James Loder articulates the correlation between pneumatology and Trinity in this way:

> That God *is* Spirit (John 4) and that the Spirit is also one member *of* the Trinity (John 17, Eph. 2:18, 4:4–6) is not an internal contradiction. The potential confusion is resolved if it is recognized that it is inherent in the nature of the Spirit to be relational and at the same time in relation to relate to itself. That is, God both *is* Spirit and *has* Spirit. (1998, 195)

In short, the relational logic of pneumatology translates into a relational trinitarianism.

Others, however, have insisted that this relationality at the heart of divinity ad intra be understood to also characterized the divine life ad extra. This is predicated on the fact that there is at least one world—this one—and as such, there must be an intrinsic relationality between God and the world if in fact God ad intra is relationally constituted. There are certainly stronger and weaker forms of this claim. Among the former are those who would insist that the world is necessary in some way to the divine life (e.g., process theology, robust panentheism, pantheism), while those advocating the latter would insist only that creation, incarnation and Pentecost portray God as intimately and immanently related to the world while preserving essential relations only for the triune persons ad intra (cf. Gunton 1997, 137–57; Peters 1993). Resolving this debate is not essential to the task at hand. Rather, I call attention again to what might be considered the logic of pneumatology that permeates these discussions. Insofar as the central features of pneumatology include relationality, rationality and dynamic life and freedom, so also, arguably, are these characteristic both of God vis-à-vis the world, and, by extrapolation, of the world itself insofar as it represents the creative work of God. As Elizabeth Johnson says in a striking passage which deserves to be quoted at length:

> What is immediately striking is that there is no possible aspect of the Spirit of God, either *ad intra* or *ad extra*, that can be spoken about without factoring in the idea of relation in an essential way. Can there be an unrelated Spirit, existing in splendid isolation? The history of theology shows that the notion has been and is unthinkable. Relationality is intrinsic to her very being as love, gift, and friend both to the world and within the holy mystery of God. At the same time that she is intrinsically related, the Spirit is essentially free, blowing like the wind where she wills, not, as feared, cramped, or diminished by relation but being distinctively Spirit precisely in and through relation. In contrast to the idea of god that equates relation with necessity or dependence and thus opposes relation and freedom, the ways of the Spirit show divine being to be characterized by a dynamic relational autonomy that overcomes such dichotomies. In fact, her ways of operating signal that far from being contradictory these two elements, freedom and relation, are essential to one another and enhance one another in a correlative way: "While remaining in herself, she renews all things" (Wis. 7:27). (Johnson 1993: 148)

Whatever else Johnson's theological agenda may be, my point is a pneumatological one regarding the centrality of the Spirit to both trinitarian theology and to the God-world relationship. This theme will be reinforced from another angle in our exploration of the mutual love theory in the next section. For the moment I simply note the developments in the preceding discussion. Beginning with Irenaeus' metaphor of the Spirit and Word as the two hands of the Father, Christian reflection on the question of God developed into a relational trinitarianism. In this way, the tri-unity of God was affirmed preserving both unity and plurality in the divine life. Applied to the works of

God, then, pneumatological relationality may be seen to hold the key toward the perennial mysteries of the one and the many, universality and particularity, God's relationship to the world, and vice-versa. As important are the metaphysical applications of these theological insights which flow forth from the pneumatological categories. The world is not only related to the divine vertically, but is also a vast web of interconnectedness horizontally (cf. Yu 1987, 214–33). Things in the world are what they are not as individuals but precisely as coordinated and mutually interdependent forms of life. Each form is what it is because of its relationship with another or others. Symbiotic relationality, a biological metaphor I borrow from Jerry Gill (1989, 40–48), thus characterizes both the divine reality and the creation itself as well as the togetherness of the two.

2.2 Spirit as the Mutual Love between the Father and the Son

The mutuality of Spirit reflected in the two hands metaphor and developments from it has also been explicitly articulated in another dominant pneumatological and trinitarian model, that of the Spirit as the mutual love between the Father and the Son. Rooted in Augustine's anthropological and psychological reflections, the mutual love model has also had a long and illustrious career (cf. Congar 1983, I.85–92). In what follows, I want to trace its developments from the patristic (Augustine) through medieval (the filioque controversy and Richard of St. Victor, albeit ever so quickly) and finally to contemporary (David Coffey) expressions. My purposes are interwoven along three lines. First, I will continue to assess the potential of the pneumatological categories for theological (and metaphysical) reflection. As before, I will suggest that pneumatology fills out trinitarian theology. Second, the pneum-atological logic developed in the previous section will here be elaborated, complemented, and clarified. This is reflective of the structural framework of Augustine's theological movement which works from the analogy of psychology to theology, and thus from the one to the three and from the order of knowing to the order of being. Finally, I wish to explore the similarities-in-difference which another trinitarian model provides for understanding not only God but also God's relationship with the world. This serves, in addition, to not only illustrate but also heed a central hermeneutical and methodological conviction to be developed later: that concerning the crucial import of multiple perspectives, models, and approaches to any particular (theological) question.

Two caveats need to be repeated before proceeding. First, as with the preceding discussion of the two hands model, my interests are less dogmatic or historical and more theological, ontological and metaphysical. This does not mean that dogmatic or historical considerations can be neglected or that they do not influence my discussions. It does mean that I am concerned with their details only insofar as they further illuminate the pneumatology and theology I envision. Second, there is a certain fluidity in the discussion from one section to the next, from one model to the next, from one argument to the next. This is intentional and is designed to illustrate the holism of pneumatological thinking. As such, hard and fast categories can be proffered only with great trepidation. Where, for example, does Eastern trinitarianism stop and Western trinitarianism begin? Can we truly discern the distinctions between the order of knowing and the order of being? Are the models presented mutually exclusive? Only with the utmost of generalities can clear divisions be insisted upon. Theological models themselves feature clear interrelationships. To illustrate this, I propose to situate Augustine within the larger history of patristic reflections and go back to the source of the two hands model itself, Irenaeus of Lyons.

2.2.1 In looking at this point back to Irenaeus, I wish to show how his theology of recapitulation provides the basic structure for later developments of the mutual love theory without demonstrating that there are actual historical connections between the bishop of Lyons and Augustine, Richard of St. Victor, or, much more recently, David Coffey. The structure of Irenaeus' soteriology (cf. McGiffert 1932, 132–48) is particularly interesting insofar as it illuminates the trinitarian movement of the triune God as well as its pneumatological moment. With regard to the former, the works of the Father through his Spirit and Word follow the same movement from creation initially (through fall) to redemption later. These are the two missions of Spirit and Word which go forth from the Father birthing creation (downward, to use the neo-platonic metaphor most congruent with patristic reflections) and return to the Father redeeming it (upward). Now because redemption is precisely the restoration of a fallen order originally created good, it is to that degree continuous in some respect rather than radically discontinuous with creation. This allows Irenaeus to connect creation and redemption in reference to the divine hands, yet consider them sequentially with regard to God's redemptive plan:

> the Father planned everything well and giving His commands, the Son carrying these into execution and performing the work of creating, and the Spirit nourishing and increasing [what is made], but man making progress day by day, and ascending towards the perfect, that is, approximating to the uncreated One. (*Against Heresies* IV.38.3; brackets orig. to translation)

The saved therefore "ascend through the Spirit to the Son, and through the Son to the Father" (V.36.2). Pneumatology becomes here both the soteriological and the eschatological links from the perspective of the human experience of God: "...the Spirit truly preparing man in the Son of God, and the Son leading him to the Father, while the Father, too, confers [upon him] incorruption for eternal life..." (IV.20.5; brackets orig. to translation). To be sure, the Father sends the Son to accomplish the reversal of Adam's fall (the legal aspect of salvation), thus initiating the downward movement which begins the recapitulation process. Yet it is the Spirit who applies salvation to the believer by re-creating him or her into the image of Christ (the mystical aspect of salvation), thus culminating the upward and eschatological movement of the recapitulation process. The Spirit is therefore the means through which fallen human beings are redeemed and restored to living relationship with God (V.9.4).

In short, recapitulation is God going forth from himself through the Son and the Spirit and restoring humankind through the Spirit into the image of the Son so that creation can be returned fully to the Father. The work of the Spirit is therefore our starting point: the divine person whom we encounter first, and through whom we experience the salvific work of God through Christ.[5] This soteriology of recapitulation and the movement of the Spirit in it become core convictions of the early Church even if Irenaeus' nomenclature of recapitulation is not retained. As Thomas Torrance notes,

> The overwhelming conviction about the Holy Spirit in the evangelical experience and doxological understanding of the Church, was that all his distinctive operations, in speaking, saving, enlightening, sanctifying and liberating us, are *divine acts*: *in the Spirit* our creaturely beings come under the immediate impact of the holy being of God, the almighty Creator and Source of all being. (1988, 233; emphasis orig.)

This conclusion is, arguably, Augustine's starting point, by which I mean that the bishop of Hippo begins with the experience of salvation freely given by God and realized in the human soul. At least three levels of correlation are at work in Augustine's *On the Trinity*, all of which he considers to be among numerous vestiges of the triunity of God in the human being created in the *imago Dei* (cf. Sullivan 1963). First is the psychological level of theological

---

[5] Later, Athanasius' contention that our knowledge of the Spirit is mediated through the Son (*Against Serapion* III.1–3) seems to reflect less soteriological and experiential concerns than it does christological and trinitarian ones. Of course, these can hardly be divided so conveniently, but the intentions of Athanasius' polemics against the Arians are what convinces me of these distinctions.

anthropology: human selfhood is constituted by memory (contemplation directed "inward" toward the past), understanding (cognition illuminating one's consciousness of the present), and will (communication transcending the present "outward" in anticipation and realization of the future). Second is the epistemological level of the mind's engaging an external object of knowledge representationally and intentionally. Last is the soteriological level wherein salvation is considered in neo-platonic terms as recollection in the soul of its having wandered away from its divine resting place. Understanding of such in the mind produces repentance, turns one away from sin and returns one to walking home to God. Each level therefore exhibits a complex correlational structure between anthropology, epistemology and soteriology with the doctrine of God understood as ideal spiritual being (Father), reason (Logos, who both knows and makes known the Father), and activity (Spirit, representing the divine community and its dispositions toward externalization and creation).

My goal here, however, is not to provide full explication of Augustine's trinitarianism, but to explore the structure of his mutual love theory within the framework of Irenaeus' doctrine of recapitulation. Within Augustine's psychology, love is that which "conjoins our word and the mind from which it is conceived, and without any confusion binds itself as a third with them" (*De Trinitate* IX.8). Building on his analogy of mind, knowledge and love, the Spirit is correlated with love. However, since the divine attributes are predicable of the particular persons only in the divine economy but are essential to the triunity of God, love is intrinsic to the divine being itself. Under closer analysis, then, the threefold structure of love as constituted by lover, the beloved, and their mutual love is determined (VIII.10.14). The argument moves from there toward the conclusion that the Spirit is thus the mutual love of the Father and the Son; or, as Augustine puts it, the "the Spirit of both is a kind of consubstantial communion of Father and Son" (XV.27.50; cf. VI.5.7; XV.6.10; XV.17.27–31; XV.19.37). The result is a striking reconceptualization of trinitarian coinherence such that the Lover (the Giver) is who he is precisely in relationship to the Beloved (the Given) and vice-versa, even as they share (give) *and* indwell (receive from) their mutual love (the Gift).

In considering the Spirit as the bond of love (*vinculum caritatis*) between the Lover and the Beloved (cf. Kelly 1978, 271), Augustine realizes he stands on shaky exegetical grounds (XV.15.27). Arguing chiefly from the Johannine parallels of abiding in love and abiding in God (cf. 1 John 4:13, passim), he attempts to buttress the scriptural warrant for his claim by making the further correlation between the Spirit and the gift of God. The clearest statement to that effect is by Paul: "God's love has been poured into our hearts through the Holy Spirit that has been given to us" (Rom. 5:5). Elsewhere, of course, the Spirit is spoken of in terms of the gift of God (cf. Acts 1:5, 2:38, 8:20, 10:45; and cp. John 4:7–14 and 7:37–39). Augustine's query is whether or not there is any more excellent gift of God than his love (XV.18.32). Concluding negatively, he equates as synonymous the biblical references to the love and the gift of God (cf. V.9–V.12; VI.10.11; XIII.10.14).

There are certainly difficulties in Augustine's arguments, especially in the intellectualism of his approach, his questionable correlation of psychology and theology, the influence of neo-platonic categories on this thinking which prejudice him against materiality in favor of mentality, and the neglect of the eschatological dimension of the biblical narrative connected with invoking dubious psychological categories for discussing pneumatology (cf. Gunton 1996, 109–12; 1997, 30–55). Some of these will be addressed below, and others remedied later (chiefly, as we will see, by Coffey's retrieval of Augustine's mutual love theory). Two points, however, need to be emphasized here. The first is that Augustine conceives of the relationality of the triune life chiefly in pneumatological terms. The Spirit is the mutuality that not only emerges from the Father's love of the Son, but is itself also constitutive of that love. Second, one detects the movement of Irenaeus' recapitulation theory in Augustine's doctrine of the Trinity. We ascend to our knowledge of the triune God from our creaturely vantage points through vestiges of the divine image and soteriologically transformative revelations of that image. Yet this ascent is made possible only because of the prior and initial descent of God through incarnation and, especially, the pentecostal gift of love. In other words, the Spirit is not only the relational key to the triune life as the mutual love between the Father and the Son, but is also the relational presupposition to our encountering and accessing that life personally as the gift of God to the world. This leads, naturally, to Augustine's emphatic insistence on the filioque.

2.2.2 How does discussion of the filioque illuminate Augustine's pneumatology and trinitarian theology vis-à-vis the argument I am advancing?[6] First, note that Augustine rests his biblical argument not only on the familiar passages (John 15:26, 20:22) but also on the fact that the Spirit is "both of the Father and of the Son" (IV.20.29). He is referring here to the titles of the

[6] For an extended treatment of the filioque, including Augustine's contributions to the discussion, see Congar 1983: vol. III, Part One. The chief passages in which Augustine discusses the filioque in *On the Trinity* are IV.20.29, V.14.15, XV.15.47, XV.17.27, 29, XV.18.32–19.37, XV.24.45, XV.26.47, and XV.27.48.

Holy Spirit: "Spirit of God" (pervasive throughout the Bible); "Spirit of Jesus Christ (Phil. 1:19); "Spirit of Christ" (Rom. 8:9, 1 Pet. 1:11); "Spirit of Jesus" (Acts 16:7); and even "the Spirit of his Son" (Gal. 4:6). This genitive structure denotes the adjectival character of the Spirit who calls attention not to herself but instead to the other persons of Godhead (cf. Jenson 1997, 147). It also certainly sits well with the understanding of the Spirit as the mutual love and therefore gift of the Father and the Son, common to both while also originating from both. And yet Augustine does concede that the Son is the co-principle of origination (rather than an independent source) along with the Father of the Spirit only because it has been given to the Son by generation from the Father. This being the case, the Father is the ultimate and principle originator (*principaliter*) of the Spirit's procession (XV.17.29 and 26.47).

Now a tension may be thought to emerge at precisely this point which may be rooted either historically in Western conceptualizations of the filioque or in Augustinian theology itself. Either the Father generates the Son and then together with the Son generates the Spirit's procession (the filioque, at least as traditionally schematized hierarchically); or the Spirit is the eternal mutuality of Father and Son, neither of whom can be without the other, and thereby together loving each other such that it is impossible to deny their simultaneously effecting the procession of the Spirit (the mutual love theory). According to the former interpretation, it may be possible to understand the filioque as meaning "through the Son" (Tertullian, the Cappadocians, Hilary, and even perhaps Augustine). Eastern thinkers who accept this formulation, however, are inclined to state in addition that the Spirit not only receives but also reposes or rests on the Son (Gregory of Nyssa).

Augustine appears to recognize this tension and strives to reconcile his mutual love theory with the filioque instead (cf. Bonner 1960). "And the Son" is taken literally such that rather than conceptualizing the procession of the Spirit hierarchically from the Father "through" the Son, Augustine affirms (perhaps by visualizing the inverse triangle of Irenaeus' two hands model) that both Father *and* Son together send the Spirit. Thus, "the Holy Spirit does not proceed from the Father into the Son, and from the Son proceed to sanctify the creature, but proceeds at once from both" (XV.27.48). Herein is reasserted at a fundamental point the stumbling block to unity between East and West. The principal texts in the dispute—John 14:26, 15:26, 20:22—are interpreted within two different frameworks. Augustine and those in the West are concerned to up hold the consubstantiality of the Son and the Father and to distinguish the mission of the Son from that of the Spirit. The filioque understood within the framework of the mutual love theory accomplishes both of these objectives. In the East, on the other hand, the dominant concerns are the monarchy of the Father as absolute source of divinity, including the two hands, and the full deity of the Spirit. Needless to say, "through the Son" or "and rests on the Son" are much more congenial to Eastern purposes than is filioque, at least as interpreted according to the mutual love theory. Problems are apparent, of course, on both sides. Eastern theologians have suggested that undesirable political and ecclesial implications have followed from the hierarchical conception of Father-Son-Spirit (cf. Lossky 1976, 174–95). While such charges have not been ignored (cf. Congar 1986, 117–17), it is perhaps the case that the Orthodox response also produces a twofold problem: a modalistic notion of divine energies in the economy of God's work on the one hand, and a frozen and static conception of the divine essence in very being of God on the other (cf. Jenson 1997, 152–53).

One might be tempted at this point to then read the filioque apart from Augustine's mutual love theory so as to be able to move in the direction of "through the Son." Yet I would suggest this to be premature for at least three reasons. First, Augustine's mutual love theory provides a vigorous complimentary conceptualization for trinitarian coinherence which value is undisputed, at least historically. To do away with the mutual love model in the interests of re-interpreting the filioque places the doctrine of trinitarian coinherence in ambiguous light. The cost may be greater than the benefit. Further, there may be alternative means of understanding filioque within the mutual love model that yet at the same time advances ecumenical unity without the cost of losing the coinherence model. David Coffey has recently proposed to do just that. I will discuss Coffey's proposals below, but mention it here only to stall eager intentions to jettison the mutual love model.

Finally, and most pertinent to our immediate purposes at this juncture, I believe that one way to understand the relationship between the filioque and the mutual love model is to be explicit about the connection between the order of knowing (how we know) and the order of being (the way things are). My argument is that both arise out of the order of knowing, set as they are within the human experience of redemption. In the *ordo cognoscendii*, we encounter first the Spirit who leads us, as in Irenaeus' recapitulation model, through Christ back to God. This eschatological motif is then transposed soteriologically to affirm then that the divine economy of salvation reveals a chiastic taxis which turns on the incarnation of the Son: the Father sends the Son who sends the Spirit who unites the world to the Son so that the Son can return all things to the Father who will finally be all in all. The exact same chiastic structure can then be seen reflected in the divine life: the Father loves the Son whose return love for the Father is the Spirit. This trinitarian taxis is recognized as incomplete in light of the economic taxis and is filled out by both Richard of St. Victor and David Coffey. For the moment, however, I simply note that within the Augustinian framework, read protologically from creation to redemption, one finds the structure of the filioque confirmed. Read theologically within the neoplatonic framework of time as the moving image of eternity (which influenced Augustine), one encounters the mutual love theory. In short, both filioque and the mutual love theory attempt to say something about the divine being while they arise out of the saving work of God *pro nobis* wherein we encounter first the Spirit, and then only, by epistemic implication, both the protological priority and the eschatological ultimacy of Father and Son.

The question is whether or not the orders of knowing and of being should not be correlated if in fact the unified truth about God and our salvation is not to be hopelessly compromised. I am hesitant to answer this question directly because it seems to me to lie at the heart of the epistemological, hermeneutical, methodological, and finally, theological issues at stake (thus this book!). Further, my own conviction is that the interrelationship of epistemology (and in this case, soteriology) and ontology are intricately interconnected such that there is (or should always be) a dialectical movement between the two which should not be cut off prematurely. A quick glance at the development of the mutual love theory by Richard of St. Victor will confirm this basic point.

Richard is particularly instructive with regard to his building on Augustine's psychological approach.[7] He takes Augustine further, however, in capitalizing on God as love. If God is truly love, then God has to love truly and fully. In turn, the object of divine love has to be fully worthy to receive such love. Evidently, no creature or even the creation itself is fully worthy of this love because as fallen, neither they nor it are capable of receiving, realizing or responding to that love. The conclusion is that God can only be fully love if there is a plurality or community of divine persons, minimally, the lover and the beloved.

Richard, however, reasoned that duality is itself plural, but not yet triune. Movement from the former to the latter necessitated a deeper analysis of true and perfect love. Perfect love, Richard suggests, needs to be shared love: "the proof of perfected charity is a willing sharing of the love that has been shown

---

[7] Richard of St. Victor, *Book Three of the Trinity*, trans. Grover A. Zinn (New York: Paulist Press, 1979), 371–99; references will be located in the text by Richard's chapter divisions (in Roman numerals) and page number (in Zinn's translation).

to you" (XI:384). Thus, what is needed for perfect love is "union with a third" (XV:388). Reasoning along these lines, Richard writes:

> When two love each other mutually and give to each other the affection of supreme longing; when the affection of the first goes out to the second and the affection of the second goes out to the first and tends as it were in diverse ways—in this case there certainly is love on both sides, but it is not shared love. Shared love is properly said to exist when a third person is loved by two persons harmoniously and in community, and the affection of the two persons is fused into one affection by the flame of love for the third. From these things it is evident that shared love would have no place in Divinity itself if a third person were lacking to the other two persons. (XIX:392)

Now it should be noted that Richard introduces a shift in the mutual love theory. Whereas the Spirit is the love between Father and Son in Augustine, the Spirit is the third lover in Richard. Yet this is not a radical transformation of the mutual love theory, but its intensification toward a radically trinitarian love. By this, it is clear that pneumatology completes, fulfills, and perfects both triune being and trinitarian reflection. The economic "fellowship of the Spirit" (2 Cor. 13:13) reflects the immanent triune community wrought about by the Spirit who is the mutual love of the Father and the Son. Further, however, herein is illustrated (and vindicated) the present argument: that there is a dialectical correlation between our knowing and encountering the Spirit and our intuition that this encounter is itself a trinitarian experience of love between ourselves and an Other (the Spirit). Which is prior—the order of knowing or the order of being? We have traversed the dialectic between epistemology to ontology so many times (situated as we are in a theological tradition which has been perennially engaged by this question) that we lack the means to clearly define priority. Is such definition needed? I propose to further explore this question through an examination of one recent effort to retrieve and elaborate on the mutual love model.

2.2.3 A number of contemporary re-interpretations of Augustine's mutual love theory exist, including Heribert Mühlen's proposal of the Spirit as the "we" of the I-thou relationship between the Father and the Son, and Anthony Kelly's neo-Thomistic reading of mutual love theory. Our focus in what follows, however, will be on the work of David Coffey. Coffey's return model, as he calls it, will be beneficial for our task along three lines. First, he strengthens the exegetical argument for the mutual love model. Second, he advances the argument for trinitarian coinherence by developing a robust doctrine of the Spirit's mission that is situated within the framework of the mutual love theory.

Finally, his model holds promise to bridge the two orders of epistemology and ontology in connecting with Irenaeus' theory of recapitulation.

Recall that Augustine provided minimal scriptural warrant for his mutual love theory. Coffey fills in the lacuna by arguing from the following premise: if it can be shown that the Spirit is both the Father's love for Jesus and Jesus' love for the Father, then the conclusion that the Spirit is the mutual love of Father and Son can be drawn (1990, esp. 201–18; cf. Coffey 1979, 120–46). That the Spirit is the Father's love for Jesus is relatively easy to demonstrate scripturally since Jesus' sonship—as elaborated in the foregoing Spirit christology—can be seen as resulting directly from the bestowal of the Spirit by the Father on Jesus at his birth (the creation of his humanity), baptism (his confirmation toward sonship) and resurrection (the ultimate declaration of sonship). That the Spirit is Jesus' love for the Father is a bit more difficult to ascertain, but not impossible. Taking seriously the developmental aspect of Jesus' true humanity, Coffey argues that Jesus' awareness of his filial relationship with the Father in the power of the Spirit increased throughout his life. The fullness of the love of God so penetrated the humanity of Jesus as to join him completely with the Son in "unfailing obedience and answering love" to the Father (1999, 41). This culminated in his living with self-abandonment toward the Father, setting aside his own will in favor of the Father's, even to the point of death. His appropriation of the gift of the Spirit to him by the Father was so complete that he was able, on the cross, to express the depths of his own love for the Father by returning (breathing out) the Spirit to the Father (cf. John 19:30). This expression of love to the Father correlates with Jesus' intense love for the world, expressed (in turn) in his breathing forth his Spirit to the world (John 20:22) (1999, 38–39, 64, 80; cf. Rahner 1969). The Spirit who the Father had radically bestowed upon Jesus "without measure" (John 3:34) is the same Spirit thoroughly appropriated by Jesus as his own. Thus is the Spirit the Spirit of God and the Spirit of Jesus and, as such, the mutual love between the Father and the Son.

Building on this, a proper pneumatological mission can be distinguished from that of the Son's, albeit one that is intrinsically related to the Son's (cf. Coffey 1984 and 1986). Eternally, "the Son comes from the self-communication of the Father, [and] the Holy Spirit comes from the self-communication of the Father and the Son (to each other)." Thus Coffey characterizes the divine persons as such: "the Father is the Giver, the Son the Receiver, and the Holy Spirit the Gift, of the self-communication of God" (1999, 152). In the divine economy, the incarnation of the Son in Jesus is brought about through the Spirit in the movement "outward" from the Father to the world. Correlatively, the "incarnation" of the Spirit is detectable in the love that those in the body of Christ show to one another, to the world, and to God, each integral aspects of the movement in and by the Spirit "inward" back to the Father through recreation in the image of the Son. What Coffey has done is transform Augustine's theory of mutual love *from being* solely a means to image, using the psychological analogy, the (static) inner operational subjectivity (singular) of God *to that* of depicting the dynamic interpersonal (plural) life of God as expressed in the creation and redemption of the world (1999, 60). In other words, the Spirit as the mutual love of Father and Son in the divine life correlates with the Spirit as the mutual love of Father and Jesus, and, by extension through Jesus' love for the world in general and the Church in particular, the mutual love of God and the world/Church. Thus if the filiological mission of the Son is incarnation, the pneumatological mission of the Spirit is bestowal by the Father (the expression of the love of the Father: creation) and return to the Father (the pneumatically empowered expression of love to the Father by those who are loved by Jesus in the Spirit: Pentecost). This reflects the eternal intratrinitarian relations.

The mutual love theory thus includes what Coffey calls two sets of Second Testament christological (and, by implication, trinitarian) data: that emphasizing descent (primarily Johannine material) affirmed by the ecumenical councils of Nicea and Chalcedon, and that depicting ascent (the synoptic gospels). The former is driven by causal categories resulting in the filioque, a true albeit partial theological witness. The mutual love theory, however, is able to retrieve that aspect of the tradition and restore it to its rightful place within the larger theological and soteriological vision which includes the eschatological orientation of creation's recapitulation with God. Coffey's return model seeks to argue—the thesis of both *Grace: The Gift of the Holy Spirit* and *Deus Trinitas*—for a theology of mutuality recognizing *both* the Spirit as the Father's eternal love for the Son and, by extension, for the world at the level of the divine economy *and* the Son's eternally responding love for the Father and, by extension, the world's response to God in the Spirit through Jesus (again at the level of the divine economy).

Notice here the three-way movement from the biblical account to the immanent Trinity, from this to the economy of creation and redemption and the Spirit's being given by Father and Son to the world, and from the latter back to Scripture. Herein is Coffey's hermeneutical circle. For the moment, however, I want to focus on the second move. This move from the immanent to the economic Trinity is legitimate since, for Coffey, the saga of creation and redemption depicts contingently the eternal movement of the Spirit as the mutuality of the love given by Father, received as gift by the Son, and returned to the

Father.[8] Thus what are eternal subsistent relations at the level of the triune God are only temporal and dynamic relations when transferred to the realm of creation and of history. This is because the Spirit's mutuality is gratuitously transferred outward to the world as love and gift, thus characterizing this outward relationship as graced by the love of God. Graced realities are non-necessitated gifts, and in that sense, the contingency of the world is sourced in the gratuitous outflow of divine love.

The humility of this "silent member" of the Trinity thus comes forth from her self-effacing character as her personality is "entirely defined by his [the Spirit's] relationship with the Father and the Son" (Durrwell 1986, 140). She is, after all, the eternally mutual gift of the Father to the Son, and the temporal gift of God to the world. The former is emergent from the divine nature ad intra and the latter from the divine work ad extra, directed outward and therefore entirely gratuitous.[9] Thus also are the orders of knowing and of being connected. These theological conclusions arise out of the prior experience of the Spirit both for Jesus (in the development of his filial consciousness) and for us (at Pentecost) who only through the Spirit are able to received the spirit of (Jesus') sonship and are enabled to say (as Jesus), "abba Father" (Rom. 8:15–16; Gal. 4:6–7). Coffey's return model thereby affirms trinitarian coinherence at the level of the immanent Trinity, at the level of the soteriological-eschatological orientation of the divine economy, and at the mediational level of the orders of knowing and of being, albeit each in their different respects.

It is interesting at this point to note the work of Thomas Weinandy (1995), of which Coffey acknowledges parallel discoveries and conclusions. Speaking of the trinitarian reality also in relational terms, Weinandy builds on the Second Testament witness that the Father as "Abba" comes by and through the Spirit, and concludes that the Son is Son to the Father only in or by the Spirit. Thus,

> The Holy Spirit does not have a distinct name because he subsists precisely as the one in whom the Father and the Son are named. The Father subsists in relation to

[8] See Coffey's comments on method in *Deus Trinitas* (1999, 14–26). I find this a better explanation of the movement from the order of knowledge (ad extra) to order of being (ad intra) than Augustine's reliance on the Platonic notion of time as the moving image of eternity which he deploys in explaining how the Spirit can be eternally gifted if in fact the Scripture only speaks of her giftedness in the divine economy; see *On the Trinity* V.15.16–V.16.17.

[9] As Brian Gaybba states, "Love is 'faceless'. The only face it seeks and therefore has is the face of the beloved. It seeks to unite lover and beloved so closely, so perfectly, that it has no identity of its own, other than that unity. The reason for the Spirit's anonymity is made crystal clear: the Spirit is love, and love is faceless. This is also the reason why the Spirit is experienced as the presence of Father and Son, and not as a person with a clear and distinct identity" (1987, 136).

the Son (and so is named Father) *only in the Holy Spirit* by whom he begot the Son. The Son subsists in relation to the Father (and so is named Son) *only in the Spirit* who conformed him to be Son. The Spirit subsists as a pure relation together with the Father and the Son in that he sustains their relationship and so imparts or manifests their names. The Holy Spirit is the hidden or unnamed person or 'who' because the very nature of his subjectivity as a subsistent relation is to illuminate the person the Father and the Son for one another. It could even be said that the Holy Spirit is the most personal of the trinitarian persons, and thus the most relational in his subjectivity, because he is the most translucent and transparent. Through him the Father and the Son eternally gaze upon one another in love. (1995, 84; emphasis orig.)

In the same way, Weinandy also "resolves" the problem of the filioque:

By giving the Holy Spirit his proper role within the Trinity the controversy over the procession is surmounted for the entire conception of the Trinity is now transfigured and redesigned. Not only does the Holy Spirit proceed principally from the Father (the concern for the East) and derivatively from the Son (the concern of the West), but the Spirit in proceeding from the Father as the one in whom the Son is begotten now actively conforms the Father to be Father for the Son and conforms the Son to be Son for the Father. (1995, 97)

To return to Coffey, however, notice also that his return model is able to bridge the insights of both the two hands and the mutual love metaphors for the trinitarian life of God. Beginning with the scriptural witness to the work of God, the Father's radical bestowal of the Spirit on the Son is the condition of Jesus' sending the Spirit (baptizing us with the Spirit: salvation). Further, Jesus' returning the Spirit to the Father (John 19:30) is the condition of the Spirit being released by Father and Son (in)to the world (the Spirit baptizing us into Jesus' body) so as to return the world through Jesus to the Father. The return model captures the Spirit's reflecting the eternal mutuality of the love of Father and Son even while it explicates the historical movement of this dynamic interpersonal relationality through the joint workings of Spirit and Word in the divine economy. The Spirit is thereby the mutual love between Father and Son, and the link between God and the world. The latter relationship includes not only our experience of God's provision of salvation, but also our knowing such through the Spirit as the love of God which binds together creation and redemption in Jesus Christ directed toward eschatological communion with God (cf. Prenter 1953). There is thus a dual sending—of Jesus and of the Spirit, the two missions—and a dual return—of the Spirit of Jesus to the Father and of the Spirit, who hovered over and breathed life into this world, through the Son to the Father—bringing together both the two hands model and the mutual love model.

In this light, Coffey's argument that the filioque correctly represents only one aspect of the divine being and economy seems correct. In this regard, the ecumenical implications of the return model are heightened. Among Eastern Orthodox theologians, Sergius Bulgakov has developed the concept of Sophia (Wisdom), which is the Word and Spirit (as the masculine and the feminine elements), both revealing the love of the Father who is Revealer (cf. Graves 1972). This is clearly along the lines of the two hands model which rejects the filioque. Of course, insofar as the East's rejection was based on the Western understanding of "procession" as signifying the causal relationship of the Spirit to the Father as source and origin, to that extent no real possibility of the East's overcoming the inferences of John 14:26 and 15:26 existed, nor that of healing the breach between East and West. However, if both begottenness and spiration are understood in an altogether different frame of reference, that of relations, and if the framework of reflection was enlarged eschatologically to include return alongside procession, then the Eastern emphasis on the perichoretic interrelationality of the divine persons can be seen to complement the Latin doctrine of the filioque. Further, Bulgakov, while following the Eastern insistence on the immanent Trinity as apophatic, understands the economic manifestations of the Son and the Spirit as two separate yet interdependent missions of the divine energy. He thus also made another distinction: that between pre- and post-incarnation. The Spirit precedes the Son in the former, and is sent by the Son in the latter (cf. Graves 1972, 179–90). More explicitly, following Coffey, the inversion takes place in the death of Jesus on the cross. This preserves the claims of the filioque, understood then to reflect the processional aspect of the economic Trinity culminating in the incarnation and paschal mystery (cf. Reid 1997).

2.3 Spirit and Trinitarian Theology: Toward Ontology and Metaphysics

It is time to step back from the exhausting subtleties of trinitarian theology and re-engage the hermeneutical project of this essay more intentionally. The goal of this chapter has been to develop the theological underpinnings for the foundational pneumatology that follows. It therefore serves to ground as well as correlate the movement from the categories of relationality, rationality, and dynamic life to metaphysics. Herein arises, of course, the specter of the hermeneutical circle. The following will therefore take up three sets of questions. First, how do the pneumatological categories inform our theology and, by implication, our ontology and metaphysics? The movement from pneumatology to theology and metaphysics will need to be made explicit in this regard. Second, what are the main contours of the logic of pneumatology that underwrites Christian theological reflection? Part of my focus here will be to make a preliminary response to the question of the hermeneutical circle which will be defended at length in the remainder of this book. Finally, what is the role of pneumatology for Christian self-understanding in terms of the central doctrine of God? Discussion of this set of questions will proceed by way of summarizing the previous trinitarian reflections and their pneumatological connections. I will take up these questions in reverse order.[10]

2.3.1 The preceding analysis allows us to compare and contrast various aspects of the two hands and mutual love models of the doctrine of God (cf. Hoskins 2000). The key question here concerns that of how pneumatology has informed Christian theological understanding. Insofar as this is, at least in part, an historical issue, at its most fundamental level, the response would be that without pneumatology, Christian faith would be binitarian faith at best (cf. Segal 1999; Moltmann 1992, 289–98; and Milbank 1986). Trinitarian theology is only inchoately stated at Nicea and awaited specific pneumatological reflection by Athanasius and the Cappadocians before being confirmed at Constantinople.[11] On the theological level, however, what needed to be confirmed is not only the divinity of the Spirit, but also the validity of the Spirit's mission alongside with the Son's. What the two hands theory implies but does not develop is filled out by, among other means, Richard of St. Victor's theology

---

[10] The remaining remarks of this chapter can be read as a provisional update of my thinking about trinitarian theology from that of my first book (Yong 2000, ch. 4, esp. 105–11). Whereas in that volume and in a previous article (Yong 1997) I advocated the collapse of Rahner's axiom because of the apophatic character of the divine essence (adhering in that sense to the Orthodox distinctions between the divine essence and the divine energies), I have come to see how such speculative reflection is in some sense inevitable so long as it is recognized as such. I do, however, continue to hold to the intuitions of the apophatic theological tradition which resists all efforts to absolutize cataphatic theologizing in a totalistic, a priori and essentialistic sense. Toward this end, I put forth this dynamic and interrelational interpretation of the Trinity, and will in the future elaborate on this model of the divine life in dialogue with the Buddhist doctrine of emptiness.

[11] For a contrary argument for binitarianism and against the fourth century development of the doctrine the divinity of the Spirit, see James P. Mackey (1983). My theological response to Mackey is to heed his theological argumentation as valid given his hermeneutical presuppositions—which appear to remain suspicious about the development of doctrine—and to engage the debate on that front.

of the Spirit as shared love and Coffey's theology of the Spirit's mission set within the return model. Just as the Spirit both points to and lifts up Father and Son in the divine economy, so also is the Spirit the answering love of the Son for the Father who completes the inner-trinitarian loving of the divine life.

A second aspect of the pneumatology-theology relationship that has emerged is that both models recognize the distinctiveness of the Spirit's person and role in the divine life but do not subordinate her either to the Son or the Father. Neither of the two hands are subordinate to the other, nor to the Father, even while the mutuality of love in the return model militates against subordinationist tendencies. While the filioque can be understood in a way which appears to subject the mission of the Spirit to the mission of the Son, its origins have already been noted to address primarily christological rather than pneumatological concerns. Further, read within the framework of the return model, the filioque is balanced on the other side by the two hands model which calls attention to the reciprocity of the divine missions. Arguably, it would be appropriate to conceive of Spirit and Word as interdependent, mutually subordinated and mutually reciprocal (cf. Badcock 1997, 160–65, 229–34, and 266–73; Victorin-Vangerud 2000, esp. 187ff.; and Fox 2001, 244–45). Boris Bobrinskoy thus writes:

> The Spirit is in Jesus as Jesus is in the Spirit. We may not resolve to 'reduce' this reciprocal presence, this 'mutual belonging in love' to a mere 'relation' of unilateral causality. It is indeed a question of an ineffable and full 'coincidence' of the Son and the Spirit, a reciprocal transparency which cannot be expressed in human terms except by the concept of revelation and of reciprocal, simultaneous love. (1999, 98–99)

Certainly in both models the Father is the originating cause of the triune life of God, but this is considered theologically rather than temporally. What is important to note here is that which has been repeatedly been insisted on in recent work in pneumatology and trinitarian theology: that there has been a tendency historically to either neglect the Spirit in theological reflection or to theologize about the Spirit in such a way as to result in at least a practical (if not actually theological) subordination of the Spirit either to the Word or to both Word and Father. The preceding reflections have retrieved pneumatological motifs from the tradition itself in order to make the argument that even historically, there is no room for pneumatological subordination in Christian theology.

Finally, in answer to the question of what pneumatology means for Christian theology, I want to highlight the notion of trinitarian (rather than simply binitarian, between the Father and the Son) coinherence. The mutuality of the two hands together with the consubstantiality of the Father and the Son led to the doctrine of perichoresis wherein the triune persons are understood as subsistent relations and coinherent activities. On this point, again quoting Weinandy,

> While, both in the East and the West, the *perichoresis* or *circumincession* has been seen as *the result* of the begatting and the spirating, I have emphasized the *perichoresis* of the actions themselves. Because the Father spirates the Spirit as he begats the Son, for it is in the Spirit that the Son is begotten, there is a *perichoresis* of action—the acts of begetting and spiration co-inhere in one another and thus account for why the persons themselves co-inhere. Actually, the persons themselves are the co-inhering acts. This *perichoresis* of the trinitarian act gives an unprecedented dynamism to the persons and to their life within the Trinity. (1995, 79–80; emphasis orig.)

Paralleling this, the mutual love model also concludes similarly, driven as it is by the perichoretic relationality of love, lover and beloved. Triune coinherence, however, is not just the addition of a third to an existing dyadic interrelationality. If that were the case, the third is simply contingent and inessential to the already genuinely relational dyad. Pnuematological relationality, however, is a distinctively complex form of interrelationality which includes duality, transcends it, and yet preserves the distinctiveness of the transcended dyad even while such transcendence posits the third precisely as immanent in the dyad. This is especially clear in Richard of St. Victor's and Coffey's analysis of how pneumatology deepens and completes the mutuality of love between Father and Son but does so not by eliminating the distinctiveness of their identities but precisely by accentuating them. And, in line with the logic of trinitarian coinherence, the triune identities can never be individualistically conceived since they are what they are precisely as subsistent relations that synthesize personal individuality and personal relationality and nothing less.

In light of the doctrine of coinherence, the notion of reciprocity between Spirit and Word in the two hands model can be extended to defend a triune mutuality and subordination (cf. Miyahara 2000, Part II). In turn, the Father's "subordination" can be understood in terms of his self-giving love to the Son and in the essential definition of his divinity as intimately and subsistently interrelated with that of the Son's and the Spirit's. The point of such conceptualization is to grasp the radical reciprocity of the divine persons. The mutual love theory as expanded by Coffey's return model enables us to do exactly that without collapsing the intra-trinitarian distinctions. Herein lies, in my judgment, the import of a pneumatological approach to Christian theology. The pneumatological emphasis rescues the Spirit from theological oblivion—where she has been consigned, at least historically—precisely by truly filling out toward a robustly trinitarian vision of God which takes the perichoretic and reciprocal relationality of the triune persons seriously. It is part of the burden of this project to draw out the implications of this conclusion for hermeneutics and theological method.

2.3.2 This leads the question of the logic of pneumatology. The question here concerns not just the rationality of Christian faith, but the pneumatological form of that rationality. What precisely is the logic or rationale that undergirds Christian theology? My thesis is that a pneumatological rationality—what I call in chapter four the "pneumatological imagination"—drives not just Christian theology in general but trinitarian faith and practice more specifically. Since I will elaborate on this notion in detail later, suffice at this point only to call attention to the main features of this pneumatological rationality by revisiting the methodological movements of both the two hands and the mutual love models.

Both models, as we have seen, feature a triadic movement. The two hands model moves either from the scriptural witness through an interpretive category (relationality) to the theological concept (the triune persons as subsistent relations), or, arguably, in reverse [see 2.1.3 above]. The mutual love model moves from the Bible to the immanent Trinity and back again to the economic Trinity (Coffey's methodology). Earlier, however, we saw that the mutual love theory was grounded, at least in Augustine, by the experiential analogy of the human (psychological) constitution and the soteriological (Irenaean) *ordo cognoscendii*. What is interesting to observe is the triadic structure of the logic of pneumatology in trinitarian reflection. The goal of this essay is to argue the thesis (at length in Part Three) that interpretation is trialectical movement of Spirit-Word-Community. Theological reflection, I will suggest, is an ongoing triadic movement and engagement. Superficially, the biblical data in both models would correspond with Word; the interpretive category (two hands) and immanent Trinity (Coffey) would be categorial processors for the scriptural material provided by the understanding which is communally defined and situated; and the third term (the theological concept and the economic Trinity in each model, respectively) would reflect meaning (Spirit). But is the third term simply the conclusion of the movement from the Scriptures to the theological idea, or are the third terms also reflective of either the starting points or even the mediational categories for theological inquiry? On the one hand, the economic Trinity appears to be the concluding third term. But, on the other hand, if we take the baptism of Jesus as reflecting the economic Trinity, could not Jesus' filial consciousness of the Father's love experienced in part through the descent of the dove have been the starting point of theological reflection concerning the (economic) work of God? Or, alternatively, could it also not be seen that Jesus' baptismal experience mediated a previously defined textual or liturgical world that both already and eschatologically pointed to the (economic) work of God. Herein the question of the hermeneutical circle can be clearly seen.

I trust at this point in the history of human self-understanding that the hermeneutical circle is not problematic in and of itself, but rather understood as a given feature of the epistemic processes that human beings continually negotiate. Here, I want only to sketch how the pneumatological rationality engages and, potentially, transforms the hermeneutical circle. The key here, as elsewhere, lies in the categories of relationality, rationality and dynamic life. The last is especially crucial with regard to transforming the hermeneutical circle by spiraling it either inwardly or outwardly (thus the hermeneutical spiral). Pneumatology as dynamic life points to the incessant drive of Spirit for meaning. This dynamism means that while the "circle" remains unbroken since we can never completely transcend it this side of eternity, it is also neither static nor reflective of some sort of eternal return simplistically conceived. Rather, there is a deepening of the circle (the inward spiral toward interiority) even as there is a broadening of the circle (the outward spiral toward universality), both suggestive of the movement carried forward by the pneumatological rationality.

And it is precisely because the logic of pneumatology is a kind of rationality (not rationalism, as chapter five will clearly demonstrate) that there is the hope that there will be some sort of correspondence between the human knower and experiencer and what is known and experienced both in the depths of one's soul and in the starry skies beyond, as Kant mused. At this juncture the insight of Augustine's psychological analogy may be pertinent. Whatever else may be the truth about our theological conceptions, they certainly are mental and cognitive processes which arise from our human experience of and situatedness in the world. As such, the claim here is that there is a complex interrelationality between the orders of knowing and of being, already reflected in the analogical correlation between our soteriological experience and the triune life of God. The *ordo cognoscendii* and *ordo essendi* are there not mutually exclusive. There is a certain knowing even in the order of being even while there is what Eastern Orthodoxy calls *theologia* in the order of knowing. The logic of pneumatology is the connection, however obscure it may be at times, of the two orders.

In this context, Rahner's (1970) intuition that the economic Trinity is the immanent Trinity is correct, although as has been rightly noted, the reverse does not necessarily follow since the order of knowing could correspond with the order of being in specific respects without exhausting the order of being in many other—perhaps an infinite number of—respects. Further, the distinction between creature and creator, some would argue, is deepened by the fall. John Milbank puts it this way: "the fall imposes an 'impossible interval' between the economic and immanent Trinities" (1986, 224). But insofar as both the order of movement and the correlation of the orders in various respects is established, to that extent I would define the pneumatological rationality as not only dynamic, but also triadic and inter-relational, mediating between the two orders, and between the two spiraling movements of the hermeneutical process. But now I anticipate the contours of the pneumatological imagination and the hermeneutical trialectic, and need to pull back at this point in the argument to attend to the question of how the categories connect pneumatology and theology to ontology and metaphysics.

2.3.3 The groundwork is almost laid for a foundational pneumatology. We need only to summarize the gains made so far and show how the categories of relationality, rationality and dynamic life are not only specifiable in the logic of pneumatology but also exemplify their fruitfulness in thinking about ontological and metaphysical issues. It will also be appropriate in a moment to formally introduce the category of community which plays a major role in the hermeneutics and methodology defended later.

The two models, I have attempted to demonstrate, specify the pneumatological categories theologically. Relationality is at the heart of the divine life, expressed coinherently and subsistently (two hands) as well as mutually and lovingly (mutual love). Further, Spirit, as we have seen, is constitutive of the dynamic mutuality between Father and Son. Spirit can therefore be conceptualized also as the dispositional vector of the divine life. The obvious point to be made in this connection concerns the dynamic orientation of the divine life both ad intra and ad extra. There is an eternal mutuality of triune love which provides the pneumatic disposition of the divine economy via the two hands. This economy is, in turn, characterized dynamically—more specifically, eschatologically—by the movements of both hands from and back to the Father. In these ways (and others which time and space require me to leave unspecified), the categories of relationality, rationality, and dynamic life are seen to interpret the connections between pneumatology and theology, and to hint toward ontological and metaphysical issues.

Here, it is crucial to observe that both models are driven to provide relational accounts not only of God, but also of the world. This is seen in Coffey's analysis of the economy of salvation as it arises from the perspective of those who are saved, but especially in Elizabeth Johnson's exploration of the relational logic of Spirit vis-à-vis creation. In both cases, the world remains contingent in some respect, thus preserving the transcendence of God. For Johnson, this contingency is articulated in terms of the Spirit's freedom, while for Coffey, it is characteristic of the dispositional gratuity of the Spirit's economic trajectory: the world is result of the divine gift ad extra and in that sense, contingent and graced. In this sense, not only is the relationality between God and world pneumatologically conceived and enacted, but the constitutedness of the creation itself can be said to have a relational, and hence, pneumatological, shape.

Such a pneumatologically shaped (read: robustly trinitarian) metaphysics has been in the making for some time now (cf. Gunton 1993, 180–209; 1995; 1998). Reality itself is understood in relational terms, according to a chastened (in contrast to modernity's iron-clad) rationality, and as dynamically evolving. Substance metaphysics has long since given way to a variety of process-oriented and relational metaphysics, along with their attending ontologies. Although in some quarters cognition is defined wholly subjectively and solipsistically, much more prevalent is some version of critical realism which affirms the concreteness and particularity not only of the ideal constructions of the human intellect but also of the things constructed. Rationality continues to be defensible only on the assumption of the possibility of bridging self and otherness, the latter itself providing part of the conditions for intelligibility. A dynamically processive world requires a dynamically conceived epistemology, without which understanding cannot be confirmed.

At this juncture, then, the notion of community which has been percolating throughout this entire discussion can be explicitly stated. Reality, because of its relationality, rationality (understood inter-personally), and dynamism, can be characterized communally. Sociality and community are, after all, brought about by the Spirit, the mutual love of Father and Son. God is, therefore, the supremely communal being, eternally living and subsisting as a triune relationality (cf. Jüngel 1976 and O'Donnell 1983). This relationality extends to the world which comes forth from God and exists in communal relationship with God, even if such relationship is fractured in some respects. Yet the world itself, insofar as it is sustained by God and is not identical with God, functions as a semi-autonomous community, including within itself complex hierarchical sub-communities. In the words of Joseph Bracken,

A community then is not a supraindividual person, as some have thought, but a process…a dynamic unity in totality of functioning parts or members. Community as process is a dynamic unity in totality of persons in continuous interaction with one another, who thereby constitute something bigger than themselves as separate individuals, namely, the community itself as a specifically social form of process. (1985, 26; cf. Gunton 1997, 83–117)

Before moving on to develop this idea of community, however, the question should at least be raised now about whether or not the preceding reflections commit us to some form of the social doctrine of the Trinity. Bracken himself, as we will see below, certainly moves in that direction, even if, as I believe is arguable, not necessarily so.[12] The question is whether or not it is the case that, "The social doctrine of the Trinity begins with the idea of the Trinity as a *community* of Father, Son, and Holy Spirit, whose relations are conceived to be genuinely personal, and in the nature of love, rather than relational in the more abstract, ontological sense of the 'relations of opposition'" (Badcock 1997, 246, emphasis orig.)? Certainly, social trinitarianism has had its critics (e.g., Gresham 1993; Mackey 1995; Leftow 1999). Anthony Kelly's negative response to Badcock's question is to the point:

> [T]he Trinity is not a communitarian process, a social genesis, more or less conceived of in historical terms. Rather, the unique reality of God as trinitarian Loving makes history, and makes history communitarian, and even trinitarian….In short, though not a community and dialogue in the human sense, God, as the Mystery of Love, is that in which community and dialogue become. For this unique self-giving Love originates, expresses, enables and redeems the human search for community in history…. (1989, 182–83)

Fortunately for our purposes, a definitive response is unnecessary, although my own intuitions make me suspicious of the "slippery slope" between social trinitarianism and tri-theism. This rationale is especially persuasive if the various aspects of social trinitarianism can be preserved apart from the social doctrine itself. And, insofar as the medieval thinkers, including Richard of St. Victor, were availed of the social trinitarian construct but either implicitly or explicitly rejected it—the notion itself runs counter to other texts and ideas in

---

[12] Contemporary defenders of social trinitarian models of God include Jürgen Moltmann, Joseph Bracken, Leonardo Boff, Clark Pinnock, and various Eastern Orthodox theologians, among others. For a discussion of late nineteenth and early twentieth century models of the social Trinity, see Welch (1952, 295–302).

Richard's own writings[13]—to that extent the burden of proof is upon those who would now or at any other time urge its retrieval. Therefore, the notion of community as employed here should be understood analogically only at worst. Instead, it functions heuristically in response to the question: how does the concept of community illuminate our experience and serve to clarify categorically the hermeneutical process and theological method? I will later explicate and defend the position that a mutually defining and reciprocal movement of Spirit, Word and Community—what I call the hermeneutical trialectic—subsists at the heart of the hermeneutical and methodological question.

[13] On the plausibility of reading Richard as a non-social trinitarian and on the medieval rejection of social trinitarianism, see Nico den Bok (1996, esp. 458–64 and 473). My thanks to Dale Coulter for directing me to this massive and comprehensive study of Richard's trinitarian theology.

3   Toward a Foundational Pneumatology: Metaphysics and Ontology

Having explored the biblical data and extrapolated its theological framework, we are now ready to correlate our pneumatologically driven trinitarian theology with ontology—the question of being—and metaphysics—what is real and possible in this and any other world. Developing this correlation is crucial to establishing three theses on the way to the epistemological and hermeneutical discussions in the following chapters. First, the claim that was made in chapter two is that there is a connection between the orders of knowing and of being. That claim needs to be explored and defended in light of ontological and metaphysical issues. This includes, second, an analysis of claims regarding metaphysical realism. If in fact human knowledge is neither solipsistically referential nor simply intra-systematically coherent without any claims to reality external to the language game being practiced, then a critical realism will need to be argued which grounds knowledge in otherness rather than solely in cognitive processes. The way forward, I will argue, is to follow out our theological insights and develop from them intuitions about ontology and metaphysics. This means, third, tracing out the pneumatological categories and trinitarian insights of relationality, rationality, and dynamism with these questions in mind.

These three theses characterize what I call the quest for a foundational pneumatology that is through and through relational, realistic and social. Briefly stated, and to be unpacked throughout the remainder of this chapter, foundational pneumatology strives to understand reality in pneumatological—read: trinitarian—terms while remaining accountable to and hoping to engage with a fully public discourse.[1] The questions here include the following: Is there a pneumatological structure or framework by which the world is to be understood? Building on the previous conclusions, would not such understanding be suggestive of an account of the presence and agency of God (through the Spirit) in the world? How might such an account itself be

---

[1] Here, I develop previous work in foundational theology and foundational pneumatology; cf. Yong 2000, ch. 4, and 2000b.

significant universally (for all peoples, times, and places), not only in terms of explicating the diversity of human experiences (the question of the metaphysics of experience) but also in terms of laying out the basic features of the world itself (the question of ontology and metaphysics in general)? Would not the end product of this series of questions be some sort of universal rationality, and if so, how is that possible in a post-metaphysical and anti-totalitarian age?

In our contemporary era that includes the post-structuralist reaction to metaphysics, we need to be wary about metaphysical reflection that claims to proceed from any abstract or neutral philosophical foundation since such alleged foundations have been all but deconstructed by the structuralist critique. This is the reason for our beginning with the concreteness of the biblical story. Our foundational pneumatology, however, is metaphysical precisely because it attempts to envision reality itself with the help of the pneumatological categories previously developed. I do hope to arrive at the rudiments of a universal rationality, albeit one that is consciously anti-totalitarian precisely because, as I will argue, it is pneumatological. The following lays out the metaphysical scheme, leaving the defense of the accompanying epistemology to Part Two. Note, however, the warning of Robert Jenson that the tension in pneumatology between the particularity of Spirit in Jesus and in the Church and the universality of Spirit as a cosmic reality "strains the Western intellectual tradition to breaking.... [T]hose who have ventured cosmic pneumatology have not always been able to avoid producing nonsense or myth" (Jenson 1984, 165). It is therefore with fear and trembling that I set us forth on this path of exploring the implications of the claim that reality is relational, rational, and dynamic.

3.1 Reality as Relationally Constituted

The fundamental thesis I will defend in what follows has been succinctly stated by James Loder and Jim Neidhardt: "...spirit refers to *a quality of relationality*, and it is a way to conceptualize the dynamic interactive unity by which two disparate things are held together without loss of their diversity" (1992, 10; italics orig.). The claim in the second-half of the quotation will be the subject of the next section of this chapter. Here, our attention will be on the notion of spirit as "a quality of relationality." I propose to untangle this claim first by filling out the concept of relationality from a variety of philosophical perspectives, and then by exploring how the two hands and the mutual love models of the Trinity may be pressed into the service of our reflections on metaphysics.

3.1.1 The preceding discussion has focused on relationality as a pneumatological (biblical) and theological (trinitarian) category. The movement toward
ontology and metaphysics, however, means that a process of translation and
correlation needs to take place. It what ways does a relational understanding
of pneumatology shed light on the category of relations, relationships, and
relationality?

The history of the concept of relations is itself complex (cf. Weinberg 1965,
61–119). Until recently in the history of Western thought, the dominance of
Aristotle's substance-attribute ontology set the parameters for all thinking about
relations. Since relations connected two (or more) terms, relations themselves
could not be substances, but rather were attributes or accidents that depended
upon primary substances. Two alternative conceptions followed: the
neoplatonic notion of relations as signifying participation and the Stoic notion of relations as nothing more than subjective cognitions. This latter idea,
while the minority view, did assert itself at various historical junctures, such as
in the thinking of the Mutakalimun, the strict and conceptual nominalism of
the medieval schoolmen, Lockean and Humean empiricism, and, obviously,
in Kant who considered relations as no more than operative categories of the
mind. The former view, however, is more pertinent to our purposes since it
led to a variety of conceptions of relations considered as ontologically real.
What is most interesting in the history of the idea of relations is that the
Cappadocians and both Hilary and Augustine in the West did stumble upon
the fact that the divine being ad intra was constituted by real, subsistent
relationally. Yet given the ontological dependence of creation on God and the
ontological independence or transcendence of God, creation and creatures
were accidental relations to each other and to God (thus the contingency of
the world) precisely through participation in the divine ideas. Alternatively,
then, while the divine persons were real relations, God's relations with the
world was purely ideal or rational (rather than real). In short, following
Avicenna's doctrine of bilateral relations which denied relations as accidents
could exist in the same way in both terms or subjects, the way toward conceptualizing the God-world relationship was all but established. In this case, the
Christian scholastic were clear that the world's relationship to God was real
from the perspective of the creation, while God's relationship to the world was
only rational and, more importantly, contingent, from the perspective of divinity. This notion of the distinction between the divine relations ad intra and
ad extra was a consistent theme from Augustine, through Boethius and the
medieval scholastics, until the late nineteenth century.

The breakthrough comes with Peirce, Frege and Russell following upon the heels of the paradigmatic transition from the Aristotelian substance ontology to the Einsteinian universe. In the latter framework, the connection between relations and the notion of participation remains. Yet because all things are what they are precisely as mutual participants in common fields of activity, things are intrinsically relational. Further, participation is understood as unfolding through processes of internalization and indwelling. In Peirce, specifically, both strict and conceptual nominalism are rejected in favor of a realism of laws or general tendencies in nature whereby participation, internalization, and indwelling is mediated. The Avicennan distinction is retained, albeit modified in two ways. The first concerns the uni-directionality of time. Thus the past is logically related to the present and the future as their condition, while the present and future are related to the past internally via participation (cf. Oliver 1981, 101–30). The second derives from the rethinking of classical theism in the modern and postmodern world. Thus real, subsistent and coinherent relations are seen to characterize not only the divine life ad intra, but also that of the world itself and the God-world relationship. Distinctions in the triune relations of God did not mean subordination of any of the relations to the other. In a similar way, the reality of the God's relationship with the world can be affirmed, even from the divine perspective, without denying the bilateral distinctions in both directions. Retention of the bilateral distinctions should not be burdensome since even in the knowledge relation, the object of knowledge exists in a real relation to the knower even if it is true that in some cases only the knower is transformed by knowledge relationship while the object of knowledge remains unaffected.

An important question that arises at precisely this juncture is that posed by Henry Jansen. In his comparative analysis of classical theism (that represented by Aquinas and the neo-Reformation tradition of Herman Bavinck) and contemporary relational theism (the later Barth, the biblical theology movement of G. H. Wright et al., process theism, and the Jewish personalism of Buber, Moltmann and Pannenberg), Jansen raises the issue concerning the overarching character of the scriptural witness. He points out that classical theism certainly has its central texts which enable it to understand relationality and change on the part of God metaphorically and anthropomorphically. On the other side, relational theists have their central texts which reinterprets God's transcendence, perfection, etc. Is it the case then that both conceptualizations are one-sided accounts of the human experience of God as preserved in the biblical narratives? If so, then, Jansen insists, both perspectives are necessary because of Scripture's ambiguity regarding the proper ontological framework of interpretation. In certain circumstances, God's relationality would need to be emphasized, in others, God's transcendence:

> Our conclusion here was that both aspects of God (his relationality and independence of the world) need to be held in balance. One cannot take only one aspect. A full, complete doctrine of God requires both, even if they cannot finally be reconciled on a conceptual level. The relations of God and the world are of a varied nature and cannot be subsumed under one concept. It may be the case, for instance, that one aspect of God's immutability is his faithfulness and other aspects may be his imperishability and unchanging being. The two aspects do not finally have to be related. Any theory of God's acting in dogmatics and philosophical theology which overlooks the variety of ways in which the relation between God and creation or his creatures can be described falls short of the criteria to do justice to both Scripture and (religious) experience. (Jansen 1995, 231)

My own immediate response is that Jansen's conclusions follow, but should be negotiated within the framework of the logic of pneumatology. The relationality that emerges from the pneumatological reflections so far presumes both the independence *and* the interdependence of the terms related, albeit in various respects. This means that while there is always a triune movement in the divine life ad intra, there is also a triune movement in the God-world relationship such that the identities of related terms are never confused, but, at the same time, are defined variously through their relational participation and indwelling. This point will be argued in detail in a moment [3.2.3]. Here, however, I will to lay out the ontological implications of this project by sketching two metaphysical models, each of which correlates with one of the trinitarian models presented above. In so doing, I will be pursuing the intuition that whatever else reality might be, it is relational at least in the sense that its central features include the perichoresis of intersubjective communion, the mutuality of synchronic participation, and the dynamism of diachronic connectedness between past, present and future.

3.1.2 The first model of reality derives from the patristic model of Spirit and Word as the two hands of the Father. Recall that this Irenaean vision insisted on the mutuality of the two hands along with their being the means of divine creation (especially) and redemption. This models lends itself to metaphysical reflection in at least two directions since what is emphasized could be the bipolarity of either the two hands themselves or of the Father on the one side vis-à-vis the two hands on the other. The former, I would suggest, could be understood as a metaphysics of immanence considered in and of itself, and the latter a metaphysics of transcendence and immanence together. Both are seen to be exemplified in the theological reflections of Walter Wink when set against the background of process metaphysics.

Wink is first and foremost a biblical theologian rather than a metaphysician. However, his scriptural exegesis has led him to a vision of reality that provides an excellent example of a metaphysics of immanence (cf. Wink 1984, 1986, and 1992). Being interested primarily in understanding the scriptural language of "the powers," Wink proposes to read them metaphysically as indicative of the inner or spiritual aspects of material realities. Herein lies a potentially clear-cut correlation with the patristic vision of the creation being the result of the work of the Spirit and Word as the two hands of the Father. The Spirit is certainly the dynamic anointing and empowering force of God even as the Word is the incarnate—materially embodied and concrete— representation of the divine reality. Transposed metaphysically, reality can then be conceived as the togetherness of Spirit and Word: spirituality and materiality. Wink is not saying that there are two kinds of things in the world, spiritual and material. Rather things are what they are precisely insofar as they constituted in two modalities: as spiritual, dynamic, subjective fields of force and power on the one hand, and as material, concrete, and objective manifestations on the other. The outer reveals the inner even as the inner directs, shapes, and informs the outer manifestations. Applied to the human condition, the more appropriate categories would be history (meaning, interiority and transcendence) and nature (materiality, embodiment and environment).

Wink's bipolar vision of reality, however, should be set within the broader framework of process metaphysics with which he explicitly acknowledges affinities. Within the process framework of Alfred North Whitehead, especially as developed by Charles Hartshorne, a similar bipolority is at work, albeit one that envisions a metaphysics of both transcendence and immanence. In this case, the bipolarity—or, to be more specific to Whitehead's terminology: dipolarity—is that of the God-world relationship. What Whitehead called the Primordial and Consequent natures of God, Hartshorne called the abstract essence and concrete actuality of God. The former is God's eternality, immutability, absoluteness and transcendence, while the latter is God's temporality, mutability, relatedness/dependence, and immanence. Hartshorne has characterized this latter pole as the totality of the creative process of becoming itself, conceiving the world therefore as, metaphorically, God's body. Yet the abstract essence of deity which survives the passage of time does provide the lure or prompting (an "initial aim") for each emerging occasion in the cosmic process.

This processive view of reality constitutes the heart of the process vision set over and against the substance paradigm which had for so long dominated metaphysical reflection, at least in the Western world. In the Whiteheadian scheme of things, reality is ultimately and fundamentally constituted by temporal and social processes of actual entities or occasions which arise and perish momentarily, each being connected to preceding and succeeding actualities through the dynamic process called "prehension." Each actual entity thus prehends all previous occasions (whether immediately with regard to those preceding directly, or mediately with regard to all other occasions), and creatively negotiates and incorporates aspects of their influences in order to constitute itself as an at least partially novel reality. Thus the past lives on objectively, even if it is experienced to a greater or lesser extent subjectively by presently emerging occasions in their dynamic acts of concrescence. The future, on the other hand, emerges out of the creative syntheses of the present moment.

Alternatively, then, while neither Whitehead nor Hartshorne were orthodox trinitarians, there is, arguably, a trinitarian structure to their metaphysical vision. On the one side is the abstract pole of reality: God traditionally conceived, just as ultimate, although in a different way, as pure possibility rather than actuality. On the other side is the concrete pole of reality: the consequent nature of God consisting of the occasions or societies of such occasions, reality's ultimate constitutive components. Mediating between the two, then, is the process of creativity itself: the dynamic, ongoing emergence of harmonized actualities from the infinite number of possibilities and preceding occasions which structure the advance of reality. There are, then, aspects of Whitehead's philosophy which point to an understanding of "one," "many," and "creativity" as equally ultimate categories, the last being the principle of harmony and novelty between the former two which brings conjunction (the unity of the one) out of disjunction (the multiplicity of the many) (cf. Whitehead 1964, 86–91; cf. Bracken 1979, 30–43).

The question that emerges for process metaphysics, however, concerns the ontological status of creativity. The problem here is the avowed conceptual nominalism of the process ontology such that reality consists, finally, of concrete actualities which instantiate the abstract initial aims of the divine mind. But if the latter, as purely abstract, are entirely inefficacious on their own, and the former, concrete actualities, arise and perish momentarily and are therefore unable, in and of themselves, to effect the dynamic of creativity, what drives the creative process onward? Allegedly, creativity itself. Yet insofar as creativity is conceptualized nominalistically—no other option available to process philosophers given that reality is constituted ultimately by drops of actual occasions—then it remains no more than a mental notion unable to fulfill its function of effective processive transformation. It is therefore not surprising that nowhere in Whitehead's system is there an adequate explanation provided for just how creativity works to advance the interaction of the one and the many. Creativity certainly functions to illustrate Whitehead's categorial scheme, but it does not explain the latter as a metaphysical notion should. Thus, set as it is within the nominalist tradition of Descartes, Hume, Locke, and Kant, process metaphysics ultimately reduces God to the world, and defends the doctrine of creativity only rhetorically rather than actually (cf. Gelpi 1994, ch. 3). The triadic promise of process philosophy is ultimately lost either to the dipolarity of process theism or to the monopolarity of process naturalism.

For the moment, however, note that the connections between Wink's inner-outer and process philosophy's God/creativity-actuality is clear. The difference is that in the former, the bipolarity is read horizontally as a ontological vision of how things in the world are immanently constituted, while in the latter, the dipolarity is read vertically as a metaphysical vision of the relationship between God and the world, between transcendence and immanence. Wink's application of aspects of the process vision to the interpretation of the biblical powers is remarkably suggestive in light of proposals coming from other theologians who are working either within the broad framework of process metaphysics, or intentionally and dialogically with both process thought and the scientific community. In each case, there is a emerging conviction that one way to reconceptualize the category of spirit is in terms of fields of force, of energy, or of activity (cf. Pannenberg 1991, 382–84; Moltmann 1992, 195–97; Welker 1994, 235–48; and Snook 1999). The argument is that herein lies a potentially fruitful way to bring into conversation ancient theories of *pneuma*, biblical conceptions, and modern physics. The ancients in general and certainly the Bible do not divorce spiritual and material reality in a dualistic sense. Similarly, modern physicists are arguing that material reality is nothing less than energy arranged within and sustained by force fields of activity. In process terms, the Spirit is the creative field of activity which lures prehending entities toward their divinely appointed reasons for being. In Wink's terms, the spiritual realm is that inner, dynamic realm of power and activity which drives reality's manifestations.

I think there is much to commend both the vision of process metaphysics and Wink's adaptation of it for a biblical ontology since in both cases, attempts

are made to overcome the disastro॥   ॥ment rationality.
Process metaphysics reflects a par॥   ॥ classical ontology of
being to an ontology of becomi॥   ॥ that respect, provides solid
underpinnings for a relational me॥   ॥ysic. In Wink's case, the advantage of
moving toward the category and language of field or energy is that it has the
capacity to overcome the rhetorical (if not essential) dipolarity inherent in the
process conceptualization on the one hand, even while it more suitably carries,
connotes, and conveys the notion of transcendence than categories of spirit-
matter and inside-outside on the other (cf. Pannenberg 1997). In my view,
however, the cohesiveness of Wink's contribution could only be strengthened
by more intentional trinitarian thinking, which, as has been noted, is already
built into but undeveloped by process metaphysics precisely because it is
retarded by Whitehead's conceptual nominalism. In each case, the criticism is
that both do not move on from otherwise valid dyadic categorial constructs to
explore a more explicitly triadic or truly relational metaphysic. To do so would
be to follow the cue of early Church fathers in their movement from the two
hands toward a trinitarian theology of coinherence. The latter does not
invalidate the former, but rather fills it out logically. The same would occur, I
suggest, in metaphysical and ontological reflection.

3.1.3 Fortuitously for us, perhaps such a move has taken place, building not
explicitly on the two hands model, but, arguably, from the mutual love and
procession/return models. I would like to explore this correlation by looking
at the triadic metaphysics of the founder of American pragmatism, C. S. Peirce,
developed by Donald L. Gelpi. It is important to note, however, that because
Peirce was not primarily a theologian, nor was he interested principally in
theological reflection, his should not be mistaken for a theological
trinitarianism. At the same time, the suggestiveness of Peirce's triadic epistemology and metaphysics for religious studies, theology, and theological method
are far from exhausted. Peirce scholar Michael Raposa (1989), for example, has
argued that Peirce's method of inquiry—what Peirce himself identified as a
semiotic theory, a theory of signs—constitutes, in effect, a *theosemiotic*, a means
of interpreting reality in a way that is religiously and theologically significant.
My own use of Peirce—and of Raposa's interpretation of Peirce—takes his
ideas on semiotics, epistemology and metaphysics in a specifically trinitarian
theological direction, and this precisely by accentuating pneumatology—what
I will argue here to be the theological equivalent of Peirce's doctrine of thirdness.
Along the way, I will suggest that if Whitehead had availed himself of Peirce's
thought, undoubtedly known to him, the dualism inherent in his dipolar

conceptualization would have been overcome toward a more coherent and plausible process metaphysic.

Charles Sanders Peirce, logician, scientist, and philosopher, is finally being recognized as one of the preeminent thinkers in American history.[2] His metaphysics involved his reworking Cartesian epistemology and Kant's categories in dialogue with the emerging scientific method of the late nineteenth century. Against Descartes, Peirce denied the doctrines of universal doubt (because it undermined itself and because lived-reality only enables reasonable doubting rather than wholesale, arbitrary doubting) and epistemic intuitionism (because all cognitions are abstractions inferred from elementary perceptions of the senses, of the self, of memory, etc.). Against Kantian agnosticism, Peirce as a practicing scientist affirmed a metaphysical realism which aspired to universal understanding albeit without invoking either a priori or transcendental necessity (what Kant sought for, in vain). Further, this time against Kantian subjectivism, Peirce distrusted epistemic methods which were authoritarian, a priori, or transcendentally based. Rather, knowledge emerges through the engagement of a community of inquirers with the world directed toward understanding the world truly, even if it (knowledge) is always fallible given its inferential character. Such a critical realism emerged from three distinct but interrelated moments of inquiry: phenomenological (which pays attention to the data of experience); normative inquiry into the various sciences (which involves categorizing the phenomenology of experiences aesthetically, ethically, and logically); and metaphysical (which concludes to judgments regarding the ultimate character of reality emergent from the previous two moments).

I will return to Peirce's epistemology in greater detail later. For the moment, however, observe the triadic metaphysic which emerges from Peircean phenomenology. Peirce created his own technical nomenclature of Firstness, Secondness, and Thirdness to account for the distinct but interrelated universes of lived human experience. Firstness is the quality of things which enable them to be experientially present. It is the evaluated particularity—the thisness or suchness—of a certain type of texture, taste, color, smell, perception, affection, emotion, image, concept, etc., which makes that experience what it is and nothing else. Abstracted from everything but its own meaning, Firstness is pure possibility. Our thinking it in terms of its various qualities makes real possibility present to us. Secondness is the facticity or factuality of things as they resist and oppose each other. It is the decisive concreteness of things in

[2] What follows is a revision and extension of my exposition of Peirce's ideas in Yong 2000a.

their environmental rootedness signifying their over-and-againstness and their relatedness to each other. Human experience consists most vividly of Secondness: brute physical interactions, resistance and struggle—hence our experience of actuality. Thirdness is that which mediates between first and Secondness, what Peirce called the activity of law or real generality. It is the habitual disposition or tendency to act in specific ways thus orienting experience dynamically toward the future. As real universals, Thirdness provides the impulses that drive both the evolution of the world and the trajectories of lived-experience, thereby structuring our experience of the emergence of actualities from possibilities—hence our experience of legality and continuity within development. Finally, Thirdness is the intrepretant which makes meaningful Secondness' otherness over and against Firstness. Alternatively said, Thirdness is the interpretation of actual or concrete signs or symbols (Secondness) with regard to their objects (Firstness).

Note that in this metaphysical scheme there are not different three kinds of things or experiences in the world. Rather everything presents itself to us experientially through the three elemental modes of Firstness, Secondness, and Thirdness. Things are what they are precisely as the togetherness of qualities, facts, and laws—the hows, whats, and habits or tendencies of experience. Three points can be briefly noted. First, Peirce was a pioneering thinker whose triadic conceptualization bypassed the essentialisms (chiefly, the Platonic ideas and the Aristotelian substances), monisms (chiefly, pantheism and materialism), and dualisms (chiefly, Cartesianism and Kantianism) of both traditional and modern metaphysical systems (cf. Gelpi 2000, and Neville 1987, 25–52). Essences, Peirce argued, were not the underlying identities of things through their accidental changes; instead, they are the felt qualities—the *hows*, not whats—of lived experience. Further, reality consists not only of possibility and actuality, but also real laws, known traditionally as generals or universals, which mediate the two. Here, Peirce claimed to have found help from Duns Scotus who affirmed the reality of generals or laws against both strict nominalism which insisted that general rules were verbal constructs, and conceptual nominalism which defined generalities as merely mental projections. With Scotus, Peirce saw clearly what Whitehead overlooked: that apart from the reality of generals, rules or laws, there can be no cosmic process, or, in Whitehead's terms, creativity.

Second, insofar as all realities were experienced as qualitative, factual, and legal feelings, to that degree reality itself is structured triadically. Arguably, it is the coinherence of qualities, facts, and laws which constitute experience. That said, it should also be mentioned that we never have a pure experience of

Firstness itself. Rather, Firstness—the qualities of things—is abstracted from our experiences of Secondness (facts) and Thirdness (laws). Herein lies the beginnings of the possibility of correlation of Peircean metaphysics and trinitarian theology which affirms that Father makes himself present to the world not directly but through the two hands.[3]

Finally, an heretofore unmentioned aspect of Peirce's categories which he explicitly develops is that while epistemology proceeds from Secondness and Thirdness to include, via abstraction, Firstness, metaphysically, the reverse movements hold, and that in two ways: a) Secondness and Thirdness are both derivatives of Firstness, and b) Thirdness is derivative of both Firstness and of Secondness (1.521–44).[4] Secondness as facticity assumes (at least two) resisting or opposing qualities, and Thirdness as mediation assumes the dynamic relationship between qualities and facts, considered separately and together. There is the sense, then, that Thirdness mediates Firstness and Secondness, and the sense that Thirdness is relationally emergent from, and in that regard dependent upon, Firstness through Secondness.

Arguably at both of these points, the trinitarian logic of mutual love as worked out by Augustine—including his defense of the filioque—and especially Richard of St. Victor seems to be operative in Peirce's reflections. They are especially noticeable in the efforts of Donald Gelpi, SJ, to correlate Peirce and orthodox Christian theology. Bringing aspects of Peirce's metaphysics as expanded by Royce, Whitehead, and Dewey, together with Lonergan's theological method, Gelpi has devoted his life's work to the development of a distinctively North American foundational theology (e.g., 1988 and 1994). "Foundational" in Gelpi follows Lonergan's usage which denotes the set of experiential conversions—moral, intellectual, affective, religious—required for living, thinking, and willing appropriately with regard to certain ends. In Gelpi's hands, foundational theology thereby amounts to the task of establishing how it is that an integrally converted Christian both does and ought to experience the reality of the God he or she worships. The goal is a systematic reconstruction set within a triadic (following Peirce), realistic (rather than subjectivistic, relativistic, or deconstructivistic), and social (against individualistic)

---

[3] I am grateful to Donald L. Gelpi, SJ, for helping me to draw this connection with Peirce more clearly.

[4] Charles Sanders Peirce, *The Collected Papers of Charles Sanders Peirce*, Vols. I–VI, ed. Charles Hartshorne and Paul Weiss; Vols. VII–VIII, ed. Arthur W. Burks (Cambridge: The Belknap Press, 1931–58); here, and elsewhere throughout the remainder of this volume, I follow the standardized methods of citing from Peirce's *Collected Papers* by volume and paragraph number(s) within the main text.

metaphysical framework. Applying Peirce's categories theologically to explicate the divine experience, the emergent understanding is of the Father as the qualitative source of creative efficacy, the Son as the decisive sign or image of the Father through whom the Godhead is embodied and efficaciously interacts with the world, and the Spirit—the divine Breath, Gelpi's preferred title—as the interpretant of the divine relationality both ad intra and ad extra. Thus the Breath is the divine mind, interpreting generally and legally the mutual relationship of Father and Son—precisely because she is sent by the Father and Son together, as revealed by the economic missions—on the one hand, and the relationship of human beings on the other. The result is what Gelpi has called a foundational pneumatology—an abstract account of how Christians do and ought to experience the reality of God through the divine Breath.[5]

Allow me to bring us back to the overall concerns of this essay. The preceding discussions of Gelpi, Peirce, Whitehead, and Wink vis-à-vis a trinitarian metaphysic are driven by what I have called a "pneumatology of quest" directed toward issues in theological hermeneutics and theological method. My concerns here are in part to ground the pneumatic hermeneutic to be developed later theologically, ontologically, and metaphysically. Toward this end, Wink's and Gelpi's insights can be brought together so long as the former's dipolar metaphysical assumptions are held at bay. The convergence of two hands and mutual love trinitarian theories as applied to questions of ontology are fruitful to the extent that the emergent metaphysical vision is robustly relational and trinitarian in terms of fundamental structure while yet centrally pneumatological in terms of orientation, shape, and function. In that case, Gelpi's metaphysical scheme which is triadic, realistic and communitarian explicates the ontological commitments of trinitarian theology, even while Wink's insistence on acknowledging energy or fields of force at the heart of all realities contributes to the theological appropriation of Peirce's category of Thirdness in ways which supplements Gelpi's adaptation of Thirdness as legality, habits, and dispositions.

Practically speaking, foundational pneumatology captures the insight that the reality that is experienced and is to be interpreted is the interrelationality of qualities, particularities, *and spiritualities* (the latter two understood loosely in

---

[5] See also W. F. J. Ryan's (1978) parallel yet alternative account of tracing the trinitarian shape of the world from the phenomenology of experience. Ryan recourses to Husserl's phenomenology of the life-world, cultural objects, and epoche. The former two are vaguely similar to Peirce's Firstness and Secondness. In my mind, however, Thirdness considered as law and generality makes more phenomenological sense and promises more theological mileage than Husserl's notion of epoche.

Winkean terms), thus requiring discernment at all three levels. The various "spirits" at work in the world—including not only the divine Spirit, individual and corporate human spirits, but also the demonic (cf. the work of Wink along with McClendon 1986, 170–76, and Newman 1987, 94–99)—therefore need to be taken into account in the hermeneutical process, even if, according to Peirce, attention to the phenomenology of Thirdness can only proceed through Firstness and Secondness. These insights are desperately in need of elaboration. For the moment, however, suffice to say that acknowledging the spiritual dimension of reality is itself to embrace some sort of foundational pneumatology.

3.2 Relationality and Rationality

The preceding sketch of a foundational pneumatology raises epistemic questions which will be taken up later. Here, however, I wish to clear the ground for that discussion by attending to the concept of rationality itself. Of course, in one sense, the argument for metaphysical rationality cannot be abstracted completely from epistemology, and insofar as that is the case, the comments here can be no more than a promissory note anticipating things to come. Yet it is also arguable that there is a distinction between the concept of rationality— the quality or state of being reasonable—and the concept of epistemology— the nature, means, warrants, and limits of knowledge. The latter examines how we know, while the former explores how we think. Certainly, the two are connected. Insofar as how we know includes memory, cognition, and other mental activities, epistemology includes rationality. On the other hand, a certain kind of physiological wiring—a right-brain learner, for example—will tend toward a certain type of epistemology—affective, let us say, over and against pragmatic; and in these cases, one can examine the question of rationality without engaging the complexities of epistemology.

Our task in what follows, then, is to trace out what I have identified as the logic of pneumatology except that in this case, the context of deliberation is metaphysics and ontology, not trinitarian theology. The question here is not so much how do I know about the relational, realistic, and social character of reality, but how these aspects of foundational pneumatology are rationally derivative from the logic of pneumatology. Toward that end, three sets of questions will comprise our task: that concerning the nature of "foundational" in our foundational pneumatology; that concerning the logic of pneumatology with regard to critical realism, and that concerning the dynamic of pneumatological rationality as applied to metaphysical thinking.

3.2.1 The question here concerns that of the foundations of rationality in general and of the logic of pneumatology in particular. Because the contemporary discussion both for and against foundationalism is rather confusing, sorting out the various uses currently in play as well as the concerns they are addressing is crucial. With regard to the latter, Susan Haack has helpfully delineated three overarching frameworks in the present debate over foundationalism. It is invoked as (1) a theory of justification (e.g., positing basic beliefs as the foundation of knowledge); (2) a conception of epistemology (e.g., as an a priori construct undergirding the sciences specifically and human knowledge in general); and (3) a thesis that "criteria of justification are not purely conventional but stand in need of objective grounding" (Haack 1993, 186). Our concern in what follows is primarily with (3), and secondarily with (1).

Applied to the criteriology of justification, a spectrum of positions can be discerned. On the far right are classical or hard foundationalists who insist, in the Cartesian tradition, that all knowledge consists either in immediately justified or self-evident beliefs, or is mediately based on such beliefs. Applied theologically, foundationalism has gone by a variety of other names, including that of fundamental theology, natural theology and even philosophical theology. Historically, at least, theological foundations have been erected positivistically on divine revelation, historically on the correspondence of revelatory propositions with historical facts, or transcendentally on the existential correlation between human subjectivity and the way things are (see Fiorenza 1984, esp. chs. 9 and 10).

Moving from this far right, minimalist foundationalism (also known as weak or soft foundationalism) has a variety of formulations clustered around the center, including that proposed more recently by Reformed thinkers such as William Alston and Alvin Plantinga. They insist on a different sort of "foundation," one that is "properly basic" and non-justifiable on evidentialist grounds but which emerges out of doxastic (belief forming) practices and is therefore warranted and not irrational (cf. Alston 1989, 19–56, 1991, 146–83; and Plantinga 1983, 1993a, 183–85). Toward the left end of the spectrum are those who identify themselves variously as postfoundationalists, nonfoundationalists, and even antifoundationalists. Postfoundationalists emphasize the need to find a via media between the foundationalism of modernity which builds all knowledge on self-evident or indubitable items of knowledge, and the antifoundationalism of postmodernity which locates all knowledge subjectivistically and, arguably, solipsistically, within a groundless web of beliefs. They make a twofold move. First, they acknowledge the contextual and located character of *all* knowledge—

including religious and theological knowledge—thereby agreeing with the antifoundationalist insistence that knowledge is relative to frames of reference and includes previous commitments of varying strength. Second, they seek to go beyond strictly localized knowledge webs through some form of interdisciplinary, intercultural and inter-contextual conversation (cf. Van Huysteen 1997, 1999; Shults 1999; Grenz and Franke 2001).

Non-foundationalism is more difficult to locate on the spectrum. Is it closer to minimalist foundationalism which secures beliefs in basic practices, to postfoundationalism which protects the process of inquiry toward truth, or to antifoundationalism which eschews all claims to truth as resting on the outmoded notion of metaphysical correspondence between propositions and reality? It raises the question of whether or not minimalist foundationalism and antifoundationalism are essentially different. Ronald F. Thiemann, for example, argues for a nonfoundationalist theology that proceeds from the following three distinctive emphases. First, theological justification is internal and specific to Christian faith. Second and correlatively, there is a close relationship between "first order" expressions of faith and "second order" theological reflections. Finally, justification is holistic, set within a web of interrelated beliefs rather than based on causal relations between theological concepts and their external references (Thiemann 1987, 72–78). Thiemann's is, finally, a narrative theology that identifies God's providence based on the logic of promise and agency, and follows through on the divine identity as the narrated gospel of Jesus Christ and its eschatological fulfillment. On these points, he seems firmly set in the Wittgenstein-Frei-Lindbeck camp which emphasizes all knowledge as local knowledge tied intrinsically to practices. As such, Thiemann appears close to minimal foundationalism which is based on doxastic practices on the one hand, and antifoundationalism which attacks claims to universal knowledge as political instruments of totalization on the other. In contrast to Thiemann, the nonfoundationalism of James Wm. McClendon and Nancey Murphy seems closer to the postfoundationalism of Van Huysteen than to either the minimalist foundationalism of the Reformed epistemologists or the antifoundationalism of deconstruction (see, e.g., the McClendon festschrift: Hauerwas, Murphy and Nation 1994).

The point of all this potentially confusing terminology is to pinpoint an arena of intense debate, especially when connected to religious and theological issues. The clearest antifoundationalist argument I know which has been proposed by a sympathizer rather than opponent of religion is that by D. Z. Phillips (1988). Because of his deep sensitivity to things religious, Phillips' antifoundationalism is much more sophisticated than that of the original Wittgensteinian fideists—Peter Winch, Norman Malcolm, Peter Geach, Stanley Cavell, James M. Cameron, etc.—with whom he has often been associated. Phillips argues that religious beliefs are truly groundless in the sense that theories regarding their justification are confused activities since the warrant for religious beliefs lies in their being guides and norms for practice. His point is that we come to religious beliefs in a way that makes them real to us without raising epistemological issues. Luther's doctrine of predestination was not a product of cognition, but emerged as a comforting doctrine amidst existential angst and trial; Pelagius' emphasis on works was to combat the means of "cheap grace," and so on. It is only when these doctrines are abstracted from the life-world which sustains their intention and meaning that epistemological and metaphysical issues come into play. Religious beliefs, in other words, are meaningful only within the world of religious devotion and practice. They are inherent to our deepest ways of being in the world, supported by our habits, and embedded *in* our thinking (rather than being *under* our thinking in the Cartesian sense of "foundationalistic"). The task of the philosopher and theologian is to clear away the metaphysical and theoretical "rubbish" that clutters the plain sense of what ordinary people believe and do in going about being religious. Thus, rather than debilitating truly religious life with confusing ratiocination, philosophers and theologians rehabilitate the kind of life-world that in turn nurtures not only religious belief, but also the appropriate religious practices. The goal of philosophy and theology is not to stultify faith, but to defend the faith in the sense of explicating the grammar, meaning, function, and attitudes of a religious life-world.

I am in basic sympathy with Phillips' affirmations, even while I am convinced his denials are off the mark. I could respond either that his position is just as theory-laden as anything else, or that it is nevertheless foundationalistic in a basic sense because it is assumed in religious life and practice. Further, true as it may be that beliefs can be said to emerge from an inherited set of practices, human beings are rational and critical creatures who have both the capacity and obligation to inquire about the present appropriateness and rightness of received traditions. Alternatively, the entire present concern with foundationalism could also be understood as a "postmodernist" critique of and reaction to foundationalism as an Enlightenment phenomenon (cf. Lundin 1993; 1997). However, my concern is to sketch a concrete proposal regarding theological hermeneutics, and along the way, I have posited a foundational pneumatology precisely in order to defend a relational, critical, and communal realism. Toward that end, my conviction is that if foundations are equivalent to warrants, then all rationalities and epistemologies are foundational in that sense. The question then is not whether or not any particular rationality is foundational, but what kind of foundations are being appealed to and how they operate. Let me tease out three features of the meaning of foundational in the pneumatology being proposed here.

First, the foundational pneumatology I am developing is not dogmatic but, following Peirce, fallibilistic. It is therefore not an epistemological or Cartesian foundationalism that is erected on incorrigible beliefs. Instead I prefer to image it in terms of a heuristic or shifting foundationalism since it is attentive to the continuously expanding data of experience.[6] It is therefore empirically driven and fallibilistically constructed, all the while serving as a theoretical guide to inquiry, ready to shift perspectives as afforded by the emergence of new data. As such, it is also appropriate to consider it as a speculative hypothesis that is revisable and open to correction by experience and by others. This leads, second, to foundational considered in terms of the contextual and communal nature of inquiry. The movement here is from the turn-to-the-subject (Kant) to the turn-to-community (Peirce and Royce). This move has the further advantage of appeasing the concerns of antifoundationalists—whether deconstructionists or others—about the associations robust notions of truth and elaborate theoretical projects have with the totalitarian exercise of intellectual and other forms of power. My argument is that insofar as inquiry is a truly collaborative enterprise, its products, even if in the form of grand or metanarratives, are intrinsically anti-totalitarian. In the case of Christian theology, one possible response is that provided by Middleton and Walsh (1995) who argue that the biblical narratives provide a sort of metanarrative that is not totalizing because of the many fissures and breaks within that narrative itself, specifically the subversive motif of God's privileging the weak and despised of the world.

Finally, the foundational claim of the pneumatology I envision strives toward universal application, albeit without claiming a priori necessity—that is, without bypassing deductive procedures aimed at clarification and inductive procedures aimed at verification and falsification. Now certainly theology cannot cease to make universal claims, however fallibilistically proffered, and however chastened its intentions. Such claims, however, do not mean that theology is totalizing (although they certainly have been taken to legitimate totalitarian claims historically). Rather, they are evidence of theology's

---

[6] The notion of "shifting foundationalism" originated from conversations during the summer of 1998 with Prof. Lucien Richard, OMI, one of my former teachers at Boston University.

conviction both that its proper subject matter is God's relationship to all of creation, and, as a corollary, that it (theology) is accountable dialogically to all other branches of human experience and knowledge.[7] The foundational pneumatology I am proposing therefore includes Gelpi's notion of how an integrally converted Christian should experience the Spirit. However, insofar as the Spirit is at work both prior to Christian conversion and even without explicitly Christian contexts, to that extent I am inquiring also about the human experience of the Spirit in general. It is appropriate here to conceive of foundational pneumatology as a project in "transversal rationality" since the metaphor of "transversality"—used by Calvin Schrag to reconceive human thinking as interdisciplinary, praxis-oriented, and socially rooted, appropriate to the sensitivities, prejudices and concerns of postmodernity, but without giving up on the claims of reason altogether (1992, 9, 148–49)—evokes images of crossing over, intersections, convergences, participation, and indwelling, all without resulting in coincidence or the canceling out authentic difference. Herein is located my present concern with metaphysics, ontology, and common human rationality, all of which are intricately connected with but anticipate the discussion of epistemology and the hermeneutics of the God-self-world relationship.

3.2.2 Having identified more definitively the foundational aspect of this project, we can now turn toward a more explicit consideration of the logic of pneumatology undergirding the metaphysics and ontology sketched previously. The main features of the proposed foundational pneumatology include a triadically conceived relational, realistic, and social metaphysics. In order to make explicit the pneumatological rationality driving this metaphysical vision, I want to probe the two trinitarian models we have worked with so far, but approach them this time from the perspective of two interrelated questions. First, how does the relationship between the two hands inform a realistic metaphysics? Second, how does the mutual love and return theory correlate with a triadic metaphysics?

As my defense of metaphysical realism proceeds within the framework of foundational pneumatology, I will, following Peirce and Gelpi, begin with Thirdness as assuming and dependent on Firstness and Secondness. How then does the logic of incarnation inform the logic of Pentecost and vice-versa toward a realistic metaphysics? That there is a realistic dimension to the incarnation can be assessed from two directions. First, the incarnation is the revelation of

---

[7] These twin foci best capture the vision and energy motivating the theology-as-universal-science programmes of Rahner and Pannenberg, arguably two of the most important Christian theologians of recent times; see Worthing (1996, esp. 6, 63–64, and 263–64).

the Father through the Son, the uttered word—the Logos—of the Godhead, apart from which God remains silent, unintelligible and inaccessible. The Son is God present to and in the world precisely by being the over-and-against the Father, "the reflection of God's glory and the exact imprint of God's very being" (Heb. 1:3). The incarnation is therefore God's supreme self-manifestation, self-revelation and self-otherness in human form. This means, second, that incarnation is both God's present with (thus, Emmanuel) and over-and-against human beings: "And the Word became flesh and lived among us..." (John 1:14). The flesh taken on is certainly common to all humanity, yet the, particularity and individuality of Jesus Christ amidst the human condition cannot be overlooked. Jesus was certainly representative (at least potentially, if not actually) of all human beings. Yet he was also uniquely himself and, as such, a distinctive other to the rest of us. Herein lies the scandal of christological particularity: that God should have actually taken on the form of this carpenter from Nazareth, even to death on the cross. To deny the historicity, particularity, and embodied materiality of the incarnation is to affirm docetism, gnosticism, and spiritualism in its various guises.

Incarnation is thereby constitutive of both universality and particularity. Its import for a realistic metaphysic can now be made explicit. The Christian doctrine of the incarnation means that knowledge of God depends on God's initiative to reveal himself in the incarnation in all of its facticity, specificity, and particularity. One allows the thing itself to "speak." But the truth of incarnation is the truth of knowledge in general since it is the only path to be taken if anything is to be known at all. What we know is, initially, our allowing reality to impress upon us what it will. This is not to reduce reality to empirical particularities, nor is it to ignore the fact that knowledge is itself a process of human *activity*. But it is to affirm the undeniable right of allowing the other that is never totally objectifiable to reveal itself. As Thomas Torrance puts it, while it is "impossible to reduce to thought how thought is related to being, else all we are left with is mere thought; it is likewise impossible to state in statements how statements are related to being without substituting mere statements for relation to being—nevertheless, in authentic knowledge, *being shows through*" (1971, 175; emphasis orig.).

As Torrance acknowledges, however, such knowledge is mediated through the Spirit. Realistically conceived, the speaking forth of the aboriginal Logos is intimately related to and preceded by the divine *ruach* hovering over the waters. Further, the Spirit not only mediates the incarnation of the Logos in Jesus of Nazareth, but also mediates humanity's initial and ongoing encounter with this reality. But before we naïvely associate particularity with the Son and universality with the Spirit, however, note the reverse as well. First, the universal presence of the Logos is itself explicitly affirmed. He is the "true light, which enlightens everyone" (John 1:9); further, "for in him all things in heaven and on earth were created" (Col. 1:15), and "he sustains all things by his powerful word" (Heb. 1:3). Logos, in other words, is universally particular, precisely in and to every person and every thing in some respect (cf. Edwards 1995, 77–87). But, second, the Spirit is also both universal and particular, albeit in different respects. Pentecost is the Spirit's establishing the body of Christ, but in a way such that particularity and difference are not effaced by unity and catholicity. Hence the diversity of languages, tribes, peoples, and nations who bring their gifts into the heavenly city (Rev. 21:24–25; cf. Rev. 5:9 and 7:9). More importantly, the diversity of graces and gifts of Christ through the Spirit are preserved and not erased in and through the "unity of the Spirit in the bond of peace" (Eph. 4:3–12). Instead, as on the day of Pentecost, the diversity of tongues—belonging to Parthians, Medes, Elamites, Mesopotamians, Judeans, Cappadocians, Pontusians, Asians, Phrygians, Pamphylians, Egyptians, Libyans, Cyreneans, Romans, Jews, Cretans, Arabs, etc.—were present and operative since "each one heard them speaking in the native language of each...about God's deeds of power...as the Spirit gave them ability" (Acts 2:4–11). Human beings are inspired by the Spirit, but they neither lose the capacity to act (speak in tongues) nor their particular identities (their gifts, ethnicities, etc.). The universality of Spirit here touches down—is embodied—concretely, individually, materially (cf. Hendry 1980, 169–70; Gunton 1993, 180–209; Cunningham 1998, 205–07). One senses here a sanctification of the diverse tongues of Babel and the restoration of the goodness pronounced upon the primordial creation, unified precisely through its diversity and plurality by the Spirit to the glory of God.

Herein can be made clear the complementarity of Spirit and Word regarding a realistic metaphysic. As incarnation establishes the particularity of otherness not only within the divine experience but also in all its historicity in the life of Jesus of Nazareth, so also does Pentecost establish the particularity of difference, but in this case inclusively across of the width and breadth of human experience. The logic of incarnation and Pentecost together defy the erasure of difference and the reduction of otherness to self-sameness. Rather, both establish difference and otherness, each in its own place within the context of the whole. In Peircean terms, Secondness is not concreteness apart from Thirdness, and Thirdness provides the legal shape for Secondness. This is because the Spirit witnesses to, shapes, and informs the particular, the singular and the individual, in fact allowing their manifestation. While pneumatology in abstraction gives rise precisely to the theological and philosophical wrong turns of speculative or absolute idealism (Hegel), a robust pneumatological theology brings vagueness and generality together with the distinctiveness, particularity, and individuality of concrete actualities. Here the subject-object distinction or difference is not only preserved but insisted upon, yet not in the Cartesian sense of re-asserting a metaphysical dualism between the knower and the known.

It is also precisely for these reasons that the logic of pneumatology resists all forms of totalism: absorbing the other into oneself, defining the other according to oneself, or neglecting, ignoring, or abusing the other as not valuable according to standards established by oneself. Both the self-deferential character of the Spirit vis-à-vis the mutuality of the Father and Son in the immanent Trinity and the gracious donation of the Spirit to establish difference and other in the work of God economically considered combat the ideology of totalization. Further, insofar as fallibilism is also negotiated communally, it acts as a means through which the Spirit checks the abuse of intellectual power. As Delwin Brown, following Cornel West, has argued, if one defines any systematic theory as a complex hypothesis vulnerable to correction, then such becomes a means through which totalization and oppression are uncovered. In this case, "opposition to theory may be more oppressing and deluding than the disease for which it allegedly is the cure" (Brown 1994, 56).

Arguably, then, only such a theological logic instantiating the togetherness of the two hands of God preserves uniqueness and difference since it does so precisely by locating meaningfulness vis-à-vis the relational context of otherness even while preserving all three terms (the relationship and the two related terms). Thus not only is difference and otherness established incarnationally and pentecostally, but so is the intelligibility and rationality of difference and otherness. According to the doctrine of trinitarian coinherence as adapted within the framework of Peirce's triadic metaphysic, reality is what it is as both quality-fact-law and as experience-symbol-interpretation. Pneumatology thus provides the interpretive key which mediates between self and otherness even while preserving the distinctness of self and otherness in the relationship. It is the relational constitutedness of minds, other minds, and the world. The Spirit as rationality overflows from the divine life to the divine creation in a dynamic process that can only be fully comprehended communally and eschatologically.

Herein we come full circle from our previous discussions regarding the coinherence of the orders of being and of knowledge. But, as the return model depicts for us, knowledge is not to be considered solely according to the Platonic doctrine of remembrance. Rather, rationality itself is dynamic. More precisely, the logic of theology driven by a pneumatological rationality is eschatological. Again, to quote Torrance,

> Theological knowledge that is grounded in the activity of the Spirit, who proceeds from God and returns to God, participates in the one movement that can carry man above and beyond himself to real knowledge of the divine Being, the movement, that is, of God's own self-revelation and self-knowledge. It is because God is at work through His Spirit enclosing man within the circle of that movement that our questioning and answering, our knowing and speaking of Him, may reach a fruition which we could never give them. (1971, 178)

3.2.3 These insights will be fleshed out in our epistemological considerations in Part Two. It is now, however, time to explore the dynamic of the pneumatological rationality. How is it that the logic of pneumatology participates in the going forth and return to God, to transpose Torrance's description into the return model of the Trinity? How does the logic of pneumatology shape not only the foundational pneumatology, but a triadically conceived relational, realistic and social metaphysics? How does a pneumatological rationality open out toward a truly relational metaphysics?

The thesis I would like to propose here is that only a pneumatological rationality is sufficiently dynamic, historical and eschatological to drive the dialectical movement of thought. Inevitably, the one-sidedness of any speculative vision results when dialectical thinking breaks down—i.e., when one or other side is suppressed or eliminated; when one or other side is subordinated to or absorbed by the other; or when the two sides are fused into a *tertium quid* (cf. Seung 1982, 203–09). My argument here is that any truly relational theology is necessarily trinitarian, meaning—as explicated through the two trinitarian models which have guided our reflection so far—on the one hand, that it is robustly dialectical in taking account of the two (or more) sides which inform the processes of inquiry, and, on the other hand, that it is also trialectical in enabling focus on the mediational structure of the movement between the terms itself. This third "term" of the trialectic is *not* Hegel's synthesis insofar as in the Hegelian dialectic, the synthesis sublates, transcends, and, in this sense, fuses together, the original thesis and antithesis, and becomes objectified as a new thesis establishing a new dialectic. Rather, a pneumatological rationality preserves the distinctiveness, particularity and individuality of the original terms of the dialectic in an ongoing relational tension. Only thus is the radicality of difference and plurality preserved. Let me explore this hypothesis by sketching more concretely the operational trialectic of the logic of pneumatology in theology, metaphysics, and hermeneutics.

No matter how hard we try, it is only to our detriment that we neglect either pole of the various tensions inherent in Christian theological reflection. Sure, all theology begins somewhere, and in that respect, privileges one side over the others. Yet a balanced theology is one which eventually moves from that starting point to give equal consideration to the perspectives and positions which contrast and, indeed, define that starting point (for without these, there would be no identifiable starting point, the starting point itself being relative to other points). In theological anthropology, for example, there are numerous polarities: human beings are created in the *imago Dei* and yet fallen; they are aspective and yet holistic; individualistic and yet communal and communitarian; made (being) and yet unfinished (becoming); free and yet bound; saints and yet sinners; called to self-denial and to self-affirmation (see Stagg 1973). These polarities characterize the dialectics of theology in general: the immanent and the economic Trinity; the primordial chaos and the spoken Logos; the protological and the eschatological (the Alpha and the Omega); eternity and temporality in the divine life; divine transcendence and divine immanence; the apophatic Father (incomprehensibility) and the cataphatic Son (comprehensibility); mystery and revelation; sovereignty and freedom; creation and redemption; grace and nature; justification and sanctification; faith and works; revelation and reason; Scripture and tradition; Church and world; nature and the Kingdom of God, and so on. The Spirit allows us to transcend these as well as other dualisms, whether that between Gospel and culture, the unity and diversity of humankind, and the partiality of present knowledge versus the fullness of eschatological knowledge (cf. Hoedemaker 1999, 217–33). To favor one side of any of these pairs is to neglect the important truths in the other.

Let us look for a moment as the tensions between sovereignty as it is creatively associated with the protological and the eschatological Trinity by Robert Jenson in order to highlight the contributions of a pneumatological rationality to a variety of theological issues. Jenson calls here for a trinitarian revisioning of the Holy Spirit as the "post-destining" power of the future in order to resolve the conundrum of a predestining God who has elected Jesus Christ. Thus he writes that "the trinitarian dialectics can be the appropriate conceptual scheme of predestination only if the whole scheme—of Father, Son, *and* Spirit—is used and only if the Spirit's metaphysical priority ('God is Spirit') is affirmed" (1984, 138). I believe that Jenson is on the right track to emphasize the Spirit as the key both to the trinitarian dialectic and to the problem of predestination. He is also in good company in asserting the Spirit to be the power of the future—e.g., in dialogue with a host of Lutheran theologians on this point, such as Jürgen Moltmann, Wolfhart Pannenberg, and Ted Peters (not to mention process thinkers like Lewis Ford). However, I'm not sure that I want to move the Spirit's horizon to the future alone. Rather, Spirit as central to the trinitarian relationality also must have past, present, and future theological and metaphysical implications, even as both Father and Son have theological and metaphysical claims on all three temporal modes. Only in this way can both the synchronicity and the diachronicity of the trinitarian perichoretic relationality be preserved. Further, it seems to me that a distinctive contribution of a pneumatological rationality is the holding forth of the tension in Christian life and theology between God as the creator, providential sustainer, and consummator of this world. A pneumatological rationality provides equal consideration of sovereignty and freedom, of creation and eschaton, and of the protological and eschatological Trinity, not because egalitarianism in thinking is currently in vogue, but because each emerges from the biblical and experiential data and needs to be accounted for.

The same kind of strategy holds true in applying the pneumatological rationality toward metaphysical reflection. How do we avoid favoring being to the neglect of becoming or vice-versa? What about substance and process; idealism and realism; universality and particularity; eternity and time; infinitude and finitude; possibility and actuality; the question of the one and the many? Is it truly the case that metaphysically, one of each side of these two polarities is more "true" to the way things are? Even if so, how do we know so? That these questions have been perennially debated by metaphysicians is no accident. Now this fact has been variously accounted for. Perhaps it is due to the finitude of human minds questing after infinity, or temporally bounded minds inquiring after eternity, etc. Perhaps they simply reflect the bias of a diversity of possible starting points. Perhaps, these tensions reflect provisional perspectives of reality which cannot be objectifiably known in and of itself? Perhaps both are true, even fundamentally and ultimately, albeit in different respects.

My own response is that whatever the truth to these metaphysical questions, the verdict is still out. Let the inquiry continue. However, let it do so by taking seriously the insights represented by these positions established in the history of metaphysical inquiry. It is currently in vogue to dismiss these perennial tensions simply by waving them off as products of an obsolete premodern paradigm dominated by dualistic sensitivities. Not so fast, I reply. Whether or not (for example) the world is one or many still remains a question for enlightened postmoderns whether we admit it or not. This is not to deny that advances have been made on this question. Reflection has shown us that any response within a dualistic either-or framework will be misguided since the world is experienced as both unified and plural. Any further pursuit of this question therefore somehow needs to take into account both facets of experience and the resulting conclusions to which reflection is driven. And, I am suggesting that a pneumatological rationality is precisely what is needed in order to sustain this dialectical process of exploration since both terms are retained, not swallowed up by, their interrelation. Thus on this question of the one and the many, as David Cunningham puts it, "God's Triunity is not merely a compromise between the one and the many. Rather, it grasps both concepts simultaneously and defines them as requiring one another" (1998, 271).

The same kind of pneumatological logic characterizes the problematic of epistemology, hermeneutics, interpretation, and method, the subject of this book. How else is the dialectical tension to be preserved between objectivity and subjectivity; a priorism and a posteriorism; rationalism and empiricism? Translated theologically, are not both the approaches from above and from below required? Put another way, do we not need both Spirit and Word? If my intuitions in this essay are correct, approaching these perennial issues in method, ontology and theology via pneumatology is promising for a way out of the dualistic impasses—e.g., between Barth's emphasis on dialectics, divine eternity, the priority of creation and of the past, the immanent Trinity, and christological method; and Pannenberg's emphasis on synthesis, created temporality, the priority of the eschatological future, the economic Trinity, and the cosmological framework of theology (cf. Bradshaw 1988, esp. 345–61)—which plague Christian theology. The issue is not whether or not we are searching for epistemic and hermeneutic synthesis, since thought is driven toward synthesis. Rather, from the perspective of the pneumatological rationality, the question is whether or not the tension of dialectical movement of thought, of knowledge, and of interpretation, is ever cut off. If so, synthesis overwhelms both thesis or antithesis, and what is important about them is lost. In order for the system not to break down or stall on one or the other side of the pendulum of thought, a pneumatological rationality is required which drives the ongoing give-and-take of the dialectical tension even while it retains the importance of both thesis and antithesis, amidst the proposed synthesis.

Herein lies the significance of a pneumatological rationality as fleshed out earlier according to the two trinitarian models. Spirit and Word are always mutually defined and subordinated, and that because of their coinherence. Sure, theologies will come and go privileging either Spirit or Word, as they will with the other theological tensions. Inevitably, they will gravitate to that pole which is most easily defined, handled, and manipulated. And, between Spirit and Word, it is the latter which has most often provided the concreteness, particularity and stability conducive to the cognitive process. Unfortunately, what is most easily handled is also more readily transformed into an ideological tool of legitimization, domination and oppression. And, as is the case with these theological tensions, whenever ideologies emerge, so do other evils. These inevitably call forth and require the violent, unpredictable, and uncontrollable winds of the Spirit as an antidote. Theologically and methodologically, the points to be made is that both sides of the tensions which inform reflection need to be kept in play, and that this occurs through deployment of a pneumatological "engine" which drives, incessantly, the dialectic of thought and reality. Of course, the result is better conceived as a hermeneutical trialectic. More on this later.

3.3 Relationality, Realism, Community: Toward a Triadic Metaphysics and Ontology

It is time to complete the argument for foundational pneumatology. While being reminded that such is a fallibilistic account, yet as foundational it aspires toward universal validity and application albeit apart from the a priori necessity characteristic of Enlightenment rationalism. From the preceding remarks, the foundational pneumatology can now be simply defined as an abstract account of the ways in which human experiences of self, other, and God are structured, mediated, and ought to be expressed. The mediational and normative aspect of foundational pneumatology touches upon theological and philosophical anthropology and psychology. We have begun to sketch the basic contours of foundational pneumatology as specified in those arenas, and will elaborate extensively on these aspects in the discussion to follow on epistemology. The structural aspect of foundational pneumatology touches upon ontological and metaphysical issues, the subject of this chapter. I have proposed here that the basic features of foundational pneumatology are best explicated along the lines of a robust trinitarianism.

The result is, so far, a relational, realistic, and social metaphysics. The following is devoted to explicating this last strand of sociality for foundational pneumatology, a motif which has been percolating since the discussion of the life-giving Spirit as the Spirit of fellowship and communion. We will examine first the idea of community as informed pneumatologically and theologically, and then probe its metaphysical implications. This chapter concludes with a summary sketch of the relational, realistic, and social metaphysics that undergirds the following foray into epistemology, interpretation and method.

3.3.1 Community is both a pneumatological and trinitarian concept. The latter emerged, as we saw, specifically in the thought of the Cappadocians in the East and Richard of St. Victor in the West. In what follows, I want to further develop this motif by drawing on the work of one of the most penetrating contemporary Orthodox theologians, John Zizioulas. His major work in English, *Being as Communion* (1985), is actually an exploration of the christological and ecclesiological mysteries of the Christian (Orthodox) faith as being eucharistically and liturgically preserved and communicated. Yet this is by no means simply an ecclesiology for Zizioulas is, first and foremost, an ecumenical theologian. It is this ecumenical breadth and depth which opens the door to trinitarian, christological, and pneumatological reflection as well.

And, it is precisely such theological work which leads to Zizioulas' central proposal regarding reconceiving the ontology of personhood. As we know by now, the West, following Augustine, began with the unity of the divine substance and followed with the three divine persons. In the East, however, the triune persons are definitive of the divine reality. More specifically, as we saw, the divine persons are what they are as triune relations. God is not first a substance who has relationships, but is first and forever a triune, inter-subsistent, and intersubjective relationality. And this point is of crucial importance because of the necessitarianism and determinism inherent in the ontologies of the Greek philosophical tradition. It is the genius of the Greek Fathers, Zizioulas points out, to preserve the divine freedom precisely by identifying ultimate being in relational and personal terms. Thus God is God simply as

> *Father*...who 'begats' the Son and 'brings forth' the Spirit. This ecstatic character of God, the fact that His being is identical with an act of communion, ensures the transcendence of the ontological necessity which His substance would have demanded...and replaces this necessity with the free self-affirmation of divine existence. (1985, 44; all italics in this and the following Zizioulas quotations are original to the translation)

Zizioulas proceeds, on this reconceptualized ontology of personhood, to understand both christology and the nature of the Church as the body of Christ.

Here, the centrality of pneumatology comes to the fore:

> [T]he Holy Spirit is not one who *aids* us in bridging the distance between Christ and ourselves, he is the person of the Trinity who actually realizes in history that which we call Christ, this absolutely relational entity, our Savior. In this case, our Christology is *essentially* conditioned by Pneumatology, not just secondarily as in the first case; in fact it is *constituted* pneumatologically. Between the Christ-truth and ourselves there is *no gap to fill* by the means of grace. The Holy Spirit, in making real the Christ-event in history, makes real *at the same time* Christ's personal existence as a body or community. Christ does not exist *first* as truth and *then* as communion; He is both at once. All separation between Christology and ecclesiology vanishes in the Spirit. (1985, 110–11)

And, later:

> What I mean by "constitutive" is that these aspects of Pneumatology must qualify the very ontology of the Church. The Spirit is not something that "animates" Church which already somehow exists. The Spirit makes the Church *be*. Pneumatology does not refer to the well-being but to the very being of the Church. It is not about a dynamism which is added to the essence of the Church. It is the very essence of the Church. The Church is *constituted* in and through eschatology and communion. Pneumatology is an ontological category in ecclesiology. (1985, 132; cf. Fox 2001 and Hütter 2000, esp. 116–28)

Zizioulas' accomplishment is the application of the trinitarian ontology of personhood to ecclesial identity. God as communitarian relationality brings about redemption through the reconstitution of human communality and fellowship in Christ by the power of the Spirit. The Spirit is therefore the relational, dynamic, and communal life of the Church. The Church is not just the collective expression of individuals around a common purpose or vision. Rather, the Church is constituted by the new birth of the Spirit which re-establishes the body of Christ precisely as the communal mutuality of its members. And, just as trinitarian coinherence resists all hierarchicalization and subordinationism in the divine life, so also are these resisted ecclesiologically. "If the Church is *constituted* through these two aspects of Pneumatology [eschatology and communion], all *pyramidal* notions disappear in ecclesiology: the 'one' and the 'many' co-exist as two aspects of the same being" (1985, 139).

Being as Communion is a specific attempt at ecumenical theology. Thus Zizioulas' intentions are the deepening of ecclesial fellowship through Christian self-understanding. Our quest here, however, is for a foundational pneumatology which aspires to universality—a pneumatological ontology. This leads me to push Zizioulas' point one step further. Certainly the Spirit is the one who births the new creation as the body of Christ. Yet is not the Spirit also biblically imaged as the divine womb which nurtures, births, and sustains the created order as a whole? Clearly, humankind lives, moves, and finds life only in God (Acts 17:28). At the same time, God is present to the entirety of creation precisely through his Spirit, from the farthest regions of the cosmos to its innermost depths (Ps. 139:7–15). Now there are two separate questions here, one which concerns humankind at large, and the other which concerns the entirety of the cosmic order. To focus for the moment on the former, might it be arguable that if the Church is constituted pneumatologically, so is human life as a whole? The former, in this case, would be the specific instantiation of the general constitutiveness of the latter. Might the difference be that the Church knows explicitly the face of the Word through which she is co-constituted with the Spirit, while the world does not?

I would like here to replicate Zizioulas' strategy, but apply the trinitarian ontology of personhood to the social and relational constitutedness of lived experience more specifically. Life is experienced socially and relationally, at different levels. Human life exists in webs of social environments. And, insofar as the Spirit is the power of life, such environments are sourced in and through the divine breath. Relationality and community are engendered through the gift of the Spirit. In this way, the Spirit's gift which is nothing less than the mutual love of Father and Son finds economic expression. The Spirit of life enables reconciliation and healing among human creatures. The divine breath renews life through reestablishing relationality, fellowship, and community.

3.3.2 But what about the cosmic order as a whole? Can the 139th Psalm be taken seriously with regard to the pneumatological constitution of creation itself? Is the trinitarian ontology of personhood at all applicable to the world of nature? On this issue, the question of foundational pneumatology—foundational ontology, more specifically—comes full circle. I propose to explore this through the work of Joseph Bracken, SJ.

Bracken's project (1985, 1991, 1995, 2001) is to recontextualize the speculative demands of Christian orthodoxy in a post-Einsteinian world. For this task, he finds most helpful the process metaphysics of Whitehead. Now while he recognizes the strength of the tradition of dipolar theism in the process camp, especially as defended at length by Charles Hartshorne, Bracken is also convinced that drawing out the implicit trinitarianism in Whitehead's cosmology—God, world, creativity [see 3.1.2]—results in a more rather than less coherent metaphysical vision. But Bracken is not about only repeating Whitehead. He is interested in orthodoxy. More specifically, he's after a trinitarian cosmology (the subtitle of Bracken's *Society and Spirit*). To accomplish this, Whitehead's concept of society is brought into creative dialogue with the notion of spirit.

For Whitehead, a society is a set of actual occasions which shares a common elemental form or is ordered according to a defining characteristic. Bracken argues, however, that insofar as Whitehead (1978, 89) admits that societies are self-sustaining and constitute their own reason, to that extent societies are categorically as ultimate as are Whiteheadian actual entities even if societies are what they are precisely as these occasions bound together. Things are thereby constituted precisely as differentiated, hierarchical, and complex social aggregates, each aggregate consisting of various sub-societies and/or occasions, all of which retain their own sense of autonomy. Yet together, social wholes are more than just the togetherness of the various parts. And, considered cosmologically, each society retains its own integrity and ontological unity both synchronically with regard to the sub-societies and occasions that comprise it and diachronically over time. Further, it is the exercise of agency by societies as aggregates (inanimate compounds, personal individuals, social collectivities, etc.) which constitutes the world's creative processes.

But, if creativity is conceived nominalistically, as it is in the Whiteheadian universe, then there arises the problem of how occasions and societies can exercise their agency so as to drive the dynamic processes of becoming. Here, Bracken draws on advances in the sciences—in biology and physics specifically—to understand becoming through the category of energy events and fields of activity. Extended in dialogue with Schelling's notion of spirit as the power of radical self-determination and Hegel's concept of objective spirit as the structured fields of activity, Bracken proposes to understand the world as comprised ultimately of socially and serially ordered occasions of energy which share common fields of activity (1986; 1991, Part Two). Spirit is the force that energizes social formulations while societies are the concrete fields of spirit's activity. The parallels here with Wink's concept of spirit and matter as the inner and outer aspects of reality are discernible. Their mutual indebtedness to Whiteheadian categories explains their convergence here.

Spirit and society are therefore Bracken's fundamental cosmological and metaphysical categories. And, insofar as God in Whitehead's categorial scheme should be the chief exemplification of rather than an exception to metaphysical principles, God is also to be understood thereby in terms of spirit and society. More specifically, God is a tri-personal community who subsists as highly complex socio-serial fields of activity: Father, the source of creation's initial aims; Son, the "focal point of the response of all finite occasions, both individually and collectively, to the offer of the 'Father'"; and Spirit, the mediating principle between Father and Son, and between God and the world (Bracken 1991, 125–26).[8] Yet the divine unity is preserved since each person participates with the other two in a shared (infinite) field of common intentional activity such that the actions of each one are actions of the other two. This infinite field of activity—here, Bracken reworks Whitehead's notion of the extensive continuum—is itself the all-embracing and all-inclusive field which contains the structured (finite) fields of creation and creatures (thus Bracken's panentheism). The latter are, in turn, constituted as hierarchically ordered natural, personal and communal fields, each reflecting social processes in varying degrees of complexity, God, of course, being the most complex of all—infinitely so. Further, as reality is socially constituted, the various societies at each of their levels mutually interact, albeit with varying degrees of capacity to influence each other depending on their "social" or cosmological locations.

Bracken's vision is as broad as demanded by metaphysical and cosmological speculation even as it is deeply informed by an earnest engagement with Whitehead's philosophical scheme. My purpose here is not to endorse completely Bracken's retrieval and reconceptualization of Whitehead's metaphysics as much as it is to tease out the ontological implications of a foundational pneumatology with regard to the notion of community. As Zizioulas helps us to see trace the movements of the Spirit in the ecclesial community, so also does Bracken help us follow out the ontological and cosmological movements of Spirit in the social constitution of reality as a whole. Human personhood, following divine personhood, consists of the relationship between the individual and the various communities through which the individual is established. These fields of relational activity can be, for the sake of convenience, reduced to three: personal and interpersonal relations; biological and environmental relations emergent from and attending to the human constitution and locatedness as natural creatures; and relationship with God, in whose image it is that human beings are created (cf. Yu 1987, ch. 7).

Thus is ontology understood as social process entailed in foundational pneumatology. This brings together various pneumatological motifs which

---

[8] Bracken also discusses the Trinity in terms of possibility, actuality, and that which mediates between the two (1995, 63). It should also be noted that here, Bracken follows Hartshorne, John Cobb and other process theists in seeing God as a compound and serially ordered society of occasions, rather than Whitehead, for whom God was an eternally existing actual entity. For Bracken, of course, it is more accurate to identify God as a tri-personally ordered cosmic society.

have been uncovered so far, including Spirit considered metaphorically and analogously as dynamic field of force, as law and generality, and as relationality itself. Herein lies the metaphysical implications of the scriptural reference to the "communion of the Holy Spirit" (2 Cor. 13:13).

3.3.3 We have arrived at a place to regroup before launching farther (or deeper) into our inquiry. Our overarching goal has been to develop a trinitarian hermeneutic from a pneumatological starting point. We therefore began with what I called a pneumatology of quest by elucidating three motifs of the Spirit drawn from the biblical narratives. Our discussion of the Spirit as relationality, as divine rationality, and as the power or dynamic of life was and is not meant to be an exhaustive portrait for a biblical pneumatology. Rather, we simply agreed to follow the trail of the Spirit by exploring the theological implications of these categories.

The result was a resolutely trinitarian theology illuminated through two models: that of the Spirit and Word as the two hands of the Father, and that of the Spirit as the mutual love between Father and Son. The former approach began with the Irenaean intuition of the co-relationality of Spirit and Word, and opened up toward the doctrine of trinitarian coinherence in the fourth century. The latter was proposed initially by Augustine following, as I suggested, the order of experience and of knowing, from which flowed both the logic of the filioque (the bestowal model) and a pneumatologically driven eschatological trinitarianism (the return model). In both, the operational logic of pneumatology overcomes the binitarian impulse in Christian theological reflection and opens up toward a truly relational and robustly trinitarian view of God. The significance of the pneumatological categories for theology can be assessed variously. First, the relationality of Spirit reflected the relational role of the Spirit in the divine life. Further, the relationality of the divine life was seen to point not only to the God-world relationship, but also to the world itself as relationally constituted. Second, the rationality of the trinitarian mystery suggested a correlation between the orders of being and of knowledge such that the experience of the God through the Spirit reflected truly the inner trinitarian life. It was also clearly pointed out that the entire project so far illustrated the hermeneutical spiral at work. In some ways, experience evokes the interpretive categories, while in others, the categories make sense of experience. Finally, the Spirit as the dynamic of life anticipated the bestowal and return models' emphases on the movement of creation-fall-redemption—history itself—as the going forth and return of the divine missions, culminating in the hoped-for eschatological regathering of all things to God through the Word by the power of the Spirit.

he journey through trinitarian theology, however, was intended to pro-voke ontological and metaphysical reflection. Again, the pneumatological cat-egories were pressed into service—this time mediated through a relational, hermeneutical, and dynamic trinitarian theological framework—in order to ask: how does a pneumatologically driven trinitarian theology illuminate the basic and most general features of experienced reality? The resulting meta-physical vision, what I called foundational pneumatology, featured a triadic structure at two levels. First, the features of human experience as probed through Peirce's phenomenology revealed a correlation of ontology and trinitarian theology. The interrelatedness of qualities, facts and laws was seen to characterize experienced reality on the one hand, while being analogous in certain respects to the triune life of God on the other. In this scheme, the spiri-tual dimension of reality is conceived in terms of the habits, dispositions, ten-dencies, and forces which mediate possibility and actuality.

Second, the emergent categorial scheme is not only triadic in terms of the struc-ture of lived experience, but is seen also to converge with the speculative implica-tions of the pneumatological categories as applied metaphysically. Thus reality is relational insofar as relationships, interactions, and processes are fundamen-tal rather than being, essence, or substance. It is rational insofar as knowledge accurately conveys reality external to the knower and enables knowers to under-stand, manipulate, and negotiate their way in the world. It is dynamic insofar as reality is socially processive and communally interactive, the ongoing emergence of creative novelty of the one amidst the continuity of the many. The result is a relational, realistic and social metaphysic which is triadically structured on the one hand even while it aspires to explain the universal features of reality as emer-gent from experiencing and thinking pneumatologically on the other.

Having said this, we should remain cautious in thinking about any of these metaphysical categories—relationality, rationality, dynamic sociality, etc.—in a priori or essentialist terms. The categories themselves are pneumatologically driven even as we have sought empirical (i.e., experiential and phenomeno-logical) confirmation for them. In short, the categorial scheme itself is fallibilistically construed, open to revision and correction from experience, collaborative inquiry, and reflective critique.

Yet both the trinitarian and pneumatological character of this metaphysic deserve some brief transitional comments. With regard to the former, the trinitarian notion of coinherence applies to the metaphysical categories. Each of the categories can always be read in light of the other two. With regard to relationality, the fact of its rationality points to the relationality between knowing minds and the various "objects" of knowledge; and, the dynamic character of the world speaks to its temporality and, hence, the relatedness of past, present, and future. With regard to ontological and metaphysical realism, the relationality of the world means that knowledge consists of an ever spiraling (inward and outward) web of beliefs which correlate knowing minds with their objects of knowledge; and, the dynamic character of the world means that knowledge is never static, but is a process of inquiry with eschatological implications. Finally, with regard to the social and processive nature of reality, the relationality of the world points to the communal structure of all forms of life and its interconnectedness not only to other life forms, but also to the natural world; and, the rationality of the world calls attention to consciousness, cognition, mentality, all of which are signs of life.

The interrelatedness of these metaphysical categories are implicated, I believe, by the frame of reference provided by foundational pneumatology. Throughout the argument so far, spirit has been understood as that relational category which enables synthesis of two (or more) terms or poles (thus being trialectical) while preserving the integrity of the terms synthesized. Thus the advantage of a pneumatological approach to metaphysics and ontology is that it a) requires and demands the universal emphasis on the particularity, concreteness and individuality of things; b) highlights the dialectical relationship which characterizes the social and processive nature of things and serves as the dynamic that drives the back-and-forth movement of the creative process; and c) moves toward a non-duality whereby the particularities of both sides are retained and acknowledged. Here, it is important to note that Thirdness is the *relation itself* between Firstness and Secondness, rather than being either its own "thing" or a "sublation" of the other two. The latter was Hegel's mistake of identifying Spirit (syn-thesis) in a totalizing sense such that both thesis and anti-thesis were lost.[9] It is Augustine and Richard of St. Victor— who emphasized Spirit as the love between Lover and Beloved—who are to be followed here instead of Hegel. This finds resonance with Levinas (building on Buber) and Mühlen (building on Richard St. Victor himself) who both want to understand spirit in terms of the "we" that relates self and other. Of course, long before either Levinas or Mühlen, Royce had said something similar

[9] On this note, I should also say that I have come to appreciate Hegel's doctrine of spirit as synthesis. He also held pneumatology as central to a fully trinitarian theology and to a speculative philosophy that overcomes (by mediating) the tensions between nature and freedom, objectivism and subjectivism, and individualism and the community. Toward this end, Alan Olson (1992) has done much to rehabilitate Hegel's theology and philosophy from misunderstanding, especially among the theologically orthodox who complain about Hegel's philosophical intrusions into

...awing from Peirce. I will return in Part Two to more extensive discussions of both Royce and Levinas. For the moment, however, it is important to emphasize spirit as the synchronicity of Thirdness which does not overcome Firstness and Secondness, but precisely accentuates the distinctiveness and togetherness of Firstness and Secondness thereby opening up toward a truly robust trinitarian relationality.

Our journey so far has brought us full circle from pneumatology through hermeneutics and theology to ontology and metaphysics only to return us to the full force of the epistemological question. The claim was initially made that reality as rational meant a correlational interconnectedness existed between thought and reality such that knowledge accurately reflects, at least in part, the world external to the knower. Metaphysical realism is therefore presumed, grounded christologically and pneumatologically in the logic of both incarnation and Pentecost. The implications of a realist metaphysic, however, is just as, if not more important than, its factuality since if objects of knowledge exist apart from knowing subjects, then such objects have ontological status on their own right to make not only metaphysical but also ethical claims on knowers. But this begs the epistemic question. How do we know that the order of knowing truly reflects the order of being, at least insofar as metaphysical, ontological, and, that which most interests readers of this volume, theological claims, are concerned? Further, given the consistency with which the categories have transferred from pneumatology to theology to metaphysics, how can we be sure that these categories truly get at reality rather than being a sophisticated concoction of a human mind fascinated with triads like relationality, rationality, and dynamic life? At bottom, what leads us to believe that the hermeneutical spiral which we acknowledge operates in the processes of human cognition reflects not Kant's categories of thought but rather the reality of God through the Spirit? These question deserve serious consideration if in fact theological and metaphysical claims are to be given credence. More importantly, these questions are unavoidable if in fact the claims of this volume regarding a pneumatological hermeneutic and trialectical theological method are to be delivered. For these reasons, the epistemological question cannot and should not be postponed any longer.

theology on the one hand, and among secular philosophers who think it possible to read Hegel apart from his Lutheran heritage and his reaction to Schleiermacher's subjectivistic Christianity on the other. Hegel's mistake causes him to ultimately lose sight of what Peirce calls Secondness or the concrete forms of the Logos. This is a mistake that returns to afflict Hegel's christology. I will return to a more in-depth treatment of Hegel's pneumatology at a later date.

PART TWO

The Pneumatological Imagination: Epistemology in Triadic Perspective

In Part One of this book, a number of biblical, theological and metaphysical hypotheses were proposed. Some of these—the claim of a correlation existing between the orders of being and of knowing; the intuition that this correlation was traversed through the hermeneutical spiral of experience to categories of thought to objects of knowledge; the suggestion of a critically realistic metaphysics which insists that objects of knowledge truly exist apart from their being known; and, etc.—both assumed and implied epistemological conclusions or (at least) hypotheses. This chapter makes explicit the epistemic convictions underlying this project. More precisely, it mediates the preceding theological and metaphysical considerations with the hermeneutical and methodological reflections which follow in Part Three of this book. At the same time, it does not deny that the reverse approach can be (and often is) taken such that the movement proceeds from hermeneutics and method through epistemology to theology and metaphysics. In that case, different aspects and motifs will be highlighted toward variously formulated hypotheses and conclusions. I am convinced that the doctrine of trinitarian coinherence provides a lens through which analogous interconnections can be seen to hold epistemically regarding the processes of knowing and ontologically between the *ordo cognoscendii* and *ordo essendi*. In this essay, however, the interrelationship between theology and hermeneutics will be explored by proceeding from the former to the latter (thus aspiring to demonstrate one of my central claims that all theological hermeneutics are inherently theological *and* hermeneutical) rather than vice-versa (as is the case with most systematic theology texts produced during the past few generations).

The way forward will be through an in-depth examination of the logic of pneumatology, what I will call the "pneumatological imagination." Whereas

119

the previous chapter attempted to outline the rational framework of the logic of pneumatology (the *what*), the goal here is to probe the dynamic character of this logic, to attempt to discern the ways in which it operates and thus what it does (the *how*). Thus the movement here will be from pneumatology to epistemology rather than to ontology, albeit set within a trinitarian framework. Three overarching objectives frame the following discussion. First, I will seek to show how the pneumatologically conceived imagination is a viable starting point for examining the movement from human experience in general and Christian experience more specifically to the activity of discernment in general and theological discernment more specifically. Second, I will suggest how the pneumatological imagination functions and contributes hermeneutically to bridge the orders of knowing and of being, to connect meaning and reality, and to distinguish truth from falsity. Finally, the inherent capacity of the pneumatological imagination to be normed by objects of knowledge will be explicated. To accomplish these objectives, I develop the idea of the imagination as a pneumatic enterprise, the imagination as semiotic and as enabling normative engagement.[1]

Three caveats, however, are in order. First, the following is far from a comprehensive treatise on epistemology—the possibility, conditions, and justification of knowledge. Rather, it engages the discussion of epistemology specifically from the perspective of knowing as a pneumatic process, and focuses that perspective ultimately on questions of theological hermeneutics and methodology. Second, the proposals here, as before, do not amount to a transcendental proof whose conclusions follow by a priori necessity. Although (as I will argue) the pneumatological imagination provides an interpretive key to understanding the relational (read: pneumatological, opening up to triadic) structures and processes that hold between knowledge and its objects, it is also potentially dysfunctional and hence fallible with regard to its conclusions, including those reached here. A plausible theory of knowledge can, therefore, claim no more than to provide an adequate provisional account of how knowledge is deductively clarified and inductively confirmed even while it is open to be corrected by present and future insights into the epistemic process.

Finally, there are, of course, various epistemic frameworks by which we know. From a theological perspective, interpretation proceeds at one point

---

[1] Elsewhere, John E. Thiel (1991, 213–14) has called for a "pneumatology of the imagination" by which he wants to understand the role and processes of theological authorship. Part Two of this book can be understood in part as a response to Thiel's request, and in part as a thorough reworking and extensive development of my previous thinking.

analogically (Tracy 1981), at another sacramentally (Hilkert 1997), at a third prophetically (Brueggemann 1978) or even apocalyptically (Collins 1998), and (for Christians specifically), of course, christologically, among other options. The pneumatological imagination here sketched could be looked at as just another proposal on the free market of epistemologies. Rather than claiming to be a universalistic, absolutistic, bird's-eye-view on reality, it is radically particular, arising out of the experience of the Spirit, and needs, therefore, to be strenuously cultivated even as it is at the same time, mysteriously, graciously received as a gift of the Spirit. But my goal here it not just to develop one more epistemology. Instead, I hope to complement other epistemic frameworks and perhaps even integrate their strengths while avoiding their weaknesses with regard to the task of theological hermeneutics. As before, then, on with our pneumatology of quest, this time focused on questions of epistemology.

4 The Imagination as Pneumatic Activity

"The Holy Spirit is God's imagination let loose and working with all the freedom of God in the world, and in the lives, the words and actions, of the men and women of our time" (McIntyre 1987, 64). Put in terms of the pneumatological categories developed previously, the Holy Spirit is the divine mind that illuminates the rationality of the world to human minds. In this chapter, I will explore the various facets of this statement from three angles. First, I review the history of humanistic, philosophical, and religious reflection on the imagination. Second, against this backdrop, I develop the idea of the pneumatological imagination as an epistemological theory that proceeds from specifically thematized constructs of experiences of the Spirit. Here, I argue dialectically and trialectically that the imagination is "pneumatological" in terms of its being illuminated by the categories drawn from the experience of the Spirit as well as further illuminating those same categories in turn. Finally, this being a project in theological hermeneutics and method, the explicit relationship between the imagination in general—and the pneumatological imagination more specifically—and theological thinking is discussed.

4.1 The Structure of the Imagination: An Historical Sketch

Our first question should be, What is the imagination? I will sketch a variety of answers to this question from the Western intellectual and philosophic tradition which has made numerous inquiries into the nature of the imagination over the centuries. Throughout, I want to highlight three of its most important conclusions for our purposes: the imagination as a synthesis of passive and active components (being functionally relational); the imagination as a cognitive blend of the affective and spiritual aspects of the human being (being functionally integrative); and, the imagination as valuational (being functionally normative).[1]

4.1.1 Given that the history of Western philosophy can be understood, as

[1] The following historical sketch draws especially from Kearney (1988). See also Cocking (1991), which includes beneficial discussions on the imagination in Judaism and Islam.

Whitehead remarked, as a series of footnotes to Plato, it is not surprising to find rather extensive consideration of the imagination in Plato's works. Plato, it will be recalled, bequeathed to posterity the idea of the imagination as the lowest faculty of the human soul. Whether in the form of *phantasia* or *eikasia*, the imaging function is almost entirely passive in receiving from the data of the senses. True, the imagination may, at times, play a more active or mimetic role in the soul's ascent, but this occurs or should occur only when it is guided by reason.

But why should the imagination be subordinated to reason? Plato formulated a five-fold metaphysical argument in response (cf. Kearney 1988, 87–99). First, those who trade in images do so either because they are ignorant of the reality behind the images or in order to deceive others into thinking that the images are true to the reality they represent (here, the epistemological opposition between truth and falsehood is highlighted). Second, images are non-didactic—they teach us nothing about the reality they image (here the anthropological opposition between political praxis and artistic uselessness is highlighted). Third, images appeal to our erotic and animal desires, rather than to our reason—hence their irrationality (here the psychological opposition between rational soul and material body is highlighted). Fourth, images falsely represent reality such that they seduce the unwary into the imitation of faults or untruths—hence, images are inherently immoral (here, the moral opposition between good and evil is highlighted). Lastly, images are blasphemous in leading us to replace the original order of divine being and reality with humanly construed copies—hence leading to idolatrous elevation of that which is not ultimately real (here the metaphysical opposition between divine being and human becoming is highlighted). Plato's student, Aristotle, did not break ranks with his teacher on this issue. For these founding fathers of the Western intellectual tradition, "imagination remains largely a *reproductive* rather than a *productive* activity, a servant rather than a master of meaning," clearly dominated by rather then complementary to reason (Kearney 1988, 113; italics orig.).

Perhaps not surprisingly, the fate of the imagination in Christianity has gone the way of Plato and Neo-platonism. Now the biblical data on the imagination is itself ambiguous. It presents the imagination—especially the Hebrew *yetser*—as the root of both good and evil in the sense that both possibilities are present to it. Thus, "the imagination was not therefore necessarily an evil impulse *in itself*, but only became so in the light of man's subsequent transgression….[I]f the evil imagination epitomizes the error of history as a monologue of man with himself, the good imagination (*yetser hatov*) opens up history to an I-Thou dialogue between man and his Creator" (Kearney 1988, 47).

The ambivalence of the rabbinic tradition with regard to the imagination is better explained when it is seen that the Hebrews understood the imagination not in epistemic, aesthetic or even physical terms, but as an ethical category. In this sense, the connection between the imagination and the human heart is evident since the latter clearly functions metaphorically throughout Scripture as the focal point of both good and evil (e.g., Gen. 6:5, 8:21, Deut. 6:5, 1 Sam. 13:14, 1 Chron. 29:18; Prov. 6:18, Matt. 15:19, Rom 1:21, 2 Cor. 10:5, Col. 3:23, 1 Tim. 1:5). Against this background, it is easier to appreciate the rabbinic portrait of the imagination as reflective of the *imago Dei*. Their reading of the Hebrew scriptures underscored the imagination as enabling human creativity (in imitating the divine creative act), providing for human responsibility (in the capacity to choose between good and evil), and projecting human beings toward the future and the transcendent (in anticipating alternative possibilities for existence).

Given their Jewish background, the earliest Christians also imbibed Hebraic modalities of thinking about the imagination, even if such were supplemented by Hellenistic ways of thought. Over the centuries, however, Christians have generally ignored the creative, ethical and dynamic understanding of the imagination by the Hebrews in favor of a Neo-platonic interpretation. Its connotations, therefore, have been, by and large, pejorative—the medieval theologian, Philoxenes of Mabboug, for example, arguing the imagination to be intrinsically perverse and constituting the "original sin." This opprobrious reading of the imagination reaches an apex in the King James Version (KJV), where its fourteen appearances have negative connotations connected to human evil and waywardness vis-à-vis the intentions of God (Gen. 6:5, 8:21, Deut. 29:19, 31:21, 1 Chron. 29:18, Jer. 3:17, 7:24, 9:14, 11:8, 13:10, 16:12, 18:12, 23:17, Luke 1:51; cf. McIntyre 1987, 5–8). The majority of these are translations of the Hebrew *yetser*, although there are other Hebraic words involved as well (e.g., *sheriruth* and *machashebeth*; the Greek term in Luke 1:51 is *dianoia*). What is important to note, however, is that none of these are technical terms requiring their translation as imagination. This is brought out by the fact that the NRSV, for example, uses alternative renderings for every one of these KJV citations ranging from the succinct "inclinations" to "inmost thoughts" and "thoughts of the heart." Consistent with the KJV, the only two occurrences of "imagination" in the NRSV are translations of the common root word, *lebab*, in Ezekiel 13:2 and 17 where Yahweh exposes false prophets who speak out of their own heart or understanding.

Discussions of the imagination in the medieval and Renaissance periods did not, therefore, see any explicit departure from the ancient Greek understanding. Pico della Mirandola's *On the Imagination* (orig. 1501; ET 1930) is a veritable synthesis of ancient and medieval thinking on the imagination. He does make one minor adjustment when he renders the imagination subservient, not to the pure reason of the philosophers, but to the intellect as being at the heart of the soul's ascent to God. This signals the beginnings of a more sophisticated view of the imagination.

The major development, however, is brought about by a shift from the emanationist model of creation prevalent in Neo-platonism to a more causal model whereby Being is understood as the transcendental source of all spatio-temporal effects. Not coincidentally, this same period that sees the renascence of the imagination is also the one which births modern science, including the Copernican revolution in cosmology (cf. Bronowski 1978). The result was that later Renaissance mystics such as Paracelsus and Bruno were led to question the consensus against the imagination as active or productive. Rather than subordinating human subjectivity to the reality that lay beyond images, the ontological status of the human subject was recognized and imagination was considered to be a creative and authoritative source of knowledge. This same recognition of the subjectivity of human selfhood and knowledge was what motivated moderns like Hume to see the connections between the imagination and the emotions, passions and other like felt impressions (cf. Warnock 1976, 36–40). Just as the imagination enabled the processing of sense data toward intelligibility, so did it enable the processing of the same toward feelings. The stronger the felt impression, the more likely it is to stir up greater passions; the weaker the impression, the more liable it is to calm emotive states, perhaps even fading ultimately into wishful thinking, fancy, or plain error.

4.1.2 The road was thereby cleared for Kant to acknowledge what had long been denied of the imagination: its including an active or productive aspect alongside its passive or reproductive function. To put it crudely, for Kant, the imagination is that which mediates between sensation and reason, absorbing from the former and transforming what is absorbed for the consumption of the latter. If that is the case, however, is not human reason subservient to the imagination precisely in the sense that reason is at the mercy of the prior imaginative organization of sense data? More disconcertingly, what then do the foundations of knowledge consist of if not reason? Does not the imagination appears to be an arbitrary filter that forever severs the ties between the essential character of objects of knowledge and subjective human experience? This conclusion was certainly one that Kant recoiled from.

Kant's reconstruction of the imaginative functions of the human mind has had far-ranging effects (cf. McIntyre 1986, and Bryant 1989, 65–84). Romantics such as Coleridge hailed the Kantian turn as a rebirth of the imagination making possible meaning, the grasp of universals or generals, in short, the formation of the human world of signification (cf. Warnock 1976, 82–89). Kierkegaard, however, was not as optimistic. For him, the creative imagination was faced instead with the predicament of life's *angst* (cf. Ferreira 1991). Nietzsche, of course, acknowledged Kierkegaard's problematic, but chose instead to embrace it. The *Übermensch* makes a distinction between authentic and inauthentic functions of the creative imagination: "the creative imagination is inauthentic to the extent that it allows its illusions to be taken for truths. And it is authentic to the extent that it acknowledges its illusions as illusions and thereby exults in the freedom of its own creativity" (Kearney 1988, 213). This was Nietzsche's challenge: to allow the imagination to live dangerously within the abyss itself. Heidegger understood this to mean that the imagination—*Dasein*—emerges from nothingness and is thrown toward nothingness; the overcoming of humankind therefore signals the end of the imagination. Existentialists like Camus rejected the nihilism explicit in Nietzsche's vision and reinserted the creative power of the human imagination even while recognizing this creativity as an absurd quest for meaning in a meaningless world.

Other existentialists like Sartre, however, sought to recover the anthropological foundations of the imagination in order to stay the demise of both the modernist and the humanist projects. *The Psychology of Imagination* (1940) was Sartre's deconstructive effort to analyze the basic characteristics of images. First, images are acts of consciousness (emphasis on productive rather than reproductive functions of the imagination). Second, images as projections are therefore not of real perceptions that increase our knowledge, but have a quasi-observative quality whereby we re-create our own realities. Third, images are spontaneous creative actions of meanings (in contrast to perceptions which are passive) which point to the freedom intrinsic to human consciousness. Finally, images are ultimately nothingness; the activity of the imagination is understood as *néantisation*: the act of non-positing by negating the real world behind one's images and choosing to live—indeed, because we have no other choice—according to images that we recognize are temporally and spatially unreal and psychologically illusory.

In *Existentialism and Humanism* (1946), then, Sartre battled with the ethical implications of his doctrine of imagination. His response was to resort to Kant's "categorial imperative." Kant's dilemma, of course, was what in part posed the modern problem: how do we validate opting for universal reason given the primacy of the imaginative subject? In *Existentialism and Literature* (1947), Sartre therefore distinguished between two kinds of writing: poetry and prose. The former signified imagination's withdrawal into its subjectivities, and the latter imagination's engagement with the objective world (the aesthetic and the ethical). Authenticity is achieved by the one who renounces the poetic imagination in favor of the prosaic, who embraces the ethical obligation to reality. This legitimated Sartre's turn to socialism. But, herein, Sartre found himself again in a catch-22: If in fact the imagination strives for authenticity and achieves it precisely by exercising its existential freedom, is not the ethical turn counterproductive for humanism? Sartre's dual project to preserve the creativity of the existential imagination and secure the anthropological basis for humanism can thereby be seen to fall on the horns of a dilemma. On the one side, to champion the creative imagination is to liberate the self toward authenticity; in this case, it makes little difference whether one carouses in a bar or enlists in the causes of revolution. On the other side, to insist on the ethical dimensions of human existence is to affirm the collective efforts of all for the common good; doing so, however, is possible only by curtailing the creative freedom of the self toward authenticity.

Postmodern thinkers, however, have rejected this reading of Sartre in part by elaborating on Nietzsche's deconstructive project. The "self"—whether imaginative or ethical—is a fiction sustained by the onto-theological tradition and can be seen to be dissolved once the infinite interplay of texts, narratives, stories and relationships that constitute the human being-in-the-world is clearly understood. How now shall we live, given that the "we" has itself been deconstructed? Yet even at this juncture, modernity's creative imagination has not been dealt a denouement by postmodernity. Instead, it has received a boost. Never before has the imagination been as celebrated, especially in literature and the arts. For these reasons, postmodern thinkers have been much less threatened by imagination's capacities, whether in terms of its access to or formation of "pure possibilities" (cf. Casey [1976] 1979, 111–23), or of its "power of redescription" (cf. Ricoeur 1995, esp. 144; see Evans 1995), both underwriting the creative human response toward an open future.

This does not, however, mean that the reproductive aspect of the imagination has given way completely to the productive aspect. It does mean that the imagination functions relationally, at least at three levels. First, the imagination mediates the human engagement with the external world through the recording of images derived from experience. Second, the imagination enables human beings to actively construct the world. Finally, the imagination holds both of these activities—of reproduction and production—together coherently such that one and the same person moves from one to the other subconsciously and fluidly.

4.1.3 The preceding historical overview also highlights two other functional aspects of the imagination: its integrative and normative character. The former emerges from a variety of questions: why is the imagination relatively passive with regard to these perceptions and not that, why the productions of the imagination take this form rather than that, why they highlight or focus on this aspect of reality rather than that? In short, what is it about the human constitution which informs our imaginative engagement with the world? Now the ancients, of course, were quick to see the connections between the imagination and fantasy, the latter then understood as the ruminations of the mind guided by what were allegedly the baser elements of humanity rather than by reason. The Hebrews, however, understood this positively as pointing to the holistic connection between the mind (the imagination) and the heart: the human center which coordinates the affections, the will, and the spirit. Much later, Hume correlated the imagination and the emotive aspects of perception, while Edwards pointed out the centrality of the affections to the human endeavor. Since the era of Schleiermacher and the Romantics, the intimate connections between the imagination and feeling has been reinforced, especially in the contemporary postmodern reaction to the positivism of Enlightenment rationality.

Now insofar as these other features are considered as central to the human experience, on what basis can they be disparaged in connection with the imagination other than the *scientistic* (and naturalistic) bias against subjectivity? Is it not the case instead that the imagination is an aspect of cognition that is holistically imbued with affectivity, and driven volitionally toward the beautiful, the true and the good? And, can the affections be arbitrary disassociated from the other central aspect of the heart—i.e., the spiritual dimension of the human experience?

This integrative and holistic aspect of the imagination has been more fully explored by others, including Mary Warnock and William Wainwright. Warnock argues in dialogue with the modern Western philosophical tradition for the imagination as being functionally synthetic and integrative at a number of levels. First, the imagination is certainly both reproductive and productive, that is, passive and active. Second, the imagination is the integrative bridge between perception and the utmost capacities of human cognition. Third, the imagination is worldmaking in the sense of holding together what is spacio-temporally present and absent. Now at each of these levels, central to the human imaginative encounter with the world is the affections or the heart. Warnock summarizes her study as follows:

> there is a power in the human mind which is at work in our everyday perception of the world, and is also at work in our thoughts about what is absent; which enables us to see the world, whether present or absent as significant, and also to present this vision to others, for them to share or reject. And this power, though it gives us "thought-imbued" perception (it "keeps the thought alive in the perception"), is not only intellectual. *Its impetus comes from the emotions as much as from the reason, from the heart as much as from the head.* (1976, 196; my emphasis; cf. Jagger 1989)

Warnock's thesis regarding the interaction between head and heart, imagination and emotions, finds support and explication in the recent study of the epistemology of religious beliefs by the Christian philosopher, William Wainwright. Bringing into mutual conversation Edwards' doctrine of "the heart," Newman's "grammar of ascent," and James' "will-to-believe," Wainwright's thesis is that proper epistemic functioning requires the integration of cognitive, moral, affective, and spiritual equipment.[2] "A converted heart, or a sensitive conscience, or a demand for meaning and the possibility of significant action are needed to appropriate the force of the evidence for religious truths. Each [of Wainwright's dialogue partners] believes that (when properly disciplined) our passional nature tracks the truth. 'Passional reason' is reliable" (Wainwright 1995, 5). But surely, critics object, this amounts to the admittance that imaginative reason is subjectivistic, circular and relativized according to the passions, long ago deprecated by Plato! Wainwright's response (1995, 124–47), consonant with the predilections of postmodernity, is that rational processes cannot avoid subjectivity completely. Further, he suggests that the circularity of "passional reason" is not vicious. Finally, he argues that certain important dispositions are required in order for arguments to be made, evidence to be assessed and nihilism to be discerned and avoided. In other words, thinking is not only an intellectual activity; it is also affective and spiritual (cf. Plantinga 2000, ch. 9).

The normative dimension of the imagination is also seen as emergent especially in the ethical orientation of the Hebraic mentality. Briefly put,

---

[2] On Newman, see Coulson (1981). Of course, it is no coincidence that one of Wainwright's dialogue partners is Edwards, whose work was conducted under the influence of the Lockean psychology. Part of Locke's dilemma, of course, was the Cartesian bifurcation of thought and reality. The question of how human beings could experience or be beneficiaries of grace was therefore acute. The answer, it was hypothesized in the eighteenth century, was that grace was mediated to the human condition by means of the imagination (see Tuveson 1960). I will return to Edwards below.

normativity pertains to human thinking to the extent that the ideals, rules and principles by which behaviors are measured are interiorized and self-consciously applied. Modernity, however, has not been hospitable to this emphasis since the modern divorce between fact and value is a fundamentally misdirecting assumption that pits the creative imagination against the ethical demands of human life (thus Sartre's dilemma). Moderns and postmoderns both labor under this dualistic presumption. Yet if the imagination is both productive and holistic, its engagement with the world should be able to take into account the values to be found in the world. How so? Precisely by overcoming the dualism between fact and value and correlating the value structures of the world with those of human experience.

Such a conception of the imagination has indeed by suggested recently by Robert Cummings Neville's axiological metaphysics.[3] Building on Dewey's valuational transactionalism whereby the real consists of interactions which have an aesthetic dimension, Neville proposes a speculative hypothesis that things are what they are precisely as achievements of some value or other. To be is to have realized value; to become is to attain value. Values, of course, are of many kinds: certainly moral, but also aesthetic, intellectual, and religious. More pertinent to Neville's analysis is are two chief categories of essential and conditional features through which all things are constituted. These translate roughly into intrinsic and relational values. The former are *sus generis* to the thing while the latter are the thing's values understood relationally or instrumentally with regard to other things (or persons).

In this framework, thinking itself is a selectively valuational enterprise, beginning with the imagination and proceeding toward interpretation, theory and the pursuit of responsibility. Neville agrees with the conclusions of the ancients and the moderns that the imagination is both reproductive and productive, but insists (with the Hebrew mind, I would add) that the conjunction be read as pointing to a continuity across the spectrum of thinking in general rather than as connoting a dualistic opposition. The imagination is therefore world-making in the sense that it sorts out experiential data and yields the limits of possibilities for human existence. These possibilities, however, are neither completely arbitrary nor are they completely indeterminate because

---

[3] Neville is a Western-trained philosopher whose familiarity with Eastern philosophic and religious traditions makes his systematic metaphysics one of the most formidable in the contemporary landscape. For an overview of his program, see Neville (1987); for the details, see the three-volume Axiology of Thinking series (1981, 1989, 1995). Because of space constraints, my discussion summarizes the imagination in Neville 1981, Part II.

the imagination is selective, dividing what is trivial from what is important among experiential inputs in order for humans to engage the world evaluatively.

Neville's original contribution, however, is to point out that the criteria for these decisions are axiological, guiding discernment of the "whats" given to the imagination through experience as well as the process of inquiry itself. Hence, the imagination shapes and is shaped by the pragmatic orientation of thinking in the sense that it seeks to carryover the values of the objects of experience into the mind so as to enable more effective human engagement with the world. Human activity is thereby normed in this process: we should go about our business in just this way, and not in that. Here, the important point to note is that the norms are not simply cognitive constructions imposed on the world, but are rather given, at least in part, by the objects of experience to the imagination. Yet the imagination contributes to the normative categorization of the objects of experience. Thus "fire" serves as a normative symbol for danger on the one hand and for being a source of life on the other (when one is cold). In this sense, we are most closely attuned to the extrinsic values of things, especially when those are directly related to our well being, our interests, our desires, etc. However, the task of normative engagement requires further diligence on our part so as to grasp values that are intrinsic to the things we encounter. Failure to do so renders our interaction with those things superficial at best, or results in our not-engaging those things at all. The imagination is thereby axiological precisely because value is not only a psychological or a moral category, but is also a cosmological one as well. The goal of the imagination's valuational activity is to shape habits and tendencies congruent with things encountered in the world and to order practical human life.

Much more needs to and will be said about the imagination, norms, and values. For the moment, however, a summary of where we are at is in order. While the imagination has had a checkered career in the history of Western thought, several important considerations to date reveal its relational, integrative, and normative character. The imagination is relational at a number of levels. It correlates cosmologically with the way things are, thereby enabling normative human engagement with the world. Finally, it includes the affective and spiritual dimension of human experience. Herein the axiological, ethical, and religious character of the imagination can be seen to converge to guide human inquiry and engagement with the world. Each of these aspects of the imagination is sorely in need of further explication, but not before elaborating on the imagination from a pneumatological perspective.

4.2 The Pneumatological Imagination

I propose to explore the pneumatological dimension of the imagination by focusing attention on certain primordial pneumatic experiences and their "root metaphors." The notion of root metaphors is itself derived from Stephen Pepper (1942). Now Pepper defines such as formative cultural symbols or icons that enable large-scale coherent visions of the world and that thereby function normatively in the assessment of visions of those outside that metaphoric framework because of their capacity to absorb and explain the other in its own terms. My pneumatological imagination certainly fits Pepper's definition insofar as its aspirations are concerned—that of being universally relevant to the appropriate phenomena. I am much more suspicious, however, about the ability of the pneumatological imagination to function normatively in an a priori fashion because I do not think that normative reason can be imposed without undermining the very epistemic processes that undergird the human quest for truth. On the other hand, if a priori thinking is admitted to be fallible and open to correction—as proposed, for example, by Alvin Plantinga (1993, 110–13)—then my chief problems with it are assuaged. Either way, the normativity of any rule has to emerge out of the dialectic of experience and understanding, rather than being established a priori.

This dialectical movement is itself captured and preserved in my approach to the pneumatological imagination via root metaphors. By categorizing the basic features of the pneumatological imagination through metaphors which point beyond themselves to primordial experiences, I am exhibiting at another level both the passive and active aspects of the imagination vis-à-vis the divine-human relationship. Certainly, the pneumatological imagination arises from specific encounters with the divine, specifically the Holy Spirit. Equally certain, root metaphors or images given in the scriptural narratives and handed down by the tradition act as lures and provide imaginative invitations that make possible such encounters. The following discussion will thereby highlight both elements of this dialectic—the experiential and the metaphoric (or narrativistic, or scriptural)—without prejudicing either over the other. As has been and will be repeatedly emphasized, the integrity of the dialectic informing the pneumatological imagination needs to be upheld in order not only to tease out the full implications of the this study, but also to assess the extent to which experience either confirms or falsifies this speculative hypothesis.

This discussion will be limited to three primordial experiences/root metaphors. These, it will be noted, correlate loosely to the three basic categories reached in the previous section regarding the imagination. First, whereas the imagination is the relational synthesis of both passive perception and active worldmaking, the pneumatological imagination accentuates the religious life that receives the empowerment of divine grace on the one hand even while it lives in and from that pneumatic power on the other; central to this aspect of the pneumatological imagination is what might be called its anti-nominalism regarding the dimension of *dunamis*, or power, inherent in all things. Second, whereas the notion of the imagination is seen to include the affective and the spiritual dimensions of human being-in-the-world, the pneumatological imagination calls attention to the mode of this togetherness via the integration of the charismatic and dynamic dimension of the Spirit and the formal and material content of the Word; central to this integrative aspect of the pneumatological imagination is its definitive christological character. Third, whereas the imagination is formally valuational, the pneumatological imagination allows us to focus more explicitly on asking normative and material questions pertaining to the various powers at work in the world—whether divine, natural, human, demonic or otherwise; central to this normative aspect of the pneumatological imagination is the what I call its "normativism"—the rejection of a positivistic and materialistic interpretation of power in the universe in favor of an approach that recognizes power is not devoid of moral or spiritual values and disvalues within the cosmological and natural processes of the world. Let me elaborate on each in turn by noting its sources within the Christian tradition, describing its phenomenological features, and developing its epistemological significance.

4.2.1 The first primordial experience of the Spirit is captured in the related biblical metaphor of "power." As we have already seen [1.3], this aspect of the pneumatological imagination derives from the experience of the Spirit as the *dunamis* or power of creation and life. Here, the power of divinity is experienced as creating (Ps. 104:29–30), as delivering (e.g., the strength of the "east wind" that divided the Red Sea and delivered the people of God from Egypt; cf. Exod. 14:21), as anointing for service (e.g., the descent of wind, tongues, and fire at Pentecost launching the worldwide mission of the Church; cf. Acts 2:1–4), and as resurrecting (Ezek. 37:1–14). The last mentioned trait, of course, finds its clearest exemplification in the Spirit of Holiness raising Jesus from the dead, thereby declaring him "to be the Son of God with power" (Rom. 1:4). In each of these paradigmatic cases, however, the people of the covenants inevitably experienced the divine presence and activity as a numinous, awe-inspiring, and worldmaking and world-transforming reality. (Here it can be seen how ecclesial pneumatology is, ultimately, concerned with explicating the presence and activity of God among the elect, while foundational pneumatology attempts to correlate ecclesiological pneumatology with the most general features of this same presence and activity in the world.)

Clearly, as seen here and previously, the Spirit is the power of God. What, however, does power consist of? Among other connotations, power is indicative of trajectories of forces and structures (cf. Berkhof [1962] 1977; Caird 1956, 31–53), extensions of dispositions (Lee 2000; Boyd 1992), purposes behind intentions (cf. Smith 1988), and vectors of laws or habits [cf. 3.1.2–3]. The significance of the power imagery thus points to what I call the "anti-nominalistic" character of the pneumatological imagination which sees more to reality than concrete phenomena and material objects. Rather, the pneumatological imagination is attuned to the fields of force and energy which shape, structure, and configure reality. In some instances, however, the outcome of these movements are entirely novel expressions of forces, dispositions, laws, etc., such that new realities are founded (as in *creatio ex nihilo*, or the resurrection of Jesus). These all are suggestive of power as energy and activity. However, they also signify the complex configurations that make up power in that no one force, disposition or intention can be so isolated as to be considered to work on its own. Rather, power functions amidst fields, within extensional networks, between dimensions (e.g., including the horizontal and the vertical), and across currents. Power is thereby active, exercised by things, events, persons, nations, etc., on the one hand, and leaving its mark and influence on the same on the other. It is productive, and the things produced are continuously both being reproduced and (in some cases) transformed, and producing and/or transforming other things. Power is therefore inherently fluid and dynamic rather than static, and as such, revelatory of intentionality, purpose and design in the world. True, the teleological character of reality is not always easily discerned. Yet it is precisely this feature of power that alerts us to the importance of being open to its diverse manifestations, to be sensitive to power's flux, and to be sufficiently flexible so as to be able to make the necessary adjustments to power's plays.

This kind of phenomenological analysis of power is revealing about the pneumatological imagination in at least two ways. First, the pneumatological imagination is sensitive to the diversity of powers at work in the world. In particular, it cherishes the activity of the Holy Breath, even while realizing that many other powers and forces continually impinge on the human condition. Second, an imagination attuned to the reality of spirit is empowered to impact the world. One imbued with the pneumatological imagination, in other words, is not only an individual who has been acted upon, but also an active individual. Herein lies the dialectic of grace and responsibility characteristic of the tension in divine-human interaction. The pneumatological imagination is "charismatic" in both senses of the term. On the one hand, it lives from the conviction that life is a gift, generally in terms of its awareness of the contingency of all things, including the self, but more specifically in terms of the futility of life's activity apart from divine graciousness. Central to this aspect of the pneumatological imagination is its passive expectancy of the Spirit's initiative: "I am sending upon you what my Father promised; so stay here in the city until you have been clothed with power from on high" (Luke 24:49). On the other hand, it lives from the conviction that life is empowerment toward creative transformation, generally in terms of human being-in-the-world, but more specifically in terms of the anointing (charismatic gifting) for service. Central to this aspect of the pneumatological imagination is life energized by the Spirit's power: "But you will receive power when the Holy Spirit has come upon you; and you will be my witnesses…" (Acts 1:8), and, "'Not by might, nor by power, but by my Spirit' says the Lord Almighty" (Zech. 4:6).

4.2.2 We have earlier seen that Spirit as relationality derives from the biblical identification of the Spirit as both the "spirit *of* God" and the "spirit *of* Christ." I am convinced that this adjectival character of the Spirit—meaning that the Spirit "will not speak on his own; he will speak only what he hears….He will bring glory to me [the Son] by taking from what is mine and making it known to you" (John 16:13–14)—is deeply significant as a root metaphor of the fact that the Spirit never calls attention to herself, but is always rather the relational pointer to an other. Whereas the experience of *ruach* among the ancient Hebrews called attention to the presence of Yahweh in their midst, the pentecostal experience of the early Christians called attention to the risen Christ in their midst. In either case, the primordial encounters of the people of God with divinity was mediated by the Spirit. The ontology of spirit, as we have seen, is relational through and through.

The relationality of Spirit therefore highlights the integrative aspect of the pneumatological imagination. Now insofar as the imagination itself is seen to integrate the affective, the volitional, and the spiritual dimensions of human experience, the pneumatological imagination intensifies this integration by transmuting or transforming the shape of the human imagination into that of the mind of Jesus Christ's. And, insofar as both the life and mind of Jesus represents and manifests the most authentic convergence of these dimensions of experience as a model for our emulation, to that extent the pneumatological imagination has a christomorphic structure. On this point, William Lynch has

rightly called attention to the imagination's capacity, in following the exu__
of Jesus, to integrate and even hold contrary or opposite images together—
finding exaltation in humility, fullness through emptiness, strength in weakness,
hope in hopelessness, infinite in finitude, life in death—so as to experience
reality it all of its richness (1973, 77–108; cf. Bednar 1996, 82–85). The result is a
more truthful and accurate engagement with reality in all its multiplicity and
plurality—thus Lynch calls it the "ironic Christic imagination"—rather than
simply reducing reality to a single, more emotionally conducive, set of images,
and ignoring or denying what is problematic. I would only add that the dynamic
thrust of the pneumatological imagination also directs the integrative process
by transvaluing or reorienting and redirecting that human imagination toward
the eschatological kingdom of God. And, insofar as the already-but-not-yet
kingdom calls us toward eschatological wholeness, to that extent the
pneumatological imagination is theocentric as well.

The result is that the pneumatological imagination is seen to function
integratively at three interconnected levels, each of which builds upon the other.
First, the Christian's imagination is interwoven with and nourished by the
image and mind of Jesus through the Spirit. Second, the various dimensions
of the imagination—the affective, the volitional, the spiritual, etc.—are thereby
integrated so as to enable a more holistic and healthy posture toward the world.
Third, this integrated imagination is the means through which humans engage with and relate to the world.

At this third level, the imagination relates to the world affectively and, more
importantly, spiritually. This point was made earlier in this century by the
Jewish philosopher of religion, Martin Buber, and the German philosophical
theologian, Ferdinand Ebner (cf. Green 1980). The spiritual life, for both, is
precisely the divine-human I-Thou relation. Whereas Buber begins and ends
with relationality itself, the Christian Ebner begins with the relational movement of the Logos between the divine I and the human Thou (John 1) and
ends by subordinating the revelatory relation of the divine Word to the human Thou to the objectivity of what is revealed. In Ebner's words, "since the
mystery of the spiritual life conceals and reveals itself in the mystery of the 'word',
pneumatology is therefore, as far as it is possible at all, word-knowledge, a knowledge *of* the word and *about* the word, and an interpretation of the prologue of
the Gospel of John" (quoted in Green 1980, 33; emphasis Ebner's). The subjectivity of Spirit, in other words, must give way to the objectivity of the Logos.

But does not both the phenomenology and trinitarian pneumatology developed in Part One call into question this subordination? On the one hand,

pneumatology points not to itself, but to the other. It is thus the character of pneumatology precisely to deflect from itself in order to allow the other to constitute itself to the imagination as other, distinct, undeniably and particularly its own self. Herein lies the truth of the passivity of the imagination's reproductive capacities. On the other hand, even granting Ebner's presumed subordination of the relational to the concrete, one could easily conclude in the opposite direction from Ebner's that concretions give false appearances since all concrete things are what they are precisely as modal and relational realities. Often, then, the character of the other is not immediately apparent not only because phenomena can be deceptive, but also because spirit is the dynamic modality of things that occur or become through space-time. Because of this, spiritual discernment must be corrigible, fallibilistic, and open to further inquiry. So it is that the pneumatological imagination is sensitive to the infinitely dense relational strands woven into the fabric of things and cautions us against the kind of epistemic absolutism often considered accessible to Christian reflection. In this way, the dogmatic absolutism that subordinationism insists on is avoided. The pneumatological imagination leads, instead, to a relational, or chastened absolutism.

But what, then, about theological absolutism? This raises the important question of the relationship of pneumatology and christology, of Spirit and Word, for Christian life and thought. Space constraints preclude extensive discussion here. But for the purposes at hand, it is important only to recall the Irenaean model of the Spirit and the Word as the "two hands of the Father." The Christian tradition has rightly insisted that both need to retain their integrity for a fully trinitarian theology. In practice, however, subordination of either to the other continuously occurs. Take the hermeneutical task, for example. Calvin himself emphasized the importance of Spirit-inspired interpretation of the Word (cf. Forstman 1982 and Gamble 1989). In contemporary currency, the conjunctive integrity of Word and Spirit (note the order prevalent among Protestants) in the hermeneutical enterprise means, in part, our recognizing that we learn to read Scripture within communities of faith and practice, and that such reading leads back to experience and practice in communities of faith (see Johnson 1998, esp. 10–15). Historic Protestant Christianity, however, has by and large neglected the Spirit or consciously subordinated her to Word (thus the usual Protestant order of Word first, preceding Spirit). The result is that the "letter of the law" has stifled the vitality of the Spirit (cf. 2 Cor. 3:1–6). On the other side, however, charismatic Christianity has often succumbed to excesses in elevating experiential phenomena to the neglect of the norms of the Logos as revealed in Scripture. My point is that while both elements are essential to a healthy hermeneutic, in practice, rarely is such balance accomplished or, more importantly, sustained. The relationality of Spirit requires nothing less than the thoroughly dialectical process of reading the world in the light of Scripture and vice-versa. Put theologically, while the content of the pneumatological imagination is effectively christomorphic and bibliocentric, the dynamic of the pneumatological imagination nevertheless remains distinctively charismatic and pneumatic.

4.2.3 The biblical root metaphor of "wind" or "breath" highlights the third primordial experience of the Spirit. This follows, of course, from the literal translations of the biblical words for "spirit": Hebrew, *ruach*, and Greek, *pneuma*. For our purposes, the import of this metaphor points to the assumed contrast between spiritual and material reality. Jesus' revelation to the Samaritan woman that "God is spirit" (John 4:24) made the point that the time had come when true worship did not consist in spatial location neither on a sacred mountain nor in the holy places of Jerusalem. This spirit-matter contrast, however, cannot be hardened into a metaphysical dualism without doing violence to the biblical imagery. Whereas metaphysical dualism suggests clear division, metaphorical contrast, however, is suggestive of a continuum, and this is recognized by the biblical data. Jesus himself compares the movements of the Spirit to that of the wind: "The wind blows where it chooses, and you hear the sound of it, but you do not know where it comes from or where it goes" (John 3:8a). Whereas the wind is here the mysterious source of the new birth, elsewhere, its effects produce instead confusion and double-mindedness (e.g., Eph. 4:14, James 1:6).

The ambiguity of the wind imagery calls for further elaboration. For now, however, it provides a contrast to the significance of the pneumatological symbol of power. Whereas the latter underwrites the anti-nominalism of the pneumatological imagination, the former highlights its normative character in calling attention to the fact that given the diversity of spirits operative in the world, we ought to earnestly desire the experience of the divine Breath rather than pursue after the breezes of just any spirit. Whereas the imagination of modernity and postmodernity has, in general, been swept away by technological positivism and been engulfed either by naturalism or by the turn to the subject, the pneumatological imagination recognizes subjectivity not in solipsistic terms, but as indicative of the interpersonal and interrelational forces that inspire, propel, and, in some cases, haunt the universe. The powers of the world—e.g., fields of force, dispositions, laws and vectors, intentionalities—these, the pneumatological imagination asserts, are not reducible to the terms established by mechanistic naturalism. Rather, they are our best efforts to articulate the spiritual aspect of reality, the spiritual dimension permeating the phenomenal world, assuredly transcendental to the physical senses, yet just as assuredly with ethical and moral outcomes expressed in and through the materiality of the created order. Thus, insofar as the wind produces a variety of effects, to that degree, the pneumatological imagination recognizes a variety of spirits—forces, dispositions, laws, etc.—in the world, operative at diverse levels (natural, human, social, institutional, national, etc.). Insofar as the powerful effects of wind are at times either constructive or destructive, the pneumatological imagination is convinced that the spiritual is a realm of divine or demonic activity that has concrete implications and material outcomes. The imagery of the wind is therefore significant in alerting us to the fact that the powers of the cosmos are never purely neutral, but inhabit and convey a normative character, one that is either potentially good or evil, beautiful or ugly, true or false, etc.

This means, of course, that the category of spirit is axiological, and that the pneumatological imagination potentially approaches the various dimensions of reality with a greater degree of sensitivity. More important, it is able to engage the spiritual aspect of reality with a particular intensity, and is ideally suited to recognize the reality of the divine and the demonic as normative dimensions of experience. Yet the pneumatological imagination does so in ways that challenge a simplistically construed dualism in that regard. Even if we were to posit an ontological dualism between the divine and the demonic, our discernment of the difference does not follow along the same, clearly drawn theoretical line. This is the case since our categories are neat distinctions only in the abstract world of thought. In the natural and interpersonal worlds of things and people, however, spiritual realities are dynamic forces co-present and co-active to greater or lesser degrees in all things (i.e., in their dispositions, habits, and intentions, and so forth). All things have a pneumatological component, and it is only via cultivating the pneumatological imagination that one can see beyond the concrete phenomena of things into the complexity of their driving habits, dispositions and tendencies. To be able to do so enables the kind of moral and spiritual discernment that gets at the values and disvalues of things in the world. All too often, the process of discernment intuits divine and the demonic trajectories that are both at work in the same instance, providing axiological lures in opposite directions at the same time.

Combining these traits of the pneumatological imagination, the following picture emerges. The pneumatological imagination envisions the world as a complex interplay of non-material powers and forces. In that sense, it is an imagination attuned to the ways of spirit in the world. It thereby realizes and expects the palpable and tangible to be, at least in part, the effects of reality which is affectively and spiritually tinged. At the same time, it also recognizes that the spiritual realm is ambiguous in that the forces it comprises are neither neutral nor all of one stripe. One can be inspired just as easily by demonic rather than divine powers. The pneumatological imagination therefore is not only open to the influences exerted by the spiritual, but it also embraces its affective participation in the inter-dimensional play of powers and forces. Do we not need a vigorous pneumatological imagination in order to discern and resist the demonic and to embrace the divine?

4.3 The Pneumatological Imagination and Theological Reflection

We have arrived at the point where the relationship between the pneumatological imagination and theological reflection needs to be made explicit. I will proceed by sketching an overview of the role of the imagination in theology as it has come to be understood recently. Then, I will make suggestions about the imagination's aspiration toward transcendence in its inherently religious activity of worldmaking. Finally, I will outline how the activity of worldmaking exhibits the functionality of the fundamental features of the pneumatological imagination, and connect that with the foundational pneumatology developed previously.

4.3.1 The preceding discussion raises many questions regarding the significance of the imagination for theology. Certainly, the fortunes of imagination vis-à-vis theological reflection have risen with the advent of modernity in that the latter allowed for the emergence of theology understood as a constructive activity over and against dogmatic theology. It would seem obvious, as William Dych points out, "that there is a very necessary and intrinsic connection between theological reflection about God and the life of the imagination" (1982, 116). Early on, however, "constructive" simply meant "supremely rational." In that case, the results have been less than spectacular, with rationalist liberals arguing against conservative fundamentalists about whether or not the correlation and coherence of revelation with the ongoing march of historical existence requires drastic compromise of what had been understood as the once-for-all deposit of faith. In fact, it was the liberals' commitment to rationalism that required them to understand the deliverances of the imagination as enabling consistency of thought regardless of historical (i.e., spatio-temporal or contextual) differences. For these reasons, among others, the mainstream of Christian theological reflection neglected any specific reconsideration of the imagination throughout the modern period (cf. Kilby 1981).

More recently, however, the landscape has been swiftly transformed with the advent of postmodernity. On the one hand, our postmodern situation signals almost the loss of the imagination in its entirety insofar as technological humanity has succumbed to a materialistic interpretation of the world, and indeed, of reality. This has been persuasively demonstrated, for example, by individuals like Dale C. Allison, Jr. (1995), who has shown that postmodernity has taken away the mystery of the world and locked us within a fabricated world of machinery. What Weber called the "iron cage of rationality" anticipated the elimination of the interpersonal realm of spirit and the subjugation of human creativity under the taskmaster of technological efficiency. On the other hand, the explosion of images in our post-industrial age of mass communication also signals perhaps the third coming of the imagination following the ancients and the early modern romanticists and transcendentalists. Local knowledge and concrete experiences are now privileged rather than universal reason or abstractions of the mind. Allison's constructive proposal is to reconnect with nature by cultivating what he calls "the ascetic imagination." Drawing on patristic models of asceticism provided by Origen, St. Anthony and St. Simeon, he challenges us postmoderns to fortify our imaginations through conscious reflection on transcendent realities, prolonged exposure to the natural world, and development of the internal posture of stillness. All this is well and good, although it would appear from Allison's programme that his overemphasis on the active aspects of the imagination suffers from a "works-mentality" struggling to free itself from the grip of modernity. I would consider the "pneumatological imagination" being developed here as a necessary supplement to Allison's "ascetic imagination."

It is against this backdrop that we should now understand the recent proliferation of the role of the imagination in theological reflection (e.g., Hartt 1977; Kaufman 1981; Kelsey 1999, 159ff.; Hart 2000), and the emergence of a plethora of approaches that see its importance. Numerous recent works have argued at length for the imagination as both receptive and constructive. Revelation has been reconceptualized (partly in Gadamerian terms) as the imaginative engagement of tradition and the existential situation (Hart [1968] 1985). This is especially important with regard to understanding the processes of reception. Reception imaginatively transforms and even adds to what is passed on in a creative manner so as to engage what is handed down with the new situation (cf. Rush 1997, esp. 164–65, 185, and 225–29). The result is that "Imagination builds upon history to say something rather different from what the original human authors intended" (Brown 2000, 31). David Bryant, in dialogue with Kant, Gadamer, Ricoeur, and Kaufman, thus summarizes the present understanding of the relationship between imagination and theological reflection:

> The involvement of the imagination means that such a revelation does not occur without the constructive engagement of our creative capacities. On the other hand, this constructive engagement occurs within the process of our imaginative *attunement* to the ongoing play of tradition and present situation, so that construction works hand in hand with, and is dependent on, the receptive powers of the imagination. (1989, 165; emphasis orig.)

While not denying the productive aspects of the imagination, however, Garrett Green (1998) exemplifies one deeply rooted Protestant tendency to emphasize the imagination as passive in order to emphasize the priority of grace. Now Green does not deny that there is a productive aspect to the imagination. Yet he attempts to hold both together by viewing imagination as itself a theory of religion. Specifically, Green's view is that the imagination is the religious point-of-contact between divinity and humanity (e.g., 1998, 4, 27, and 40). His problematic being framed by the Barth-Brunner debate on nature and grace, Green does not interact explicitly with previous efforts—such as the eighteenth century, Lockean inspired, program—to analyze the imagination vis-à-vis religion. But in order to avoid subsuming grace to nature, his discussion of imagination as the locus of religion proceeds from the differences between its formal and material aspects. The former, the point-of-contact between human beings and the divine which is inherent in every human being, is primarily active, and thereby explains (theologically, at least) the plurality of religious ways. The latter—at least for Christians, Green gladly concedes—is "the paradigmatic image of God embodied in Jesus Christ" (1998, 104). Because this has been graciously been initiated by God, only its passive reception prevents its distortion. Is Green's formal-material distinction analogous to what I categorized earlier as pneumatic-dynamic and christomorphic-content? If so, then it seems to me difficult, if not impossible, to separate the two in the way that Green does. In order to get at this issue, it may be advantageous to explore further Green's notion of the imagination as a theory of religion.

4.3.2 Now Nelson Goodman has certainly demonstrated that it is possible to consider the processes of worldmaking as completely apart from religious dimension. His discussion highlights five elements of worldmaking (1978, 7–17).

making involves, first, composition and decomposition. This includes classification and categorization of perception and experience. It includes, second, weighting, the assessment of the relevance, importance, utility, and value of things. Third, it involves ordering, whether temporally, spatially, or otherwise. Fourth, deletion and supplementation are central aspects of worldmaking whereby the general and the vague are filled in (or, filled out), or that which is trivial is ignored, neglected, or just forgotten. Finally, worldmaking inevitably results in what Goodman calls deformation since not all data are taken in solely on their terms; rather, they are processed imaginatively toward human ends. Yet Goodman is careful to point out that this is by no means an exhaustive categorization of the imaginative activities that comprise worldmaking. Further, Goodman's notion of weighting itself raises axiological questions.

It is here that the preceding discussions of both Neville's axiological metaphysics and the holistic and integrative character of the imagination combine to highlight the intrinsically religious dimension of the imagination. Neville acknowledges, with Kant, the imagination as the difference between perceiving (passively) and experiencing (actively). Together, however, they produce images which disclose the spacio-temporal and valuational forms of the world in various respects. The latter include what Neville calls boundary elements which shape the limits of experience and what is experienceable (cf. 1981, 169–75, and 1996, 47–58). As such, the imagination constitutes the lived-world in its totality, including its farthest horizons, sometimes expanding these horizons and transforming them from possibility (fancy) into actuality, and other times going beyond them speculatively if what is yonder is effectively beyond reach. In these senses, the imagination actually makes possible the different kinds of worlds that we inhabit, and is thereby worldmaking. The language Neville uses is that imagination works to define the possible conceptions of where and how the finite borders on the infinite. For Neville, it is then the activity of interpreting and theorizing which specifies the vague possibilities suggested by the imagination. Herein lies an important difference between Neville and Green. Whereas the former correctly sees the imagination as distinct from, even if continuous with, interpretation, the latter blurs the distinction by understanding the imagination an interpretive faculty. Better, I think, to say with Neville that the imagination is the synthesizing faculty from which interpretation emerges.

This said, it will also be recalled that the imagination is itself emergent from the complex fusion of valuational and affective habits, dispositions, and tendencies alongside spiritual ones, even as the last, in turn, effectively shapes each of these other dimensions of human life. It is precisely this which explains the imagination's inherently religious character. To use Nevillean lan~~_~~ _ . humans negotiate the boundaries of the finite and the infinite as valuational, affectional and spiritual beings. Put more conventionally, human beings exist not only in a world of things, but in a world of values, of affections, and of spiritual quest and longing. Certainly the world of things impinges on what human beings value, what they get passionate about, what they aspire for and to. Equally certain, nothing exists solely as its phenomenological manifestation since all phenomena participate to a greater or lesser degree in the many dimensions that intersect with human existence in the world.

In this way, Neville has provided vigorous argument for the essentially religious function of the imagination in terms of the totality involved in the imagination's worldmaking or world-envisioning activity. In Tillichian terms, the imagination is responsible for casting the spectrum of worldly possibilities ranging from the mundane to that which is of ultimate, and thereby religious, concern. Paralleling Neville's discussion about the religious origins of the imagination is Pannenberg's argument about the locating the origins of language alongside and with the emergence of the religious consciousness of humankind (1985, 340–96). And, those who have worked with Chomsky's transformational-generative linguistics arrive at a similar view regarding language itself as revelatory of religious preferences. Thus Irene Lawrence concludes in her theological study of Chomsky: "…implicit in the use of human language itself is the choice among the 'gods'….a speaker's *overall* linguistic performance is not only dependent on, but revelatory of, that speaker's God or pantheon" (1980, 168).

Thus it is that the activity of worldmaking has both immanent and transcendent aspects, and this in at least three ways. At its most basic level, the world that is encountered through the imagination is never simply itself. Rather, the imagination transcends the phenomena of the world precisely by constituting it according to the values, affections, and intentions of the perceiver and experiencer. Here, the empirical world takes shape, even if it cannot be reductively explained as such. Second, there is a mutuality to this process of imaginative engagement when two (or more) human beings perceive and experience each other. In this case, two (or more) sets of values, affections, intentions, etc., are operative, resulting in two (or more) ways of transcendence of selves vis-à-vis others. Truly personal relationality results, at this level, in the mutual transvaluation of individual perspectives and frames of reference, as well as transmutation of specific habits and dispositions. Finally, there is the human experience of and relationship with God through the Spirit. Here, the imagination constructs, inhabits, and continuously reformulates the boundary of immanence and transcendence. Yet the result is not simply speculative abstraction (although there is certainly plenty of that), but deeper spiritual and moral living.

Theology, Neville therefore says, is theoretical activity that brings coherence to truthful inquiry (interpretation) of revelatory data processed by the imagination, and that issues forth in responsible spiritual and moral living. In less technical terms, theology is the cultivation of imaginative, interpretive, and practical skills with regard to religious images, metaphors and symbols (cf. Forbes 1986).[4] In this sense, theological reflection and articulation ensures that revelation is being adequately engaged, even if not altogether understood. Imagination, in this process, is the necessary mediator that enables theologizing—considered as orthodoxy and as orthopraxis—to take place. From the specifically Christian perspective, the goal of theological reflection is what might be called "patterns of discipleship" (cf. Brown 1999), the putting on of the mind of Christ and the following in the footsteps of Christ, both as enabled by the Spirit. This brings us back full circle to the pneumatological imagination and its contribution to worldmaking and the human engagement with the transcendent.

4.3.3 In what follows, I want to continue to explore the relationship between the imagination, worldmaking, and theology by approaching the discussion from the perspective provided by the pneumatological imagination. Further, the discerning reader will note that the central features of the pneumatological imagination being developed here—as correlative with expressions of power, as essentially integrative albeit with a christomorphic form, and as inherently normative vis-à-vis the experience of the world—are arguably inversely correlative, however loosely, with the metaphysical categories of foundational pneumatology—relationalism, realism, and social dynamism—developed previously. I therefore also want to supplement the present discussion through its connection with foundational pneumatology.

We have seen that the process of worldmaking involves the self's engagement with and situation of itself vis-à-vis the world, with others, and with the

---

[4] This leads naturally to the phenomenology of signs and sign-interpretation. Neville has, accordingly, developed a full-blown semiotic theory of interpretation from which I will draw selectively at various points in my discussion in the following chapter. At the same time, theologically speaking, Neville's trinitarianism is dominated by the second moment—the Logos, as in his explicitly Logos-christology; Spirit—the third moment—is of much less significance in Neville's overall theological system, relegated as it is to the traditional area of sanctification (cf. Neville 1991). My argument in this book, however, is that an authentically pneumatological theology is central to a rigorously trinitarian theology, and Neville's theological work needs to be corrected insofar as its anemic pneumatology is a handicap to the trinitarian theology that he defends and aspires to.

divine. The pneumatological imagination goes about this task of worldmaking at least at three levels. First, it recognizes that whatever there is to be encountered is multi-dimensional at least insofar as it is a result of being acted upon as well as being a creative and more-or-less powerful actor in its own right. The world is the result of various powers acting and being acted upon. In Wink's terms, the things of the world exhibit an outer manifestation driven by inner dynamics. In Peircean terms, things are not only qualitative and factual, but are also legal, habitual and dispositional. Potentially, the pneumatological imagination may misdiagnose and confuse the many natural, interpersonal, social, and even demonic powers at work in anything. Alternatively, it may discern correctly that things are often the result of the complex operations of a multitude of forces. The pneumatological imagination will not, usually, err toward rendering a solely positivistic, naturalistic or mechanistic judgment on the world.

The essentially modal and dynamic nature of reality, however, requires that one exercises patience in discernment. This is important because the temporal features of spiritual manifestations often initially surprise us or leave us in the lurch. And while the character of the legal, habitual and dispositional aspects of things may not be immediately apparent, careful attention to and prolonged engagement with them will be revelatory of their pneumatic nature and identity. A pneumatological imagination, then, is not only prepared to pursue the ways of the Spirit, but is also in some sense constrained or empowered to respond with discernment, over time, to the variety of shifting situations it encounters in accordance with its own position vis-à-vis the other forces and vectors that comprise each occasion.

Second, the pneumatological imagination engages the process of worldmaking holistically, combining valuational, affective, and spiritual sensitivities to the task. As Christians, moreover, those imbued with the pneumatological imagination desire to engage the world with the mind of Christ, at the same time as such engagement proceeds through the enabling of the Spirit. This means that the pneumatological imagination is alert to the paradoxical interconnectedness of the knowing self with the objects of knowledge. There is, one might say, a sort of mutual participation—a perichoretical indwelling—of subject and object such that the evaluative, affective, and spiritual habitation of the self and of things in the world correlate. Yet this does not reduce knowledge to the cognitive imposition of the self's evaluative, affective, and spiritual images on the other since, according to the intuitions of foundational pneumatology, Spirit enables the other to exist as other rather than dissolving the other into the self.

At this point, however, the tension emerges between the attempt to engage the world through the mind of Christ on the one hand and the insistence of protecting the integrity of the world that is engaged on the other come to the fore. Does not the christomorphic form of the pneumatological imagination effectively cancel out the important and essential terms which constitute the object that is engaged? In other words, is there not an epistemic bias which leads Christians to engage the world christomorphically and, as such, neglect things on their own terms or, in the worst case, misrepresent or abuse them for "christian" purposes? It would have to be admitted that the latter danger is always present insofar as Christians ideologically legitimate their own agendas even if such do not authentically reflect the life and mind of Jesus. However, given that both the incarnational and pentecostal missions exhibit the providential extension and constitution of otherness itself [3.2.2], it is, arguably only in the form of Christ and the power of the Spirit that true integrity, authenticity and autonomy is achieved. The triadic, relational and realistic metaphysics of foundational pneumatology provides the conceptual framework to see how things are what they are not in isolation from other things but precisely in their relationships with and to other things. The pneumatological imagination then enables recognition of such relational autonomy and integrity, of the social character of individuality and particularity. Further, it sensitizes the imagination to the multi-dimensional—evaluative, affective, spiritual—constitution and dynamic movements of things in the world of many others. In short, the pneumatological imagination provides the epistemic corrective to the ideological tendencies which otherwise plague human knowledge.

Finally, the pneumatological imagination engages the task of worldmaking axiologically and normatively, and this at two levels: that of discernment and that of engagement (see Yong 2003). The former also proceeds at two parallel levels whereby discernment of the values and disvalues are directed toward both the self and the other that is known. Here, the pneumatological imagination enables the kind of honesty which identifies, names, and resists all that the scriptures declare to be "of the flesh," of the "form of the world," and of the demonic. As directed toward the individual, the goal is to "take every thought captive to obey Christ" (2 Cor. 10:5b). With regard to the other— the world, other persons, the divine—the goal is to discern their sources, intentions, values, and purposes. Engagement obligates the knower to engage self and other in ways that are morally and spiritually responsible. One ought to walk in the Spirit rather than continue in the flesh; one ought to work toward the Kingdom of God rather than preserve the form of this world which is

[handwritten marginalia: "NO", "?", "isn't it", "of", "bias", "→ assumes", "all", "viewpoint", "have", "same", "value", "Sure"]

[handwritten note at bottom: "Spirit enabled Adam to name"]

passing away; one ought to resist rather than entertain the devil. Further, the things engaged—the world, other persons, the divine—make diverse normative claims on us, and therefore need to be attended to differently. I will elaborate on this important point later. For the moment, suffice to note that together, discernment and engagement are axiologically informed and normatively framed at one level according to the life and mind of Jesus Christ.

Yet it is also crucial to see that the life and mind of Jesus is not spiritually mediated a-historically through biblical osmosis or in a vacuum by charismatic experience. Rather the life and mind of Jesus are mediated by the Spirit through the body of Christ. Herein lies the import of the social or communitarian element of foundational pneumatology. Christians are followers of Jesus as an *ekklesia* of believers and worshippers even as they are more generally individual selves only in community. It is only in and through community that norms and obligations are meaningful and necessary. Even the discernment of normative living is a communal affair since criteriologies of discernment are the result of social consensus. Implementation of moral and spiritual responsibility, finally, presupposes the interests of the group to resist the devil.

We began this chapter with an overview of the imagination as a historical construct. We then correlated the basic features of the imagination with one inspired by the Christian experience of the Spirit. The particularity of the emergent pneumatological imagination therefore in some senses both inhabits and participates in the imaginative activity of human beings in general. Further, insofar as the pneumatological imagination reflects the logic of pneumatology that underwrites foundational pneumatology, it also to that degree aspires toward universality, although one that is not a priori or by necessity. Yet the question nevertheless persists: how is it that the pneumatological imagination bridges the *ordo cognoscendii* and the *ordo essendi* so that what we think we know corresponds to the way things are other than just verbally or by fiat of declaration? How does the hermeneutical spiral enable truthful claims about the world external to the knowing subject, and, more importantly, about things demonic and divine? Following from this, insofar as the pneumatological imagination drives both discernment and engagement axiologically and normatively, how can we avoid imposing our own values and norms subjectively and inappropriately on what is known and engaged if indeed the latter has its own ontological reality according to the critical realist metaphysics we have posited? The claim that the pneumatological imagination engages us with objective others both truly and normatively needs to be elaborated upon and defended.

5 The Pneumatological Imagination and Truthful Discernment

The purpose of this chapter is to provide some justification for understanding the pneumatological imagination's truthful engagement with reality. To do so, I will pick up and elaborate on the semiotic aspects of Peirce's thought and attempt to show how it underwrites a pneumatological account of the epistemic process. This will, in turn, open up to a triadic conception of truth and its warrants. Of course, the possibility of accessing the truth means it is also possible to entertain falsehoods. The last section therefore attempts to provide an account of epistemic fallibility. Altogether, the following discussion therefore aspires to finally fulfill previous promises to account for not just the correlation but the connection between knowledge and reality. More than that, its explication of the triadic character of the interpretive process lays the groundwork for the hermeneutical and methodological trialectic this essay seeks to defend: that all theological interpretation consists of an ongoing spiral of Spirit and Word in community.

5.1 Engaging the Other Semiotically

How does the pneumatological imagination engage the world? In one sense, no differently than any other imaginative engagement: with images. In another sense, however, the pneumatological imagination is, as we have seen, poised and sensitized to organize and integrate its images holistically to reflect the multi-dimensionality of lived reality. Here, Peirce's triadic epistemology provides an alternative, albeit technical, account for how the imagination functions to engage the world. What follows is an exposition of Peirce's epistemology, an explication of his semiotic system, and the extension of both toward a hermeneutic of religion in general and a pneumatological (read: trinitarian) hermeneutic in particular.

5.1.1 For our purposes, the central motif which drives Peirce's epistemology is his notion of thinking as inferential and proceeding from the logic of abduction. Peirce is here waging war on three epistemological fronts: against the Cartesians who insist on knowledge as building from indubitable intuitions; against Kant who argues deductively from transcendental and a priori truths; and against the empiricist tradition (of Bacon through Locke and Hume) insofar as it attempts to solely argue inductively from experience. Peirce certainly agreed that knowledge is intimately related to our experience of reality since his critical realism insisted that it is reality, finally, which shapes our beliefs. But how does this occur?

Experience, Peirce theorized, emerges from two elementary procedures. The first Peirce termed the *perceptual judgment*: the uncontrollable operation of grasping, assenting and acting on sensation. This primary stuff of experience played a similar role in Peirce's epistemology as the notion of the *sense datum* did in the British empiricists. However, against their atomistic conception of sense datum, Peirce anticipated James' theory of mind as a "stream of consciousness" and regarded perceptual judgments as a continuous current of felt, intuitive, and affective inferences. As continuous, they are abstract, vague, and not segregatable, thus being uncontrollable, uncriticizable and indubitable in themselves. In holding to the existence of indubitables, Peirce anticipated Plantinga's retrieval of Thomas Reid's Common-Sense philosophy, and is rightly called a "foundationalist" (Robin 1981). But Peirce saw that if perceptual judgments are not consciously identifiable and dubitable, a fallibilistic epistemology requires that they be open to correction. In denying immunity to and positively criticizing these "basic beliefs," Peirce distinguished his own philosophy—what he called "Critical-Commonsensism" (5.497–501)—from that of Reid's Common-Sensism (and thereby also from classical foundationalism, and perhaps even from contemporary Reformed epistemology). His quarrel with Reid was that he did not develop a means by which to address the emergence and resolution of doubts which arise from experience: "the Common-Sensism now so widely accepted is not critical of the substantial truth of uncriticizable propositions, but only as to whether a given proposition is of the number" (5.497).

But how are indubitable perceptual judgments analyzed and criticized? Peirce was led to identify a second aspect of experience which he called *perceptual facts*. These are the controlled cognitions or ideas which follow upon perceptual judgments. He described them as "the intellect's description of the evidence of the senses, made by my endeavor. These perceptual facts are wholly unlike the percept, at best; and they may be downright untrue to the percept" (2.141). This is the case because perceptual facts are not immediate but temporally removed from perceptual judgments, and therefore inferentially dependent upon memory. Memory, however, is fallible, and since perceptual facts in their final form are propositions produced by controlled cognition, thinking can only grasp reality partially and inexactly. Arguably, the perceptual judgment is emergent from the interface of the world, experience and cognition, and belongs to the field for psychology and the philosophy of cognition, while the perceptual fact is emergent from the process of translating and articulating the basic perceptual judgments, and belongs to the fields of semantics and philosophy of language.

Peirce's next realized, against the Cartesians and the empiricists, that inferential procedures are not limited to deductive or inductive thinking. Both presumed the more fundamental inference of abduction. *Abduction* is the emergence of a broad inference, a hypothesis, that ensues from the general classification of perceptual judgments. *Deduction* is the prediction of what should follow from the hypothesis. *Induction* is the concrete, piecemeal testing of the deduced predictions to see if the hypothesis holds in reality. All three work together as we can see from Peirce's consideration of rules, cases, and results. Abductions proceed from results (Enoch was mortal) and rules (all men are mortal) and conclude toward particular cases (Enoch was a man). Deductions proceed from the universal rules (all men are mortal) through the particular cases (Enoch was a man) to results (Enoch was mortal). Inductions proceed from particularity (Enoch was a man) through results (Enoch was mortal) to general rules (all men are mortal).

Two points need to be made from the preceding. First, from a phenomenological analysis of perceptual experience, Peirce was led to see that abduction, deduction and induction all assumed each other and collaborated in the thinking process. This is because our engagement with the otherness of the world and of reality (Secondness) results in the sensations of qualities (Firstness) according to the general and vague legal features (Thirdness) governing the object of engagement. Peirce's distinction between generalities and vagueness is not unimportant (cf. 5.447–48; 5.505). The former are interpretants given over to interpreters for completion: "tables are four legged utilities with flat surfaces" is a general statement from which you or I could specify by pointing to desks or dining room furniture, etc.; here, the law of the excluded middle does not apply. The latter, vagueness, are interpretants which call for further semiotic specification: it is false that "this is a table" (in a vague sense) means that it is either made of wood or not made of wood (it could be a combination of wood and plastic); here, the law of contradiction does not apply. Thus, our sensation of a table is fundamentally of the laws or generalities to which things such as tables conform: hardness, coarseness, color, etc., and our beliefs about such a table is vague to the extent that what we know about the surface of this table leaves us more or less in the dark about its specific constitution. As general on the one hand, we are called to specify the type of hardness, the texture of coarseness, shade of color, etc. As vague on the other, only further inquiry of the table can provide the semiotic detail needed to fill out our knowledge of it.

Experience of generalities leads to cognitions which are equally, if not more so, general, abstract, and universal. In Peirce's own words,

> [P]erceptual judgments contain general elements, so that universal propositions are deducible from them....[T]he perceptual judgments are to be regarded as an extreme case of abductive inferences, from which they differ in being absolutely beyond criticism. The abductive suggestion comes to us like a flash. It is an act of insight, although of extremely fallible insight. It is true that the different elements of the hypothesis were in our minds before; but it is the idea of putting together what we had never before dreamed of putting together which flashes the new suggestion before our contemplation. (5.180)[1]

As such, we can see that perceptual judgments are thirds that connect our sensations with the world. From this, Peirce saw that generality and inference are replete throughout experience and the process of reasoning. Both are thereby movements from vagueness to specificity. But, more important, that perceptual judgments are thoroughly general and vague means that experience puts us in touch with the laws, habits and tendencies that structure reality. As Robert Corrington comments, "if these beliefs were anything *but* vague, they would make it difficult for the self to function in a variety of situations, each with its own complex variables" (1993, 55, emphasis orig.). This, in my view, is one of Peirce's most important contributions.

Second, and following from the first, is Peirce's insight into the basic continuity between perception and abduction. Abduction is thereby connected with perception and occurs continuously with it. In fact, Peirce specifically said that a percept or sensation "fulfills the function of an hypothesis" (5.291). The various hypotheses are initially refined in vague perceptual facts, deductively theorized, and then tested inductively in more specific ways. Hypotheses which

---

[1] The history of science and the advance of knowledge also led Peirce to this conclusion. Einstein, for example, posited that the creative insight which advances the scientific enterprise is driven by "a jump of imaginative insight: a bold leap, an informed, speculative attempt to understand, a 'groping' constructive attempt to understand" (quoted in Loder and Neidhardt 1992, 177). This is what Peirce called abduction.

prove themselves as reliable guides for the course of experience are solidified into habits of thought and action. The process of thinking is then nothing more or less than the drawing of inferences from the generalities of sensations, and the continuous filling in the blanks or making determinate the vague aspects of these perceptions, both by connecting them with previous cognitions and by integrating novel experiences through the ongoing process of reasoning. Because generality or thirdness "pours in" upon us continuously in sensation, percepts and perceptual judgments are codified over time as mental signs (interpretations) that grasp the laws and habits of things.

Beliefs, then, emerge from thinking that proceeds inferentially from perceptual judgments and perceptual facts, and concludes with the establishment of habits of action relative to the object of belief. This led Peirce to define the meaning of anything as the habits it involved. He put it this way in his famous Pragmatic Maxim: "Consider what effects, that might conceivably have practical bearings, we conceive the object of our conception to have. Then, our conception of these effects is the whole of our conception of the object" (5.402). (Peirce added in a footnote that his Pragmatic Maxim was "only an application of the sole principle of logic which was recommended by Jesus; 'Ye may know them by their fruits,' and it is very intimately allied with the ideas of the gospel".) If effects are inconceivable for any thing, such a "thing" is probably meaningless and, as such, neither true nor false. To get at the truth of anything is to formulate a hypothesis about its effects. True beliefs are those reached when the effects predicted are borne out in experience. This leads to *full beliefs*—in contrast to mere *opinions*—to which we assent and upon which we are willing to risk ourselves.[2] Opinions that do not lead even to insignificant actions probably either mean that hypotheses about them have not been properly framed or that there is no truth to them.

The essence of pragmatism therefore follows the logic of abduction. Pragmatism is the process of inquiry which seeks to establish firm beliefs about reality from the inferences of perceptual experience. The pragmatic elucidation of truth asks the question: what can be expected to follow from a true hypothesis? The logic of pragmatism is that the vagueness of perception and perceptual judgment lead us to formulate equally vague inferences (abductions), from which more specific predictions are made (deductions), which

---

[2] This thesis of Peirce's—that the meaning of signs is determinable by the habits it produces—has been largely accepted in the discipline of semantics (e.g., Morris 1955). There is also ample evidence that this Peircean account of the attainment of knowledge is true to the ways in which human beings learn (see, e.g., Swartz, Perkinson and Edgerton 1980).

are in turn finally tested in a variety of ways (induction). As these are continuously confirmed, inductive experience is shaped into provisional habits that inform our action. As Peirce put it, "the only method of ascertaining the truth is to repeat this trio of operations: conjecture, deductions of predictions from the conjecture; testing the predictions by experimentation" (7.672).

5.1.2 Having established Peirce's logic of thought as inferential through and through enables an understanding of his claim that thinking proceeds from the images and signs that are the stuff of abductions, deductions, and inductions. Herein we come to the heart of Peirce's semiotic or theory of signs: that all human experience, from the perceptual feelings to perceptual judgments and on through the entire process of cognition, is wholly semiotic (5.283–317).[3] Thus the imagination traffics in semiotic representation, translating the self's engagement with the world into hypothetical images and signs to be tested.

Now Peirce defines a sign in triadic terms as anything which stands for something (an object) to someone (an interpreter or subject) in some respect (an interpretant, the idea produced). More formally, "A *Sign*, or *Representamen*, is a First which stands in such a genuine triadic relation to a Second, called its *Object*, as to be capable of determining a Third, called its *Interpretant*, to assume the same triadic relation to its Object in which it stands itself to the same Object" (2.274). Alternatively put, a sign is "Anything which determines something else (its *interpretant*) to refer to an object to which itself refers (its *object*) in the same way, the interpretant becoming in turn a sign, and so on *ad infinitum*" (2.303). This is because a sign is a third, interpreting, term. So when I am driving along and see a stop sign on the road, I think to myself, "Halt-and-carefully-proceed-as-appropriate"—the interpretant. In turn, this interpretant becomes a sign which could require interpretation: what is "appropriate"? What kind of intersection? Are there pedestrians who have the right of way? Did I get to the stop sign before that vehicle on my right? And so on. Each of these in turn become other signs fit for interpretation. Thus it is that a sign mediates an object to an interpreter on the one hand, even while, as an interpretant in its variously vague respects, it is a datum that calls for further clarification (becomes another sign) on the other (cf. Savan 1987).

Note here that the triadic relationality of both Peirce's inferential logic and

---

[3] As he drew from the scholastic Duns Scotus in his metaphysics, so also did Peirce draw from the *Tractatus* of *Summule logicales* of Peter of Spain (1205?–1277) in his semiotics (see Ponzio 1990, 77–93). For arguments since Peirce about the semiotic character of all human experience, see Deely (1994). The Whiteheadian doctrine of sense perception is itself framed in terms of "symbolic reference" (see Franklin 1990, Part Two). Alternatively, at the other end of the perception-cognition continuum, the symbol, as Ricoeur says, "gives rise to thought" (1969, 347–57).

his theory of the signs presents an advance over dyadic epistemologies. Saussurean inspired semiotic systems, for example, hold to a dyadic notion of signs whereby signs are simply relations between signifier and signified. In Saussure, then, the orientation is primarily psychological: signs are socio-psychological constructs representing mental relations. Peirce's explanation for this dyadic relationship is in terms of Secondness: our brushing up against the brute facts of resistant reality. Transposed into the triadic system of Peirce, however, signs become interpretive thirds (cf. Parret 1983, esp. 25–32; Sheriff 1989). They are logical and, at some level, ontological, relations, but not psychological. As such, each sign mediates between and thereby interprets signs and/to their objects on the one hand, even while it serves itself as a sign on the other, calling for further interpretation.

But what then prevents a sign from slipping completely into instability given its function to evoke yet further interpretants? Are not the (especially French) deconstructionists here correct that all interpretation is no more than the continuous encounter with signs and symbols within an infinite semiotic system? If that is the case, then no interpretations can claim to get at reality truly. The Peircean, however, has a twofold response: that this is a semiotic system that accounts not only for interpretation, but also for reference; and that semiosis is directed, finally, toward the establishment of habits of activity. Let us take each in turn.

First, signs in Peirce's semiotics do not refer only to other signs. Rather, as indicated earlier, signs refer to objects meaningfully by producing interpretants (other signs). Peirce therefore gave extensive thought to the ways in which signs referred to their objects, the three most important for our purposes being signs as icons, indicia, and symbols. An icon refers to its object by virtue of its character of reproducing the qualities of said object, thus being able to serve as a substitute for the object of reference, whether or not the object exists. Examples include maps, paintings, photographs, fictions, diagrams, images, algebraic formulas, and so on, all of which refer according to the immediacy of Firstness. An index refers by being causally affected by or spacio-temporally related to its object. Examples include stop signs, physical symptoms, clouds, smoke signals, pointing fingers, weathervanes, sundials, barometers, and so on, all of which refer through physically resisting as Seconds. A symbol refers not to particularities but to generalities, and that by virtue of the established rules, habits or conventions which determine the interpretant. All words, sentences, books, arguments, etc., are symbols. Symbols are purveyors of Thirdness. They are carriers of laws, regularities or habits which are grounded in what is real, inform the future, and shape the advance of knowledge. Thus, "Symbols grow. They come into being by development out of other signs....A symbol, once in being, spreads among the peoples. In use and in experience, its meaning grows" (2.302). Now together, icons, indicia, and symbols refer precisely by producing qualitative, relational and representational inferences in human minds.[4]

This leads, second, to Peirce's pragmatic response to Descartes. The gist of it is that human beings do not need to be skeptical about what they know or believe insofar as the referential signs we negotiate enable us to grasp the qualities, facts, and laws of things in such a way so as to manageably predict with greater rather than lesser accuracy the way the world will respond. If that is the case, we can, in turn, respond to our environmental stimuli under variously specified conditions, and in that case be practically confident that we have understood reality truly, even if fallibly so, in just those respects. Dewey adopted just these features of Peirce's semiotic realism in developing his own pragmatic and instrumentalist logic of deliberation (cf. Gelpi 2001, ch. 6). In Dewey's account, there is an ongoing transactional interface between lived experience and reality itself such that human beings can respond and manipulate the world to a greater or lesser degree, always subject to being corrected by the way reality itself responds and behaves. Within the pragmatist framework, signs are meaningful indicators of how reality acts, and facilitate our interactions with the world. In the case of reading and understanding textual symbols, given Peirce's Pragmatic Maxim, our interpretations run up against and are often corrected by the responses we get by other semiotic realities (other interpreters and interpretations of the same text). In this sense, the kind of relativism which sees interpretation as driven by arbitrary wills bent on exercising particular forms of power is resisted. Instead, Peircean pragmatism is constrained by how reality—including the actions of other interpretive agents (cf. Lamb 1992)—responds in return.

Yet at the same time, it is also important to point out that since cognition is nothing but inferences from the vaguely hypothesized images or signs of perception, and since there is (at least potentially) an infinite series of interpretations that follow upon the presentation of a sign, all knowledge can only be provisional. This is the case because inductive reasoning can only engage in a finite number of verification or falsification experiments even if extended

---

[4] Thomas Seebok has developed Peirce's semiotic categories in numerous publications (see, e.g., Seebok 1991 and 1994). On the complexity of the notion of reference according to various respects, see Neville (1989, chs. 13 and 14), and Fodor (1995, chs. 3 and 4). A concrete working out of the many levels of reference with regard to biblical interpretation is Lategan and Vorster (1985).

indefinitely by an entire community of inquirers, and all that is needed is one falsifying instance to undermine the initial hypothesis. Given the provisionality and fallibility of all knowledge, Peirce insisted that "there are three things to which we can never hope to attain by reasoning, namely, absolute certainty, absolute exactitude, [and] absolute universality" (1.141; cf. 5.587). He therefore admonished the investigator to be watchful for exceptions to the rule (cf. 1.55). So long as things are encountered as anticipated, thinking proceeds in smooth continuity from perception through to action, and our habits of thought and action are solidified and confirmed. They begin to be consciously criticized, however, when we are surprised by the unexpected (1.336). Surprises, Peirce said, are "very efficient in breaking up association of ideas" (5.478; cf. 5.512). The result is that what is experientially indubitable in perceptual judgments can be and is cognitively dubitable when propositionally asserted as perceptual facts and tested and resisted by experience.

If a *belief* is understood as a self-satisfied habit, *doubt* is defined as "the privation of a habit" (5.417), or as that which "really interferes with the smooth working of the belief-habit" (5.510). Peirce insisted, however, that genuine doubt exists not in the laboratory of thought but is, rather, the "uneasy and dissatisfied state from which we struggle to free ourselves [in order to] pass into the state of belief" (5.372). For this reason, it is never the case that the entirety of one's belief structure is upset, even when thoroughly surprised. The unexpected surprises we encounter jolt us from the specificities of our habituatedness, trigger doubt on just those specifics, and inhibit our ability to function in a limited way vis-à-vis those specifics. But they do not lead us to doubt the totality of what we do know since such doubts can neither be meaningfully expressed nor can they ever be tested. Rather, genuine doubts spurred on by experience leads us to a process of inquiry that has as its goal the resolution of said doubts and the establishment of new modes of belief and action. This new *modus operandi*, however, will be satisfactory only if and insofar as it enables us engage the world successfully. To do so would be to regain a truthful understanding our relation to the world in just those respects. In short, it is precisely because human cognition is designed to enable our functional engagement with the world that relativism, skepticism, and nihilism are avoided. Then, it is only the surprises arising from experience that return us to inquiry.

5.1.3 Is Peirce's semiotic conducive to understanding religious experience, and even the task of theology? Many who know Peirce much better than I certainly believe so (see, e.g., Orange 1984; Raposa 1989; Power 1993; Gelpi 2000 and 2001). And why not, since Augustine long ago admitted that all Christian instruction is "either about things or about signs; but things are learnt by means of signs" (*On Christian Doctrine* I.2). Our focus, however, will be on how the preceding exposition can be informative with regard to the pneumatological traits of the religious and theological imagination. In order to make these connections explicit, I will focus on a triad of correlations: that between the pragmatism, realism, and communitarian character of Peirce's epistemology with the empowered activity, the integrativeness, and the normativeness of the pneumatological imagination. The goal will be to experience these correlations as mutually illuminating, and provide, in rough form, the primordial shape of the hermeneutical trialectic of Spirit, Word and Community.

To begin, Peirce advocated a pragmatic epistemology whose objective was to resolve doubts so as to enable more efficient and truthful engagements with reality. Because human knowledge is fallible, its ongoing correction is to be expected. But more important, Peirce provided an account for how this corrigibility produces more accurate and truthful beliefs: through an inferential process circulating between abductive, deductive, and inductive reasoning.

The pneumatological imagination is able to benefit from Peirce's pragmatic epistemology. First, Peirce's nuance assessment of how thinking proceeds both transformatively and inferentially connects well with what the Scripture calls "living in the Spirit." The Spirit speaks in a "still small voice," inspiring faith and leading the believer in the process of sanctification. This is best understood in terms of a spiritual journey, advancing appropriately on one front, perhaps only to digress on another; making headway on this issue, but lapsing on that; being transformed in some respects, resisting transformation in others. The inferential and probative character of transformative knowing is clearly evident in this process. Further, the pneumatological imagination is especially open to the ongoing encounter with novelty and surprise—no a priori limitations can or should be imposed on what life in the Spirit might bring about. Finally, the pneumatological imagination is able to embrace the Peircean dictum of the fallibility of knowledge. As pneumatically inspired, all emergent notions—in Peirce's terms, hypotheses—have to be judged by selves-in-community.

Yet the processes of pragmatic and habitual transformation left to themselves lack a qualitative dimension. The pneumatological imagination provides just such an aspect in its goal of transforming the knower into the image of Jesus by the power of the Spirit. James Loder speak of this pneumatic process in terms of *analogia spiritus* (1989, 93–94; 1998, 112–18). The *analogia spiritus* includes two moments: that of *mortification* of sin and its perversities which have obfuscated the true face of the human spirit as the image of God; and of *illumination*, of the face of Jesus as a restorative act which reveals not only the image of the invisible God in all its glory, but also the truth of human nature as it was created to be. These two moments are translated into two reciprocal and ongoing movements: that of *centeredness* on the true image of God as revealed in Jesus, thus its christomorphic character; and that of *exocentricity*, whereby the Christ-like individual is who he or she is precisely as transformed by the Spirit and given a transcendent horizon which drives his or her engagement with the world and with its creator. The *analogia spiritus* is therefore the "point of contact" between the human spirit and the divine Spirit, wherein the vestiges of the *imago Dei* are reactivated and through which its healing commences to restore the human spirit into the likeness of Christ as its original ground and reason for being. The result is the ongoing process of conversion in each dimension—affective, intellectual, socio-moral, and spiritual—of human life (cf. Gelpi 1998).

Yet Peircean pragmatism inculcates appropriate responsive habits ultimately with the goal of engaging reality accurately and truly. This is accomplished through signs which refer to the qualities, facts, and laws which constitute lived experience. Here, Peirce's semiotics and the pneumatological imagination are mutually illuminative in a number of ways. First, Peirce's insistence that others are encountered semiotically converges with the pneumatological imagination's intuition that others are encountered relationally through mediators. Signs call attention not to their interpretants but to their objects. Similarly, the Spirit shows not her own face, but that of the mutuality of the Father's and the Son's. Second, Peirce's insistence on the irreducibility of otherness—Secondness—parallels the pneumatological imagination's emphasis on the integrity and autonomy of the terms mediated. Herein the critical realism of Peircean metaphysics and of foundational pneumatology are mutually reinforcing. Finally, insofar as Peircean semiotics truly engages qualities, facts and laws holistically, it bolsters the claim that the pneumatological imagination engages the affective, emotive, and spiritual traits of the world, each distinctively and yet wholly together in every inferential act.

To see the specific contributions of the pneumatological imagination, it might be helpful to look at one concrete proposal for a semiotically informed biblical hermeneutic. Daniel Patte points out that semiotic theory applied to biblical studies highlights not only the construction of the sacred text, but also the various discourses of interpretations—the multitude of methods employed in the discipline of biblical interpretation—which are applied to the text (2000, esp. 19–23). Further, alongside illuminating these critical goals of biblical studies, semiotic theory also insists on correlating such with the didactic and ethical goals of reading Scripture as Scripture. Thus, critical biblical studies includes three specific transformational moments: the informational, related to "knowing" the text in its context; the hermeneutical, related to understanding the text and how it functions in the interpreter's context; and the pragmatic, related to the gaining of skills by which the text applies to our lived reality. None of these moments are divorced from the other, and each implicates the other. The value of semiotic theory is recognition of this interrelationship not only in biblical studies, but in all interpretation.

What is missing, of course, is a pneumatologically nurtured imagination. Such an imagination therefore seeks not only the habitual application and transformation of the text to our lives, but also our transformation according to the christomorphic character of the living Christ. Such an imagination, further, not only seeks to know the text in its context, but also seeks to know the text in its radical otherness, apart from which its integrity is compromised. Finally, such an imagination recognizes that the text engages us not only pragmatically, but also affectively and spiritually. The pneumatological imagination touches both what we do as well as the relational qualities which constitute the axiological, affective, and spiritual dimensions of who we are.

This leads, then, to the third correlation: between the Peircean notion of community and the normative dimension of knowing insisted upon by the pneumatological imagination. In Peirce's system, symbolic references assume linguistic and intellectual conventions and arrangements which are socially originated. The triadic structure of signs—involving objects, interpretants, and interpreters; requiring perception, cognition, and interpretation; including a sign initiator, the sign itself, and a sign receptor—assumes a community of inquirers or interpreters. For Peirce, the ideal community was that of science since diverse perspectives and continuous testing characterize scientific inquiry. Given the provisional and tentative nature of all knowledge, Peirce preferred instead to speak of practical certainty and to rely on the accumulated wisdom of human experience and the consensus of the community of inquirers to establish both truth and reality. As he observed, the real is that which

> sooner or later, information and reasoning would finally result in, and which is therefore independent of the vagaries of me or you. Thus, the very origin of the conception of reality shows that this conception essentially involves the notion of a COMMUNITY, without definite limits, and capable of a definite increase in knowledge. (5.311)

Peirce's optimism in this regard reflected an earlier period of his thinking which was later chastened. Yet the centrality of community as a motif in Peirce and in the hermeneutic tradition inspired by his semiotics cannot be denied. Josiah Royce, Peirce's colleague and friend, developed Peirce's notion of communal inquiry in dialogue with Pauline ideas of communal loyalty. Along the way, it may perhaps have been inevitable that Royce extended Peirce's idea toward the universal, ecclesial, and beloved community of the Spirit (cf. Royce 1968, vol. 2; Corrington 1995, 1–30). In doing so, Royce realized he was departing from the absolute idealism which characterized his earlier metaphysical ruminations toward what might be called a genuinely Christian—i.e., pneumatological or trinitarian—metaphysics. He actually insisted that only a truly pneumatological theology and philosophy was worth the name "Christian," since even a Logos theology and philosophy was, on its own, attained from Greek metaphysical reflection (Royce 1968, 2.16). His making this move leads me to believe that one could make one's way toward a triadic metaphysic by beginning with the notion of community as did Royce, or one could follow out a foundational pneumatology through a trinitarian metaphysics toward the notion of community as we did here.

In any case, the pneumatological imagination would insist on interpretation not only as a communal act, but also as an act of engaging others in community. And perhaps more important, the pneumatological imagination insists that communities are not concerned with interpretation for interpretation's sake—even for the sake of interpreting oneself to another communal member—but so that it can derive, formulate, and follow normative guidelines for communal relationships. The pneumatological imagination thereby insists on interpretation as a normative act. The normative character of all discerning interpretation is intricately connected, of course, to the social nature of lived experience. In our time, we are slowly beginning to realize that lived community extends far beyond human relationships to include environmental, natural, cosmic and spiritual (even demonic) dimensions as well.

Much more needs to be said about the normative functions of interpretation, and to that we shall return later. But note the basic emergent structure of so far. Interpretation can be said to be an intentional, teleological and transformative activity. It can be said to aspire to engage an other while enabling the other to retain its integrity and autonomy. And, it can be said to be communally defining as well as communally engaging. Herein lies the basic triadic structure—what I call Spirit, Word and Community—of the hermeneutical trialectic which will occupy our attention in Part Three. For now, however, other epistemic issues need to be attended to, the chief of which is the question of how interpretation engages otherness truthfully. We have already seen hints of an answer to this question in Peirce's semiotic theory. It is appropriate, however, not only to tease those out toward a more complete response, as well as to provide an account of truthfulness from the perspective of the pneumatological imagination.

5.2 Engaging the Other Truthfully

The question of truth lies at the heart not only of metaphysics and epistemology, but also of hermeneutics and theology. What kind of concept it is, what it means, how it functions linguistically and socially for human beings, among many other questions, has been extensively debated. In our postmodern context, concern with relativism also returns religious and theological communities repeatedly to this question (e.g., Kirkham 1992; McCallum 1996; Kennard 1999). I do not intend to recreate the wheel in what follows. Having suggested that hermeneutical and interpretive engagement with reality proceeds semiotically, larger concerns with religious and theological issues demand that I now take up the question of how it is that semiotic engagement can be truthful. The following will provide three avenues of response to this question utilizing the traditional notions of truth as pragmatic, truth as correspondence, and truth as coherence.[5] I hope only to provide insight into how these various traditional perspectives on the truth-question are illuminated by a pneumatologically-inspired imagination.

5.2.1 There are certainly a variety of pragmatic theories of truth, ranging from Peirce's realist version on the right to James' almost purely psychological view and Dewey's thoroughly instrumentalist account on the left (cf. Martin 1979, and Westphal 1998). Given the critically realist metaphysics we have adopted, those on the latter end of the spectrum will not concern us here. In Peirce's view, the truth of any proposition depends on the meaningfulness of ideas which operational consequences are clearly hypothesized and confirmed inductively. The key question is whether or not the proposition leads us to correctly predict the behavior of the thing in question. To do so leads to reliable practices and habits, thereby directly connecting thinking with acting in the world. This is an important point since the pragmatic theory of truth is focused on obtaining desirable results, not in the sense of that which human

---

[5] I leave aside here other, more recent, notions of truth such as the logical superfluity theory, the semantic theory, and the non-descriptive theory, since these have not gained such a following among contemporary philosophers as to have replaced the traditional theories; for a summary and assessment of these recent theories, see White (1971, 91–101).

beings simply wish or want, but in the sense of harmonizing or comporting with the way reality is.

Peirce's logic of consequences follows from the two-fold belief that the world will reveal the truth through its behavior, and that our grasping that truth will lead to the transformation of our behavior. A word needs to be said about each of these components with regard to related theories of truth as disclosure and as performative. The former, advocated primarily by phenomenological philosophers, has sought to return to the ancient Greek understanding of truth, *aletheia*. Here, truth is intrinsically unveiling or manifestness (Heidegger). It is that which opens up or creates possible worlds of habitation (Ricoeur). It is the process of un-concealing, presencing, or truth*ing* on the subjective side, and that of the unconcealed, the made present, the revealed truth on the objective side (Husserl). Here, truth is revelation of that which is otherwise hidden, the manifestation of that which is otherwise unmanifest, and grasping and being grasped by that which is otherwise ungrasped and even ungraspable. The result, of course, is existential transformation. Put religiously, truth is salvific (cf. John 8:32; cp. Guerrière 1990).

Alternatively, truth is related to performance. This is not to endorse the notion that truth statements are only performative utterances. It does, however, agree with performative theories insofar as the truth of the statement at a wedding ceremony, "I do," is born out in the lifelong commitment of each spouse to the other. Thus it is that the pragmatist notion of truth is predicated on the assumption that truth makes a difference in practice, both in terms of what it demands and in terms of our affirming truth. Thus, to seek after truth is to intend to commit oneself to it and to embody it in one's life and activity (cf. Apczynski 1977). As important, however, living truthfully also means that one's life conforms to the values and structures of one's natural and social environment.

Here we can see the import of Neville's hypothesis that the imagination is the means through which the values of things experienced are carried over into the experiencer or knower. In this case, "truth is the properly qualified carryover of the value of a thing (or situation, or state of affairs, or fact, or any complex harmony that might become an object of interpretation) into interpreting experiences of that thing" (Neville 1989, 65). The qualification mentioned concerns the various constraints—e.g., biological, cultural, semiotic, and so on—which bias human engagement with the world, and the various respects and intentions which guide that engagement. Yet such qualifications do not amount to enabling one to sidestep the full force of the challenge about whether or not truth is finally grasped, because to grasp that which is true would be to embody that truth in some respect. Truth is thereby experienced such that our activities and habits are transformed as a result of engaging the world (cf. Neville 1996; Yong 1998).

This means, however, that truth is not only (or maybe even primarily) a cognitive category, but an ethical one. Arguably, this is also the presumption of the biblical authors who discuss or mention truth, especially in the case of the Johannine literature. When read against the background of Qumran, as it should be, the extreme dualisms associated with the Johannine Spirit of truth (John 14:17, 15:26, 16:13, 1 John 5:6) are understood soteriologically and ethically rather than metaphysically or ontologically (cf. Breck 1991, 125–64).[6] Sure, the Spirit reminds us of the truth and leads us to the truth. But, the truth is and in the person of Jesus (John 14:6; Eph. 4:21) whose ways are to be followed, and whose image it is that we are being conformed to. Thus the Spirit convicts the world of sin, righteousness, and judgment (John 16:8–11), brings about the new birth (3:6–8), and gives life (6:63). The result is, finally, nothing less than that the truth is supposed to abide in us (1 John 1:8), and us in it, by the power of the Spirit (John 14:17): "…the anointing that you received from him abides in you, and so you do not need anyone to teach you. But as his anointing teaches you about all things, and is true and is not a lie, and just as it has taught you, abide in him" (1 John 2:26–27).

Now we certainly need to be cautious about reading more into Scripture than warranted, especially if we think we are going to find a theory of truth in the Bible (which we will not). Yet there is much food for thought about the pneumatological and trinitarian nature of truth, particularly in the Johannine writings. And, when read against the broader biblical background, the theological affirmations of God who speaks the truth (Ps. 19:9; 119:160) and acts truthfully in accordance with what is spoken (Rom. 15:8) translates into the view of truth as good news (Gal. 2:5, 14) which sets human beings free (John 8:32). Here again one finds soteriological and ethical pointers to God's dependability, constancy, fidelity, and reliability—the Hebrew *emet* connoting firmness and faithfulness, moral rather than metaphysical characteristics. And, insofar as we grasp these truths, such grasping can never so solely cognitive in nature, but

---

[6] The Johannine community and the Essenes were not exceptions in thinking in this way, but representative of Greco-Roman culture in the first century. As Ben Witherington III says, "Not only was there interaction between the inner and outer person, the inner and outer world, but a hierarchical ordering was assumed to exist in the universe, in society and in the human body" (1998, 38). Dale B. Martin also notes that ancient Greco-Roman views of the body included pneumatic, psychic, aesthetic, and cosmic dimensions rather than understanding these as ontologically distinct (1995, ch. 1).

will effect the very way in which we relate to—trust, follow after, inquire into—God. And, to the extent that truth shapes our activity and habits in these ways, to that degree will we have to affirm the pragmatic theory of truth.

5.2.2 That said, it is also important to recall that for Peirce, truth is fundamentally "the conformity of a representamen [the sign itself] to its object, *its* object, ITS object, mind you" (5.554). In the long run, a community of inquirers, if so motivated, will converge on a set of beliefs that accurately and truthfully reflect or correspond to the world as it objectively is. To the degree that this element of Peirce's view of truth is recognized, the pragmatist theory cannot be divorced from the correspondence theory of truth which affirms truth in dyadic terms as the accurate representation of any assertion—proposition, statement, sentence, judgments—to any fact or state of affairs that exists independently of such assertions (cf. Austin 1964; Searle 1995, ch. 9; Alston 1996; Groothuis 2000, esp. 83–110.). Truth as correspondence therefore builds on a critical realist metaphysics that affirms external reality as distinct from knowing selves, and therefore given perceptually through sensation and memory.[7]

Now this definition certainly raises numerous complexities, not the least of which pertains to the notions of "correspondence" and "fact." Taking the latter first, there are particular facts and general facts. Facts also appear to be "slices" of events reduced to conceptualization and language. Facts, therefore, seem to also be social and linguistic constructions (see O'Connor 1975, esp. chs. 7–8). One can get caught up in these complexities and forget that both the correspondence theory of truth and a critical realist metaphysics affirms factual reality as prior to and independent of human engagement, knowledge, and linguistic expression. But, nevertheless, what does "correspondence" mean? Two explanations have been offered: correspondence as congruence and correspondence as correlation. The former argues for a more rigid structural isomorphism—i.e., like two halves of a paper, or a one-to-one conformity—between truth statements and states of affairs, while the latter is satisfied with less than exact or rigid equivalence—i.e., like that between the British Parliament and the American Congress, or the parallel that exists between the numbers 1 to 26 and the letters A to Z. Most theorists now seem to think that the case for correspondence as congruence is weak since words, sentences, statements, etc.,

---

[7] For a nuanced defense of the doctrine of the given against its detractors—especially those in the Anglo-American tradition of analytic philosophy—who insist on it as a myth, see Russman (1987, 7–13). An alternative strategy which views philosophical reflection as engaging with the gratuity and givenness of lived-experience is that suggested by Continental postmodernists like Derrida and Marion.

are different kinds of things altogether than actualities, facts, and states of affairs. Thus theorists seem more willing to defend a correlational rather than congruence view of the correspondence thesis.

This move makes eminent sense when applied to statements regarding theology proper. Now one can certainly make truth claims about the historical Jesus, about the Church, and perhaps even about the resurrection (to be confirmed eschatologically, of course). But how can one make claims about God the Father who is neither empirically accessible nor an existing entity— especially if one follows Tillich and the apophatic tradition—like created things? Here, the predominant belief that all theological language is analogical at best hinders an application of the correspondence theory of truth to claims regarding God in Godself. For that, metaphorical, symbolic, and mythical language is required, which truth needs to be measured through other means. Thus Paul Avis distinguishes between a critical realism applied primarily but not exhaustively to created reality, and a symbolic or mythical realism through which we conceptualize and talk about the transcendent (1999, Part IV).

The breakdown of the correspondence theory has not, however, been limited to assertions regarding the transcendent. Rather, with the advent of postmodernity, this view has come under intense and sustained criticism even with regard to the human experience of the world. Among those rejecting the correspondence theory are neo-pragmatist philosophers like Richard Rorty who advocate an anti-representationalist view that denies truth matches propositions with external realities (1990, 1–6; 1991; 1998). In dialogue with the early Wittgenstein who understood language as a tool rather than as a mirror for reality, and with Dewey's vision of a pragmatic society, Rorty suggests that what philosophers have called epistemic justification is "not a matter of a special relation between ideas (or words) and objects, but of conversation, of social practice" (1980, 170). Thus, statements are relative to schemes, contexts and frames of reference, and function as guides to determining not what things are in themselves, but how and why they work, what we can expect of their behavior, and so on. Rorty's guiding vision is a fully tolerant, creative, pluralistic, and democratic society open to ongoing conversation, and he finds philosophical debate on epistemology, mind-dependency versus independency, idealism versus realism, etc., to be besides the point at best and altogether mistaken at worst. Rather than speculating about (what he calls) the spectator theory of knowledge, philosophers should be about the struggle for a just and democratic society.

Arguably, however, Rorty may have confused meaning and truth. This is a crucial distinction, as Donald Davidson points out (1984, 17–36). One can, for example, present meaningful fiction, but that does not translate into truth. Further, since even fiction depends on truth in order to communicate effectively, in that sense, truth is more fundamental than meaning. Now Davidson recognizes that the affirmation of correspondence can only be expressed linguistically, thus involving multiple sentences or assertions, each of which needs to sit coherently alongside with the others.[8] And, he is clear to insist that we cannot justify the totality of our beliefs (the inverse of Peirce's previous denial of our ability to doubt the totality of our beliefs all at once). However, for the meaning of anything to be adjudicated, its truth or truth-conditions have to be apparent. Divergent meanings cannot only with difficulty be adjudicated if their references are unknown, unverifiable, or false to begin with. Understanding and negotiating meanings therefore depend on and follow from truth, its conditions, and whether or not these conditions are met. In short, beliefs about what is true ultimately determine meaning, not vice-versa, even if meanings are accessible only through a coherent set of affirmations (cf. Marshall 2000, 91–100).

Now Davidson's adoption of a correspondence theory of truth alongside a coherence theory of justification points out a further weakness in Rorty's position since it appears that the latter also seems to have confused the difference between what the truth relation is and how we go about demonstrating that relation. Neville puts it this way: "Whereas an interpretation is either true or false in a dyadic sense, determining what it means and whether it is true is a matter for more interpretation, and perhaps a re-engagement of the object" (1996, 242). In Peircean terms, demonstrating truth is a semiotic (and, therefore, interpretive) process that is potentially infinite, except when it satisfies doubt so as to enable resumption of habitual activity. For this reason, even if one were to trade in Peirce's definition of meaning as pragmatically defined [see 5.1.1] for Vanhoozer's (1998) definition of meaning as intrinsically related to an author's communicative action, one is still no better off in accessing meaning since doing so requires the ongoing activity of interpretation (involving what Peirce calls interpretants and what Vanhoozer calls signification). It is in this strict sense that Alan White (1971, 102–29) is correct to argue that coherence and pragmatist theories are criteriologies for assessing truth, while the meaning of truth can only be that what is said corresponds to the facts of

---

[8] Thus the justification of beliefs requires that "they are supported by numerous other beliefs (otherwise they wouldn't be the beliefs they are), and have a presumption in favor of their truth. The presumption increases the larger and more significant the body of beliefs with which a belief coheres, and there being no such thing as an isolated belief, there is no belief without a presumption in its favor" (Davidson 1986, 319).

things as they are.[9]

The persistence of the correspondence theory of truth is thus not so easily disposed of. And, certainly, the biblical authors also assumed truth to be the correlation of language and reality in some way. As Pharoah admonished Joseph, "…in order that your words may be tested, whether there is truth in you…" (Gen. 42:16; cf. Deut. 17:4, 22:20). Lying, the bearing of false witness, and the deceitful tongue—all are abhorred because the truth is thereby compromised, and that which obtains in reality has not been faithfully witnessed to. Ultimately, however, the notion of truth as correspondence is presumed to function most intensely with regard to the central christological and trinitarian claim of Jesus as the "image [eikon] of the invisible God" (Col. 1:15) in whom the whole fullness of God dwells (Col. 1:19, 2:9), and the one who "is the reflection of God's glory and the exact imprint of God's very being" (Heb. 1:3) (cf. Schillebeeckx 1963; Haight 1999; and Marshall 2000, 108–17 and 265–75). The Johannine witness further identifies Jesus as the one who reflects the fullness of the grace, glory and truth of the Father (1:14; cf. 8:19, 10:30, 14:7–11, 17:5); who does whatever the Father does (5:19, 36, 14:31) and speaks whatever the Father has spoken (8:28, 12:49–50, 15:15); who both receives honor (5:23) and bears hatred (15:23–24) on behalf of the Father; whose acknowledgment or denial qualifies as the acknowledgment or denial of the Father (1 John 2:22–23). In fact, Jesus identification with the Father is of sufficient iconic intensity such that he not only carries and reveals the name of the Father (17:11), but also proclaimed, "Whoever has seen me has seen the Father" (14:9).

On this specifically christological and trinitarian point, the truth of Jesus Christ is affirmed to be the truth of God the Father. However, even granted this correspondence between Jesus and the Father, two caveats need to be registered in light of the preceding discussion. First, the correspondence requires, seemingly, to be explicated in terms of congruence rather than correlation simply because of the transcendental or apophatic character of divinity. Whatever and whoever else the Father is, he is neither Jewish nor male nor a car-

---

[9] James White arrives at a similar position in arguing the correspondence thesis: that there is "ultimate unity in the concept of truth, but practical diversity; thus allowing for ontology and epistemology to be separated methodologically but unified metaphysically in God's knowledge" (1994, 204). I think reference to the divine knowledge to secure the distinction between the correspondence theory of truth and the epistemic or hermeneutic access to truth is unnecessary once the triadic structure of semiotics is understood. Understandably, however, White's concern is to protect the correspondence view in order to preserve evangelical doctrines of especially the inspiration and inerrancy of Scripture. But of course, the last notion is problematic to begin with.

penter, etc. More will be said about the apophatic aspect of theological reflection in due time. Second, that Jesus and the Father are one does not mean that access to such truth is unmediated, directly intuited, or fundamentally foundational. That any statement or claim truly describes or corresponds to a reality or state of affairs does not mean that interpretation, a triadic relation, is bypassed. Our accessing the truth of Jesus revealing the Father is still necessarily a trialectical act of interpretation.

5.2.3 This leads to the coherence theory of truth whereby the truth of any one statement follows from and depends on its relationship to and consistency with other statements and claims (cf. e.g., Rescher 1973; Walker 1989; and Lehrer and Cohen 1987). Thus any particular truth claim is to be tested systematically for consistency (is this claim inconsistent with everything else we know?), connectedness (does this claim fit well or oddly within our system of knowledge?), and comprehensiveness (are there limits to this claim's scope of applicability?). At the same time, coherentism is clearly a non-foundationalist theory of justification since it acknowledges that all claims to truth are provisional since they are made within particular contexts, frameworks or systems, even if, finally, the coherentist aspires to universal systemization (cf. Malcolm 1977). Thus the coherence theory of truth has tended to be more dynamic with regard to the fluctuation of terms which need to be systematized given the ongoing advance of scientific (especially) knowledge, and more socially oriented with regard to the emphasis on inquiry as a communal enterprise. These factors undergird its eschatological sense (cf. Finger 2000, esp. 82–85; Henn 1987, 73–102) whereby it anticipates the elimination of contradictory claims as falsehoods and the unveiling (revelation) of reality as holistic and integrated in its plenitude and purity. Put eschatologically, the final truth will account for all provisional beliefs insofar as these are true. So, even if the notion of truth references the dyadic correspondence between assertion and reality, accessing that truth involves triadic acts of interpreting interpretants upon interpretants, potentially *ad infinitum*. The result is that truth necessarily emerges through the coherence of the entire set of interpretants.

The momentum of truth as coherence has gained especially in the postmodern movement toward truth as modeled after notions of "indwelling" and aesthetic experience whereby completeness, roundness, harmony, and feeling are the dominant criteriological frameworks (cf. Vattimo 1993). The promise and perils of the coherence theory are therefore best seen in light of the emergence of hermeneutical strategies which have taken advantage of the postmodern turn. Narrative theory is one such phenomenon. Briefly put, narrative theory is an adaptation of ancient mythological worldviews for the postmodern world. Following the Wittgensteinian analysis of words as finding their meaning in sentences, sentences in paragraphs, paragraphs in grammars, etc., narrative theorists argue that truth claims have to be assessed not as abstractly isolated propositions, but as members of the larger narrative sets— stories, myths and mythologies, language games, etc.—within which they find themselves. Not surprisingly, many have been thus drawn recently to narrative approaches to theological truth. Thus Henry Knight argues—in dialogue with a host of evangelical thinkers: Clark Pinnock, Stanley Grenz, G. C. Berkhouwer, Thomas Torrance, Donald Bloesch, Alister McGrath, Gabriel Fackre, Stanley Hauerwas, to name a few, even if we should not forget that the dominant evangelical view of truth remains the correspondence theory—that narratives are needed to convey the richness of the world we experience and are called to; that they preserve the unity of truth amidst the plurality and difference of lived experience; and that they are requisite to an adequate portrayal of personality, especially that of divinity (1997, 99–104).

The most rigorous attempt to justify narrative theology to date is Michael Goldberg's. Goldberg argues that any proposal to establish theology on non-narrative foundations is not only confused, but impossible since the convictions central to all theology (and ethics) have "*got to have* some story—or else be unintelligible and/or insignificant" (1982, 235; emphasis orig.). And how would stories or narratives provide justification, one could ask in return? Goldberg's response is that narratives a) disclose meaning by providing the primary conditions for understanding; b) reveal the world by providing the representative conditions for truthfulness; and c) transform persons by providing the affective conditions for engaging life and reality (1982, ch. 6; cf. Tilley 1985, 182–214). The justification of narrative, it is clear, includes criteria of coherence, correspondence and pragmatics/performativity. While one might read Goldberg's criteriology hierarchically, nowhere does he claim this to be the case. He does emphasize that failure to assess any narrative by each of these criteria in turn would be to neglect fully justifying it. Ultimately, however, one can assess neither the truth of narratives nor their truth conditions by employing non-narrative criteria. In this sense, the category of narrative—the coherence of the entire story or plot line—is itself primary or holds a position of epistemic priority and privilege.

The issue seems to me, however, more complex than this. On the one hand, yes, it appears undeniable that the test for truth goes beyond that of the question of meaning. The Wittgensteinian and Lindbeckian cultural-linguistic theory of truth seems right on this point. On the other hand, as we previously saw in Davidson's response to Rorty, it also seems right to affirm that something is meaningful because it is true rather than vice-versa. The issue is that of truth as correspondence versus truth as coherence. In the narrative or coherentist view, truth is understood in terms of coherence in that Christian doctrine and theology are meaningful only within their own internal framework. But this raises some difficult questions about the nature and reach of Christian truth claims. What then becomes of its applicability to those without the Christian community? Would narrativists theologians be willing to admit that Christian truth thereby becomes no more than a function of or appendage to the Christian narrative? How would narrativists defend the truth of their claims apart from this story when doctrinal or theological truth is primarily intrasystematic and performative rather than ontological or propositional (cf. Lindbeck 1984, 47–52 and 63–72; Pailin 1990)? The result has been that truth can no longer be universally asserted but is only meaningfully embedded within particular traditions. More specifically, truth as Christians consider it is relative to the Christian narrative.

Perhaps the way to hold both together is to recall that getting at whether or not something is true to begin with is an interpretive process that involves meaning and signification. One can therefore agree with the gist of the coherence theory of truth, but understand it more with regard to warrant and justification than as actually definitive of what truth is. If this is right, then, the truth of the coherence theory highlights the dynamic character of epistemic justification. Here, I am referring not only to the process of inquiry, but to the criteriological tools brought to bear in inquiry itself. Historically conscious persons and communities of inquiry cannot deny that each generations' conditions of plausibility differ, even if ever so slightly. The very criteria for accessing and assessing truth therefore have to be dynamic. In a curious way,

> truth becomes tradition-dependent or 'relative' only if the criteria are nailed down and prevented from changing in any way. In this case traditions face each other like rocks in the desert, with no possibility of communication. [Ironically,] it is the anti-relativistic defender of special traditions who provides dogmatic relativists with their strongest arguments. (Feyerabend 1990, 260–61)

Here, Feyerabend sounds out explicitly the logical conclusions regarding criteriological frameworks of the Kuhnian paradigm change theory of scientific advance. The result is, as Evan Howard reminds us, "no list of criteria is failsafe" (2000, 348).

If this is right, then it makes eminent sense to understand not only coherence but pragmatism as theories of justification rather than of truth. As such, they function more as meta-theories or frames of reference by which to assess truth claims. Now, if truth and falsity apply specifically to propositions, criteria of adequacy and non- or inadequacy apply best to the "frames of reference" within which beliefs are set. In this case, neither coherence nor pragmatist theories can literally be said to be false since "one never asserts or denies as such the frame of reference in which one makes propositional affirmations.... An adequate frame of reference allows one to ask and answer all the questions necessary to understand fully the reality one seeks to interpret. An inadequate frame of reference does not" (Gelpi 2001, 293). Herein lies the truth of coherentism understood as a frame of reference since it assumes, as Goldberg points out, both the pragmatist theory of justification and the theory of truth. The coherentist position is necessarily inclusive regarding all the relevant data, at risk of otherwise denying itself.

It is therefore not surprisingly that the theological analogue to the correspondence theory of truth is the christological representation of divinity, while pneumatology—Thirdness: interpretation, justification—best functions with pragmatism and coherentism understood as frameworks of reference. That the Spirit is truth (1 John 5:6) now takes on greater significance. First, the Spirit who is the mutual love between the Father and the Son is the divine mind who interprets the Father in and to the Son and vice-versa. The economic work of the Spirit thereby involves interpreting the world (the Word of the Father) ontologically and epistemically. The latter means, for human cognition, that all interpretation, justification, and reasoning are nothing less than pneumatically inspired efforts to correlate our understanding of the whole with the whole. Theologically, it means that the Spirit's work is to reveal the truth of the Father and the Son, to remind us of what is Jesus' precisely because what is Jesus' belongs to the Father (John 16:13–15). More important, second, the work of the Spirit is to enable not only our knowledge of Father and Son, but our mutual participation or indwelling of that relationship itself (cf. Marshall 2000, ch. 8). To know the Father and the Son is to keep the commands of and love Jesus. It is in this context that Jesus promises the everlasting presence of the Spirit of truth who not only walks alongside us as an advocate but abides in the very depths of our interiority (cf. John 14:15–21). In this way, we are enabled to love Jesus and one another, through which the world will come to realize who Jesus is. Finally, the purpose of knowing and loving the Father and the Son is to be conformed to them truly. The Spirit is the Spirit of truth in that she conforms us to the truth who is Jesus. More specifically, the truth which Jesus is simply reflects the truth of the Father, and our being conformed to the image of Jesus means the restoration of the image of the Father in us as well. It is thus the divine power of the Spirit which enables us to become "participants of the divine nature" (2 Pet. 1:3–4), and to thereby embody the truth individually and ecclesially as its ground (cf. 1 Tim. 3:15).

Much more would need to be said to fill out a coherentist reading of theological truth from a pneumatological perspective. My limited objective is to develop a robust theory of truth that includes a pneumatological component whereby truth is not an abstract relation between a proposition and certain facts or states of affairs, but is a personal, affective, existential and embodied relation whereby to know the truth both implicitly and explicitly demands and, in some sense, brings about conformity of life to it. The Spirit of Truth is not just a demonstrated theological definition but is the one who brings about correction of error, healing of brokenness, reconciliation of fractured relationships, in short, who orients human selves wholly—affectionately, spiritually, and materially—to truthful living. As personal rather than abstract and ethical rather than totalistic, truth is that which is transformative and directive toward eschatological fulfillment. It therefore has to be a thoroughly relational affair that involves communities of knowers in the knowing process. Theologically speaking, it is nothing less than the triadic or trialectical process of engaging the Spirit, the Word, and the divine Community.[10]

5.3 Dis-engaging the Other: An Account of Epistemic Fallibilism

Yet it is also the case that the quest for truth implies, and often involves, error, illusions, falsehood, and even deceptions. To affirm that the mind aspires to discern the pragmatic import, referential connections, and the systematic coherence of beliefs requires, in turn, that one affirms the fallibility and corrigibility of those same beliefs. To put it in Peirce's terms, experience has

[10] Parallels to my Spirit-Word-Community, considered as hermeneutical categories, abound. Donald Marshall, for example, suggests viewing truth as based on choosing right actions (*phronesis*), reasoning (*episteme*), constructing (*techne*) (1997). D. Z. Phillips' epistemological categories are actions, propositions, and communal relationality (1997). Following Wittgenstein, Phillips himself prioritizes the last, what he calls the "dance" whereby propositions and choices are grounded in community. My argument, of course, is that it is not beneficial to prioritize either of the other two at various moments of the hermeneutical spiral: thus the mutual interdependence of these categories for a fully developed epistemology. Other parallels will be mentioned in Part Three.

taught us that we have been wrong before, and will continue to do so if we are vulnerable to correction. Now, beliefs can be wrong for many reasons (cf. Gilovich 1991). In what follows, I want to explore the sources of epistemic fallibility along three fronts: the partiality of knowledge; the perspectival character of knowledge; and the finitude of knowledge. This discussion will provide a broader context within which to take up the question of how the imagination engages the world not only truthfully but also normatively.

5.3.1 That human knowledge is partial should go without saying. However, an examination of what partiality entails and its role in the epistemic process will contribute to our understanding of both truth and error. To begin with, the previous analysis alerts us to the partiality that attends to the accumulation or increase of knowledge. Things are not known directly or immediately. Rather, all knowledge, as we have discussed, is inferential and semiotic. As inferential, knowledge is reliant on memory (perceptual facts) drawn from sense perceptions (perceptual judgments). Knowers are always already one step removed from the things known.

This applies also to knowledge of ourselves. Is it the case that self-knowledge is immediate? Although the Cartesian *cogito* at one point counted as evidence for non-mediate knowledge of the self, it no longer carries much authority. Is it not rather the case that self-awareness is itself a cognitive construct that is entirely mediated? The Buddhists understood such mediation to occur through the five aggregates: form, feelings or sensations, perception or experience, discrimination or will, and consciousness. The underlying question, of course, is whether or not there are any direct, immediate, intuitions which count as knowledge. Peirce, as we know, answered in the negative. At the level of perceptual facts, knowledge is intuitively and affectively felt. But, brought to full consciousness and articulation, all knowledge proceeds inferentially through signs.

Another way to make this point is to observe that knowledge is predicated on the absence—i.e., "distance"—of the known object from the knowing subject. The distances between knower and known cover a wide range. In some cases, knowledge is mediated through a teacher, an elder, tradition, or some other kind of authority. In the case of religious knowledge, perhaps the known is mediated by faith. In the case of the knowledge of God, the distance is, in one respect, infinite. As W. Stephen Gunter reminds us, we are dealing with the one of whom Scripture says, "There is none like you" (Ps. 86:8; Isa. 45–47, passim), and therefore the one without analogy. Gunter's response is that such authentic theological and religious knowledge therefore arises precisely through our participating in the reality of God (1999, 87).[11] Put in other words, the knowledge of God indwells us even as we indwell the divine reality, and both mutually precisely through the Spirit who has been given to and poured out upon us. Theological knowledge is pneumatologically mediated if it is to be knowledge at all.

Knowledge is also partial since it is semiotic. As mediated by signs, knowledge is fundamentally conveyed by ideas. Now ideas are generals. They are universals abstracted—in Peirce's terms, abduced, inferred, or hypothesized—from the reality that is experientially perceived. Thus all knowledge is general and universal even if the objects of knowledge are determinate particulars. If the preceding account of movement from experience through perceptual judgments through perceptual facts provided by Peirce is correct, then knowledge (perceptual facts) is one step removed from basic, inarticulate beliefs (perceptual judgments) and two steps removed from the richness of the world and of our experience of the world. Process thinkers make similar claims using an alternative vocabulary. Ronald Farmer, for example, writes:

> [B]ecause process thought conceives of reality as a fluid environment composed of myriads of internally related momentary events (actual entities) rather than a world of discrete substantial objects, words can never be understood in a univocal sense. The application of a name to a group of entities—such as those entities comprising this "page" at this moment—requires that *some* aspects of that actuality be lifted out of the complex and dynamic set of relationships within which it occurs (its concrete connectedness) and that *other* aspects of the actuality be ignored—such as its relationship to the tree from which it came and the hand which now holds it. Consequently, language is always abstract—an imprecise, incomplete, and indeterminate representation of concrete actuality. The plurisignificant nature of language so conceived is obvious. Due to the "elliptical" character of language, each word is potentially capable of designating a whole host of meanings; no word can indicate precisely one singular and individual meaning. (1997, 104, emphasis orig.; cf. Franklin 1990, 266)

Whatever else one may think about the details of Whitehead's cosmology, that we no longer think in the static categories of Hellenistic philosophy scarcely needs to

---

[11] Gunter draws primarily from Polanyi's notion of "tacit knowing" and applies it to the knowledge of religious faith. Alternative conceptualizations of this aspect of the pneumatological imagination might include Kierkegaard's notion of knowledge and truth as subjectivity, William Lynch's knowledge as grounded in faith, and Wilfred Cantwell Smith's argument for faith and truth as personal.

be argued. Given this shift to an ontology of becoming, the fluid nature of thought and language is assumed to reflect the dynamic nature of reality itself.

This means, however, that knowledge is partial not only because of the mental processes—inference, semiosis, universals, etc.—involved, but also because the very nature of what is known is, in this respect, partial or incomplete. The world is not static but evolving or becoming. Things are incomplete in this sense. Sure, they are what they are from moment to moment, and in each moment, constitute themselves as some value or other. This axiological aspect (to which we will return below) does not, however, mean that no further developments of the thing will occur. Rather, Thirdness shapes and guides the legal, habitual, and vectoral trajectories of becoming. As the biblical author writes, "what we will be has not yet been revealed" (1 John 3:2).

The dynamism of reality means knowledge is itself dynamic and partial, not only since the future is vaguely knowable, but also because the richness of the specious present is gone before it can be fully delineated, and only fragments of the past remain—memories, archaeological sites, geological strata, history texts, etc.—to be interpreted. Knowledge is therefore always *in via*, partial, and obscure, as through a glass darkly or as a dim reflection in a mirror (cf. 1 Cor. 13:12). Theological knowledge is especially so since God is "able to accomplish abundantly far more than all we can ask or imagine" (Eph. 3:20b; cf. 1 Cor. 2:9). It is eschatological in that it increases as inquiry progresses across spacetime toward the eschaton. This eschatological orientation of theology is critical and should not be overlooked (cf. Grenz 2000; and Grenz and Franke 2001).

The partiality of knowledge means not only that knowledge is incomplete, but that error is possible. Errors occur because we fail to be discerning or discriminating about our experiences; because we misjudge inferentially; because our memory fails us. Error occurs when our teachers are wrong; when our authorities are undependable; when our traditions fail. Error occurs when we presume to have overcome the distance between ourselves as knowing subjects and what is known. Error occurs when we confound the partiality of our ideas with reality as it is in its exhaustiveness. Error occurs when we mistakenly assume yesterday's knowledge holds for today, or that today's will hold for tomorrow. Sure, it might, but we would need to check from day-to-day to ensure that it does.

5.3.2 As Peirce noted, however, even eternity is an insufficient amount of time for a community of inquirers to exhaust all inductive experiments regarding a certain item of knowledge. This is, in large part, because all experimentation proceeds perspectivally. Human investigators and entire communities of researchers are specifically located and particularly situated its various respects. No one has the God's-eye-view on reality. Knowledge thus arises out of our being "located" in particular "places" and is (to put it one way) relative to those locations and places, or (to put it another way) infected with the biases which accrue from those contexts. Things are "observed" or "experienced" by human beings from particular perspectives. Inferences and interpretations of those inferences (signs) therefore need to be qualified as appropriate by our understanding of the contexts within which those experiences and interpretations emerge. Three in general stand out: the biological, the cultural-linguistic, and the intentional/purposive (cf. Neville 1989, ch. 4).

The biological aspects that impinge upon knowledge are complex. To begin with, biological embodiment means we are confined to being at one place at one time. Here, biology connects with geography. Growing up in Taiwan results in certain habits of thinking that growing up on Pretoria does not inculcate. Second, are we male or female, right-brain or left-brain dominant, blessed with a high IQ or ordinarily equipped, etc.? Answers to these and other like questions are important in mapping out various cognitive tendencies. Third, are our bodily organs healthy? Are they functioning as they should? All too often, we take for granted the role that our organs of sense play in what we know. Fourth, what about the physiological and psychological aspects of ourselves? We are often unconcerned about these until we experience depression, mental fatigue, stress, etc., and our normal functionality is impaired. Yet since our bodies need to be sustained—by food, rest, physical exercise, interpersonal interaction, etc.—we have, generally speaking, cultivated the appropriate habits by which such sustenance is ensured. Biological, physiological and psychological considerations all determine, at least in part, our ability and to infer, discern, and interpret fairly clearly about some things (those that have direct impact on our well being), and less clearly about others. In short, knowledge is that which emerges from what Plantinga calls properly functioning cognitive equipment operating in congenial cognitive environments according to a process that has been successfully designed—whether by evolution or by God (Plantinga favors the latter hypothesis)—to produce true beliefs (cf. Plantinga 1993, esp. ch. 10; 1993a; 2000). Our interests and attention spans, of course, follows this trajectory set out by our epistemic equipment.

The cultural-linguistic dimension refers to the environmental context of inquiry. This includes, first, the geographical, topographical, and social features of the landscape—i.e., deserts versus coastal regions; rural versus urban; a country home versus an assisted-living situation, etc. Certain skills required for success in some situations are not at all helpful in others. Second, the cultural dimension involves the narratives, myths and traditions with which one is raised. These are deeply rooted not only in the actual stories that are told but in the ways in which the entire culture is itself organized, from its architecture to its rituals of interpersonal interaction. As such, certain values are highlighted as crucial to cultural awareness and survival, others are neglected or ignored. Third, and interconnected to the previous two, the language(s) available present(s) ways of imagining and talking that get at some things better than it does others. A culture's language encodes semiotically its values, and provides it with the means of engaging those values. Further, a culture's language reflects its landscape. Urban cultures have complex semiotic systems which order traffic or predict weather patterns, etc.; rural cultures have equally complex, but much less technologically sophisticated, semiotic systems to do the same. One's cultural-linguistic locatedness therefore shapes the perspectives that drive engagement and thinking.   *Siked*

Nevertheless, the intentional/purposive dimension cannot be overlooked in any discussion of epistemic perspectivalism. Habits are the result of long processes of interpretations directed toward successful living. Thinking is itself a process of habituated activity. But why pursue the development of some habits and not others? This is the teleological aspect of interpretation, even if such is intrinsically connected to one's biological constitution and cultural-linguistic conditioning. All knowledge is teleological to the extent that it seeks to provide some sort of order, whether that be of thought, of self, of self-in-society, etc. To go back to habituated activity, these arise so as to enable efficiency in our engagement with the world. Practical exigencies drive other kinds of thoughtful activity. In more theoretical activities such as philosophizing or theologizing, the purposes are intrinsically connected to the unresolved or problematic aspects bequeathed by the cultural-linguistic tradition(s), as well as to practical issues related to biological and/or cultural situations.

The point is that all thinking is conditioned by the biological, cultural-linguistic, and purposive contexts of inquiry. These contexts determine, in some ways, what is considered to be valuable or important. Truthful knowledge therefore requires multiple—perhaps an infinite number of—perspectives, each approaching the object of knowledge with various motivations for inquiry from a particular angle and asking distinct questions (cf. Poythress 1987). The more perspectives are available, the better our overall understanding of any particular phenomenon. In this regard, four Gospels are better than one, and better to have Pauline, Lukan, Johannine, etc., schools of early Christian thought

Why? what was the nature of the Fall? Was there always necessary? will sin always be?

rather than just any one. In our contemporary context, emphasis is therefore placed on multi- and inter-disciplinary investigation since diverse starting points, habits, languages, and motivations provide differing, albeit complementary, lenses on the object of inquiry.

Now as the pneumatological imagination should always alert us to the fact that the syntheses it provides holds together two (or more) perspectives or facts without compromising them, so is it the case that there is and is not a "distance" between the knowing subject and the known object. Yes, given metaphysical realism, the one is not the other. However, our situatedness amidst the buzzing developments of the world means that human knowers are not only transcendent to what is known, but also thoroughly immersed in the knowing process. Human knowers are not subjects completely detached from known objects. Ironically, then, while there is certainly partiality of knowledge which arises from the "distance" between knower and known, there is also distortion that arises out of the coinherence of the knower and known whereby both participate and indwell, albeit in different ways, the same world, location, or "space." Hence the self's situatedness vis-à-vis the objects of knowledge does not enable truly objective epistemic engagement.

But if human knowledge is always perspectivally emergent and therefore can never exhaust the object(s) of knowledge, how then can true knowledge be attained? Can the limitations of perspective be overcome? To be honest means to admit, No, at least theoretically. Practically, however, successful engagement with the world is the product of more rather than less valid knowledge. Thus Evan B. Howard (2000, 123, 270–75, and 286), following Jonathan Edwards (see his discussion of the twelfth sign in the classic *Religious Affections*) and Gelpi, speaks of moral but not absolute certainty.

As such, error could be the result of illusions generated from the standpoint of inquiry. Error could also derive in part from not discerning the proper respects or contexts of any particular interpretation or claim to truth—i.e., not understanding how one's biological constitution, cultural-linguistic formation, or purposive intentions produce, develop, and follow out certain inferences rather than others. Finally, error may just be the presence of bias developed from one's locatedness. Bias itself is unavoidable since it means nothing more than having a specific perspective, which we all do. However, not realizing one's particular perspective means we remain ignorant that other perspectives exist. At worst, bias develops into prejudice which minimizes the value of other perspectives or arrogantly asserts one's own perspective regardless of the merits or demerits of that perspective vis-à-vis others.

5.3.3 Finally, knowledge is fallible because it is affected (or, infected, as the case may be) by finitude. Now finitude in and of itself simply points to the fact of creaturehood. Human beings are creatures, and as such, subject to the conditions of contingency, ontological dependence, and relativity. Such is the human condition. In this sense, insofar as epistemic fallibilism is a trait of human finitude, it characterizes what it means to be truly human rather than divine. Adam and Eve in the garden (however they are to be understood) were epistemically fallible as finite creatures. It is this fact which explains (in part) the fall from grace, rather than arguing the reverse, that the fall explains epistemic fallibility (cf. J. Smith 2000). Even in the case of Jesus, insofar as he is understood to be truly human, his personal, social, and religious life should be understood in developmental rather than static terms, with all of the attendant ambiguities which characterize human growth and social development (cf. Gelpi 2001a, vol. 1, chs. 6–8). As such, error may be the result of under-developing or not cultivating properly one's habits of engagement.

Yet there is more to be said about finitude since it characterizes not only creaturehood, but fallen creatureliness. Here, the human condition is not just one of innocent participation of knowing subjects and known objects in the common field of creation. Rather, our mutual indwelling is fallen creation: subjects and objects are enmeshed in, entangled by, and thoroughly caught up with the world of sin. In theological terms, human being are not only potentially but effectively fallible, and fallen. Kierkegaard thus recognized the human situation to be enveloped by despair, fear, anxiety and melancholy. As such, humankind's existence is, as Heidegger remarked, a "being-toward-death." Mortality and death is not only possible but inevitable, uniquely individualized, non-relative, indefinite, and cannot be outstripped (cf. Schrag 1961, esp. 67–118).

Given the finitude that is endemic to fallen human existence, human knowledge is thus radically marked by sin, understood here both in the biblical sense as falling short of the mark (perhaps hampered by finitude), and in the existential sense of the willful resistance against and rejection of God and the divine intentions for creation. Here, it would be less appropriate to speak of error since there are connotations to the making of errors which do not imply a thoroughgoing culpability. But epistemic fallibilism in this case should be understood in moral terms. It is, as Ricoeur puts it, the "fault" which not only makes error possible, but the tear or the rift which signals weakness and thereby entertains temptation, and the flaw which has already given into that temptation (1965, esp. 203–15). Fallibility is thus willful activity, whether that be willful negligence of the facts of experience, willful disengagement with the world,

no, b/c it ignores issues of culpability

[handwritten margin notes: "assuming phenomenological constraints / projects them back", "begs the question / assumes the answer", "anti teleological / ignores", "?", "cause", "effect"]

willful misrepresentation of such engagement, willful and irresponsible exercise of epistemic judgment, or, finally, the willful denial that one's knowledge is partial, perspectival, finite, and fallible, this last normally called idolatry. Moreover, each of these cases could be compounded by extraneous factors. The emergent knowledge claims in each instance could also be misused or abused by the self-centered or egocentric will to power of personal agents, could be intentionally directed toward deceptive and sinful ends, or could be the means by which destructive habits of thought and activity are fostered, this last perhaps characterized as the work of the demonic. In each case, there is a determination on the part of personal agents to conspire against the work of the Holy Spirit. The result is deception, isolation, segregation, suffering, tragedy, evil, and, perhaps most importantly, injustice (cf. Plantinga 2000, ch. 7).

[handwritten margin note: "why would eschaton be different?"]

For these and other reasons, human knowledge is inevitably fallible (at least on this side of the eschaton). It is always in process, partial, perspectival, and infected with finitude. It is never infallible, absolute, and exhaustive. While any statement or assertion about reality or fact is either true or false, determining its truth or falsity is a triadic affair of interpretation. The conclusion might be the declaration of the statement's truth or error. Alternatively, it also could be determined to be "undecided"—what Philip Clayton calls "three-valued logic" (1999, 78–95), akin to Peirce's notion of vagueness that is subject to the law of non-contradiction but not to the law of the excluded middle—thus awaiting further investigation. Certainly, the world does not stop because of what may be undecided at any particular moment. Inquiry continues with the previous conclusions held not incorrigibly but made vulnerable to correction by the community of interpreters.

Our discussion of the fallibility of knowledge so far pertains to the epistemic processes in general. One more word needs to be said here about the pneumatological imagination specifically. Insofar as the pneumatological imagination is especially attuned to the legal, habitual, and dispositional aspects of reality—the internal aspects of things, if you will—it needs to be especially discerning since it that recognizes the import of piercing through the phenomenal manifestation of a thing toward its inner aspects. This is a complex task in part because we are dealing with Thirdness is all of its complexity—legal, habitual and spiritual realities—even though we are most sensitive to and most adept at engaging with the phenomenal world of Secondness—concreteness, materiality and embodiment. Thus the pneumatological imagination is one that realizes it should be epistemically patient in waiting for the object of knowledge to more fully reveal its habits, dispositions, and laws. The

[handwritten margin notes: "?", "yes", "pneumatological imagination"]

pneumatological imagination is therefore aware of the tendency to prematurely and inappropriately discern any phenomenon. Hence the provisionality and fallibility of the pneumatological imagination.

The argument so far is that knowledge and interpretation is ultimately of reality—our engaging it and our being corrected by it. Reality is therefore the measure of our interpretations and misinterpretations. In this sense, metaphysics and ontology precedes epistemology and interpretation itself. Now certainly all metaphysics is hermeneutically discerned, and truth in the robust sense is therefore necessarily eschatological. Equally certain, human knowledge is fallible for a variety of reasons. But this does not lead to epistemological skepticism or relativism in the here and now because we do engage reality, our engagement is more or less truthful, and it is normed by reality itself. The question that will concern us in what follows is how reality is normative. How then does normative engagement with reality that is truthful occur? How do the values of reality carry over and norm our interpretations and engagement? How does the pneumatological imagination discern normativity? How is it grasped or normed by reality?

6 The Pneumatological Imagination and Normative Engagement

The following discussion focuses on the ethical and aesthetic norms which shape our interpersonal relationships and our engagement with the world. In the process, some insights will be gleaned on how engaging others and the world (which always goes together, never separately) leads us to encounter the divine. If indeed Peirce is correct all human experience is mediated semiotically, then the human being is, indeed, an *animal symbolicum* (see Cassirer 1944, 26). As such, I will argue that norms are intrinsically connected to the sense of obligation which emerges in the encounter with otherness insofar as otherness is *sign*-ificant—i.e., bears the imprint—of the divine (which it always does, to a greater or lesser degree). I will suggest that the pneumatological imagination is especially attuned to recognize these connections because it realizes that interdependence, intersubjectivity and interrelationality characterize the knower and known relationship, and because its rejection of metaphysical nominalism and materialism frees it to acknowledge the axiological and spiritual dimensions of reality which are semiotically communicated. This chapter therefore explores how axiological and normative issues are emergent in the movement from epistemology to theology. Given the previous argument regarding the interconnectedness and interrelatedness of human beings with the world and with the divine, I will proceed to discuss in order our experience of each other, the natural world, and the divine, with the goal of sketching what might be called a symbolics of human community, a symbolics of nature, and, finally, a symbolics of God. Together, these remarks constitute a nascent theology of symbols, perhaps a theological semiotics, that will serve to transition us from epistemology to theological hermeneutics proper.

6.1 Normative Engagement: Toward a Symbolics of Human Community

Insofar as knowing has a pragmatic course, it raises moral and ethical questions, especially in our relationships to each other. But how and when does the ethical question arise? How is that that we recognize or experience our obligatedness to others? How are human relationships normatively experienced? Our ever-increasing consciousness of the fact that history is replete with injustice legitimated in the name of truth drives these questions (cf. Beuken, Freyne and Weiler 1988). I begin with a clarification of norms in general and ethical norms in particular, and proceed to explore the thesis that our experiencing otherness normatively derives from our mutuality which is signified or given expression in the face of the other as Other. In the second and third sub-sections that follow, I draw on the work of Emmanuel Levinas to flesh out this hypothesis.

6.1.1 The claim has been made so far that the world is constituted by values and disvalues, and that lived-experience therefore includes an axiological or normative dimension. It is now time to clarify and defend this claim. The word "normative" is the adjective form of the noun "norm." As it is used in discussions of ethical theory, a norm is a level of achievement or a standard or rule with which human conduct is expected to comply and according to which human conduct is thereby judged. That human beings ought not to kill other human beings is a norm, and failure to live up to this (or any other) norm may involve punishment or retribution related to the normative expectation. What is normative, however, may not necessarily be normal. It is normal for human beings to go to sleep at night, but no punitive social consequences follow the decisions of those who choose to work graveyard instead.

But why are certain rules normative and not others? How are norms formulated, if at all, or how are they recognized? Are ethical norms simply the result of social constructs relative to the interests of those in power at particulars places and times? One of the ways to begin addressing this set of questions is to reconnect norms with values. To talk about norms is to talk about values: can things be envisioned to be better than they are? Can things be more rather than less well ordered? Is the intellect more or less satisfied about its assessment of what is true? The imagination engages these and many other normative questions that reflect the human aspiration after the valuable. Usually we are more adept at applying normative measures to our experiences and to the things we experience in order to maximize the values enjoyed by human life than we are at theorizing about norms.

Yet theorize we must, at least for the purposes at hand. Lived experience includes a number of realms of values. There are truth values that are graded according to intellectual norms. There are personal values, sometimes gauged according to character traits or a list of virtues. There are interpersonal relationships, most often judged according to ethical codes or rules which guide behavior. There are social values such as the flourishing of individual persons as creatures of intrinsic worth on the one hand and of human society and civilization as a whole on the other. The development and articulation of socio-ethical norms address the values envisioned at this level. Finally, there are values derived from nature itself, which can be classified into those which are intrinsic to nature and those instrumentally attached to nature. The former are judged according to aesthetic norms, and the latter according to norms for sustaining and preserving the environment. In point of fact, as we shall see, the intrinsic-extrinsic distinction—norms which gauge how we should engage others in their otherness, what or whoever that may be, and norms which gauge how we should engage otherness in their or its relationship to us and vice-versa—is applicable not only to environmental ethics or an ethic of nature, but also across the board. The discussion of an ethic or symbolics of nature will ensue shortly. For the moment, however, our focus will be on an ethic of normative engagement with human others.

And here, the waters begin to muddy. This is because we are attempting here to answer at least two kinds of questions: that exploring what kind of thing values and norms are and how they are known, recognized or discerned; and that pertaining to the contents that mandate what we ought to do. The first has traditionally been identified as belonging to the realm of meta-ethics or theoretical ethics, while the second is usually identified as normative ethics. The debate among ethicists has traditionally been twofold: what is or should be normative for human conduct and behavior? Is there agreement on the content of normative ethics? Are not normative ethical codes universal in the obligation which they impose upon all rational human beings? No consensus has been attained on any of these questions. This has led to the argument that philosophers and ethicists should not actually be about trying to come to agreement on what is or is not normative and ethically binding for human behavior. Rather, they should be about the task of meta-ethics, which is to clarify what norms are to begin with; or to analyze the meanings or normative ethical statements; or to probe the logical status of moral claims and arguments, etc.

The problem in a nutshell is that while human beings order their world according to a variety of ethical norms—this being a descriptive fact of human societies—how do we get from the "is" to the "ought"? Just because we've always believed such and such, and done things so and so, does that mean that we should always continue to believe such and such and do so and so? Here, the two dominant ethical traditions respond in different ways. Deontologists hold that the "ought" is implicit in the "is"—that what is normative for any situation can be determined upon close inspection of the situation itself since the values to be pursued are intrinsic to the experienced situation. Therefore the situation will reveal the "rules" that apply, and the proper response is to fulfill one's obligation in that situation by heeding those rules regardless of the outcomes. Consequentialists, on the other hand, hold that the "ought" follows the larger context within which the situation is to located. This context should be analyzed not only synchronically (as the deontologists emphasize) but also diachronically in order to determine the potential results of alternative responses. Actions that result in the greatest good for the greatest number is normatively binding. The problem, of course, is that what is good for one may not be good for another, or may not be good for the natural environment which holds the two parties, and so on. Here, the intrinsic-extrinsic distinction made previously can be seen to apply to the two theories under discussion. The question of how we get from the "is" to the "ought" can therefore be rephrased to ask: are ethical norms emergent from factors intrinsic to the situation at hand or from other implicated factors? Perhaps both. In fact, if our previous analysis of how the logic of pneumatology drives the dialectical movement of thought holds [3.2.3], then the pneumatological imagination will preserve the insights of deontology and consequentialism in ethical decision-making.

But here I am not only jumping the gun, but am doing meta-ethics rather than taking on the epistemological question, namely, how is it that we know in general, and how is it, more specifically, that we know about values and norms at all? It is at this point that the earlier sketch of both Neville's axiological metaphysics and Peirce's semiotic metaphysics come together to illuminate our problematic. If facts and values are not bifurcated, and if knowledge is semiotically mediated, then semiosis itself is a value-laden process which interprets a world of values. In this case, meta-ethics—the epistemological question—cannot avoid normative ethics, and vice-versa. How does fleshing out this hypothesis clarify our normative experience of human otherness, and direct us toward a symbolics of human community?

6.1.2 The work of French phenomenologist and philosopher, Emmanuel Levinas, is pertinent to our question. Having imbibed Husserlian phenomenology and Heideggerian onto-theology, Levinas' turns from the question, "What does ethics appear to be?" to the question, "What ought to be?" The latter is identified as being the important ethical question. For him, the ontological question of freedom has to be subordinate to the metaphysical and ethical question of justice—more explicitly, justice of and for the other.

Morality, Levinas says, is not simply one of the branches of philosophy, but first philosophy itself (1969, 79 and 304).

But how does one recognize the other? How does one engage the other? How is one confronted with one's obligations to the other? Through the face, Levinas responds, which, as the "expression [and] source of all signification," makes the other present to myself (1969, 297). Levinas disclaims providing a phenomenology of the face, but that is what he does with deep perceptiveness. The significance of the face is summarized by Levinas as follows:

> There is first the very uprightness of the face, its upright exposure, without defense. The skin of the face is that which stays most naked, most destitute. It is the most naked, though with a decent nudity. It is the most destitute also: there is an essential poverty in the face; the proof of this is that one tries to mask this poverty by putting on poses, by taking on a countenance. The face is exposed, menaced, as if inviting us to an act of violence. At the same time, the face is what forbids us to kill. (1985, 86)

Four points are apposite for our purposes. First, the face reveals the depths of the other as an infinitely complex reality. To ask what or who the face symbolizes, we can be given any number of roles or personae in response. She may be a child on the one hand (to her parents), or a parent on the other (to her children). She is a student (to her teachers) and a teacher (to her students). She is servant as one who meets the needs of others even as she is master as one who lords it over or makes demands of others; and so on. Each of the other's persona has its own time and place, relative to particular situations, needs, and contexts. Yet none of them individually nor all of them together exhaust the face's identity as other. While these variant roles comprise one or another aspect of the other, the face remains inexhaustibly significant. Its identity cannot be finally captured, contained, or encompassed. While her personae is describable, her person finally eludes categorization and definition. She resists thematization and objectification. She cannot be possessed, and, as such, remains irreducibly other in the face-to-face relationship. She is without defense, but no offensive maneuver can finally overtake her. The face therefore signifies radical alterity. In Levinas' words, "The face is signification, and signification without context….[T]he face is meaning all by itself" (1985, 86).

Second, the face is symbolic of the relationship which binds me to the other. The face is living, evocative, dialogic, and interactive. The face demands a response, and calls me into relationship insofar as it presents the vulnerability of the other to me. At the same time, while the face does provide me with an opportunity to dominate that other, it also exposes me to interrogation. Thus

I am tempted to violence in part because the nakedness of the face is a threat to my own naked solitude and privacy, gazing upon me intimately. In the face-to-face relationship, my own self is subject to the deep searching of the other, and my own nakedness is revealed before the gaze of the other. As such, the other is stranger to me, radically over-and-against me, inviting but also threatening.

Third, and most important for the purposes at hand, the face obligates me—it unveils my own sense of obligation to the other. As radically other, the face discloses herself as destitute and impoverished, and thereby reveals herself as my master. This is not just because of the face's blemishes or material needs, but because the other is ever free over-and-against me, always superior to me. "To recognize the Other is to recognize a hunger. To recognize the Other is to give. But it is to give to the master, to the lord, to him whom one approaches as 'you' in a dimension of height" (1969, 75; reference to "height" denotes the "you" of majesty rather than the "thou" of intimacy, so comments the translator in a footnote). The other cannot be put down or subordinated to me, just as I cannot just simply waive away my own needs, pains, frustrations, and hunger. In fact, these experiences enable me to feel the ethical demand and moral obligation that confronts me in the face of an other. In that sense, the other's face echoes my own pleading, begging, and crying out for justice. And because this demand for justice can never be satisfied, it means that my obligations to the other will always remain unfulfilled. Alternatively, it means that the demands signified by the face are relentless, encroaching always upon me, growing and ever-increasing as a burden I bear for and toward the other. So it is that "the face opens the primordial discourse whose first word is obligation…" (1969, 201; cf. Farley 1996, ch. 4).

The last word, however, is judgment. This follows from the guilt I realize in the face-to-face relationship. Levinas puts it this way: "The infinity of responsibility denotes not its actual immensity, but a responsibility increasing in the measure that it is assumed; duties become greater in the measure that they are accomplished. The better I accomplish my duty the fewer rights I have; the more I am just the more guilty I am" (1969, 244). This guilt is exacerbated since most often, I reject the other as alien; I use or abuse the other; I reduce the other to myself, or an extension of myself; thus incurring the judgment of the other. This is not only because the other, by virtue of being other, resists my continuous efforts to dominate and possess her, but also because the destitution of the other means that I owe all that I am and have to her. And, because of the face-to-face relationship, two results inevitably follow. First, this obligation is not transferable: I cannot have someone else fulfill my obligation so that my culpability can be alleviated and my guilt assuaged. Sure, someone else may meet the other's actual need. But this satisfies only that third party's obligation to the other, not my own. Second, the other remains always the standard by which judgment is meted. And, because the other's demand upon me is context-less and hence infinitely deep—as represented by the face's significance—this means that the other's judgment over me is infinite. Levinas puts it this way: *[handwritten: More Particulation in the garden]*

> The other's face is the revelation not of the arbitrariness of the will, but its injustice. Consciousness of my injustice is produced when I incline myself not before facts, but before the other. In his face the other appears to me not as an obstacle, nor as a menace I evaluate, but as what measures me. For me to feel myself to be unjust I must measure myself against infinity. One must have an idea of infinity, which, as Descartes knows, is also the idea of the perfect, to know my own imperfection. The infinite does not stop me like a force blocking my force; it puts into question the naïve right of my powers, my glorious spontaneity as a living being... (1987, 58)

If I thereby stand infinitely obligated in the presence of the face of the other, I can purchase my freedom only in laying down my life for the other. Here, I realize that this infinite judgment under which I stand condemned serves as a pointer to the transcendent.

6.1.3 But notice that the transcendent is manifest not immediately but in the face-to-face relationship. Transcendence is disclosed in the excessive, albeit deeply ambiguous, meaning of the face. I can always only hope to begin discerning the identity of the face as I fulfill my obligation to her, but I can never complete such discernment. Thus it is that the other is present, revealed in the face-to-face relation, but yet also infinitely distant. This paradoxical situation is captured in Levinas' notion of *proximity* whereby the other,

> my neighbor (*le prochain*) concerns, afflicts me with a closeness (*proximité*) closer than the close of entities (*prae-ens*). The relationship with alterity, which is what escapes apprehension, exceeds all comprehension, is infinitely remote, is, paradoxically enough, the most extreme immediacy, proximity closer than presence.... (summarized by translator Lingis in Levinas 1991, xix)

Here, connections can be made with the previous discussion along two fronts. First, Levinas' face representing the other echoes Peirce's semiotic self whose communicative agency is manifest phenomenologically (outwardly) as that which resist, opposes, or is established over-and-against us (cf. Colapietro 1989). In both cases, human selfhood is characterized by intersubjectivity, by a dialectical tension between inwardness and outwardness, and by the pragmatic (Peirce) or ethical (Levinas) relation. Second, might it not be said that what Levinas calls proximity is what Christians call the Spirit—the Spirit of God being that same breath that animates myself and the other, and causes me to recognize the other, empathize with the other, and fulfill obligations in response to the demands of the other? From the perspective of the pneumatological imagination, is it not precisely the worship of God in Spirit and in truth by which self and other are brought into relationship, obligation, and *koinonia*? Turning away from self toward the other in and of itself might accomplish little, if the Marxist-socialist revolution is historically suggestive at all. It is not the other as other that makes demands on me, but the other and myself—together bearing the divine image and standing under God—that puts me, and us all, under obligation (cf. Hodgson 1995).

In other words, the other not only reveals, confirms, and exposes myself and us, but deeper still, through the face of the other, I become aware of the infinitude, the depths, which envelop our relationality, the significance of which can never be fully plumbed. Thus the other reveals my obligatedness to that which is paradoxically supremely immanent and supremely transcendent. It is as if whatever I would do to and for the other, I do to and for divinity. To look into the face of the other, then, is to peer, however dimly, into the face of the divine. This is stated in a round-about way by Levinas' translator, Alphonso Lingis:

> And in transferring religious language to the ethical sphere, Levinas no doubt divinizes the relationship with alterity; indeed he will say that the description of the other in his alterity is less a phenomenology than a hagiography. But Levinas does not mean purely to employ a language now without proper object to describe human relations, in order to exalt them with the sentiments that once transcendent divinity inspired. He rather means to locate the proper meaning of God—the one God—in the ethical bond. Not so much that God would be a postulate required to render the ethical imperative intelligible, not that God would be revealed in ethical phenomena—but that God is the very nonphenomenal force of the other, that God "exists" in his voice, which speaks in the ethical imperative. And that all responsibility bears witness to the Infinite who is God….Sacred, in a literal sense, it is the transcendent instance that contests and judges being. It is the Good that calls unto being and to expiation for the wants and faults of being. Here God figures not as a compensation for us for the wants of the universe, nor as healer of our mortality, but as judge and as imperative which calls us into question. (Lingis in Levinas 1991, xxxiii)

Levinas' challenge to reconceive of the divine Infinity as "otherwise than being or beyond essence" should be applauded. The whole point of *pneuma* in the Christian theological tradition is to point away from being toward relationality. Yet, it is also true that, as his translators put it, "the structure of transcendence [in Levinas] is exemplified not by religious experience but by the ethical" (Peperzak, Critchley and Bernasconi in Levinas 1996, 129). Is ethics the be-all and end-all of religion? Does the second commandment explain or replace the first? Is religion predominantly about action, or is religion predominantly about the one, infinite, reality to whom worship is due? Surely, the Jewish and Christian traditions have representatives affirming both sides of this debate. Some insist that the divine-human relationship is wholly encapsulated in the ethical relationship itself. Others insist that divinity is the source of human ethical experience, but is itself exempt from ethical categories.

Levinas appears to align himself with those in the Jewish tradition that emphasize the priority of morals and ethics—perhaps as the only imperative relationship that should concern human existence. The question is whether or not Levinas intends the phenomenological infinitude displayed in the face as equivalent to the ontological infinitude behind or beyond the signifyingness of the face? Does he wish to and succeed in preserving what he calls the "glory of the Infinite" in the face of the other (cf. Levinas 1985, 105–09)? Or, does Levinas truly believe that the infinitely deep ethical relationship that emerges from the face-to-face encounter *is* the essential human-divine relationship? At one point, Levinas says that

> to bear witness [to] God is precisely not to state this extraordinary word, as though glory would be lodged in a theme and be posited as a thesis, or become being's essence. As a sign given to the other of this very signification, the "here I am" signifies me in the name of God, at the service of men that look at me, without having anything to identify myself with, but the sound of my voice or the figure of my gesture—the saying itself. (1991, 149)

Thus it is that Isaiah's response to the divine address is, at the same time, a response toward otherness: "Here am I; Send me!" (Isa. 6:8b). To respond to the divine Other is to fulfill my obligation to the other whose face I behold. Here, the love of neighbor and the love are God are intertwined, and my response to the face of the other is my response to the one whose image her face reflects (cf. Matt. 25:31–46). As Levinas says, "There can be no 'knowledge' of God separated from the relationship with men. The Other is the very locus of metaphysical truth, and is indispensable for my relation with God" (1969, 78). To deny the one is to deny the other and to attempt the impossible and yet damaging stance of not-being-in-relation (cf. Heyward 1982, 73–106).

The face is therefore an epiphany, revelatory of other, of self, and of divinity. With this, the face signifies normatively our understanding of human community. Its truth is found not in my measuring the other propositionally, but in the other measuring my actions ethically. It is a symbolism of obligatedness, whereby I come to a recognition of who I am vis-à-vis the other—human and divine. Yet it is important to emphasize, on the one hand, that the other always remains other, and never becomes myself. Here, the pneumatological imagination recognizes the other's radical alterity. My obligation to respond to the other is, at this level, purely for the sake of the other; thus its inconvenience to me. The truly ethical act is the one which does not expect, nor receives, anything in return. It is, finally, the laying down of my life for the other. On the other hand, the face of the other is a mirror through which I myself am defined, identified, and revealed. Here, the pneumatological imagination illuminates the mutual indwelling, the perichoretic interrelationality, that constitutes the face-to-face relationship. My obligation to the other is at the same time to myself—in fact, to love the other as I love myself. To neglect, ignore or injure the other is, finally, to scar my own self. Together, the face-to-face relationship enables a symbolics of human community to emerge wherein the alterity that characterizes my relationship with the other finds its mutuality—including hope, healing, and reconciliation—only in God.

6.2 Normative Engagement: Toward a Symbolics of Nature

Might we be able to detect a similar movement which grounds our interaction with nature normatively? During the past generation, the field of ethics has expanded rapidly and now includes, among other new areas, environmental ethics. Is this what normative engagement with nature means? But even if so, how and when does the ethical question regarding nature arise? How is it that we recognize or experience our obligatedness to the natural world? Here, the intrinsic connection between ethics and aesthetics comes to the fore. I therefore begin with a cosmological theory of value (in dialogue with Neville), proceed to explore a cosmological semiotic (in dialogue with Rahner), and conclude toward a symbolics of nature (in dialogue with Edwards). Along the way, as in the preceding discussion, we can trace the movement of the pneumatological imagination from its engagement with nature to its engagement with the divine.

6.2.1 From a theological perspective, it would certainly be valid to begin reflection on how nature is engaged normatively by recalling that creation was declared to be good and that humankind was given charge to tend for it. This raises, however, the age-old question: what makes creation good? God's simple declaration that it is (was) so, or the fact that there is some normative measure for recognizing creation's goodness which God evaluatively discerned? The former calls for theological analysis that finally rests in a posture of faith. Better to begin with the latter question to see if light can be shed on the original question.

So the issue before us is that regarding nature's norms and our access to those norms. Norms presuppose values: better or worse, minimally. The disastrous move during the modern period was to divorce things and values. The realm of values was considered to be socially constructed attitudes which were relative to places, times, and cultures, and thereby utterly subjective. The realm of things, on the other hand, was concerned with the ultimately real components of the world, and the scientific enterprise emerged precisely in the attempt to engage that realm objectively, apart from the subjective biases that infect human knowing. The paradigm has now shifted so that we have come to understand all human knowing—including scientific knowing—as involving subjectivity, affectivity, and values. But are values therefore to be categorized only epistemically or psychologically? Doing so would simply perpetuate the notion that whatever values "discerned" in nature are imposed there by us rather than inherent in nature itself. What is needed is an understanding of values as a metaphysical and cosmological category.

At this point I want to reintroduce Neville's axiological metaphysics but focus on his theory of cosmological value rather than on the imagination as such. Recall that for Neville, things are what they are as harmonies of essential and conditional features. Harmonies are ordered wholes that integrate various components which are themselves harmonious wholes of other components, and so on, *ad infinitum*. Harmonies therefore range in complexity. Yet it is the case that a thing's identity and value is found in its being a de facto harmony. More technically put, "the value of a thing is determined by its form, the complex possibility it realizes, which combines its components in certain ways" (Neville 1995, 117). This means that our analysis of any thing needs to be sensitive to its complexity even as our assessment of its values (its identity) should proceed from a variety of perspectives. Neville (1995, 44–53) provides five such approaches to the understanding of value which I will discuss in under two categories: that for others, and that considered on its own terms.

Under the former, each thing has *extrinsic value*, *relational value*, and *perspectival value*, each of which provides a unique angle on the cosmological relationality of things.[1] The focus of the first is the value that one thing has for another thing (or other things). Extrinsic values highlight how a thing conditions or causally relates to another (or others). The sun is valuable for the heat it produces; breathable air for human sustenance; water for the quenching of thirst, the cleansing of filth, the renewal of the soil, etc. Relational value is a variation of extrinsic value and focuses on the general patterns or environmental systems which integrate and structure the togetherness of things. Scientific theories and historical narratives capture the relational values of things, albeit not comprehensively. Closely related to both extrinsic value and relational value is perspectival value, of which there are two aspects. This is not the human perspective of the thing in question, but the perspective that thing itself has on a) the various values of the components which it integrates in order to constitute itself, and on b) its own place in the environment it finds itself. Perspectival value thus captures the processes through which a thing integrates the variety of things that condition it, picking out and preserving some aspects of its predecessors as more valuable and neglecting or discarding others that are less. The importance of perspectival value is most clearly seen in the history of marginalized people groups. Their perspectives are now being forced upon the consciousness of the majority as we have seen the destructive effects that can result from neglecting their perspectival values. In a similar way, the perspectives of nature itself need to be taken into account whenever we attempt to discern nature's values and norms.

Now each of these three sets of values are central to environmental ethics— among other applications—at two levels of analysis: how things relate to and effect other things; and how things relate to and effect human life and vice-versa. Of course, insofar as the human species is intent upon self-preservation, it is driven to develop an environmental ethic that enables preservation of the natural world and its flourishing. In short, we are most concerned with the values of anything "for others," especially for ourselves, and have worked hard to engage the world normatively precisely because our own well being is at stake. For these same reasons, the imagination is most at home when attempting to discern especially extrinsic and relational values since we are most interested in those things which bring us the greatest comfort, ease, and satisfaction. Our harmonious co-existence with and in the environment and its relationship to

[1] Note that I am bringing together here what Neville treats separately and in different order. I am not sure if he would agree with my re-arrangement, specifically in my categorizing perspectival, extrinsic, and relational value as highlighting cosmological relationality. So this is my own reading of Neville for my own purposes. I would like to think that I am being faithful to his own ideas, and just adapting them for another discussion.

us most efficiently accomplishes these human objectives. Perspectival values are a bit more difficult to access. Our efforts to do so has brought about multi-disciplinary approaches to human inquiry. As important to registering the perspectival values of things is the development of empathy. Insofar as the pneumatological imagination illuminates not only the other's radical alterity, but also, paradoxically, the perichoretic interrelationality that envelops the self and the other, to that extent the pneumatological imagination sustains the self's quest to engage the other not only as other, but as oneself. This nurtures the self's capacity to look at the world from the perspective of the other.

However, close attention to the question of why things have perspectival, extrinsic and relational value leads us to see that these values are intimately connected to the *intrinsic value* and the *singular value* of things. Things have value for others only insofar as they are valuable on their own terms apart from whatever benefits we may derive from them. In fact, a thing's perspectival value of itself in its environment—aspect (b) above—informs its perspectival evaluation of what to integrate or discard from the values brought to it by its components—aspect (a) above. This is why multi-disciplinary approaches to aspect (b) of perspectival values are so important: nature does not talk to us as marginalized people groups do, and discernment thus needs to proceed empirically in order to identify the norms by which nature makes it integrative decisions. The same goes for discerning intrinsic values that identify the achievement of values in the thing itself regardless of—even if connected with—its perspectival, extrinsic, and relational importances. Here, the focus is most explicitly on aesthetic value. The person's intrinsic rationality, the painting's intrinsic excellence, the sunset's intrinsic sublimity—each points to the ordered harmony of a multitude of components. Yet it is precisely each thing's intrinsic value derivative from its utter uniqueness as a harmony of just these components in just this order, which are, in turn, harmonies of other components, and so on, which points to that thing's singular value. A thing's singular value is that thing's immense worth, its "infinite and incomparable value" (Neville 1995, 85–90). Now since a thing's value is infinite, it is not representable or expressible in any theoretical language. Herein we re-encounter the partiality of knowledge which we then saw emergent in the context-less signification of the face. Yet confessing our inability to articulate a thing's infinite worth does not mean we ignore its singular value. In fact, our imagination does recognize the utter uniqueness of objects of knowledge and does register its complexity, even if always only partially. In that sense, the imagination acknowledges singular values.

Neville thus uses the language of "pious deference" to refer to the ways in which we should therefore approach each thing, unable to discourse about its infinite worth, but conceding its singular presence and developing attitudes appropriate to the fact that we are in the presence of such things that make certain claims upon us. As such, engagement with anything is measured by what Neville calls "norms of deference" (1995, ch. 5, esp. 124–27). These norms obligate our conscious engagement with the world to affirm singular value, to register intrinsic value, and, to some degree, to inquire into perspectival value. Practically, norms of deference focus on

> the independent careers, the independent natural integrities, the centered perspec-
> tives of the components on the world, noting the prices paid by the imposed or-
> ders. It means attending to family connections and feelings, to the impulses and
> passions of kinship, friendship, ethnicity, and other components of social life that
> might be subordinated for the sake of a just order. It means honoring for their own
> sake the plants and animals society uses as food, the natural environment ordered
> as a human habitat, the natural processes of metabolism, formation of atmospheres
> and ecological systems, geological processes, the forces of weather, the changes of
> seasons, microbes, and the social institutions that have their own history and worth
> somewhat irrespective of their contributions to or impedance of just social order.
> (Neville 1995, 118)

I would add that the pneumatological imagination should be most adept at recognizing singular value given that it seeks first and foremost to call atten-tion to the other rather than to the knowing self. As such, the pneumatological imagination recognizes the norms and values inherent in the other as other, and not just the other as related to us.

6.2.2 The preceding outlines the rationale of *why* we do engage nature nor-matively. Descriptive and normative responses were provided. On the one hand, nature in some ways imposes its norms on us and we learn, even if very slowly sometimes—witness our delayed response to the greenhouse effect—to pay attention to nature's values. On the other hand, we ought to pay attention to nature's norms insofar as we are creatures that find enjoyment in aesthetic value. Our discerning the norms by which nature's harmonies are produced and maintained enables us to appreciate nature's values with far greater inten-sity. Together, we see that both dimensions of nature's values—those for us and those in nature itself—combine to norm human engagement with nature ethically and aesthetically. Our task is to submit to the various norms of defer-ence in order to develop alternatives habits of engagement with the world so that we can interact responsibly with our environment and not only in a utilitarian fashion.

But *how* do we engage nature normatively? As already briefly noted, our phenomenological analysis of the face has been deepened through millennia of human relationships, through the dialogues and conversations we have had; through learning from each other where we have things right between us and where we do not, and so on. Yet our "conversation" with nature, while certainly not verbal, is no less dialogical. Nature does not present itself to us through the human face (although insofar as humans are natural beings, to that degree, the face does depict nature's identity as well), but through the broad spectrum of inferences derived from perception and sensation. Given that these inferences are the sole keys which unlock the secret of nature's mysteries, it is indeed remarkable that the human mind has so often abduced the correct hypothesis out of the very many false options available in order to understand nature. Peirce conjectured that since abduction is based on inference and all hypotheses are actually guesses, and since false hypotheses are infinitely far greater numerically than true ones, our remarkable guessing ability can be seen as evidence of the adaptation of the human mind to the world (5.591, 6.417, 7.39, 46). While Peirce drew from the terminology of Darwinian evolution in calling this ability Insight or Instinct (5.173, 7.687), he did not succumb to the Spencerian materialistic or mechanistic interpretation of the universe. Rather, this led to the view that both the world and humanity are signs to be interpreted (5.119, 314), which is in turn suggestive of the theological doctrine of the *imago Dei* (5.588, cf. 6.307). This is consistent with those working in contemporary physics who see the anthropic principle as affirming that "human intelligence is uniquely designed to disclose the patterns of order hidden in the physical universe" (Loder and Neidhardt 1992, 285; cf. Miller 1993).[2]

In drawing these connections, however, Peirce and contemporary physicists are simply participating—whether they are aware of it or not—in a conversation which has ancient roots. At the heart of this tradition is the conviction that the divine is symbolically revealed in two books: that of scripture and that of nature. The Psalmist declared long ago that "The heavens are telling the glory of God; and the firmament proclaims his handiwork" (19:1), even as Paul affirmed that God's "eternal power and divine nature, invisible though they are, have been understood and seen through the things he has made" (Rom. 1:19). The belief that nature and history were indeed revelatory of the

---

[2] It is therefore arguable that Peirce's is a naturalistic epistemology if by this is meant the continuity between mind and reality; see Maffie (1990).

divine motivated the development of the fourfold hermeneutic during the patristic period since it provided a means to account for the allegorical, moral and spiritual senses of the biblical text without dismissing the literal sense. In fact, the allegorical sense of Scripture is incomprehensible to us unless it is recognized as a premodern attempt to discern what was revelatory in the biblical accounts of natural and historical events. This conviction about nature and history as having deeper symbolic significance intensified during the medieval, Reformation and early modern periods. Individuals like Paracelsus, Bruno and Boehme were representative of movements such as hermeticism, Rosicrucianism, Renaissance, Reformation and Romantic mysticism, and later New England transcendentalism, all of which emphasized correspondences within and between the visible and invisible universes, between nature and the self, and between nature/history and the Bible (see Faivre 1994, and Faivre and Needleman 1992). Parallel developments included science's access to the mysteries of the world at an increasingly rapid rate. This expansion of knowledge buoyed confidence in the belief that nature was indeed correlated with the human imagination. Not coincidentally, of course, these same periods in the history of the Western world saw the emergence of the imagination as a productive faculty.

My point at present is not to jump into the hermeneutical issues which are the subject of the next part of the book. Rather, it is to highlight the long-standing idea that the natural world is not only what appears to the human senses on the surface, but is deeply significant and symbolic beyond its phenomenological manifestations. Here, I want to interact briefly with Karl Rahner's neo-Thomistic notion of symbolic representation as intrinsic to being's self-expression in order to come at the question of how nature is engaged normatively from another angle.

Rahner's theology of the symbol (1966) is focused on clearing the way for understanding the symbolic function of the heart of Jesus within the devotional practices of Roman Catholic piety. While the more strictly theological aspects of his theory will concern us in due time, for the moment, it is the philosophical underpinnings of Rahner's ideas of symbolism—the general meaning of the notion of symbol—that is interesting. This is characterized by the following summary statement: that all beings—"being" as a central Thomist category is synonymous with "thing" in the American philosophical tradition—are, by nature, symbolic since they necessarily manifest or express themselves in order to attain their own nature; and, conversely stated, that a symbol or symbolic reality is the self-realization or self-actualization of a being, and constitutes that being's essence. Now Rahner wants to distinguish genuine symbols from what he calls "arbitrary 'signs', 'signals' and 'codes' ('symbolic representations')," and attempts to do so by arguing that the former—genuine symbols—are those primary or primordial symbols which are ontologically grounded in the realities which they render present or which allows the things they symbolize to be re-presented, or "to be there" (1966, 225). But how do beings ground their symbols ontologically? Here, Rahner recourses to the neo-Thomistic metaphysics of being and develops the argument that all beings are pluralities-in-unity, the pluralities deriving from, expressing, disclosing, and fulfilling the original unity. In this way, "the symbol is the reality, constituted by the thing symbolized as an inner moment of moment of [sic] itself, which reveals and proclaims the thing symbolized, and is itself full of the thing symbolized, being its concrete form of existence" (1966, 251). One observes at work here the Platonic doctrine of images as participating in the reality of their exemplar.

Now Rahner's examples are all theological, connected as they are to the Catholic theology of sacraments. Yet it would be instructive to follow him a bit in this discussion at this point not in order to jump from a philosophy of the symbol to a theology of the symbol, but in order to explore further how nature is engaged semiotically and normatively. Certainly, the Church as the sacrament of salvation is "the persisting presence of the incarnate Word in space and time" that makes God's saving grace present to human beings; the plurality of the Church's members are each a symbolic expression of the presence of Jesus by the Spirit. Equally certain, the seven sacraments of the Church effectively mediate the grace of God which constitutes them as sacraments precisely by passing over into them (Rahner 1966, 240).[3] To enter into relationship with the body of Christ and to partake of the sacraments is to enter into a (saving) relationship with the triune God. But from these considerations, Rahner proceeds to follow out the distinction made previously between primordial and derivative sacramental symbols: "The only question is whether sacred images in the strict sense—statues and pictures—may be explained without more ado in terms of the symbol of the primordial type which we have discussed; or whether such images belong to the class of derivative and secondary symbols, which of course exist, as a result of relatively arbitrary arrangements and conventions" (1966, 243). While the seven sacraments are considered as belonging to the former class of symbols, Rahner is raising the

---

[3] For more on Rahner's theology of the sacraments, see Rahner (1963; 1982, 411–30). Stephen M. Fields, SJ (2000, ch. 3), also discusses Rahner's symbolic theology of the sacraments within a larger historical discussion of the idea of symbol from Aquinas through Heidegger and Neo-Thomism.

question, I think, of whether other kinds of relics, iconography, the (community of) saints, the sign of the cross, and the like, are primordial symbols of the same order as that of the sacraments.

It is here that I think Peirce's classification of signs can be of assistance. Recall that there are three types of signs: iconic, which signify by reproduction (or, re-presentation), indexical which signify by causal connectedness, and symbolic, which signify according to social conventions. Since Rahner's musings about symbols in general are situated within the Platonic framework of participation, arguably his philosophy of symbolism elevates indexical signs as more primordial than what Peirce calls iconic or symbolic—the latter two dubbed by Rahner as derivative or secondary symbols. But if Peirce is right, and I believe he is, then sacraments, relics, iconography, liturgies, etc., each convey certain qualities, facts, and laws to the devotee, even as different kinds of signs might refer iconically, indexically or symbolically, or, alternatively, the same sign could refer in this triadic way on different occasions. Partaking of the Eucharist, for example, would refer iconically to the Last Supper, indexically to common fellowship of believers with each other gathered in unity around the risen Christ, and symbolically to the bread and wine representing fellowship or consumption of Jesus as the source of new life. More important, to partake of the Eucharist can also be understood qualitatively as the process of ingesting the bread and the wine, factually as engaging the otherness of the bread and wine which function indexically to bring to memory the paschal suffering of Jesus, and legally as participating and indwelling the field of force unleashed by the life, death and resurrection of Jesus and manifest by and through the eucharistic community.

In this regard, the exercise of the pneumatological imagination is especially crucial since its christomorphic character mediates the field of force instantiated by the incarnation, death, and resurrection of the Word. Jesus is made present (in Rahner's terms) in the eucharistic fellowship precisely by the Spirit's symbolic reconstitution of Jesus' activity, words, vision, and sacrificial life. Thus it is that the pneumatological imagination alerts us to the underlying currents, the legal dispositions, and the affective and spiritual power released through the incarnational and pentecostal events, and which continue to infuse the semiotic world that Christians interacts with. In this sense, both Peirceans and Rahnerians can agree that engagement with the sacraments is not just a psychological or existential exercise, but a means of relating to a deeper world of meaning and significance.

6.2.3 Having said that, there are also differences between Rahner and Peirce. Chiefly, Rahner begins with the pervasive "need" of being to constitute itself symbolically while Peirce begins with the pervasive activity of human knowing that engages the world semiotically. These two approaches actually complement each other. In order to see this clearly, I want to draw into the conversation the work of Jonathan Edwards as a bridge between the ontological and epistemological orders.

The typological exegesis central to Edwards' theology of nature enables us to further appreciate the Scripture-and-nature-as-the-two-books-of-revelation tradition. Now it should certainly be denied that Edwards participated wholly in the occultism that stretched from Paracelsus to Boehme. This is clearly seen in his rejection of the spiritual exegesis of the Cabalists and certain Anglican and Catholic movements of his time. The result, to be avoided, was their "turning all into nothing but allegory and not having it to be true history" (Edwards 1993, 151). On the other side, Edwards also polemicized against deists and Enlightenment rationalists who denied the validity of typological reality altogether. Against these, Edwards affirmed, anticipating Peirce, the mind's affinity with nature (1993, 74).

Yet for Edwards, the significance of this affinity was not only epistemological but ontological and theological. This is because nature as a whole contains types—or, images, shadows, representations, vestiges, traces, or symbols, each of these being synonymous with types in Edwards' reflections on this topic— which point to the truth of the spiritual world. As he put it:

> The system of created beings may be divided into two parts, the typical world and the antitypical world. The inferior and carnal, i.e. the more external and transitory part of the universe, that part of it which is inchoative, imperfect and subservient, is typical of the superior, more spiritual, perfect and durable part of it, which is the end and as it were the substance and consummation of the other. Thus the material and natural world is typical of the moral, spiritual and intelligent world... (1993, 191)

This insight contains Edwards' response to two specific deistic objections: the theological one that God is far removed from the mundane events of the world, and the moral one regarding the inaccessibility of specific revelation to the majority of the world's inhabitants. Yet the revelation of God through nature's signs is not only for unbelievers but also for believers who yearn to be instructed about the character and reality of God. Thus Edwards concludes the "Images of Divine Things" by saying:

The immense magnificence of the visible world, its inconceivable vastness, the incomprehensible height of the heavens, etc. is but a type of the infinite magnificence, height and glory of God's work in the spiritual world: the most incomprehensible expression of his power, wisdom, holiness and love, in what is wrought and brought to pass in that world. (1993, 129–30)[4]

In saying this, Edwards was not undermining the crucial role of Scripture in divine revelation. In fact, however, his insistence on the priority of Scripture for understanding divine revelation underscored all the more the import of discerning revelation in history and nature as well since the Bible itself testified to such revelation. But Edwards went one step further. In as much as the Scriptures witness to the books of nature as revelatory, only a theological semiotic that—again anticipating Peirce—insisted on an ongoing, dynamic, and eschatological hermeneutic could take seriously the book of nature and the infinite complexity of nature's signs. Such a hermeneutic was, therefore, prerequisite to the task of correlating natural and specific revelation in a genuinely dialectical manner. Edwards therefore affirmed:

I am not ashamed to own that I believe that the whole universe, heaven and earth, air and seas, and the divine constitution and history of the holy Scriptures, be full of images of divine things, as full as a language is of words; and that the multitude of those things that I have mentioned are but a very small part of what is really intended to be signified and typified by these things: but that there is room for persons to be learning more and more of this language and seeing more of that which is declared in it to the end of the world *without discovering all*.... To say that we must not say that such things are types of these and those things unless the Scripture has expressly taught us that they are so, is as unreasonable to say that we are not to interpret any prophecies of Scripture or apply them to these and those events, except we find them interpreted to our hand, and must interpret not more of the prophecies of David, etc. *For by the Scripture it is plain that innumerable other things are types that are not interpreted in Scripture* (all the ordinances of the Law are all shadows of good things to come), in like manner as it is plain by Scripture that these and those passages that are not actually interpreted are yet predictions of future events. (1993, 152; emphases added)

---

[4] Here, Edwards' proximity to the medieval mystical tradition which understood the universe to be the self-expression of God, the divine exemplar, is evident. He also anticipated Emerson's pantheistically tinged vision of nature as symbolic of spirit, and Royce's idea—inspired by Peirce—of a metaphysics of universal community interpreted by the Spirit of that community. For more on the American context of Edwards' ruminations about typology, see the "Introduction" by Perry Miller (1948, 1–41).

Edwards provides linkages between Rahner and Peirce at two levels. First, he affirms, with both, that nature is symbolically (Rahner) or semiotically (Peirce) revelatory of the divine. Rahner provides the most explicit theological rationale for this in his christological starting point: that the Father expresses the divine nature in the Logos, and that through the Logos, "All things are held together by the incarnate Word in whom they exist (Col. 1:17), and hence all things possess, even in their quality of symbol, an unfathomable depth, which faith alone can sound" (1966, 239).[5] The result is a thoroughgoing semiotic conception of the world—effectively, a symbolics of nature. This means that phenomenal reality is revelatory—of its own depths, of its connections (its relations), and of its otherness (Edwards' "antitype"; Rahner's "being"; Peirce's "reality"). Neither in the neo-Thomism of Rahner nor in the American tradition of Edwards and Peirce is reading the book of nature to be understood in the esoteric or occultic senses. Whereas esoteric traditions look for the deeper cosmic meanings finally focused on self-transformation within a pantheistic worldview, the semiotic and theological approaches described here include self-transformation in the give-and-take relationship between God-self-and-world.

Second, Edwards understanding about nature's typological character derived from his conviction that creation is the extension, the repetition in time, of God's eternal movement. God's living actuality does not preclude in the divine life a dispositional dynamic which shapes first and foremost the eternal self-communication of the intra-trinitarian relationality. More important for our purposes, however, is that this dispositional essence communicates ad extra, and in doing so extends "being" to the world in order that the world may reflect the glory, power, and character of God (cf. Lee 2000 and Boyd 1992). In this sense, the world is an expression of the dispositional overflow or effulgence of divine glory, and creation as a whole reveals, piecemeal to be sure, the glory of God. Thus nature is to be understood as the interpretant (to use Peirce's term) of God's glory, and our interpretation of the world is our engagement with the glory of God, refracted, that is, through the created order. Edwards' notion of disposition as characterizing the divine activity parallels Rahner's insistence that being constitutes or realizes its unity symbolically through the plurality of otherness. Further, and more importantly, Edwards' disposition

---

[5] For more on Rahner's theology of symbol applied to christology, see Wong (1984: esp. Part Two). But note that while Rahner is explicit in this essay that the christological starting point is also a trinitarian one, as I have argued in chapter two of this book, a truly trinitarian starting point is necessarily pneumatological. On this score, Rahner's theology of the symbol is insufficiently pneumatological and hence, not fully trinitarian.

also anticipates Peirce's Thirdness (law, habit, tendency).[6] In Peircean terms, the world is revelatory precisely because lived experience engages not only qualities and facts, but laws and generalities. Put another way, it is because the habits of thinking are shaped by the habits of the world that the mind is able to grasp the patterns, purposes, and intentions of the created order, and hence of the world's creator.

Here again reflection on the means through which human beings engage nature normatively unveils the activity of the pneumatological imagination, even if such operates most often at the unconscious or subconscious levels. As already noted, in as much as the pneumatological imagination is oriented not only toward the factual and concrete but also toward the dispositional or spiritual dimensions of the world, it is thereby sensitized and attuned to engaging just those features of reality which are ignored or denied by nominalistic and materialistic worldviews. Further, and more to the present point, if normative engagement with the world involves deferring to the qualities, facts, and laws through which the other presents itself, then insofar as pneumatological imagination insists on pointing away from itself toward the other, it is to that extent poised precisely for such normative deference. Finally, the pneumatological imagination is at home with the triadic and communitarian structure of normative engagement. The world is engaged semiotically (inferentially utilizing signs) and communally (involving communities of inquirers). Human beings learn pragmatically and from one another about the qualities, facts, and laws of nature. In the process, they develop and transform habits and tendencies that enable more and more efficient engagement with nature even while continuously learning to defer to nature's perspectives and values. The goal is to nurture transformative practices which are congruent with the kind of world in which we live, which respects the worlds and is sensitive to its demands on us, and which recognizes not only our dependence on nature but the delicate mutuality and interdependence of nature and history.

6.3 Normative Engagement: Toward a Theological Semiotic

We are on the home stretch of the epistemological problematic that clears the way for the hermeneutical and methodological inquiry that is at the heart of this essay. But one more set of questions needs to be addressed before taking

---

[6] It is doubtful if Peirce ever read Edwards. Sang Hyun Lee (2000, 16 n 3) is probably correct to speculate that the similarities of their positions here and at other points can be traced to their grappling with the limitations of Locke, Hume, and the nominalist tradition of the West.

up that task. If, in light of the preceding discussions whereby both the symbolics of community and the symbolics of nature opened up toward the encounter with the divine, is there, then, a specifically theological semiotic? Is there a distinctly religious experience, or an explicitly religious encounter through which the divine is truly and normatively engaged? The answer may already be included in the framework of the question in that a theological semiotic presupposes that signs in all of their variety mediate human encounter with and knowledge of God. The implications of this move, however, needs to be addressed in some detail, and I propose to do so by dealing with the normative implications and the normative demands of a theological semiotic. The concluding sub-section will summarize the findings of the book so far.

6.3.1 The argument so far is that normative engagement with other persons and with the natural world at some point lead to our encounter with the divine. Levinas' insistence that the face-to-face relationship confronts us at some level with the person of God is deeply rooted in the Hebraic imagination which considers the ethical realm as the normative barometer of the individual's and the community's interaction with Yahweh. It also finds expression in Jesus' teaching that judgment will be meted out according to how we treat the hungry, the thirsty, the stranger, the naked, the sick, and those in prison since our response to those in need is precisely our response to him (Matt. 25:31–46; cf. James 2:14–17; 1 John 3:17 and 4:20–21). Yet the face of God, otherwise hidden, is revealed not only in the face of our neighbor, but also typologically and semiotically in the natural world. Edwards and Peirce, along with Rahner, each understood in their own way that to engage with nature is to be engaged with signs and symbols pointing to the divine. Both in our engagement with the others and with the world, the pneumatological imagination is at work, carrying over the divine reality into lived experience.

The question is whether or not there is a direct experience of the divine apart from our experiences of and with each other and the world. The surest way to confront the full force of this question is to examine the most explicit theological mediations acknowledged by Christians: that of incarnation and Pentecost—i.e., the historical Jesus and the living ecclesia. Is it the case that both are direct experiences of the divine? Is looking into the face of Jesus phenomenologically different than looking into that of Levinas'? It would be difficult to make this argument for a variety of reasons. For one, even Jesus himself affirmed to Peter that his confession regarding Jesus' messianic identity was not something that Peter arrived at on his own cognitive capacities, but, rather, was revealed to Peter by the Father (Matt. 16:17). For another, according to the previous accounts, even the face-to-face relationship is perceptually mediated. The encounter with the divine through Jesus of Nazareth is therefore unavoidably semiotic—in Peirce's terms, the inferential activity of interpreting perceptual judgments and perceptual facts emergent from engaging the Galilean. Finally, and most importantly, Jesus' own divine identity could only be discerned through the Spirit's inspiration, what I have called here the pneumatological imagination. And, of course, prior to Jesus' glorification, the Spirit was not yet given (John 7:39). *how broadly?*

The question therefore turns to whether or not there is a direct pentecostal experience of God through the Spirit? Mystics, enthusiasts, charismatics and modern Pentecostals—nothing pejorative is meant with these characterizations—have all claimed such direct encounters with God throughout the ages. If Peirce is right, and I believe he is close to the truth, then the cultural-linguistic argument has got the better of the experiential-expressivist argument—to use Lindbeck's (1984) terminology—on this question.[7] To say that theological reflection is mediated semiotically is to affirm that religious knowledge is communicated through a variety of forms—i.e., through evoking a sense of the plenitude or depth dimension of perceptible signs (as in glossolalic prayer, or meditative contemplation); through propositional or literal statements (as in the recitation of a creed, or the reading of Scripture); through experiential attitudes, feelings, and activities (as in liturgical participation), and so on (cf. Dulles 1992, 18–19). Put epistemically, all knowledge is semiotically mediated and therefore at least one step (or sign) removed from the richness of experience. Put experientially, the first Christians experienced the Spirit through the violent rushing wind, through the tongues of fire which alighted on each of them, through stammering lips and strange tongues, all of which were interpreted or understood, at least in part, through the sacred writings (cf. Acts 2:16ff. draws from Joel 2:28ff; and 1 Cor. 14:21 quotes Isa. 28:11–12). Put theologically, Christians experience Jesus through the pneumatically constituted body of Christ. To be sure, the Spirit's work to inspire a specifically pneumatological imagination is required in order for a more accurate apprehension of the significance of each of these encounters as more than just particular experiential phenomena. The same pneumatological imagination is also of central import for a graciously transformed life. And, certainly, apart from the activity of the

---

[7] My agreement with Lindbeck here is not a complete endorsement of his theory. Wittgenstein and the Yale School taken in certain directions runs up against the problems of truth and that of cross-cultural engagement; I make the necessary adjustments to Lindbeck's main point elsewhere [see 5.2.2 and 9.3.2].

pneumatological imagination, the normative bearings of the encounter with
Jesus and the body of Christ are either ignored or overlooked altogether.

The important point to register here is that the emergent epistemology of
the divine—how human beings can experience and come to know divinity—
can be conceived as a theological semiotic which would include within its com-
pass a symbolics of human community and a symbolics of nature. And, insofar as knowledge of the divine is conveyed semiotically, it provides a norm by
which to gauge claims regarding the human encounter with and experience of
God. The normative implications of the theological semiotic—respecting what
it tell us about itself as an abstract account of how human beings know divinity—can now be explicated briefly along two lines.

First, as mediated, all theological knowledge can be characterized under
the rule of analogy which says that all theological symbols communicate the
divine reality through similarities-in-differences. "The Lord is my shepherd"
means that God cares for us like a shepherd cares for her sheep; but it also
means that God is unlike human shepherds who slumber and sleep, are for-
getful, and oftentimes negligent, etc. Analogies always break down at the point
of difference. This applies to the various cognitive and linguistic tools (semantics) which carry semiotic meaning. In fact, given that knowledge in general
and theological knowledge more specifically emerges from the convergence of
evaluative, affective, and intellectual operations, it should not be surprising to
note that religious language includes not only propositional assertions but
also a variety of genres appropriate to the affective and imaginative dimension
of engagement such as poetry, lyric song, prophecy, metaphors, myths, narratives, parables, etc. Yet for theological purposes, each of these semiotic carriers
operate analogically. More importantly, they are, by their very nature, "open-
ended" (Green 1998, 69–70). Religious metaphors most clearly illustrate this
analogical rule: "The Lord is my shepherd" evokes distinctive feelings in those
at home in agrarian and rural cultures compared to those adapted to urban
environments. Its metaphorical power, however, is demonstrated precisely by
its translatability into the latter context, whether it be into the language of a
video culture—God as the "all-seeing eye"—or into the language of efforts
amidst the nuclear age to restore community—"God's care over us exceeds
that provided by the neighborhood watch."[8] Of course, this openendedness

[8] For an overview of the importance of semiotics to religious studies in general, see Fawcett
(1971) and Long (1986). On religious and theological language as metaphorical, see, e.g., The
Entrevernes Group (1978), McFague TeSelle (1975), McFague (1982), and Avis (1999, 93–102). J.

Christians in dialogue w/ postmodern ideas should be even more aware of their presuppositions.

now

means that religious metaphors, as with all semiotic carriers, should never prohibit ongoing inquiry by posing as the "final word." But such open-endedness is intrinsic to the processes of human knowing in general as well, so that it applies theologically should be of no special concern. Further, as we have seen earlier, such open-endedness marks an essential feature of the pneumatological imagination itself.

Second, as mediated, analogical, and conveyed semiotically through finite signs, symbols, metaphors, etc., all theological knowledge both reveals and conceals its object simultaneously. God is thereby always both disclosed and hidden, and theological semiotics is both cataphatic and apophatic. Here, the analogy between the openendedness of epistemic processes in general and the openendedness of theological knowledge more specifically holds ontologically as well. If the face is infinitely significant because it transcends all contextualization, and if nature at each of its levels is infinitely dense and valuable thereby requiring ongoing interpretation and engagement for understanding, why would we consider the theological "object"—God—to be an ontological exception to the rule? The face reveals, even as it conceals. Nature reveals precisely because much is concealed and awaits further inquiry. And, as Gareth Jones notes, since theology proceeds from the interplay of rhetoric, event, and mystery, then divine revelation—manifestations, narratives, discourses, even the Christ event—will always both reveal and conceal as well; in short, "revelation is always simultaneously concealment" (Jones 1995, 243) ? *it*

Yes, / infers /bual / conceal this / but this

Here, all the conditions pertinent to epistemic fallibility in general are applicable as well. Human fallenness hinders us from the full knowledge of the glory of God (Exod. 33:20). Human embodiment limits our perspective on the divine to that which emerges from our fragmentary experience of Holy Saturday—our locatedness in Hell's "silence," our wandering in the wilderness, our living in exile from the land of promise, all of which symbolize the endless deferral of human signs, of language—that is situated between the creation and fall of Good Friday and the anticipated eschatological unveiling of Easter Sunday (cf. 1 John 3:2b) (cf. von Balthasar 1990; Lewis 2001). Theological knowledge is always partial not only because our finite minds can only comprehend finitely (1 Cor. 13:12), but also because of the inexhaustibility of what is knowable about all things, and especially about the "object" of theology: God. Here it is important to insist, with Eberhard Jüngel (1983, esp. 250–55), that

Wentzel van Huysteen (1989, 126–42) correctly points out that the contemporary fascination of the role of metaphor in theology is not new, but is rather the medieval notion of analogy—understanding differences through partial similarities—reworked by recent philosophy of language.

God is mystery not only in the negative epistemic sense of being incomprehensible to finite human minds, but also in the positive ontic sense of being uncircumscribable even when grasped through revelation. This points to a theological and eschatological (rather than metaphysical) sense in which the divine life remains incomplete. God as eternal creator is *actus purus* between Alpha (aboriginal finishedness) and Omega (eschatological consummation and unfinishedness). Thus, rationality does not exhaust reality in the sense that there is also a non-rational (not irrational) element to all knowing which represents the vague—not wholly determinate—possibilities of the future. In this sense, theological knowledge is inexpressible (2 Cor. 12:4). Yet to make the apophatic move at this juncture is not to endorse the claim that nothing can be known of the divine since, as Christian faith asserts, God has revealed himself incarnationally and pentecostally. As D. Z. Phillips notes, "religious mysteries are not epistemological mysteries" (1988, 265) because while the latter admits the perplexity that follows on our inability to know things, the former does not (we make all kinds of claims to know God, etc.). In the end, theological knowledge has the apophatic moment built into it, as in the notion that we know a mysterious God.

6.3.2 Is it the case, then, as Sharon Warner (2000, 257) says, that "to know mystery is to realize that knowing is not essentially about gaining certitude but about embracing ambiguity"? Here, I want to probe the normative obligations of theological knowledge as that which requires a robustly dynamic hermeneutical stance. My entryway into the discussion will be to return full circle to the starting point of this discussion on epistemology and re-engage the pneumatological imagination.

The ambiguity of meanings inherent in the pneumatological symbols has already been briefly noted (1.3.1). To quickly recapitulate, the biblical data is itself replete with ambiguity, paradox and conflict regarding the biblical symbols of the Spirit (cf. Wallace 1996). This other "darker" side of biblical pneumatology needs to be recognized in order not only to deconstruct the symbol, but to highlight that the healing, reconciling and renewing work of the Spirit in the biblical narratives is meaningful precisely because it emerges through discontinuities, caesuras, and "dark nights" of the soul. Not just with regard to the new birth accomplished by the Spirit from the darkness of the cross, the primary pneumatological symbols in Scripture—water, fire, and wind (cf. Oden 1994, 41–44)—are also suggestive here. Water is a source of life and yet also a means of death, especially when unleashed as floods. Fire is heat-producing and yet destructive. Wind is refreshing on the one hand, and unpredictably destructive on the other. Because "spirit" as wind serves as a contrast with material or concrete reality, it is at times utterly ambiguous and, as the Johannine account indicates, unperceptible in terms of its sources and unpredictable in terms of its outcomes (John 3:8). And yet, its effects always appear to be tangible, whether positively or negatively construed. Thus, on the one hand, wind can be seen to work creatively and constructively, as in the creation narrative whereby the Logos comes forth from the Spirit's hovering over the waters; as in the wind that dried the earth after the primeval flood; or as in the wind that brought quail to the Israelites in the desert. On the other hand, it can also be seen to function destructively, as in the havoc wreaked on Egypt by the locust-bearing winds; as in the means of the devastation of Pharaoh's army in the Red Sea; or as in the source of death for Job's household. The ambiguity of wind is perhaps most clearly seen in the analogy of human life as ephemeral breath (e.g., Job 7:7, Ps. 78:39, 103:15–16).

Here, it is prudent to heed to admonitions of Robert Corrington, himself a Peirce scholar and subtle philosophical theologian. Corrington's retrieval of Peirce is accomplished with the help of Dewey's naturalism and Justus Buchler's ordinal metaphysics. His semiotic theory of nature is a radical alternative to Rahner's neo-Thomistic and Platonic theory of symbols sketched above. The result is that Corrington warns against the kind of utopian idealism which the later Peirce himself was cautious about. Such idealism overlooks the decay, conflict, tragedy, waste, caesuras, fragmentariness, disorder, ambiguity, melancholiness, and, indeed, meaninglessness, both in nature and in lived-experience. Yet if nothing else, work in psychoanalysis since Peirce has alerted us to what Corrington calls the *underconscious* of nature, the mystery of all that "spirit" represents, not that which is beyond language, but that which is underneath language. Corrington therefore proposes a psycho-semiotic perspective that emphasizes the vastness of nature's signs, much of which has yet to be engaged by our anthropocentrically motivated concerns. Such an approach would be more sensitive to and better able to call our attention to the ruptures, tragedies, conflicts, and ambiguities inherent in lived-experience which narrative frameworks either neglect, ignore, or are unable to register fully (cf. Corrington 1992; 1994; 1996; 1997; 2000).

Two normative demands follow with regard to theological knowledge. First, the pneumatological imagination's engagement with the divine needs to ride the tension between its distinctively christomorphic shape that unveils the divine with clarity on the one hand, and its ambiguously anthropocentric intentionality that veils the divine with obscurity on the other. Yes, the pneumatological imagination leads us to the knowledge of God by pointing to Jesus. Yes, the same imagination also leads us to the knowledge of God through the ambiguities inherent in the faces of others, and in the book of nature. But, insofar as both avenues are traversed semiotically, accessing the meaning of Jesus, others, and the world itself are ongoing dynamic and unfinished acts of interpretation.

Second, and derivative from the first, that the pneumatological imagination consistently points beyond itself toward the other requires that the semiotic character of theological knowledge also be taken seriously as continuously pointing beyond itself. The human tendency is to alleviate doubts by developing habits of thought and practice which are fairly stable. Yet, as any spouse will testify, relating to one's significant other only habitually leads to a stagnant and unfulfilling marriage relationship. To be sure, no marriage relationship survives on spontaneity. What is normative for most is spontaneity amidst stability, or discontinuity amidst continuity. Translated theologically, our knowledge of God as unavoidably semiotic (continuity) should include moments when such habits of interpretation are interrupted, as when the Spirit freely "breaks into" our rituals and liturgies. On the anthropological side, this points to the tension between our theological and religious symbols having some kind of stability on the one side, while yet also being radically provisional on the other. This means that the signs and symbols through which we encounter and engage the divine should never attain the kind of ultimacy that belongs to God alone. Recognizing the semiotic character of theological knowledge ought, therefore, to alert us to continually recognize that they point to the divine reality only fragmentarily, in certain respects, from various perspectives, for different purposes, etc., and never absolutely. As such theological semiotics demands resistance against the tendency to absolutize the signs and symbols that mediate the divine. In the language of Paul Tillich, religious and theological symbols taken to refer absolutely to the divine should be broken in order to neutralize their capacity to function as idols. If not broken, symbols reduce the divine reality to the symbolic phenomena and cease to point beyond themselves to their divine object (cf. Tillich 1957, 48–54; 1960; 1961).

The problem with idolatry in this context, however, should be made clear. In the first place, idolatry is the result of insisting on the reduction of the infinitude of the divine reality to solely finite terms. Over time, this means that attention is focused on the symbol itself and habits are formed which engage the symbol rather than that to which it points. As a result, the symbols loses the capacity to enable true engagement with the divine. When this happens, multiple idols emerge since finite realities can never satisfy ultimate concerns, and the habits of interpretation will transfer allegiances from one interpretant to the next in search of its holy grail. Alternatively, idolatry breeds destructive habits that derive from the self-absorbing nature of the idolatrous symbol. Emergent are demonic realities bent on intensifying the radically finite character of all religious and theological symbols such that not only do the symbols not point beyond themselves to the divine (a passive stance), but they mobilize habits of resistance to the very divine realities they originally witnessed to (an active field of demonic force). In fact, it is fair to say, given the dispositional character of all reality, that there are no purely neutral signs, symbols or semiotic systems as such since all habits, tendencies and legalities—reality's Thirdness—are trajectories in one direction (the divine) or other (the demonic). Thus, the spiritual gift of discernment of spirits enabled by the pneumatological imagination is crucial for identifying and countering the qualities, reactions, and illegitimate forces of demonically inspired symbols. More to the point, normative engagement with the divine cannot proceed effectively or in a sustained manner apart from the discerning function of the pneumatological imagination.

When actively engaged, however, the pneumatological imagination grasps the divine reality with ever-increasing intensity not only in the ecclesial context, but in and through every single perception or apprehension. The mundane otherness of history (Levinas) and of nature (Edwards and Rahner) become revelatory of the divine as inspired by the Spirit. And, insofar as such revelation does occur, human beings are placed under obligation to respond normatively in certain ways. Of course, one's capacity to discern the divine could simply be dulled, and one could resist the Spirit's work of bringing about a transformed imagination. Or, one could refuse to acknowledge the normative structures of what is engaged, or insist on imposing one's own perspectives, values, and structures on the historical or natural other. Or, one could use the other as a means toward one's own ends, and deny either the integrity of the other or the other's mediatory significance regarding the divine. Such idolatry that elevates either the self or the other to ultimate status is directed toward the satisfaction of self-serving and destructive ends. In each case, only a pneumatically inspired imagination can counteract the emergent habits of interpretation because it continuously directs attention beyond itself to the other as other.

6.3.3 The main lines of the hermeneutical and methodological framework has now been established and should be quickly summarized. We began our journey with the intention of testing out the hypothesis that pneumatology characterized vaguely according to the categories of relationality, rationality, and dynamic life may provide insights into the perennial human mysteries of being, of knowing, and of interpretation. Seeking understanding in faith, we turned first to the biblical narratives to see if such a vague categorization could be sustained exegetically and hermeneutically. The results were sufficiently promising so as to enable our exploration of the theological implications of pneumatology so conceived.

We next tested the hypothesis that pneumatology was crucial to a robustly trinitarian theology. This was confirmed in both of the trinitarian models we analyzed, and that in more than one way. The two hands model was seen to open up to a truly relationality mutuality between Spirit and Word so as to be rich in resources to combat the historical subordinationism of the Spirit to the Word; it also brought home the truth that knowledge of the Father is mediated through the Word and the Spirit. The mutual love model featured not only the Spirit's completion of the Father-Son relationship, but also the Spirit's donative character of deflecting attention from herself and bestowing such on the Father and the Son; it also highlighted the fact that knowledge of the divine is experienced soteriologically and dynamically, thus unveiling an eschatological dimension to the trinitarian life of God. Together, the two models emphasized the triune coinherence of the divine life. Further, the claimed correlation, at least in some respects, of the order of knowing and experience with the order of being assumed at least a distinction between the orders rather than assuming human selves to be locked up solipsistically in the former or reducing either to the other. Finally, both models were suggestive with regard to understanding the God-world relationship itself, as constituted by Spirit and Word on the one hand, or as replicating ad extra the eternal divine movements on the other.

These aspects of trinitarian theology approached pneumatologically opened up naturally toward understanding reality ontologically and metaphysically in relational, realistic, and social terms. The process of establishing this proposed foundational pneumatology was guided by Peirce's phenomenological analysis of lived experience in terms of qualities, facts, and laws. That all experience reflects this triadic structure is significant not only epistemologically (the order of knowing) but also ontologically (the order of being). That our experience of qualities are abstracted from our experiences of facts and laws reflects the Christian conviction that the Father is known only through the Spirit and the Word. That facts are the undeniable over-and-againstness of experience—that given otherness confronts us at every turn—converges with the critical realist conviction that objects of knowledge exist apart from their being known, and with the trinitarian conviction that divinity is revealed in and through the historicity, particularity, and concreteness of the incarnation and Pentecost realistically conceived. That laws are real generalities that shape and interpret reality's processes hints at the presence of a pneumatologically inspired imagination that overcomes or is capable of overcoming the materialistic, positivistic, and nominalistic mentality characteristic of both the ancient world and the modern age. This discussion of the order of being—as relational, realistic, social—if true, would be epistemologically suggestive as well.

Part Two of this book turned to explore the epistemological implications of the foundational pneumatology. Starting with the Spirit, as this essay insists is not only appropriate but intrinsic to Christian theological reflection, provides the human imagination with specifically pneumatological features. If the imagination is both passive and active, holistically affective and spiritual, and intrinsically evaluative or valuational, then the pneumatological imagination is empowered actively by the divine breath, is attuned especially to the spiritual components of reality, and is structured normatively according to her christomorphic shape and trinitarian character.

Further, insofar as the Spirit consistently points beyond herself to the Father and the Son, so is the pneumatological imagination driven to engagement with the other that stand over and against the self. Such engagement, I argued, is thoroughly semiotic and therefore intrinsically hermeneutical (involving signs), triadic (signs as representing something to someone) and fallibilistic (interpretative processes as partial, perspectival, and finite). It is, however, directed toward the truth as constrained by the need to negotiate human life successfully and efficiently in a complex world of relationally given others and otherness. In this sense, truth can be understood in a dyadic sense as pointing to the correspondence between thought and external reality, even if access to such is triadically interpreted through pragmatic and coherentist criteria.

Finally, the pneumatological imagination's semiotic and truthful engagement with otherness is also normative with regard to the ethical and aesthetic dimensions of knowledge as both relate to human persons and the natural world. The normative aspects of lived experience assume and confirm reality as social and human life as communal. As important, normative engagement recognizes that otherness—human persons-in-community and the world itself—is the ultimate measure of our interpretations. And, insofar as our semiotic engagement with otherness mediates not only our encounter with divinity itself but also our indwelling and participating in the divine life, to that extent, all interpretation is potentially theological, normative, and revelatory both of the divine and of God's relationship to human selves-with-others-and-in-the-world.

The journey thus far from pneumatology to trinitarian theology to a triadic metaphysics has thereby opened up toward a triadically structured epistemology. Theological knowledge can therefore be said to emerge semiotically by way of the pneumatological imagination's quest for truth as constrained normatively by the object(s) of engagement. Theological hermeneutics and theological method are thereby inherently triadic as well, both with regard to the activity of interpretation which is semiotically structured, and with regard to the three moments of imagination (Spirit), engagement (Word), and truthful normativity (Community). We are now finally ready to explore in earnest the hermeneutical and methodological implications of this triadic metaphor in an attempt to develop a pneumatological and trialectical approach to the knowledge of God.

PART THREE

Theological Interpretation: The Trialectic of Spirit-Word-Community

The time has now come to complete the argument for a pneumatological and trinitarian hermeneutic and theological method. The hermeneutical trialectic that is developed in the following pages is only in one sense a constructive proposal. It is more accurately defined as a consensual hermeneutic in that it attempts to bring together some basic Christian convictions regarding the circle of interpretation. I have called these convictions Spirit, Word, and Community. My argument to this point is the beginning with the Spirit leads toward a robust trinitarianism, and that this movement reflects both the shape of a hermeneutical theology and the intuitions of a theological hermeneutics. I have therefore argued that the activity of interpretation both includes theological, metaphysical (ontological) and epistemological assumptions even while such activity leads to the formulation of these aspects of a worldview. There is, therefore, a trialectical movement which sustains the activity of interpretation. Alternatively said, theological interpretation also can be said to involve the ongoing interplay of three factors: the activity of an interpreting subject, the data of an interpreted object or a set of interpreted objects, and the various contexts which interpreters and interpreting communities find themselves.[1] Each of these factors, however, is intrinsically related to the other two, albeit in different ways. Not insignificantly, it is this togetherness that signifies the convergence called theological interpretation.

The objectives of the last three chapters are threefold. First, I wish to provide a fairly detailed argument regarding theological interpretation as necessarily *trialectical* (with regard to given structures) and *trialogical* (with regard to methodological movement), modeled as it is after the perichoretic interrelationality

---

[1] Gabriel Fackre (1987) discusses these under the category of "authority"—options in authority; the text of authority; the context of authority—within the broader framework of Christ as the center, Scripture as the source, and the ecclesia as resource.

of the divine persons. Second, starting with the Spirit does not mean the neglect of the Word. The metaphysical insights regarding the inviolability of the object of knowledge here come into play, even while such "objectivity" is tempered by the recognition, since Descartes, of the three epistemological turns: to the subject, to language, and to community. Further, while the mutual love model justifies our starting with the Spirit, the two hands model requires the mutuality and reciprocity of Spirit and Word for theological hermeneutics and method. Finally, theological method, as Lonergan (1972) puts it, consists of recurrent operations performed by a community of inquirers which yield cumulative results. My thesis in this volume is that method in theology begins with the Spirit which is always informed in some respect by Word and Community, and moves through, not necessarily in sequential order, the moment of Word which is also never entirely bereft of either Spirit or Community, and the moment of Community which is also never entirely disconnected from Spirit and Word. Herein lies the relational, perichoretic and robustly trinitarian nature of the hermeneutical trialectic of interpretive acts (Spirit), interpretive objects (Word), and interpretive contexts (Community). Theological method itself is therefore also envisioned as consisting of these three interpretive moments analogous to Lonergan's recurrent operations—although metaphorically understood either in terms of a circle or of a spiral—and yielding cumulative theological results.

One caveat before proceeding. This proposal is set squarely within the framework of the fallibilistic epistemology previously proposed [5.3]. In this case, it claims no a priori necessity, and, if true, should provide a means for correcting the deficiencies of the model—a means that lies internal to the hermeneutical method that is being proposed. In other words, the question needs to be asked: How would the flaws, if any, of the hermeneutical trialectic be recognized? Let me suggest that insofar as the unpredictable winds of the Spirit provides the dynamic engine that drives the method, to that degree, the first moment has within itself the task of calling attention to whatever problems need to be addressed. Put another way, the preoccupation with theological hermeneutics and theological method since Schleiermacher may itself be read as a provocation of the Spirit to pay attention to the question of meaning (spirit) itself. If that is the case, then the Spirit is calling us to critical reflection on the linguistic and communitarian turns from a perspective that includes the turn to the subject. The result may be a transformed understanding of the turn to the subject toward an even more robustly trinitarian, and hence, trialectical, hermeneutic and methodology.

7 The Acts of Interpretation: Spirit

In this chapter, I will elaborate on the activity of interpretation as a subjective enterprise which nevertheless retains certain objective and communitarian aspects. The subjectivity of theological interpretation can be assessed from at least three perspective. First, the activity of interpretation involves persons in communities attempting to understand each other and the world around them. Given the previous discussion regarding persons as subjects created in the image of God, and, as such, understood as spiritual beings who have communion with the divine subject present and active as the Holy Spirit [1.2.3], theological interpretation is necessarily subjective because of the interpersonal relationships that comprise human existence and experience. Second, the activity of interpretation is a cognitive endeavor which is semiotically funded and, as such, trades on inferential abstractions [5.1.1 and 5.3.1]. In this way, interpretations are more or less vague ideas of experiences isolated for the purposes of understanding. The goal of interpretation is the generation of ideas that are true to the facts of experience. Curiously, then, the activity of interpretation results in a fusion of subject and object in a dynamic and dialectical relationship. Put another way, interpretation consists of a subjective reading of an objective fact. Finally, the activity of interpretation is always motivated by a problematic recognized by and relevant to the interpreter's situation and goals. Interpretive acts are, like everything else, not value-free, but teleologically driven. They are directed toward certain ends to the exclusion of other ends. The goal of interpreting truly or rightly is therefore motivated by the intuition that what I know includes a normative component requiring further activity: what ought I to do?

Much more can and should be said about the turn to the subject vis-à-vis theological interpretation. My goal, however, is not a treatise on subjectivity. Rather, the following discussion is motivated by the conviction that interpretation considered subjectively is itself a complex pneumatic activity involving persons in relationship to things (others and the world), and persons constituted by teleological intentions. Interpretation therefore includes an undeniably subjective moment. That said, interpretive subjectivity cannot be divorced from the other two moments of the trialectic. These will be the focus of our

221

attention in the next two chapters. For the moment, however, our attention is on the activity of interpretation.

7.1 The Activity of Interpretation and the Work of the Spirit

Central to the Christian tradition is the conviction that theological under-standing is a gift of God the Spirit (I Cor. 2:9–16) whereby the interpreter relies on the gracious (charismatic) activity of the Spirit to reveal and illumine di-vine truths. This requires the interpreter to be open to the unpredictable move-ments of the Spirit who "breaks in to" (or "breaks through") the interpreter's situation and enables interpretive activity to commence in and through the same Spirit. Key features of the Spirit's inspirational role in interpretation can be seen expressed in basic human activities such as the when the imagination is exercised creatively, when personal agency is freely and responsibly exhib-ited, and when the human being is grasped by what is otherwise transcendent. The following will discuss each in order without assuming that these features exhaust the Spirit's operational role in inspiring human interpretation.

7.1.1 Awareness of the historical situatedness and social locatedness of the interpreter has raised one of the central hermeneutical questions of our time: how is it that truly novel interpretations emerge? I will argue, according to the argument previously developed, that such novelty emerges in part through the creative faculty of the imagination. The imagination is not only world-affirming (re-productive) but also world-making (creative) [4.1.2]. It is the vehicle through which the self negotiates its engagement with the other so that both self and other are brought into a new relationship such that each is no longer opposed to the other. Clearly, the imagination is not a dis-incarnate vehicle that is abstracted from the conditions of the human body or the constraints of history. Rather, the imagination is valuational, affective, spiritual, and materially embodied. As such, it enables the full range of human life in the world precisely because is it partici-pates fully in these various dimensions of human existence.

But how does creative novelty emerge imaginatively? According to foundational pneumatology, through the process of conversion. I would suggest, following Donald Gelpi (1998), that there are five basic forms of conversion: affective, intellectual, moral, sociopolitical, and religious.[1] Each form of conversion, taken separately, inform or transvalues (sets in a different

---

[1] Gelpi himself sets these five conversions within what he calls seven conversion dynamics. I do not follow his treatment of the seven conversion dynamics; for my rationale, see Yong (2002, 16–18).

frame of reference) the other forms—e.g., affective conversion shapes the other types of conversions, and so on. It is conversion in any one of these areas that brings about a qualitative transformation in the individual in mediational ways such that the other dimensions of life are transmuted. At the same, there is also a cumulative effect whereby any combination of two, three, or four realms of conversion could bring about conversion in a non-converted realm. So sometimes, moral, affective, intellectual and sociopolitical conversion bring about religious conversion, or moral, affective, intellectual and religious conversion bring about sociopolitical conversion, and so on. In short, the five conversions which are dynamically interconnected so that conversion in any one or two or three, etc., realms can bring about conversions in one or more of the other realms.

The imagination in general and the pneumatological imagination in particular are driven by conversion experiences. Thus on the one hand the imagination searches for new applications of the system of values it inherits; on the other hand, it is also affectively, spiritually, materially, etc., sensitive to new social and cultural contexts such that it creatively reconfigures the axiological system so that what emerges is both continuous with and yet discontinuous from before. Again, on the one hand, the imagination is the means through which one's spirituality sustains one's attitudes to life; on the other hand, it is also the means through which one renews and energizes a vibrant spirituality after walking through the valley of the shadow of death such that what emerges features both continuity and discontinuity—something new—with the previous experience.

This creativity can be understood to be inspired by the Spirit through whom the living God breathes new things into the world (cf. Sherry 1992, 110–32). What is emergent should be understood across a spectrum. On the one side is the work of the Spirit in our hearts and minds that remind us of what has been previously deposited and perhaps neglected (John 14:26b). In this case, there is an imaginative retrieval and reappropriation of familiar truths and convictions. What would otherwise be dead letters of the law is vivified by the Spirit and applied in fresh ways (cf. 2 Cor. 3:6). On the other side of the spectrum is the work of the Spirit that not only leads us into *all* truth (John 16:13; 1 John 2:26), but, arguably, into *new* significations and appropriations of the truth. As previously argued [1.3.3], the work of the Spirit includes the new things of creation, redemption, and eschaton. In some respects, what is new will always retain features of continuity with that which is immediately preceding. Yet the power of imaginative extension is such that when compared and contrasted over longer periods of time, the continuities fade while the discontinuities grow in prominence. That there is certainly a tension between the creative imagination and the authority of tradition and of the ecclesia cannot be denied. At the same time, perhaps there is also the gift of the Spirit, a type of "creative fidelity" or *habitus* whereby theological reflection proceeds responsibly vis-à-vis what is handed down or inherited (cf. Thiel 1991, 129–37). Ironically, perhaps such a Spirit-inspired *habitus* is required for the retention and reappropriation of tradition itself since the latter, especially when temporally distant, loses its power to engage the imagination. As St. Paul puts it, what we once saw with veiled faces to be fading glory, we now see face to face through the enlightening power of the Spirit who opens our eyes to the radiant glory of God (cf. 2 Cor. 3:7–18). Be reminded, however, that even this fullness of glory pales in comparison to what shall be. In eschatological light, our vision now through a glass dimly (1 Cor. 13:12b) is but a shadow of the truth as will then be revealed (1 John 3:2).

As the imagination is precisely the faculty that bridges the gap between the self and the other, it is therefore well suited to mediate the creative human engagement with the transcendent. It is no wonder that we often image our encounter with the Spirit according to the categories of irruption, interruption, and disruption. Even here, the terms themselves are suggestive of a spectrum of experiences. As irruption, the Spirit breaks forth from within our lives, from inside, as it were, to transform us, our ways of living, understanding, anticipating. As interruption, the Spirit intrudes, from outside, as it were, confronting us with the radical alterity of otherness in such a way as to demand our attention, and possibly, our transformation. As disruption, the Spirit is experienced as invasive, from above, as it were, in a way such that what results is (sometimes radically so) discontinuous with what preceded. In the latter case especially, our world is turned upside down. Given the capacity of the imagination to be attuned to wholly new ways of understanding, thinking and experiencing, the capacity of the Spirit to bring about profoundly new things over time should never be underestimated. This fundamental aspect of human creativity thus also underscores the unpredictability of the acts of interpretation.

7.1.2 This unpredictability is also related to the constitution of the human being as a free creature, understood either in the compatibilist sense of spontaneity or in the libertarian sense of having the capacity to do otherwise. Certainly in either case, freedom should not be defined absolutistically since human freedom is constrained at least cosmologically, socially, and biologically. The way the world is sets certain limits on where and how we live. The environments within which we have been raised shape our worldviews, form our habits, inclinations and dispositions, and nurture our values and aspirations. I will return to these issues momentarily. At present, however, I mean only to suggest that this being the case, freedom is best understood in relationship to the structures and experiences within which humans exist and from which they wish to extricate themselves. These latter can be understood personally, socio-structurally, and religiously, among other ways. Insofar as human beings find themselves in conditions of suffering, experiencing existential anxiety, held captive by others (whether physically, socio-economically, or otherwise), or alienated from what fulfills ultimate concerns, they will make efforts to liberate themselves from these situations (cf. Patterson 1991). Such efforts are a signal mark of human freedom. Human beings do exercise their freedom by thinking, willing and acting toward greater and greater realizations of freedom in the various dimensions of their lives. Of course, the situations of "slavery" or "bondage," however these may be construed, themselves fund the possibilities open to or establish the parameters controlling the activities of those aspiring for liberation.

Here, however, it is important to emphasize that biology, culture and cosmology constrain but do not, strictly speaking, determine what ensues. This is the case simply because thinking, willing, and acting are expressions of the freedom that attends to the human-being-in-the-world and correlate with personal intentions as guided and inspired by the Holy Spirit. Human beings intend to maximize their freedoms within the constraints they find themselves, and inevitably exercise their intentions toward that end. What do I think? What connections do I make? What alternatives should I explore? What options are most plausible and viable? What actions do I pursue? How do I go about transforming my world into a better world? These and many other similar questions constitute the fundamental processes that underlie the activity of interpretation. Inevitably, the drive for freedom resists conformity to the declarations, pronunciations, and interpretations of the status quo. Beyond resistance, however, new readings of familiar material are produced. Under more difficult circumstances, efforts may be made to shift the shape of the received canon, or, alternatively, to seek to establish entirely new canons.[2] Ultimately, such acts may be best understood as expressions of the human response to experiences of alienation that are connected somehow to the ways in which the received canon is perceived to be oppressive (cf. Farley 1996a, 138–39). The quest for liberation achieved in part by knowledge of the truth (John 8:32), and in part through the work of the Spirit of truth (John 14:17, 15:26, 16:13; 1 John 4:6) is

---

[2] On the processes of canon reception and re-formation, see Rush (1997, esp. 265–73). I am grateful to Bradford Hinze for directing me to this book.

directed toward enabling the life of freedom (Gal. 5:3–26) (cf. Ottmar 1988).

That human beings are imaginative, creative and free creatures who react to what they have received in order to actualize greater and greater freedoms for themselves in itself opens up the possibility of error, oversight or neglect of pertinent data, and even the possibility of wrong conclusions. In the effort to redress their situation, wrong deductions may be drawn; erroneous data consulted; other facts overlooked; and misguided options actualized. In some instances, human beings seize on conclusions they realize are clearly unwarranted by the evidence, or persist in activity which is morally, legally, or otherwise wrong in pursuit of what they conceive as greater self-satisfaction even to the detriment of others. In this sense, the possibility of sin is concomitant with the possibility of doing good and actualizing liberation for oneself and for others. To realize the former, however, is to forfeit one's quest for freedom and to be re-captivated by that which is ultimately enslaving. One can, finally, either resign oneself to be a slave to sin, or be carried on the road to freedom by the Spirit of God (Rom. 6–8).

The possibility of legitimizing one's enslavement to sin by way of appealing to the work of the Spirit raises the question regarding the criteria for discerning the liberative and truthful activity of the Holy Spirit from that of other lesser spirits. This ultimately returns, for Christians, to the question regarding the normative authority of Scripture. While I will deal in more detail with this issue in the next chapter, a few thoughts are apropos here proceeding from the relative independence and interdependence of Spirit and Word in the two hands model. First, given the fallibility of human beings, discernment will always be provisional. This does not mean that discernment should never occur, only that our discerning should always proceed with the allowance for correction. Second, the interdependence of Spirit and Word in the divine economies means that we should take Scripture seriously as the primary means through which the Spirit's liberative activity is accomplished. That Scripture is Spirit-inspired means not only that it has spoken to the people of God in times past, but that it continues to be Spirit-inspired to all those who have ears to hear the Spirit today. Third, the relative independence of Spirit and Word also points to the distinct possibility of being led to novel readings or applications of Scripture by the Spirit, even as the Spirit preceded the Word in hovering over the waters, and as the Spirit conceived the Word in the incarnation. Here, it is crucial to distinguish between the Spirit creating new significations of the Word, rather than bringing about a completely new word altogether. The latter claim should always be checked by the Johannine insight that the Spirit "will not speak on his own, but will speak whatever he hears" (John 16:13).

7.1.3 This said, it is nevertheless imperative to insist that the possibility for error is especially real when interpretation attempts to engage the transcendent. Yet engage the transcendent we must since unless one presumes a completely immanentist pneumatology, the human spirit continually reaches "beyond" itself. Further, the human spirit has to be open to that which is truly transcendent in a theological sense in order to engage with and be engaged by the divine Spirit. Of course, "the transcendent" in this case needs to be understood in more than just psychological, social, or temporal terms. Certainly, human beings are open to self-discovery, to others, and to their future. Equally certain is the possibility that the Holy Spirit could meet us in the depths of our own hearts (Augustine), in the face of the other (Levinas), and in the future that beckons and welcomes us (cf. Pannenberg 1970, 1–13). Yet having said this, Kierkegaard's qualitative distinction between time and eternity, between creation and the creator, needs to be noted. This means that the transcendence toward which the Spirit inspires us must always be more than what we encounter in ourselves, in others, and in our futures. And it is this genuine openness toward eschatological transcendence that is the condition of and suggestive regarding the unpredictability of human interpretation (cf. Gunton 1996, 119–23).

But does this mean then that our encounter with the Spirit is to be conceived dualistically in terms of subject (ourselves) and object (the Spirit)? Does the human openness to transcendence mean finally that we encounter the divine Other as one who is over and against us? Our tendency might be to conceptualize the human openness to transcendence in exactly this fashion. These questions reflect, however, a dualism which a trinitarian theology of coinherence and indwelling effectively undercuts. A trinitarian conception is able to affirm the second but sets it within the framework of "St. Paul's statement that we are in the spirit provided that the Spirit of God dwells in us" (Hamilton 1966, 34; cf. Rom. 8:9). Thus a triadic, pneumatological conceptualization of this relational indwelling enables us to overcome the dualism inherent with traditional understandings of this transcendental relationship.

How this is the case can be understood by looking at what the *ressourcement* theologian, Hans Urs von Balthasar, refers to as the transcendental experience of the Spirit. Von Balthasar is explicit in terms of defining the relationship between the human spirit and the divine spirit as one that is "unmediated" (1993, 21; cf. Sachs 1993). Undoubtedly, in our time, many cringe at even that denial of mediation to human experience. However, I would urge that we pay close attention to Von Balthasar's proposal before dismissing his claim. In the

Balthasarian framework, the divine Spirit is not conceived of as the other beyond the human experiencer. Rather, the Spirit is the ontological prerequisite for human experience and it is precisely this fact that creates the possibility for self-transcendence. Von Balthasar's portrayal of this pneumatic overcoming of the subject-object dualism needs to be quoted in full:

> But if God the Spirit is the One through whom we "see" God, in that we receive an inner experience of what God's being is as love, then it is superfluous to pose the question whether there exists something like an (objective) beholding of God. The question can be answered both with yes and with no. The One through whom we "behold" God is the Spirit, the least objective mystery that breathes eternally beyond all objectification but in whose light everything that is at all capable of being illuminated becomes clear and transparent. But this light clarifies for us essentially what has the form of the world and, highest of all, the God-Man in whom Church, humanity and cosmos are incorporated: in him, we shall behold the God(-Man) who reflects God to us and shows us what the Father is; and since we shall see him with eyes and hearts that are divinized by the Spirit, we cannot say that this "seeing" will only be "mediated," indirect. We shall "see" God to the extent that it is at all possible to see him. His mystery will be the light in which we shall see his light that is twilight in the mystery. (1993, 112)[3]

Von Balthasar's point is an important one that connects well with the Augustinian tradition which emphasizes the Spirit as the togetherness (love) of the Father (Lover) and the Son (Beloved). Theologically speaking, the Spirit is the transcendental condition of the human experience of God. Stephen, for example, is able to see the risen Christ only as filled with the Spirit (Acts 7:55; cf. McClendon 1994, 291). This enables us to experience ourselves both subjectively and objectively, in different respects. It also enables us to encounter God in ways analogously to how we encounter ourselves—both subjectively and objectively, or, to use Lyle Dabney's term, "transubjectively" (1996, 161). Our encounter with that which is "beyond" us remains beyond us in a real sense, but is also internalized insofar as what is encountered is truly engaged. The Psalmist points to this experience of God as Other and yet as the one known within one's inward parts (Ps. 139:5–18) Thus also the scriptural reference, "In him we live and move and have our being" (Acts 17:28), can be appropriately paraphrased: "in the Spirit of God do we live, move, and encounter ourselves, others, and God" most fully. Conversely, apart from life

---

[3] Killian McDonnell puts it this way: "we must use the Spirit to understand the Spirit...because the Spirit is the universal comprehensive horizon within which any and all theological reflection is possible" (1985, 216).

in the Spirit, human experience would remain tragically solipsistic. In the Spirit, however, the horizons of what are at the edge of our experiential possibilities continuously expands. As the apostle Paul reminds us, "What no eye has seen, nor ear heard, nor the human heart conceived, what God has prepared for those who love him" (1 Cor. 2:9).

Ultimately, while Balthasar's notion of "unmediatedness" may still assume too much since finite human minds cannot fully access the infinite God. It is important not to exalt the human imagination as an autonomous faculty or human freedom as an autonomous capacity. In fact, as contingent creatures capable of engaging the transcendent, human beings are also fully dependent on and related to God, or, for our purposes, the Spirit of God. Von Balthasar's radical "unmediatedness" should therefore be qualified as a "mediated immediacy" (cf. Rust 1981, 49–76). This captures the togetherness of both aspects of the process of religious knowing: that of our knowing in the Spirit, and that of our knowing only by and through the Spirit. Here it is important to emphasize, therefore, interpretation as a charismatic or graced activity. Theological interpretation related to things divine is especially implicated since apart from God's revealing of himself in ways accommodated to our modes of perceiving, the imagination's access to the divine transcendence would be blocked and the will's intentions toward freedom inhibited. In other words, all theologizing is charismatic in the sense that it is enabled by and through the Spirit. One receives and develops a charism for theological reflection. And, of course, as a gift of the unpredictable Spirit (John 3:8), the emergent interpretations can themselves never be completely predetermined. It is this unpredictability that in part enables the possibility of critical assessment of the "givens" of interpretation, and which thereby advances, perhaps, theological knowledge (cf. Jeanrond 1988, 68–70).

In saying all this, however, we need to point out that while the imagination as creative, free, and open to transcendence provides for novelty in interpretation, these same features of the imagination function, at the same time, to correct any speculative deficiencies in one's metaphysical, hermeneutical, or even theological scheme. This is an important element of the trialectic since all human interpretations are finite, perspectival, and hence, fallible. The value of any speculative proposal therefore has to include within itself a self-critical component. I am suggesting that the pneumatic moment in the hermeneutical trialectic serves, in part, this corrective function.

I have argued so far that human acts of interpretation are graced by and through the Spirit such that unpredictable novelties emerge over time. Such

novelties exhibit features of both continuity and discontinuity from what
precedes, the former more pronounced in view of what is more contiguous to
the creative moment, and the latter in view of the larger interpretive process.
Another way to view the relationship between what is continuous and
discontinuous is the emphasize the latter as emergent from the interpretive act
as engaging with and being grasped by transcendence, and the former
engagement as that which influences, shapes, and constrains the interpretive
act. I will discuss later the "givenness" of interpretation in terms of its objective
features. For now, however, I want to focus on the "given" in relationship to the
Spirit and the acts of interpretation.

7.2 The Activity of Interpretation and the Subjectivity of the Given

My focus in what immediately follows remains on the subjective aspects of
interpretation. Now it is certainly the case, as has already been alluded to, that
the activity of interpretation always engages a given other. Yet it is also true to
say that the given is engaged or interpreted not as radically other in a purely
objective sense, but as an other-in-relationship-to-us in a somewhat subjective sense. This is in part because what is given, while objective in one sense, is
also unobjectifiable in another sense. The analogy to this, as I have previously
suggested [1.1.1], is that while Christian theological interpretation engages the
given and clearly objective historical Jesus, the person of Jesus is supremely
subjective and hence unobjectifiable because he is the man anointed by and
full of the Holy Spirit (Acts 10:38). Further, the trinitarian notion of subsistent
relationality and perichoretic indwelling leads to the idea, both with regard to
the human relationship with God and to human relationships with others and
the world around them, of the mysterious intimacy enjoyed between the knowing subject and the known object even in its radical alterity. My argument at
this juncture is that the givenness of interpretation is unobjectifiable precisely
because the structures of the given fluctuate according to the movements of
the divine Spirit and the indwelling of human spirits in space and time. Such
movements and fluctuations can and should be assessed at the level of the
biological, natural, cultural, and ecclesial worlds.

7.2.1 For starters, what is undeniably given to interpreters is what we might
call our interpretive "hardware." This consists, at least minimally, of brain cells,
neuro-physiological components, and perceptual equipment. Human
interpreters are not disembodied minds, and this would be true, according to
Christian belief in the resurrection of the body, even for the postmortem state.

Further, human bodies are situated environmentally now here in this place and next there in another. Thus, it would certainly be true to say that a blind man given a Braille education in the modern West will make interpretive connections in significantly different ways from that of a fourth-century Desert Father (cf. Burton-Christie 1999) simply because the habits shaping and options confronting both are drastically different. Similarly, a mother of a nuclear family in Chicago will envision her interpretive possibilities in ways that contrast with that of wheelchair-bound nun in the Andes mountains.

Yet even at this level of biology and the world of nature, it is not the case that interpretation is mechanistically derived from biology, environment, and cosmology. Rather, the activity of interpretation would still be set within dynamic processes at each of these levels. This flows from our biological framework as developing continuously from the birth through adulthood and onto old age, and from the fact that one can choose to disposition one's biological givens in certain directions rather than others through training, discipline, education, and so on. Our environment also cannot be understood in static terms. The continental divides and glaciers surely move at imperceptibly slow rates, but hurricanes, floods and earthquakes can transform the landscape almost momentarily. Finally, whether or not the rapidity of the world's geologic transformation is at issue, it is certainly the case that our knowledge of the world continues to increase at exponential rates. We now know much more about the processes of life on planet earth than the authors of Scripture did two thousand years ago. And, as mobile beings whose addresses do not stay the same, we learn sometimes simply by moving from one place to another. My point is that both materially and epistemically, what is given even in terms of our hardware and our setting in the natural world is not finally static or completely objectifiable.

An unobjectifiable biological and natural world in itself therefore demands adjustments to how we discern its signals. This means, in part, that we should now use dynamic categories to understand the world of nature, which includes ourselves as biological beings, since such a move would enable us to better attend to the complex movements of the world which both funds our interpretive acts at one moment, and is part of the object that we attempt to interpret at another moment. Even as objects of interpretation, things in the world, including ourselves, are not purely objectifiable givens. This is not only because as far as we are concerned things do not exist only in themselves but do so in relation to us; more importantly, the "subjectivity" of things as given to us follows from the unpredictable and the continuous working of the Spirit in and through the various given "objects" of nature. The shifting character of the biological and natural world thus requires us to make a transition to what might be called a pneumatological theology of nature which emphasizes the Spirit's dynamic presence and activity (cf. Pannenberg 1997). Interpretation or discernment in this framework would need to include these backdrops against which our interpreting occurs. Failure to discern the shifting character of the biological and environmental context within which interpretation proceeds results in the incapacity to understand both how these factors act conservatively on the one hand, and how they contribute to birthing novel and sometimes radical alternatives on the other.

Herein lies the value of connecting with the notion of natural revelation, more precisely understood as the unveiling of God in and through natural signs. As we become more discerning about ourselves and the world in which we live, we become more aware of how the Spirit does work through our biological hardware along with our environmental and geographic situatedness to mediate our perceptual encounter with the world, to prohibit certain activities, and to motivate us toward others. A more sophisticated pneumatological theology of nature (or pneumatological theology of natural revelation) should inform not only our vision of who God is, but also our understanding of who we are as interpreting beings. And, it goes without saying, it is all the more important to recognize these "objects" in all their dynamism and complexity especially when we're engaging in the task of understanding ourselves and the world theologically. Interpretation, after all, builds as certain options are actualized within the constraints of biology, environment and cosmology which are themselves continually shifting.

7.2.2 This shifting character of reality has long been acknowledged with regard to the social dimensions of what it means to be human. The dawn of historical consciousness has alerted us to the fact that humans are historical beings, constrained to a large extent by the vagaries of space and time. This raises the question, of course, of the larger socio-cultural and historical situations within which Christians find themselves engaging the Spirit and the scriptural and later traditions. It is now a truism to insist that our social locations shapes both the ways we experience the Spirit and the ways in which we read and understand Scripture and the theological tradition. Theology no longer proceeds either formally from the data of revealed Scripture alone (as in Protestant fundamentalism) or only deductively from Scripture as discerned by the community of faith (as in Catholic or Orthodox traditionalism). Rather, it is just as crucial to discern what kinds of interpretive lenses, besides that of one's faith tradition, are brought to the reading of Scripture. Responsible theologizing cannot avoid inquiring into how natural as well as social, economic, and political forces converge to influence, shape, and perhaps even dictate interpretation. Herein lies the importance of Fernando Segovia's call to acknowledge the reality of flesh-and-blood readers who interpret texts, traditions, and themselves (1995 and 2000; cf. Tompkins 1980, Dyck 1996, and Powell 2001).

For the moment, however, I want to follow the preceding discussion of the Spirit's prior activity in the natural world by briefly unpacking the dynamic (perhaps even Spirit-led) aspects of our socio-cultural and communal identities. In the first place, it needs to be observed that our social and cultural matrices are just as dynamic and fluid, if not more so, as the biological, environmental, and ecclesial dimensions of our lives. This dynamism should give us pause when attempting to understand how theological interpretation occurs since discernment of our socio-cultural conditions now needs to be an ongoing affair. In some ways, this project can be understood as the effort to discern the spirits—divine, demonic and otherwise—present and active in the world. This ongoing activity requires nothing less than our ongoing attention since the legalities, habits and forces of the world do not allow experienced phenomena to stand still.

Yet the forces that shape our social world are certainly not limited to those analyzable by sociological, economic, political, or other such categories. Nor is it the case that the relationship between our socio-cultural world and the biblical and theological tradition proceeds only in one direction, from the former to the latter. It is also certainly the case that the latter influences and shapes the former. Christians are also called to be salt and light in the world. As such, they are in some instances prophetic voices to the world, being in the world but not of it. Christian engagement with the world therefore not only results in their being transformed by the world, but also in their transforming the world. Yet Christians to not witness to the world in and of their own strength. Better to say that the Spirit of God is continually present and active in the world, convicting it of sin and transforming it in part by and through the power of the divine Word as preserved and mediated by those in the Christian community of faith.

In this sense, the traditional givens of theology—Scripture and tradition—have been understood to be normative and prior to our subjective engagements with them. Yet my thesis so far has been not only that humans are open to the transcendent, but also that the transcendent has come near to us in, by and through the Spirit of God. My focus in the remainder of this section will therefore be on the subjective aspects of our interpretations as a scriptural and ecclesial people.

7.2.3 Ecclesiality refers to the distinctive Christian way of being in the world. More specifically, it is a way of life that is birthed, sustained, led, and consummated by the Spirit. I wish, therefore, to highlight the total givenness of Christian Scripture and tradition as dynamic and continually emerging realities brought about by the activities of the Spirit of God. My argument is that while Scripture and tradition do stand over and against us in some ways (and even as authoritatively given in some respects), yet the distance between the interpreter and the text and tradition, however minute in some cases, will always mean that there is slippage that occurs between what was once meant and what the interpreter takes the current meaning to be. Now, rather than bemoan this fact, it should simply be recognized as the human condition, and perhaps in some ways, as divinely intended with regard to humans as knowing beings. My objective in what follows is to trace out the (trialogical) connections between this conditionedness and the work of the Spirit on the one hand and our socio-cultural situatedness on the other.

To begin with, Christians unanimously agree that "All Scripture [*graphè*] is inspired [*theopneustos*] by God and is useful for teaching, for reproof, for correction, and for training in righteousness" (2 Tim. 3:16). I will return to the purposes of the Spirit's inspiration of Scripture in the next chapter. For the moment, I want to focus on the product of inspiration by calling attention to the tension which emerges immediately in this regard. Now whereas Christians have generally agreed that theological application of this text pertains to the totality of the Christian Scriptures (Hebrew Bible and Christian Testament), attention to the context and author's horizons of understanding would only with difficulty be able to deny its original reference to the writings of the still contested (during the first or even into the second centuries, C.E.) Hebrew canon. Some may thus insist on applying this text comprehensively to the entire Bible on the basis of its final canonical shape.[4] The Jew would certainly be within his (*she* never had any such rights) rights to apply this principle to the final canonical shape of the Hebrew Bible, with the proviso that he probably would not want to do so since he does not see this Pastoral Letter as having canonical authority. But on what grounds would a Christian do the same to the final canonical shape of

---

[4] This is Peter H. Davids' strategy (2001, 2–20, esp. 3 and 17). Curiously, Davids, in a footnote, refers the reader to the chapter on canonical criticism in the same volume that contains his essay, but such is nowhere to be found. I would argue that a canonical approach to Scripture would call for a much greater continuity between Scripture and tradition than I suspect Davids allows. More on this below.

the Christian Scriptures if he or she insisted on the normativity and priority of the text over the ongoing ecclesial tradition?

To confront the full force of this question, let us turn to James Sanders' notion of canonical criticism. As he portrays it, canonical criticism understands the Holy Spirit to be

> at work all along the path of the canonical process: from original speaker, through what was understood by hearers; to what disciples believed was said; to how later editors reshaped the record, oral and written, of what was said; on down to modern hearings and understandings of the texts in current believing communities. (Sanders 1984, xvii; cf. Abraham 1981, esp. 58–75)

One might immediately object to Sanders that a canonical view of Scripture would need to understand the special working of the Holy Spirit to persist only during the process of canonical compilation. Post-canonical developments would be qualitatively different works of the Spirit once the final shape of the canon is secured. Two questions arise here. First, since when has the final shape of the Christian canon been secured? One can only assume there is a definitive canonical shape if one arbitrarily defines the canon according to certain traditions of Catholicism, Orthodoxy, or Protestantism since what counts as Scripture differs among these communities. Second, even if Christians could agree that just this clearly defined set of texts was scriptural and not others, on what basis would they determine the workings of the Spirit after the final shape of the canon is established to be qualitatively different from what went on before? Certainly this could not be determined on biblical grounds alone.

Scripture and tradition, therefore, cannot be divorced from the workings of the Spirit, and all of them combine to determine ecclesial existence. To begin with, certain individuals were inspired to articulate in speech and writing just what God had done among them (2 Pet. 1:21). Scripture itself, I would then argue, reflects interpretive accounts of a people's experiences with God along with subsequent re-interpretations of these experiences, whether such be the Chronicler's re-writing the Kings, the exilic community's wrestling with the Torah, or the early Church's re-visioning the Hebrew Scriptures. Further, the Church has been led over time by the Spirit to recognize certain texts and not others as the Word of God to them and therefore as trustworthy for life and faith. Finally, I would argue that the post-canonical community's ongoing development can only be understood in terms of a process of tradition-making such that the people of God are transformed by its continuous encounter in and through the Spirit with the biblical and later traditions even while the content of Scripture itself is in some sense transformed by the Church for the Church as it engages the world. I will return to this point later.

The interpretive situation is therefore supremely complex. Theology emerges from the ongoing activity of the Spirit in the world, such that the world, the community of faith, and the understanding of the divine Word is continually transformed along with the readers and interpreters themselves. Discernment is therefore required of the dynamic situations, locations, and contexts within which Scripture and tradition are mediated and the Spirit is encountered. This wide-ranging capacity to discern is akin to Wilhelm Dilthey's notion of a hermeneutics of life or hermeneutics of the human sciences (*Geisteswissenschaften*) whereby what needs to be understood is the full range of human experience (*erlebnis*) (see, e.g., Dilthey 1986, esp. 35–40; cf. Palmer 1969, 98–123). As such, it also include Claude Geffré's "hermeneutics of human existence" (1974, esp. 43), Langdon Gilkey's "hermeneutic of (secular) experience" (1969, 234–302), and perhaps even James Wm. McClendon's "theology of life" understood against his larger project of theology as experiential and biographical (1974, 170–203), insofar as the presence and activity of divinity itself can be detected in each of these dimensions of human endeavor. Thus a fully developed theory of interpretation is no less than what might be called a "hermeneutics of reality" that is able to discern the ideas, actions, and aesthetic expressions of human beings in all of their variety and through all of their interactions with reality as a whole. Texts are both given with lived experience and read against the backdrop of experience. Hermeneutics is therefore always a more-or-less subjective enterprise not only on the interpretive end but also with regard to the given.

7.3 The Activity of Interpretation: Telos as Subject and Object

There is one more cluster of questions that I wish to address in order to bring together the discussion so far concerning subjectivity in interpretation. As aforementioned, "All Scripture is inspired by God and is useful for teaching, for reproof, for correction, and for training in righteousness" (2 Tim. 3:16). Clearly, there are specific purposes for Scripture, some of which are identified here. Theological interpretation builds in part on Scripture as well as the purposes here adumbrated toward specific teloi. These teloi are subjective in the sense that they arise out of the convergence of Spirit, Word, and Community. They can also be said to be objective in the sense that they are oriented toward certain goals. Yet even these goals can only be generally formulated, subject to the ongoing process of inquiry and the interpretive gains made. In order to see this, I will briefly explicate on interpretive teloi with regard to orthopraxis, orthodoxy, and cognitive doubt. In each case, my focus will be on their emergence and refinement as aspects of life in the Spirit on the one hand, and as features of the existential quest of human beings-in-community on the other.

7.3.1 Arguably, all interpretation is motivated by practical concerns. Mention was made during the earlier discussion of human freedom that the quest for liberation springs forth from the experience of bondage or slavery. Analogously, interpretations are posited in the process of seeking satisfaction of both basic and complex human needs. Needs demand to be met. The question of how such needs are met launches human beings on the path of inquiry. At one level, we learn about our needs and their satisfactions from our religious and socio-cultural environments and traditions. At another level, we find ourselves increasingly dissatisfied either with previous articulations of such needs or with the answers handed down to us. Insofar as the former pertains, our quest focuses on "what the problem is"; insofar as the latter is applicable, we inquire into alternative solutions. At a third level, it is also the case that the intersection of the human spirit and the divine Spirit brings forth the existential response that drives our search for meaning in life as a whole as well as our realization of particular needs more specifically. Even our recognition of the fact that we do have needs and what such needs might be is brought about by the work of the Spirit in us. Of course, it follows that recognition of particular needs leads to particular responses designed to meet just those needs. In other words, it is the work of the Spirit both to alert us to "what is broken" as well as to direct our attention to how to get such "fixed" (see Schlitt 2001, esp. 78–87).

In theological terms, it is arguable that the preceding describes the Christian path of sanctification. The Christian way of being in the world suggests, at the most basic level, that sin is what plagues human existence, that Jesus Christ is the central symbol of how that plague has been dealt with, and that being assimilated into the mind and way of Jesus by the power of the Holy Spirit is the most effective human means of experiencing such freedom. Christian interpretation may therefore be understood as the pursuit of sanctification that requires discernment of God, self, and world directed toward spiritual praxis. Interpretation therefore involves discerning and assessing oneself, one's situation, and one's prejudices (what Gadamer calls horizons or foreunderstandings), looking for possible resources, and charting the appropriate response (cf. de Nicolas 1986; Newell 1990, 27–49; Thiselton 1995, esp. Part Two).

At the same time, since one is never alone, discernment of the self requires discernment of the self-with-others. For Christians, interpretation is discerning what the Spirit has said and done (and is now saying and doing) through the Church precisely in order to determine what the Spirit wishes to do next in and through us whose identity is that of being members of the ecclesial community. For this reason, among others, the sources of theology include both one's "personal relationship with Jesus" (to use an evangelical phrase), and the lives of the saints (cf. Wicks 1994, 84–86 and 133–38). The result sought for is not only enlightenment of the mind, but transformation of the heart and redirection of the will by the Spirit in accordance with the example of Jesus and after the model of those who have gone on before us (cf. Heb. 12:1). And, of course, such transformation and direction is never complete at any point in this world since the next moment would itself be a new problematic situation whereby the old situation is set into a new context by the preceding transformative moments.

In this sense, transformation should be understood both as a moment in the hermeneutical spiral and as the telos of interpretation. As Theodore Stylianopolous puts it, the transformative level of interpretation is more so a spiritual experience than a cognitive method or technique. When transposed to second-order reflection, what Stylianopolous calls "transformative hermeneutics" understands and grasps "the dynamics of how biblical teachings are actualized in personal and corporate life, that is, how they become the living Word of the living God in the present" (1997, 216). I would simply want to expand the media of actualization from what Stylianopolous calls the "biblical teachings" to the complex of truths mediated by the conjunction of Spirit, Word and Community. In this sense, sanctification is the Christian way that seeks, on the one hand, to imitate the divine "actions" of the Spirit in the past— as preserved in the community's memory—even while it aspires, on the other hand, to be sensitive to the fresh workings of the Spirit in the present. It is therefore both a goal, and yet a supremely subjective process or orthopraxis, transforming us from moment to moment and from day to day as individuals-in-community into the likeness of Christ (cf. 2 Cor. 3:18).

7.3.2 The important point to be underscored here is that interpretation is not simply a cognitive affair. Rather, as suggested by recent speech-act theory, interpretation is spiritual and holistic activity that brings mind, body, soul, will, and affections together in asking the questions, What then should I (we) do? and How then should I (we) live? These questions are suggestive of the two greatest commandments: to love the Lord our God wholly, and to love our neighbors as ourselves. Interpretation therefore strives toward maximal interpersonal and intersubjective relationality, categorically identified in the theological sense as reconciliation with God, and in the ethical sense as shalom with our neighbors. If orthopraxis captures the sense of the latter, orthodoxy—literally, right worship, as in *orthodoxa*—does so the former. I want to explore more specifically what it means to understand theological hermeneutics as rightly worshipping God.

Certainly, worship is at least a cognitive matter, and the content of our cognitions varies according to our being grasped by various texts, traditions, liturgies and interpretations. Yet Jesus' challenge was to worship God not only in truth, but also in spirit (John 4:24). Theological interpretation therefore includes not only grasping certain conceptual truths about God, but also the cultivation and development of the proper affections for God, and the appropriate orientations, attitudes, and approaches to God. Certainly, as with everything else, these all go together, and it would be not only impossible but immaterial to attempt to determine which precedes the other. In this sense, then, it is appropriate to say that theological interpretation cannot avoid the question of what it means to relate to God. The driving questions include not only, Who is this God?, but also, What do we do before him? Orthodoxy in this sense is not just right doctrines or right thinking about God, but right approach and worship of God. And, since God is spirit, theological interpretation strives to understand and encounter God not solely as other to ourselves. This certainly is meant to be understood in a sense inclusive of von Balthasar's statements cited above. More than that, however, theological interpretation is spiritual activity that emerges out of the convergence of two dynamic trajectories— that comprising our own lives-in-communities and that of the life of God. How are the two brought together? In and through our life in the Spirit.

This life in the Spirit is best understood through the metaphor of a journey. The way of Jesus Christ in the Spirit is in this sense as an ongoing discovery of the reality of God. We begin, as Gregory of Nazianzus speaks of Moses, with concrete knowledge of the reality of God and of the divine name: "I AM WHO I AM" (Exod. 3:14). Yet this revelation of the divine name is not wholly new since it is connected to the God of Abraham, Isaac, and Jacob (Exod. 3:6). Further, this name is reflective of a "more" that attends to what is revealed: "I AM WHO I AM" should also be understood as "I will be what I will be." As we proceed with Moses, we ascend into the dark cloud of Sinai. For the Christian, this moment, while now enlightened through the face of Jesus (cf. Heb. 12:22–24), remains imposing and forbidding (cf. Heb. 12:28–29) and, finally, even unapproachable (cf. 1 Tim. 6:16). The end of Moses' life includes a glimpse of the back of God—since, as Yahwah responded to Moses' request to see the divine glory, "you cannot see my face, for no shall see me and live" (Exod. 33:20)—that anticipates the Seer's heavenly vision of a faceless God (Rev. 4:2).[5] Theological interpretation therefore wrestles with the tension of a God who has both revealed himself and yet always remains unknowable. It does no good to simply repeat Deuteronomy 29:29 at this juncture—"The secret things belong to the LORD our God, but the revealed things belong to us and to our children forever, to observe all the words of this law"—for a number of reasons. First, the same difficulties as we saw pertaining to our understanding of 2 Timothy 3:16 above attend to our understanding of what "the revealed things" mean here. Second, even what is revealed—whatever we finally decide that to be—cannot be understood apart from interpretation. Finally, interpretation can only in a very arbitrary sense distinguish between what remains secret to God and what has been revealed to us.

Better, I suggest, to understand the thrust of this text as directed to both orthopraxis—"that we may follow all the words of this law"—and orthodoxy— right understanding and right worship together. Theological interpretation as a strenuous activity never ceases its drive for understanding. Thus is life in the Spirit characterized by the continual and ongoing unveiling to us of what no eye has seen nor ear has heard (1 Cor. 2:9–10). Insofar as we understand and are grasped by revelation, God is not other than we are to ourselves. Insofar as we remain in darkness, God is the infinitely far-off one who lures us through and toward orthopraxis and orthodoxy. In between is the space within which we grow in grace, truth, and love.

7.3.3 It should now be clear that the motivating engines that drive theological interpretation cannot admit of termination. Orthopraxis—sanctification— is a lifelong concern. Orthodoxy—our best efforts to think truly about God— is a never ending project. With regard to theological interpretation, both orthopraxis and orthodoxy, I now want to argue, emerge out of existential, cognitional and spiritual doubt. As previously discussed [5.1.2], human inquiry is motivated by the experience of doubt. Existential doubts need

---

5 "His" in Rev. 22:4 appears to refer to both God and to the Lamb of the preceding verse. Perhaps the author of the Apocalypse has in mind both the Johannine saying that "No one has ever seen God, but God the One and Only, who is at the Father's side, has made him known" (1:18), and Jesus' claim that "anyone who has seen me has seen the Father" (14:9b). In any case, God and the Lamb are repeatedly paired together at least from Rev. 21:22 onwards, and are functionally equivalent. This does not, in my judgment, count against the fact that the Christian vision of the Father is always mediated through the Lamb.

B/c before we had no doubt - ☆

soteriological solutions; practical doubts need corresponding resolutions; spiritual doubts require holistic transformations, and so on. None, of course, can be said to be completely unconnected with any other since all are intertwined at some level. Theological doubts are no exception. Theological reflection proceeds for various reasons: to envisage what incarnation and trinity mean; to resolve the problem of theodicy; to attain epistemic certainly regarding one's salvation; to confirm human freedom in the face of determinism; to understand the spiritual world; to reconcile the plurality of what is with the unity of God, and so on.

The theological and intellectual traditions within which doubters find themselves provide the starting point for theological reflection. The doubts themselves are handed down from generation to generation in the form of unresolved questions and inadequate answers. One generation may, because of the social, intellectual, and historical matrix within which it finds itself, be led to deal extensively with one set of questions, perhaps leading to satisfactory albeit momentary (even if for a few succeeding generations) resolution, perhaps reframing the problematic altogether. Alternatively, engaging any particular problematic could result in an even greater obfuscation whereby multiple sets of other connected questions are opened up. Of course, the same generation could bypass previously unresolved issues altogether, leaving such basically untouched for posterity. It is fair to say, using the Kuhnian language of paradigm shifts, that each generation is subject to the plausibility conditions of theological reflection whereby certain venues are opened up for (re)consideration and not others.

But again, theology as an imaginative enterprise is a second order affair that traffics in abstractions, generalities, and speculative hypotheses. Truly creative advances can indeed be made in one generation which are not recognized as such until a much later time. And, of course, the gains finally received may not necessarily command consent even for later generations. One thinks of the initial rejection of the Nicene settlement such that Christian orthodoxy would have been preserved in the doctrinal platform of the twentieth century's Jehovah's Witnesses if not for Athanasius' "stand against the world." And then again, securing the *homoousious* against Arius led through Apollinarius, Nestorius, Eutychus, et al., to the Chalcedonian creed. The "two natures" doctrine of Chalcedon itself immediately drew reactions from monophysites and Nestorians, just to name two groups. Even today, the value of both the Nicene-Constantinopolitan and Chalcedonian statements are suspect from various quarters, ranging from postmodern relativists on the one side to biblical primitivists and others who adhere to the "hellenization of dogma" thesis on the other.

Where do we go from here? Conservatives call us to return either to the pure revelation of holy Scripture or to the received orthodoxy of the patristic period. Liberals and postmoderns want to keep our focus on the times. Others suggest alternative responses, including orthopraxis or mystical solitude. In any case, none can stay long where they are at unless doubts are simply silenced and pronounced illegitimate. Part of the genius of Christian faith, it seems to me, is that it is open to critical questioning and even encourages and delights in the process of inquiry (cf. Ps. 34:8; Acts 17:11). The same God who identified historically with humankind in the Jew from Nazareth is the God who took upon himself the vicissitudes of history in all its finitude, frailty, and fallenness. The Galilean wondered during his passion whether his fate was truly avoidable and then went on from there to his death with the cry, "My God, my God, why have you forsaken me?" on his lips. That question, of course, was asked previously (Ps. 22:1), and continues to be asked down to the present day. Unlike cultic groups who deny their followers the privilege of questioning asserted authority, doubt drives theological inquiry until our hearts finally find rest in God (Augustine).

In and through all of this, the Spirit is simultaneously subject and object of theological inquiry. As "deep calls to deep" (Ps. 42:7), the Spirit calls us beyond ourselves even as she carries us where we are unable to go on our own. Theological work periodically comes to a resting place where doubt—especially that motivated by soteriological concerns—is alleviated by the Spirit's inner witness. Certainly the Spirit's inner soteriological work includes epistemological effects (cf. Abraham 1990, esp. 435–40). This comes about in part through the Spirit's reversing the noetic and affective consequences of the fall into sin, thereby restoring proper functionality to the believer's epistemic capacities (cf. Plantinga 2000, chs. 8–9). At these moments when the Spirit's saving and enlightening work is experienced, human beings are enabled to transcend the subject-object dichotomy since satisfied doubts overcome, at least momentarily, the chasm between the knowing self and the unknown other. Here, truly theological knowing in the form of doxology occurs (cf. Rom. 11:33–36).

My argument so far is that theological interpretation is activity that is inspired and guided by the Spirit. Let me make three summary observations by way of transitioning at this point. First, it would here behoove us to be reminded by Charles Wood that the inspiration of Scripture should not be considered simply as a historical claim. Inspiration, as we have seen, is a pneuma-tological category. The implications of this for theological hermeneutics is that the Spirit's inspirational activities can only be understood in dynamic terms, whether such be applied to Scripture, tradition, revelation, or otherwise. Yet Wood is also correct to point that that Christians certainly desire that their reading of the text be inspired by the Spirit. And this involves, at least in part, the decision by the reader to receive the scriptures as God's word to him or her. In other words, this would be a self-conscious hermeneutical decision to read Scripture in faith—faithfully, and with humility (cf. Wright 2000, 243–45)—even if one also believes, as many increasingly do, that the Bible consists of fully human documents (cf. Wood 1993, 67). Even in these cases, however, the Spirit is certainly capable of vivifying such words at various times and places.

Second, the issue of theological reference is now much more complex in light of the preceding remarks. If theological inquiry is inspired in unpredictable ways by the Spirit's working in and through our imaginative engagements with the world; if such proceeds from the converging matrix of particular and yet dynamic perspectives, locations, and traditions; if it is driven by various needs, aspirations, questions, and doubts; if its teloi are both objective and subjective, intending, at different moments, assortments of soteric, pragmatic, doxastic, epistemic, and properly theological notions variously configured; then theological beliefs, doctrines, and even dogmas need to be properly interpreted at each of these various levels. The potential for confusion is legion since inquiry carried out to resolve practical issues may lead to a theological formulation that is later dislocated or abstracted from its original context of inquiry. When extracted from the context of the socio-historical problematic it was originally intended to address, misunderstanding inevitably results. (An excellent case in point is the unintentional elevation to dogma of the metaphysics of substance undergirding the patristic creeds when in point of fact, the Church Fathers were motivated primarily by soteriological rather than by metaphysical concerns.) Now of course, my whole argument calls us to attend to the interrelatedness of these various dimensions and questions, and to such interrelatedness I will return to discuss in more detail below. Yet my point at present is to demand specificity with regard to theological reference precisely because theological interpretation arises as a holistic activity directed to a multitude of teloi.

Finally, a preliminary word on discernment. Theological interpretation requires discernment of the divine presence and activity in the various concrete particularities, including religious, intellectual, cultural, political, and socio-historical traditions, that situate selves-in-communities (cf. Gorringe 1990). Theological knowledge emerges from these particular matrices as the Spirit manifests herself through interpretive actions by such selves-in-communities on datum that are continuously shifting and evolving. Theological interpretation therefore of necessity focuses on discerning both the forms of the past as they bear on the continuously shifting present, and the specious present itself, precisely in order to discern appropriate responses directed toward suitable goals. This discernment includes, but it is not limited to, the self, the self's various communities of inquiry, the world at large, epistemic processes themselves, and the potentially confusing influences of trajectories of truthlessness or falsehood (idolatry or the demonic). Theological reflection on this side of the eschaton remains an open-ended and ceaseless task in the Spirit through whom we live, move, have our being, and interpret.

8 The Objects of Interpretation: Word

As one might object, treating theological hermeneutics purely as a pneumatological enterprise would leave us with the persisting difficulties of dealing with the innumerable false claims presented by those who profess to have been inspired by the Spirit. These are those whose subjectivity has apparently been unconstrained, and whose imagination knows no bounds. How do we confirm any particular interpretation to be inspired by the Spirit of God? How might we realize another interpretation to be demonically inspired? What about the subtlety and sophistication of human aspirations and creativity to produce interpretations motivated by self-interest driven by corruption and depravity? Or, what about human finitude and fallibility? How would cognitive errors be corrected?

My thesis is that theological interpretation is the continuous interplay of Spirit, Word, and community. In this chapter, I expand on the objective givens that fund and constrain theological interpretation. My goal is to deal specifically with the question of how to discern the objects of interpretation—revelation that is mediated experientially, scripturally and ecclesially—that are relevant to the theological task. The following therefore seeks to sketch explicitly a hermeneutics of religious experience, a hermeneutics of the Word of God, and a hermeneutics of the ecclesial and theological tradition.[1] These are especially pressing concerns since, as I have argued so far, all are "given" to and lay claim on our lives in some way on the one hand while being responded to in a subjective manner by human-beings-in-community on the other.

8.1 The Hermeneutics of Experience

In beginning with what may be called the hermeneutics of experience, three preliminary remarks are in order. First, interpretation at some point requires self-reflection. Theological interpretation needs to be discerning about how the experiences of the self-in-community are intertwined with how one

---

[1] Even a Reformer of the stature of Calvin understood the notion of revelation in these (trinitarian) terms (see Butin 1995, esp. 55–61).

understands God and the world. This is because experience is both phenomenologically and logically prior to reflection and the second-order activity of theologizing. As such, the norms emergent from our experiences operate powerfully, most often underneath our full consciousness. At times, such experiential norms override whatever else we may be confronted with. Thus, we neglect consideration of experience as a given for theological reflection to our own peril since, as I will make clear, we all exegete our experiences (or lack of them, as the case may be) whether consciously or not. Thus, for instance, our experience of the finality of physical death makes it difficult for us moderns and postmoderns to take the physical resurrection of Jesus with full seriousness.

Second, a brief word should be said about what I mean by experience. Donald Gelpi has called it a "weasel word" since it connotes such a wide variety of meanings (1994, 2). Among the variant definitions, Gelpi enumerates four: 1) the non-technical meaning of practical wisdom gained from prolonged exposure to reality; 2) the medieval notion of the "powers of sense" derived from the five external senses, the emotions, the imagination, and sense-judgments; 3) all uncritical or pre-reflective cognition; 4) the entire spectrum of human evaluative responses. My use of the term includes the last two meanings identified by Gelpi. Certainly, language is inextricable from perception as such once we think about it and attempt to articulate it to ourselves or others. Yet our reflections do not engage the entirety of our experiences, not only our sense experiences, but also our non-perceptual experiences of ourselves, our memories, our imaginations, etc. Further, what we do (and experience) at any given moment is not always later thought about or articulated, even as we sometimes do things without conscious forethought or awareness of so doing. (Of course, there are also times when we do plan and execute our plans, even as we then later reflect on how those plans went.) What I would like to do here is to point out how some of our experiences affect our theologizing when brought to reflective consciousness.

Finally, I wish to make a few remarks about how it is that our experiences function as objects for theological interpretation. As already noted, thinking is a second-order activity that grasps by way of abstractions our experiences which are continuous and dynamic. All thought and reflection, in this sense, emerge out of experience. By asserting the possibility of experience serving as an object of reflection, then, I mean simply that human beings consciously carve out slices of experience, now smaller, now greater, for categorical reflection. Thinking is a more or less continuous activity; however, thought contents are discrete and inferential representations of rather arbitrary slices of experiences since the human mind is finite rather than infinite and unable to comprehend the whole of experience all at once. These representations follow each other in succession mentally. And, as representations, such mental objects (thoughts) are always-already semiotic interpretations of perceptual experience from the start. It follows then that aspects of our experiences emerge as objects for theological reflection precisely as interpretations from the beginning.

This said, it should be clear that our "pure experiences" are unavailable for reflection. Thinking involves interpretation all the way down. Theological reflection thus aims at its subject matter—God, self, world, etc.—but needs to recognize such always as second order interpretations. Scripture itself is interpreted experience, the genre of narrative and testimony that fills its pages being most indicative of this. Similarly, tradition is available to us only as historically reconstructed (or, as theological portraiture, to use Edward Farley's term). Further, we do not interpret either Scripture or tradition directly, but rather interpret our experience of reading Scripture and tradition. In a sense, then, we are at least twice removed from the reality described by what has been understood as the primary (biblical and traditional) sources of theology. Yet our most direct path to that reality is through the experience of reading both. If, as previously argued [6.1.2], experience mediates and relates self and other, then our access to the other is therefore through the experiences of the self. Interpretation thus begins with the self—more specifically, with the discernment of the self, and that always understood as the self-in-community. In what follows, I want to briefly examine only three of the many categories of experiential objects given to theological reflection: enthusiasm, ritual, and the mystical encounter.

8.1.1 By "enthusiasm," I mean nothing more than our experience of God (*en-theos*), what we have previously described as the in-breaking of the Spirit's presence into our lives. Paul's encounter with Jesus on the road to Damascus and his later infilling with the Holy Spirit resulted in a radical conversion, a abrupt turning of his life in the opposite direction, literally, southward to Arabia instead. The one who had passionately disbelieved in Jesus and persecuted his followers was now confronted with the reality of the risen Lord, and given the ability to believe. Similarly, Augustine's incapacity to attain peace of heart, truth of mind, and rightness of will was overcome through the word that awakened him at the right hour (cf. Rom. 13:11), and Luther's penitent but guilt-filled life was alleviated only upon encountering the message that "the righteous will live by faith." Now it is arguable that Augustine's was a fair response to the scriptural injunction. Yet it is also arguable both that Luther's understanding of Romans 1:17 can only with difficulty be reconciled with Paul's intentions regarding the letter to the Romans, not to mention the larger canonical witness (remember that Luther rejected the authority of James), and that Paul's cited usage of Habakkuk 2:4 deviates significantly from the message of the prophet. My point, however, is that life experiences shape—either by confirming, extending, checking, or even sometimes correcting—our reading and interpretation of received scriptural traditions, and that we therefore need to pay attention to the experiential matrices that birth our theological interpretations.

This is perhaps more clearly seen than in the theological explication of glossolalic experiences on the one hand, and the doctrinal insistence on the cessation of the charismata on the other. The earliest Christians "began to speak in other languages, as the Spirit gave them ability" (Acts 2:4), and tongues and interpretation of tongues as well as other charismatic or spiritual gifts continued throughout the first century Church even if there were occasions where certain congregations misunderstood and misused them. The emergence and decline of the Montanist movement during the latter half of the second century, however, served as the occasion which marked in some respects the triumph of the Church institutional over the Church charismatic. By declaring Montanism a heretical movement, guilt by association was attached to tongues, prophecy, and other charismatic gifts, among other things (cf. Trevett 1995). Overt charismatic manifestations continued occasionally throughout Church history, but always with the stigma of Montanist heresy appended. The Reformers polemics on two fronts—against the abuses of medieval Christendom on the one side and against the enthusiasms of the radical *Schwarmerei* on the other—led to their emphasis on *sola scriptura*, their exaltation of the sacrament of preaching, and the centrality of the pulpit in the Protestant liturgical environment. The convergence of these various factors led, over time, to the emergence of a fairly sophisticated theology of revelation which argued for the cessation of the charismata following from a dispensationalist understanding of the completion and canonical reception of the enscripted Word of God. The onset of Deistic Christianity during the seventeenth and eighteenth centuries did not help the cause of those arguing for the ongoing validity of either miracles or spiritual gifts. This cessationist theology, as it has come to be known, received its most elaborate articulation and vigorous defense in the work of the nineteenth century Princeton theologian, Benjamin B. Warfield.

The early twentieth century Pentecostal revival launched at Azusa Street, however, was a turning point in the Church's understanding of both glossolalia in particular and the charismata more generally. Modern Pentecostal narratives of what they called "Spirit-baptism" or the "second (or even third) blessing" has featured the experience of being grasped radically by the sense of the numinous presence of God. To be sure, the early Pentecostals were accused by Protestant fundamentalists in the cessationist tradition of speaking in the tongues of demons rather than by the Spirit of God. Rather than quenching the revival, such polemics seemed only to encourage it, the extended result being the charismatic renewal movement in the mainline and Catholic churches in mid-century, and the Third Wave movement since the 1980s. Today, few of even the most staunch dispensationalists care to argue a cessationist theology regarding miracles, signs, wonders, and spiritual gifts.

My argument here is that experience functions as an object for theological reflection. In the case of contemporary Pentecostals and charismatics, their experiences of glossolalia and other spiritual gifts led to theological reflection wherein such features were prominent. Arguably, the cessationist polemic of Warfield and others against miracles and the charismata was driven as much by their own experiences, including, as it were, a lack of experience of the phenomena they strove the refute (cf. Ruthven 1993; Stronstad 1995, esp. 58–71). In either case, God was experienced concretely in certain ways and not others, resulting in emphasis on certain points, neglect of others, and polemics against doctrines and positions which ran counter to one's experiential horizons.

8.1.2 Similar things may be said of ritual experiences. Arguably, religious rituals are evolutionary means through which humans construct and shape sacred meanings, beliefs, and practices (cf. Rappaport 1999).[2] As such, Christian liturgical rites can be understood as premeditated structures designed to cultivate and nurture Christian life. At the same time, rituals are complex phenomena that serve multiple socio-cultural, psychological, and religious functions. So, Christian ritual activities are not meant to be walked through by rote, but are meant to be effective with regard to our experience of God and our corresponding transformation so we can live faithfully and truthfully in the world. Taking the sacrament of the Eucharist for the moment, it is arguable that no matter what one believes about the presence of Christ, the result

[2] Alternatively, Catherine Bell's theoretical proposals need to be heeded. Her deconstructive analysis have shown how understandings of ritual have impinged on ritual studies to date (Bell 1992). Further, she has also argued that ritual is not a universal feature of human behavior and experience, but is, rather, a scholarly construct designed to explicate social, cultural and religious situatedness and the ordered relationships of human beings to mediated sources of power and authority (Bell 1997). My use of ritual should be understood heuristically rather than ontically. It is designed along with the categories enthusiasm and mysticism to specify how the density of human experiences function as objects of theological reflection.

is encouragement for Christian life. Sacramentalists would argue that such encouragement is the direct result of the grace mediated through the partaking of the eucharistic elements (for Catholics, the consecrated host and wine). On the other side, non-sacramental eucharistic theologies would also agree in the mediation of grace, except that such would come through the community of faith's obedient remembering, celebrating, and anticipating of Jesus' life, death, and parousia, rather than through the elements themselves as such.

In either case, a comprehensive theology of the Eucharist would emerge not only from reflection on the scriptural witness, but also from the Church's reflecting on its actual experiences of the Eucharist throughout history. When and how often should the community of faith gather around the Lord's table? Where in the liturgy does the Eucharist belong? Who should administer the Lord's supper? Who is eligible to receive the elements? What is the ritual process for the eucharistic feast? These are just some of the questions about which the apostolic witness is itself ambiguous and to which only Christian experience as preserved in the ecclesial tradition begins to answer. In fact, there is some evidence that the earliest (post-Pentecost) Christians celebrated the Lord's supper as they fellowshipped around the daily meal (Acts 2:46). Today, most Christians call these occasions potlucks and reserve the eucharistic meal for more solemn expressions, no doubt in the wake of Paul's rebuke of the degenerate form of the meal shared among the Corinthian Christians (cf. 1 Cor. 11:20–22). My point is that our theology of the Eucharist derives as much, if not more, from our ritual experiences of it than from consultation of the biblical texts.

This applies to all forms of Christian ritual and not just "high Church" Christianity. Pentecostal ritual, for example, is probably as "low Church" as one can find within Christendom. Yet it is designed in very specific ways to enable worshippers to imitate what Pentecostals consider the spontaneous movements of the Spirit of God. In Daniel Albrecht's (1999) analysis, from the pre-service gathering or greeting rites, on through to the opening chorus (call to worship), the praise and worship, the congregational prayer (often for physical healing or other needs), the sermon (unless pre-empted by the Spirit of God), the altar call, and the dispersal and final farewell, the Pentecostal worshipper encounters God visually, audibly, kinesthetically, and even physically. In a real sense, Pentecostal ritual is thereby supremely embodied. It has its own logical of sacramentality whereby the spiritual realm is mediated through the material and ritual dimensions of healing, song, glossolalia, the dance, the shout, the lifting up of hands, the experience of being "slain in the Spirit," and so on.

Three aspects of Albrecht's discussion are important for our purposes. First,

Pentecostal worshippers participate fully in the service and are transformed by contemplating, expressing sorrow and contrition, and celebrating God's presence through their ceremonial experiences. Second, Pentecostal commitments to being led by the Spirit enables them to combat stagnation and ensure that rites evolve dynamically and vary in terms of format and/or performance. Finally, Pentecostal ritual provides opportunities for the expression of human concerns (e.g., faith in prayer rites, repentance at altar rites, or communal solidarity in greeting or dispersal rites), social configurations (e.g., distinguishing pastoral from lay leadership, confirming prophetic roles or even calling, or allowing the emergence of charismatic giftings and perhaps vocations), and theological relationships (e.g., within the local congregation, in mission to the world, or vertically toward God himself). These expressions, however, serve a pragmatic function as well, whether it be in terms of fostering community, nurturing wholeness, motivating action, or enabling transformation.

It should be sufficiently clear, then, that congregational rituals are a central means of engaging the divine, of being confronted with the divine Word, and of undergoing spiritual—personal and communal—transformation. Theology therefore emerges, at least in part, from the human experience of God's self-revelation in and through ecclesial liturgy and ritual. In fact, I would go so far as to say that the ritual structures of the Church are necessary components to the processes of socialization of the individual Christians into the community of faith and nurture their ongoing development and maturation. As will be suggested later, theology as a second order activity by the Church and for the Church cannot exclude explicit reflection on ritual, first experienced and then considered as an objective datum.

8.1.3 Last but by no means least to be considered is what goes under the category of mysticism. As in the preceding discussion of enthusiasm and ritual, my purpose here is not to untangle the scholarly debates on these topics (about which there are too many to detail), but to illuminate the claim that aspects of experience serve as objective data for theological reflection. To begin with, consider Paul's repeated refrain about being "in Christ." In what ways is this a theological versus ecclesial, existential, psychological, or other kind of claim? How might we begin to understand this union with and in Jesus? Might this have anything to do with Paul's own self-assessment as having "been crucified with Christ" (Gal. 2:19b)? Might it also not refer to what Paul later describes as freedom in Christ and life in the Spirit (Gal. 5)? And what might all of this have to do with his insistence that "God's love has been poured out into our hearts through the Holy Spirit that has been given to us" (Rom. 5:5)?

Let me suggest that one way to unpack these statements is to understand Paul's own mystical experiences of union with Christ in and by the Spirit. We are given hints of such in his praying and singing hymns at midnight with Silas in the jail in Philippi (Acts 16:25); in his experiences of life amidst death, of sustenance through persecution, trial and hardship, and of strength in weakness(cf. 2 Cor. 4:7–12, 11:23–33, 12:9–10); in his gaining Christ over and against other gains, and being content in every situation (Phil. 3:3–14, 4:11–13); and in the peace and courage with which he faced death (Acts 21:13; and, if authentic to Paul, 2 Tim. 4:6–8). The portrait that emerges is that of a man wholly given to God and the work of the Kingdom of God. Such a portrait, one might counter, is hardly mysticism at all, at least not in the traditional sense of having rapturous or ecstatic experiences. Looking closer, however, I see a strong connection between the traditionally defined mystical sense of the loss of self in union with Christ and Paul's claim, "I have been crucified with Christ; and it is no longer I who live, but it is Christ who lives in me" (Gal. 2:19b–20).

This connection is certainly made explicit in at least one instance in the Pauline corpus: that of being caught up to the third heaven (2 Cor. 12:1–6). This event included much of what the later mystical tradition would emphasize: visionary experience, out-of-body "travel," the apophatic moment wherein silence is the only appropriate response, and so on. Even in the last mentioned case, however, what is experienced can be understood either as the fullness of the divine presence (which explains, in part, the eclipse of the sense of the self) or as the radical otherness and absence of God (whereby God can only be conceptualized or categorized negatively—in terms of what God is not). In either case, one reaches the point where language no longer serves to convey theological content since language itself assumes the kataphatic nature of the subject/object identity-in-difference which the mystical experience has obliterated. The result is that mystical experience, whether in its "everyday" sense seen in the life of Paul and other saints, or in the apophatic tradition of Paul's third heaven experience, the Cappadocian Gregories, Pseudo-Dionysius, Eckhart, etc., serves in its own way as an objective datum for theological reflection.

My purpose so far has been to argue that the Christian experience of God, whether breaking upon the believer as radically other or mediated liturgically, ritually, mystically, or otherwise, is fundamental to the data of theological interpretation. At the same time, it is critically important to remember that not all experiences classified under the preceding categories qualify as legitimate experiences of the divine. Paul himself warned about the one who was capable of masquerading as an angel of light (2 Cor. 11:14), and it is certainly possible that charismatic, ritual and mystical experiences are demonic trajectories with harmful or destructive effects. Experience, as has often been said, needs to be discerned. My claim is that religious experience is discerned in part by way of theological reflection, and that such discernment should always take place, as does the experience which is being discerned, amidst the self-in-community.

One more important set of questions needs to be heard before proceeding: how are experiences normative, and what are the ways in which they function normatively? Further, should experience function normatively, and if yes, then how so? To take the second couplet of questions first, an affirmative response seems unavoidable. How else would norms arise (even scriptural ones) if not out of experience (in the case of scriptural norms, through reading, recitation, memorization, liturgical reenactment, etc.)? If that is the case, then the former set of questions includes its own answers. Because our experiences are, in a real sense, given to us, at the level of description, it seems to me impossible to deny that they function normatively—in the formal sense—as general constraints on our capacity to understand. Much of what we experience becomes engrained in us so as to guide and shape future possibilities of thought and action. I would therefore want to be open to the possibility that our ongoing experiences may actually bring about understandings that correct previously selected perceptions and interpretations of either the scriptural and/or later theological traditions. In this sense, experience serves up a set of formal norms for theological understanding that in turn brings about novel or creative ways of being-in-the-world.

Having admitted that experience functions as formally normative at least in certain ways, it is also imperative to remember that experiential criteria do not operate on their own, even if other norms emerge only from the experiential matrix. This is in part because experience serves as both the medium and as object of interpretation. As medium, experience is normative with regard to how we interpret. As object, experience is abstracted as a semiotic datum for interpretation. Therefore, just as experiential abstractions focused as objects of theological reflection may correct Scripture, so also the reverse may occur. This leads to the topic of Scripture as object for theological interpretation.

8.2 The Hermeneutics of the Word of God

My goal here is to sketch what may be called a hermeneutics of the Word of God. Even as experience mediates ourselves and the otherness of the world, words arise out of our experience and, as previously discussed [5.1.2], are symbols that relate our thoughts to reality. In what ways, however, can we understand God's word to arise out of our experience? I would suggest this happens in the sense that God speaks to reveal himself to us and to call us toward himself. "And the Word became flesh and lived *among us*" (John 1:14, my emphasis). In so doing, the divine Word is always to us, for us, and in our midst. It is experienced as an other that demands our response. Simply put, as we go about the business of living, we are sometimes gripped by the divine Word thundering in our hearts, other times sensitized to the word of the Spirit as she speaks softly. I want to look variously at how the spoken, lived, and written word of God confronts us and lays claim on our lives.

8.2.1 What does it mean to say God speaks? One could argue that divine speech occurs through deputized or authorized representatives (i.e., the prophets), or through God's appropriating the discourse of human beings as his own (see Wolterstorff 1995; cf. Abraham 1981). Yet early on in the Christian tradition, Ignatius of Antioch had already distinguished the "three speeches" of God as creation, incarnation and Scripture (see Vanhoozer 2000, 72). Leaving the latter two modes of divine speech aside for the moment, I want to briefly explore the significance of the creative Word of God through Austin's (1975) speech-act theory which understands words simply uttered (locutionary acts), words doing something (illocutionary acts), and words bringing something about (perlocutionary acts). God's Word is illocutionary insofar as God is creating with it, and perlocutionary insofar as it produced the world as we know it, e.g., "And God said, 'Let there be light'; and there was light" (Gen. 1:3). My immediate interests, however, lie in how God's speaking functions objectively for theological reflection and by so doing, also serves as a check and balance for our acts of interpretation.

Let us begin with God who has spoken "to our ancestors in many and various ways by the prophets" (Heb. 1:1) On the one hand, the Word of the Lord to "speak tenderly to Jerusalem, and cry to her that she has served her term, that her penalty is paid, that she has received from the Lord's hand double for all her sins" (Isa. 40:2) is simply a locution describing a certain state of affairs; it is, however, at the same time also illocutionary with the intent of comforting the people of God (Isa. 40:1). On the other hand, observe the illocutionary force of the divine Word to Nebuchadnezzer—"You shall be driven away from human society, and your dwelling shall be with the wild animals. You shall be made to eat grass like oxen, you shall be bathed with the dew of heaven" (Dan. 4:25a)— which came to pass soon enough (4:33) and thereby brought about (perhaps in an indirect perlocutionary sense) a different state of affairs in the repentant and transformed king than had previously existed (4:34–37). Last but not least, consider the perlocutionary effects of Isaiah's prophetic word to Hezekiah who was sick to the point of death: "Set your house in order for you shall die; you shall not recover" (Isa. 38:1b). The result was Hezekiah's repentance in prayers and tears and extension of his life (38:2–5). As spoken through Deutero-Isaiah: as rain waters the earth and seed yields produce, "so shall my word be that goes out from my mouth; it shall not return to me empty, but it shall accomplish that which I purpose, and succeed in the thing for which I sent it" (Isa. 55:11).

Similar analyses of the creative and prophetic Word of God can be found in the Christian Testament. Matthias Wenk (2000) argues, for instance, that the Holy Spirit in Luke-Acts is more than just the divine person who inspires the speech of the people of God. Rather, inspired speech through specifically appointed representatives—the divine Word—is but the intentional (illocutionary) work of the Spirit of God through which the believing community is transformed (the perlocutionary effect). Thus the Spirit-inspired speeches in the infancy narratives (Luke 1–2) herald the new, restoring work of God that is about to transpire through Jesus (Luke) and the believing community (Acts). Jesus' ministry of reconstituting a liberated community is itself anointed by the Spirit of God (Luke 4:18–19). Luke's version of what we have came to identify as the Lord's prayer (11:2–4) is the means through which the people of God ask and receive the life transforming and community-forming power of the Spirit of God (11:13). Pentecost (Acts 2) is a liberative event of the Spirit that results in the formation of the new messianic community (2:42–47). Elsewhere in volume two of Luke-Acts, the Spirit's words and works level out socio-economic, ethnic, and gender differences, even while these same words and works identify, mark, and guide the people of God. Wenk's exposition of Luke-Acts thus highlights the illocutionary and perlocutionary work of the Spirit of God that restore and reconciles human relationships with God and with each other.

This means that my listening to what the Spirit is saying includes my being open to being transformed by what is said, and not just myself, but all those claim to be of the Spirit of God and are claimed by that same Spirit. The prophetic Word of God should be understood not only as inspired speech, but as a complex interactive process between God, the prophet, the inspired utterance, and the audience to which such utterance is directed. Thus, the prophetic message of John the Baptist, for example, is the means through which God addresses Israel, the tax collectors, and the soldiers, and which produces in them repentance (Luke 3:1–14). Yet, it was also a message which left a mark on the messenger himself since John could not be a voice proclaiming in the wilderness (3:4; cf. Isa. 40:3) without having his home in the desert. Spirit-inspired speech thus has transformative effects on both the speaker and the audience. At the same time, rejected prophecy is not only a rejection of the prophet, or the word of the prophet, but also of (the Word and Spirit of) God. Thus the intertestamental period is better understood as reflecting the unwillingness of the people of Israel to hear, engage, or be transformed by the Word of God than as the period during which prophecy ceased (cf. Wenk 2000, 122–33). In other words, it is not—either during the intertestamental centuries, the early Christian period, or since—that the Spirit of God has ceased to speak the prophetic word; rather, a hard-hearted and hard-of-hearing people have refused to accept the message, the messenger (the inspired prophet), or God (cf. Acts 28:25–28). Arguably then, the prophetic word of God never ceases; it is, instead, denied, ignored, neglected, rejected or resisted by the unfaithful community.

The spoken Word of God thus confronts us as an other, a locution. It also makes demands of us, as an illocution. Finally, it actually transforms us, as a perlocution. Thus is the Word of God "living and active" (Heb. 4:12). For the Church, this effectiveness of the divine Word demonstrates the power and life of the Spirit of God since the words of God spoken "are spirit and life" (John 6:63b). In these ways, to say that one interprets the Word of God is true only in a weak sense since the divine Word is not an object that can be manipulated according to our own wants and wishes. More accurate would be to say that the divine Word "interprets" us by the power of the Spirit.[3] In this sense, the Word of God spoken stands over and against us as an other. It is this word that calls us beyond ourselves, lays claim on our lives, demands our response, and, in the end, transforms us in our inabilities.

The interpretation of Scripture could therefore be said to be constrained in at least these three ways: as locution, as illocution, and as perlocution (see Watson 1997, ch. 3, and Vanhoozer 1998). The parameters of the text are established on the one side by the world of the text, including the text's original meaning as intended by the author and as received by the audience. On the other side, however, is the world "created" or opened up by the text, including the transformations brought about by the text in its readers. A diversity of transformations do ensue from the reading of scriptural texts. But even if not all of

---

[3] That the Spirit's work is and must be present for the divine Word to be transformative is an old theme. For earlier statements, the first which represent a classical liberal theological perspective, see Gore (1889). More contemporary treatments include Henry (1979, Theses 12 and 13), Klooster (1984, 451–72), Maier (1994, 45–64, 308–19), Pinnock (1993 and 1993a), Stein (1994, ch. 3), and Vanhoozer (1998, ch. 7).

these could be said to have been originally intended by the biblical authors, the criteria for determining those which are valid from those which are not may not be purely textual. "Let two or three prophets speak, and let the others weigh what is said" (1 Cor. 14:29) requires the kind of spiritual discernment which is not simply a matter of applying the principle of "Scripture interprets Scripture," as important as that might be. Rather, such criteriology reintroduces the real and yet necessarily healthy tension between Spirit and Word whereby both are distinct and yet interdependent, mutually reciprocal, and mutually subordinated to the other. In short, meaning and interpretation is grounded at least in a two-fold manner: in author(s) or text(s) insofar as the biblical language functions communicatively (Word), and in performative or interpretive activity insofar as the biblical language functions transformatively (Spirit).

8.2.2 This transformative power of the Word of God is most clearly seen in the life, death and resurrection of Jesus Christ—the living Word of God. Jesus is the Christ, the one anointed by the Holy Spirit. The same divine breath who hovered over the waters and carried the creative Word of God is the one through whom Jesus is conceived (Luke 1:25; cf. Matt. 1:18b), through whose filling his life and deeds were empowered (Luke 4:1, 14, 18–19, passim). and through whom Jesus gives up his life (Heb. 9:14). More important, as Lyle Dabney (2000) has pointed out, is that it is the Spirit of life who is the "presence of God in the absence of the Father"—note Jesus' cry on the cross, addressed not to Abba, but to "God" (Matt. 27:46)—and who raised Jesus from the dead (Rom. 1:4), from the very abyss, darkness, and forsakenness of the cross which was nothing less than the breach in God himself. In this sense, it is true to say that Jesus was who he was only as subordinate to the power of the Spirit of God, and that the Spirit is the measure of Jesus' anointed life, death, and resurrection.

Having said this, it is imperative to recognize also that the Spirit of God is none other than the Spirit of Jesus, sent to remind the Church of his words, to glorify him and lift him up. As the divine breath of life for all humankind (Gen. 2:7), the Spirit proceeds from the Father to the world in order to testify of the Son (John 15:26). To have the mind of God is impossible except by or through the Spirit who bestows upon us the mind of Christ (1 Cor. 2:11–12, 16b). Similarly, as the breath of God for the community of faith, the Spirit is given by Jesus (John 20:22) in order to enable his followers to do even greater things than he did (John 14:12). The work of Jesus, it is thus arguable, is to baptize with the Holy Spirit (Matt. 3:11b; Mark 1:8; Luke 3:16; John 1:34) resulting, in part, in the endowment of power for witness (Luke 24:49; cf. Acts 1:5, 8) to the saving person and name of Jesus (Acts 4:7–12).

It is therefore better said that there is a mutual subordination of the living Word of God (Jesus as the incarnate Logos) to the spoken Word of God (the Spirit) and vice versa, with both, in the end, being eschatologically subordinate to God the Father (1 Cor. 15:24–28). Word defines Spirit, and Spirit defines Word. Together, they are, as already noted, the "two hands of the Father," and yet the Spirit herself is the legal field of force through which the togetherness of the Father and the Son is revealed to the world. But this revelation of Jesus the Christ is the living Word of God who is over and against us, and who confronts us by the power of his Spirit. It is this Jesus who calls us to repentance and discipleship in anticipation of the impending Kingdom of God (Mark 1:15). It is because of this Jesus that the community of faith gathers around the Lord's Table to celebrate Jesus as the object of faith on the one hand, and fellowship with him in an interpersonally subjective manner on the other. It is this Jesus who is preached, and in that proclamation draws near to us.

Christian theological interpretation is therefore confronted on every turn by the concreteness, the social and historical materiality, and the undeniable particularity of the person of Jesus the Christ, the living Word of God. It is the Son whose face is "the reflection of God's glory and the exact imprint of God's very being" (Heb. 1:3a), and in whom "the whole fullness of deity dwells bodily" (Col. 2:9). As such, the living Word of God silences and exorcises the demonic powers from our midst; he confronts us in our idolatry and demands that every thought to be taken captive and made obedient to his mind; he reflects upon our lives as a mirror, penetrating into our innermost recesses of our hearts in order to unveil, expose, and deliver that which is opposed to the things of God. The living Word is therefore interpreted only insofar as he is engaged concretely, interpersonally and intersubjectively. Better, understood in the Levinasian sense, Jesus as the face of God demands us to look upon and respond to the one who is radically other. Yet he is not only other, but also the one who shares with us in the depths of our humanity, made like us in every way, sin excepted, in order to enter that place that none of us would rather be. Thus the living Word of God cries out for interpretation, even while, at the same time, enabling mutual encounter, (self-) understanding, and transformation. Whatever other data theological interpretation may work with, it cannot do without, much less ignore, the central given for theological reflection: the living Word of God in Jesus Christ. It is, finally, this person who is the inexhaustible way, truth, and life that serves as the concrete and material norm for all theological interpretation.

8.2.3 The living Word continues to serve as both formal and material norm, even without being materially present since the ascension. Certainly, the living Word is present by the power of the Spirit. Yet it may also be said that the living Word continues to be effective through the written Word of God. Within two generations after the Pentecost event, gospel accounts were generated to preserve the details of the life and teachings of Jesus. Initially, the concern of the early Church was with the apostolic witness. Only later did these witnesses take on the form of an authoritative canon. I will here pass over issues connected with the process of canonization. My concern in what follows is on how the written Word of God functions as object for theological interpretation. Let me make three general remarks toward that end.

The first thing to note is the diversity of genres in Scripture. There are historical narratives, literary texts, wisdom traditions, socio-political tracts for the times, letters, prophecies (both of the forthtelling as well as the foretelling types), gospel accounts, and so on. Diversity is characteristic not only of the genre categories in Scripture, but also within those categories themselves. There are, therefore, Jahwist and Elohist voices in the Torah, a variety of wisdom texts drawn from a variety of ancient Near Eastern cultures, major and minor prophets, a multiplicity of Writings in the Hebrew Bible, four (canonical) gospels, Catholic, Pauline, and perhaps deutero-Pauline epistles, etc. The fact is that each of these genres along with the pluralism that reigns in each category require a diversity of interpretations, a diversity of methods, a diversity of perspectives of approach, and so on (cf. Dulles 1983; Goldingay 1994; Fackre 1997; Gillingham 1998).

Yet not only do the various biblical genres need to be interpreted each on its own terms, but a further distinction should also be noted. As Clarence Walhout (1999) has recently pointed out, some texts are more conducive to "closed" readings (those connected, e.g., with the author's intention) while others are more amenable to "open" readings (e.g., those directed toward obtaining the reader's response). This is the case since, as illuminated by speech-act theory, certain texts are more so objects of action (from their authors) while other texts are more so instruments of action (on their readers). Finally, along this vein, a "pluralising hermeneutic" (as opposed to "singularising hermeneutic") is required not only to adequately handle pluralism at the source of theology, but also the plurality that accompanies the processes of traditioning and reception (cf. Rush 1997, esp. 326–30).

Now it is precisely through these different voices that Scripture makes its claim on our lives. I would argue that this reflects, at least in part, the richness of the various trajectories of early Christian experience. Helmut Koester and James Robinson (1971) paint a rich portrait of the milieu wherein what came to be recognized later as canonical Christian Scripture existed alongside gnostic (from Nag Hammadi), apocryphal (e.g., the Dead Sea Scrolls), pseudonymous, apocalyptic and other texts from the intertestamental period, and together informed developments in Judaism and early Jewish Christianity during the first and second centuries C.E. As historical beings, Christians have always struggled to hold together to unity of the Christian message as they have read, heard and attempted to live out one strand of the gospel today, another tomorrow, the first in an altogether different way on the third day, and so on.

My reference to hearing Scripture leads to the second point regarding how Scripture functions as object of interpretation. The written word, it is arguable, was never meant only to be read. Certainly the invention of the printing press has made texts available in such a way that we can now enjoy relatively quiet reading for its own sake. However, Scripture as the written Word of God was always meant to be experienced—imagined, spoken, heard, recited, memorized, interpreted, and obeyed—and that as directed toward a variety of liturgical, social, devotional, formational, and spiritual ends (cf. Coward 1988, 34–80; McCready 2000; Hart 2000a). This was certainly the original Hebrew understanding of Torah, as exemplified with the following facts. First, there were no vowel points in the original Hebrew script. This led to an ambiguity of pronunciation which was meant to be "resolved" by interaction between individuals in particular reading and reciting communities with the consonantal structures of the text. Second, Torah has always been understood to consist of a written and an oral tradition—the one illuminating the other and vice-versa—a dual tradition which has continued to the present with the relationship between Torah and Talmud, Mishnah, and so on. Finally, Torah was ultimately about how life should be lived. Emphasis on the textuality of Scripture as the Word of God has therefore been misplaced from the beginning. The Hebrews were constrained during the Babylonian exile to locate the living Word of God textually and script-urally because they were cut off from the vital structures and dynamics which nourished their participation in the divine Word, viz., land, temple, and sacrificial system (cf. Abram 1996, 239–50).

On the Christian side, it has also certainly been the case that the canon of Scripture itself is a relatively late development, provoked from the time of Marcion in the mid-second century onward by various doctrinal debates. But even then, until the development of the printing press, Christian life and piety revolved not around the written Scriptures but around the rules of faith, the liturgies, the sacraments, the iconographies, and so on. To claim that the Word of God is only textually and script-urally located would be to deny access to the divine Word for most Christians in history and many (who are illiterate) today. For this reason also, the Reformers emphasized the Word proclaimed and preached, not only the Word read, even if out loud. If Scripture was meant to be proclaimed, expounded and heard rather than simply recited, it should also be understood to represent or point to rather than contain or circumscribe the Word of God. Alternatively put, Scripture is not the Word of God but makes present the living Word of God in Jesus Christ (Barth and Bultmann). As such, Scripture serves as a guide to life, opening up possibilities for life, pointing to a world in front of, or beyond the text (Ricoeur). If that is the case, theological interpretation that engages Scripture needs to be attentive to that dimension of its function. In other words, theological hermeneutics may be as much an effort to understand how Scripture itself shapes both us and the ways in which we theologize (by virtue of Scripture's capacity to form, inform, and transform the way we live, read, think, etc.) as it is an effort to understand what Scripture says about the many items of doctrine or topics of theology which we theologize about (see Work 2001).

This leads, third, to the difficult issue of Scripture's authority, at least vis-à-vis theological interpretation. Here David H. Kelsey (1999), has helpfully distinguished between two modes of Scripture's authority: *de jure*—theological theories about authority—and *de facto*—actual, usually functional and operational, uses of Scripture in theological reasoning and argument. He proposes through an analysis of theologians across the spectrum of Protestantism that the normativeness of Scripture lies less in its being a source for theological reflection as it does in providing a variety of normative patterns—e.g., conceptual, doctrinal/propositional, recital/narrative, historical, expressive—for cultivating, assessing, and critiquing the theological imagination. Thus the relationship between Scripture and theology is much more complex than one would assume from (at least conservative Protestant) discussions of scriptural authority and normativity. My own view assumes Kelsey's conclusions with regard to modern theology with the one caveat that while not denying his positive thesis, it seems to me undeniable that Scripture also functions, at least in part, as a source for theological reflection. In what follows, however, I am more interested in the genealogy of *de jure* notions of Scriptural authority than in debating this point.

In order to get at this question, we need to pick up on the previous story of the developing concept of scriptural canon and authority as received and reformulated by the early Christians who were also Jews. These Christians, as Edward Farley (1982, Part I; cf. Farley and Hodgson 1982) has pointed out, inherited both the concept of written scripture, and the diasporic mentality from intertestamental Judaism. The written word thus served the needs and purposes of a fluid and missionary movement, but only to a point. This was because Christians—as sectarian Jews or, if Gentiles, following the Jews—began to relocate the Word of God within the confines of the written text. Such relocation occurred for a number of interrelated reasons that correlate antithetically with the trajectory of Jewish religion. First, the Jews have been, are, and always will be a specific people of explicit ethnicity. Christians, on the other hand, are mostly Gentiles who have always been, are, and always will be multi-ethnic. Whereas the notion of a specific, concrete and materially written Word of God suffices as a vehicle of self-identity for a specific ethnic and cultural group, it serves less easily as such a vehicle for a community of faith that knows no ethnic boundaries. This leads, second, to a consideration of the emergence of enscripted Torah in Judaism as flowing forth from its particularistic self-understanding as an elect people of God, chosen for specific reasons at specific points in space and time. The Christian self-understanding, by way of contrast, is as a universal community that seeks to be the people of God across space and time, "to the ends of the earth" (here, "ends" referencing extension throughout both space and time). Such a universalizing self-identity can only be constrained in a negative way when a strict correlation is asserted of the Word of God and the written text of scripture originally written in Hebrew, Greek and Aramaic. This explains the tension in Christian mission and witness between thoroughgoing contextualization/inculturation and syncretism. Certainly, the Bible has been the most translated book in the history of humankind, and it is arguable that its translatability testifies to the universality of the Christian message on the one hand, even while it has served as the vehicle for cultural preservation on the other (cf. Sanneh 1989 and 1993; Beeby 2000). At the same time, it is also undeniable that the translation of the Bible into other languages results in a transformation of its meaning over space and time. Finally, because of the particularity of Jewish religion focused on the land, exile demanded what might be understood as "the portability of authority"—viz., authoritativeness as shifted from temple to script. Christian authority, on the other hand, has always been the person of Jesus Christ, by, in, and through the Spirit. Farley concludes, then, that the collapse of the "house of authority" (the stronghold of the understanding of the Word of God as the written text) during the modern period is a good thing because it frees Christians to once again grapple with the Word of God as mediated, rather than circumscribed, by Scripture.

My own reading of the problem of scriptural authority follows Farley's up to a point. The collapse of the house of authority Farley depicts refers only to the collapse of the humanly constructed edifice which some Christians have called the inspired, inerrant, and infallible Bible. I agree with Farley that these are problematic categories for historically conscious persons. Yet historical consciousness is not antithetical to biblical faith since, if Christians take the incarnation seriously, the God who has revealed himself has done so by taking a form shaped by all the vicissitudes and ambiguities of history. Why would Scripture be any less important or valuable in its making demands on its readers precisely through its radical alterity? Does not Scripture demand, at least in some respects, a hermeneutics of consent, to use Peter Stuhlmacher's term (1977, esp. 83ff.), in the same way as any thing demands our acknowledgment of its density and infinite value [cf. 6.2.1]? The purpose of Scripture has always been to witness to the apostolic tradition—the episcopate, the liturgy, the sacraments, the iconography, and so on—and its authority lies in the fact that it not only is there as an undeniable historical datum, commanding our attention, but it is also here, in our hearts and in our minds, entreating our allegiance.

How then is Scripture normative for theological interpretation? The only possible response, it seems to me, is to note that the Bible's authority (its normativeness) does not work in isolation, but in conjunction with the norms intrinsic to human engagement with reality in all its multidimensionality. Certainly, Scripture may be insisted upon as the final norm—or, according to the classical formula, as *norma normans non normata*—since Christian life and practice was initially defined by the apostolic tradition and witness. In this case, what the apostles wrote (the biblical texts themselves), and what the earliest Christians received from them, preserved, and handed down (the canonical shape of the text) has normative force for defining what Christianity means. But even here, the reality is that human beings do not come to Scripture with a blank slate. It thus seems clear that the norms evoked by the plurality of human experiences cannot be overlooked or "trumped" simply by declaring "what the Bible says." In fact, logical norms, aesthetic norms, moral norms, socio-cultural norms, the norms of the Christian tradition and community of faith—e.g., the various standards by which readers and doers of the Word at different times and places hold themselves accountable—among others (cf. Gelpi 2001b, 22–38), are all brought to bear on every situation. As such, these norms require discernment precisely in their convergences in order that appropriate response and action in any situation can be decided, and proper theological conclusions can be drawn. Further, even if one were to respond that the scriptural norms nevertheless need to retain primacy, the truth of the matter is that biblical principles are, in general, vague and in need of application or specification in the various situations human find themselves. Such a process of determining the significance of biblical norms is, as previously argued, a hermeneutical and therefore triadic one. The upshot of all this is that practically speaking for theological hermeneutics, there will always be a dialectical struggle between Scripture as *norma normans* and tradition as *norma normata* (cf. LaCugna 1982). Put another way, the theologians will always struggle with the tension that derives from the difficulty and, indeed, practical impossibility, of determining if, when, and how intra-theological norms over-ride extra-theological norms (cf. McIntyre 1976, 226).

The discussion of the Word of God as object of theological interpretation thus in some ways brings us back to where we started: the importance of discernment of the Word of God as spoken, living, and written. In each of these forms, the Word of God understood as the story or narrative of the Church mediates reality (the world of the text emergent from or reflecting the world "behind" the text), enables the ongoing experience of that reality (the world "within" the text), and funds the ongoing (re)construction of reality (by providing possibilities for another world, one which lies "in front of" the text). There is a strong tendency, given human orientation toward activity and the future, to emphasize this last dimension of the world "in front of" the text (e.g., Wallace 1995). I would also underscore the point that the world in front of the text cannot be arbitrarily disengaged from the world of the text or the world behind the text without such becoming an illegitimate attempt (that still ultimately fails) to break through the hermeneutical circle. Keeping all three worlds together—the world behind the text and the world in front of the text being connected by the text and the world of the text—is the crux of all interpretative activity; otherwise, we would be fantasizing or dreaming, not interpreting. But, perhaps more importantly, even if we were to believe ourselves doing the latter, would not our fantasies and dreams also be shaped, however subconsciously, by our experiences, etc., which have themselves emerged in part out of textual traditions we have inherited, replete with their own worlds within and behind? All the more reason to pay attention to the hermeneutical trialectic if our intention is to interpret and live responsibly.

The upshot of this discussion is that theological knowledge consists not just in a simple arrangement of scriptural proof texts according to certain categories. Rather, theology emerges as an arena of knowledge constrained by reality as objectively given to us. That which is given—which includes, in our discussion so far, experience and the Word of God, spoken, living, and written—therefore measures both how we know and what we know. Yet it is also the case that reality in all its multifacetedness is knowable only from various perspectives. This includes Scripture, which is bequeathed to us only through an historical and theological tradition that is equally given. To that aspect of the given the argument now turns.

8.3 The Hermeneutics of Ecclesial Tradition

The discussion focuses here on what may be called the hermeneutics of the ecclesial tradition.[4] Christian tradition, of course, is not to be understood apart from either Spirit or Word. It is the one continuous work of the Spirit through the biblical and ecclesial traditions, on down to the present traditioning Church. A hermeneutics of the ecclesial tradition enables us to discern the factors intrinsic to Christian faith that shape our presuppositions, that influence the categories of theological inquiry, and that drive our questions and therefore also our answers. And it does so specifically by raising pointed questions about the hermeneutical process: that regarding historical consciousness (tradition as past history), that related to historical locatedness (tradition as present-ness), and that related to historical activity (the act of traditioning directed toward the future).

8.3.1 In the first place, tradition is, simply put, the unending endurance in and transmission of the past to the present (cf. Shils 1981; Coady 1992, Part II). This accounts for the human experience of stability and change. Traditions shift due to internal and external factors. The former includes the processes of rationalization, the exercise of the creative imagination, and the emergence of anti-traditional mentalities such as progressivism, while the latter results from tradition's engagement with other alien worlds, from social developments, and from intentional resistance. Yet through these dynamics, the changes are always that of discontinuities within continuities. As Peirce denied that one could truly doubt the whole all at once, so also the past is never radically abrogated as a whole since the present cannot be sustained except through its connections with that which has gone before.

Therefore, a valid hermeneutics of tradition requires that it emerge through the fires of a thoroughgoing baptism into historical consciousness (cf. Kaufman

---

[4] On the continuity between the biblical and later traditions, see, from an Eastern Orthodox view, Florovsky (1972); from a Protestant perspective, Williams (1999); from Catholic vantage points, Blondel (1964), and Congar (1967, esp. Part Two).

1960; Michalson 1963; Stuhlmacher 1977). In this regard, the work of contemporary Mennonite theologians like J. Denny Weaver (2000) parallels the call of historicist and liberation theologies to take the creeds of the Church seriously only insofar as we are ready and willing to recognize them for what they are: socio-culturally, politically, and historically contingent efforts to understand the biblical text, rather than normative, absolutistic and universalistic pronouncements for all time. My question to the current generation of Anabaptist and Mennonite theologians concerns whether or not they are as historically conscious about the biblical text itself. The Reformation motto of *Ecclesia Reformata Semper Reformada* ("A Church must be reformed and always reforming") needs to be taken seriously, as does the insistence of contemporary hermeneutical theorists that tradition is the background horizon from which interpretation proceeds. In fact here Gadamer (1994) joins with the Reformers in insisting that human historicity and tradition-dependence are by-products of human finitude (cf. Smith 1991). Inevitably then, this historicity that conditions thought is given also to all theological reflection.

If this were all that were needed to be said about the theological tradition, however, theological interpretation may just as well ignore the it. But, of course, the tradition is not only historically embedded and in that sense, contingent, it is also historically effective and in that sense, is normative in at least the following three ways. First, in a simplest sense, the tradition is given to ecclesial memory and therefore constitutes Christian identity: who and what we are. This dovetails with my discussion below about tradition as presentness. In this sense, tradition is normative to the extent that we cannot step completely outside of it in order to engage it as objective other. This claim that tradition lays on us is the second aspect of its normativeness. The ancient rules of faith, the ecumenical creeds, the Reformation confessions, etc., are representative summaries of the faith which have defined us in the past, and lay claim to defining us today and our children tomorrow. There is therefore a power that tradition wields over us, a power of the past that cannot be taken lightly because it has been internalized in our memories, our liturgies, and our self-conscious, subconscious, and unconscious identities. Finally, tradition also reveals theological developments which are untrue to the objects being interpreted. Theological interpretation cannot neglect these wrong turns—heresies, as they are known—since to do so would risk their repetition. At the same time, of course, the decision to reject certain turns as wrong ones during a previous age should be considered fallibilistically. These may in fact be wrong turns for all times and for all places, but determining that would require an ongoing process of traditioning.

Theological method therefore requires, at some point in the hermeneutical spiral, engagement with the Christian tradition on whatever the topic at hand might be. This would be a kind of theological portraiture that brings to explicit consciousness the given data of ecclesial reflection (Farley 1982) and lays bare the ways in which tradition norms theological activity. Such portraiture, however, would include moments of historical excavation—the archeology and genealogy of thought (Foucault)—whereby the various socio-historical reasons why the Church has believed in just this way and not that are detailed, so far as such can be determined. Both moves are requisite in order for the creeds, doctrines, pronouncements, and beliefs of the Church and its members throughout history (no less than the scriptural texts) to be remembered, interpreted, appropriated, and translated afresh in each successive age. Such interpretation and translation may conclude in a renewed appreciation for tradition, or in a better understanding of ecclesial identity. Certainly, any reappropriation itself requires the strenuous work of understanding the tradition in its "thickness" (Geertz) so that its translation may be true both to its own places and times and to ours. Or, it may be decided that the tradition has taken a wrong turn which needs to be exposed, rejected, and/or corrected. Nothing, a hermeneutics of ecclesial tradition avers, is theologically sacrosanct, and that precisely because it is not immune from the ravages of either history itself or the inquiry of historically-conscious beings.

8.3.2 Having said all of this, part of the problem with tradition is that it also is, in some respects, completely other to us, foreign to our contemporary modes of thought and sensibilities, at times a strange relative that calls to us from our distant past, at other times lost, buried, or plain forgotten (cf. Farley 1996, ch. 3). The problem in these cases may be that of retrieval itself. My thesis in this book is to argue that even the act of retrieving tradition itself involves a trialectic of Spirit-Word-Community (or, tradition). Following from this, the hermeneutics of tradition cannot avoid the question of historical locatedness with regard to contemporary interpretation. Thus a hermeneutics of tradition needs to follow the various lines of development that lead to the horizon informing the present situation. Such a hermeneutic will therefore uncover the roots of contemporary ecclesial faith and its categories of understanding. It also enables us to discern the present needs and questions of the interpreter and his or her interpreting community, and helps to identify the specific context of theological inquiry. Here, the various hermeneutics of suspicion—socio-economic, political-ideological, race, gender, etc.—apply. The anticipated result is a better understanding of the interpreter's situation within his or her immediate community of faith as both are related to the larger historical tradition and contemporary Church catholic. These moves are crucial in order to guard against developing a parochial, ideological, or historically naive theology.

This means that any religious tradition needs to be considered in part as the cumulative sum total of its sequentially ordered local theologies (cf. Schreiter 1985, 75–94). This is because all theologies are local theologies framed not only geographically but also historically. They emerge from the continual interaction between persons of one time and space both with their contemporaries of other spaces and with persons of preceding times albeit of similar as well as different spaces. Local and located theologies thus require that prolonged attention be given to both synchronic and diachronic questions of translation, adaptation, accommodation and inculturation. The synchronic issue focuses on the variety of present situations spatially distributed and their demands on the attempts to give theological accounts faithful to the gospel. The diachronic matter focuses on the claims made by previous accounts of the gospel on the theologian, accounts which include differing elements which may be problematic because of their locatedness in different times (and perhaps also spaces). Yet to acknowledge one's own theologizing as being located in a variety of respects means that one ignores both the demands of the present and those of the past to one's own peril. To neglect both is to misconstrue not only the connections between past and present (and the power of the former over the latter), but also the spatial diversity of the contemporary theological horizon (and the potential power of ideology to distort theology).

But clearly not all preceding trajectories of local theologies count as valid developments which inform one's present theologizing. Certainly one should not deny that one is shaped through, influenced by, and even acted upon by heterodox developments which have gone before. Yet only by being aware of such heterodox presences in the tradition is one better able to counter its infectious influence. But how does the theologian weed out the invalid traditions from the valid? A variety of criteriological sets have been proposed for this task, beginning with Newman's investigation into the development of doctrine (1989; cf. O'Collins 1982). Criteriologies for discerning orthodox from heterodox traditions are undeniably needed, and useful so far as they go. But observe that to decide true from false traditions and traditionings from within the tradition(s) in question results in an infinite regress since the very criteria which is put in play to judge antecedent developments have emerged precisely out of those developments themselves. In one sense, of course, this cannot be helped. It only puts the theologian and the believing community on the alert that the criteria themselves are at best only fallible guidelines to assessing the past. It is the case, then, that even one's criteriology is always in dynamic flux, shifting (ever so slightly, perhaps) as the theologian-in-community reflects on the past in light of the present. Even this process, I would argue, reflects the hermeneutical trialectic of Spirit-Word-Community.

Of course, since there is no neutral vantage point for theological reflection, all emergent theological conclusions will always, to some extent, retain these features of locality, even if one hopes such extent will be lesser and not greater. Thus tradition as presentness is given to theological method. The interpreter can never avoid his or her locatedness. He or she can (must) only work hard to identify such locatedness within the tradition so as to become aware of the presuppositions that are at work (cf. Bultmann 1960) and to avoid bias. Yet caution should also be given regarding theologies that proceed from explicitly defined socio-historical locations since such may develop into apologetically driven agendas for specific groups, ideologies and traditions. If theology is, in part, the quest for truth, then the tension between the local and the global, the particular and the universal, needs to be respected. The tradition in its historicity is present at any moment of theological reflection, but that does not mean that the tradition fully determines the outcome or conclusion.

8.3.3 This leads to the good news regarding tradition: that theological interpretation as an ongoing historical activity of "traditioning" (cf. Irvin 1998) means that the parochial, ideological and naïve features can always be corrected. Now certainly there are times when the needed corrective is long delayed. Yet, the ecclesial tradition is a dynamic reality and always holds forth the possibility of recovery. Its past is given, comprising of the biblical and historical tradition; its present is being given, taking shape as theological reflection emerges from the various Christian faith communities; and its future is to be determined by what happens in the present as led by the Spirit of God. In short, the tradition is continuously shaping the community of faith, even as the latter is re-shaping the former in the continuous process of handing it down. What is passed on from one generation to another will always differ in some way—sometimes markedly so—from what is initially received unless the tradition is passively absorbed. In this case, the traditioning process it itself disregard since to care about it is to reflect on and take responsibility for it. In most instances, at least theologically speaking, this process of traditioning is actively engaged, and therefore central to the existence of the ecclesial tradition as an organic entity.

The "given" of ecclesial tradition is therefore always in flux. This means that the objects of theological interpretation—the data of revelation—is therefore

constantly shifting as well (cf. Hart [1968] 1985). The ambiguity of interpretation derives in part from the realization that pluralism has always reigned in
history. No less in Christian theology, theological signs and symbols have functioned in dynamic ways, been taken up by different interpreters-in-communi-
ties for different reasons and toward different ends, and led to a multiplicity of
meanings. All of this serves to highlight the broad scope of what is given in
tradition and the ongoing process of traditioning. Theological interpretation
can never fully "catch up" with its own processes; it only participates in the
activity of traditioning, sometimes more consciously and other times less.

How this comes together may be evidenced by the developments of the first
Jerusalem council as recorded in the book of Acts. The early Church is here
confronted with a theological question of wide-ranging implications: whether
or not the Gentile believers in the Christian way should be compelled to be
circumcised as their fellow Jewish Christians. The church at Antioch sent Paul,
Barnabas and others to Jerusalem to convene and consult with the apostles
and other elders. Much discussion ensued (15:7a), of which only the contributions of Peter and James are recorded. Considerations were given to the initial
experiential developments (15:7b, 14, referencing, undoubtedly, Peter's own
conversion toward openness to the Gentiles recorded in Acts 10) which gave
rise to the situation and the question; to the ongoing work of God (15:4b, 12);
to the testimony of Scripture (15:16–17, alluding to the words of the prophet
Amos 9:11–12); and to the precedence of tradition (15:20–21). The decision of
the council to refrain from insisting on circumcision is communicated as what
"seemed good to the Holy Spirit and to us" (15:28a). Here one finds the hermeneutical trialectic clearly at work in the convergence of Spirit and Word within
community of faith (cf. Thomas 2000, esp. 119). Discernment is multi-dimensional, in no particular order: of the situation in all of its complexity; of tradition; of history; of experience; of Scripture; and of what the Spirit is doing in,
and therefore saying to, the churches (cf. Orsy 1976, 15–18; Fowl 1998, 109–15).

By now it should be clear that my understanding of tradition is not separable
from either the Spirit's presence and activity in history and human experience
or the Word, whether prophetic, living, or enscripted. All intertwine to influence
and correct the other—thus what I call the hermeneutical trialectic. The enthu-
siast may say "taste and see that the Lord is good," but is not able to check his or
her experience except against the givenness of Scripture, or properly interpret,
discern, and judge experience apart from being held accountable by and within
a community of faith. The biblicist's insistence that "this is what the Bible says!"
avoids dealing with the fact that all reading is through various experiential and

traditional lenses, possibly distorted or ideologized. The traditionalist, of course, has to realize on the other side that the core convictions, values, and beliefs of the community of faith have emerged from concrete particularities (including, for Christians, the biblical traditions) and historical experiences. Each element of the trialectic is required to check and balance the other two in theological interpretation. It does no good to insist that reversing the Protestant priority of "Scripture and the Church" (e.g., Bloesch 1994) to the Orthodox priority of "The Church and Scripture" gives us the "correct historical and theological perspective" (Stylianopoulos 1997, 233 n 39). This also misses the mark since once again, both are set off, each against the other, vying (in a sense) for supremacy. Better to consider Spirit, Scripture, and Church in a relational and triadic sense, a move that correlates better with the trinitarian sensibilities of both traditions. (Note that Stylianopolous' own constructive restatement is a trinitarian hermeneutic of sorts that includes exegetical, interpretive and transformative levels in the hermeneutical engagement with Scripture.)

What is required is for interpreters to cultivate the necessary skills of discerning the breadth and depth of the theological tradition, from the past through the present and even toward the anticipated future, in order to be able to understand how it functions in the processes of theologizing and how it serves as an object for theological reflection. A thoroughgoing historical consciousness will avoid coming to conclusions too swiftly about the data of theology, whether that be about the significance of historical events, about regulative interpretive principles, about the norms or essence of Christian faith, about the validity of theological categories, and so on. This is because a hermeneutics of tradition will be sensitized to the pluralities embedded in historical processes. There thus needs to be a de-essentializing of tradition, even as there needs to be a de-essentializing of the Spirit and the Word. Just as no one experience, sign, or symbol captures absolutely the reality of Spirit, and no one text, principle, or norm preserves absolutely in an objective manner the reality of the Word, so also no one event, creed, doctrine, etc., can carry the weight of the entire Christian theological tradition. Rather, in each of these cases, there needs to be a plurality of features or components in play, some functioning definitively and in some ways normatively at some point and others at other points, and only some (not all) of which need to be either present at any point in order to define Spirit, Word, or Christian tradition and community.[5]

---

[5] This is akin to what the scholar of religion, Jonathan Z. Smith, calls "polythetic classification," whereby the essence of anything is defined not by a specified set, but by a range of categories distributed unevenly across exemplifications of the phenomenon in question (1982, esp. 1–5).

To deny this non-essentialism will inevitably lead one to assume in an a priori and uncritical sense that the categories or experiences of a previous time and place (e.g., either of the first century for primitivists, that of the third and fourth centuries for classical theists, those of the sixteenth for those in the Reformed tradition, those of the 1900s and 1910s for Pentecostals, and so on) are and should be absolutely normative. To affirm such non-essentialism would be to confront and embrace the historicity and what Stephen Sykes (1984) calls the "essentially contested" identity of Christian faith. It would be to acknowledge that the incarnation of the Word enables the incarnation of the gospel in and through the vagaries of space and time. It would be to insist that the ongoing process of traditioning is at the heart, rather than at the periphery, of Christian identity. Ormond Rush puts it this way with regard to the question of the reception of Christian faith, a lengthy comment that needs to reproduced in full:

> Contrary to a substantialist notion of the content/form schema, a rejuvenating reception of a doctrine is here understood as the understanding, interpretation and application of doctrine. In rejuvenating reception, no doctrinal 'content' takes on new 'form'. Rather, the rejuvenating reception *is* its meaning, conveying truth within a new horizon of understanding. In future reception of this interpretation, future interpreters will in turn, by virtue of their interpretation, be able *retrospectively* to distinguish 'the form' in which the present generation has expressed 'the content' of the doctrine. *But, from the context of the present horizon, the interpreter is not able to do that.* The 'essence' is not first extracted in order to then clothe it in contemporary clothes. The reconstruction of the answer as the content *is* its new form. The reception is the content. The interpretative reconstruction of the author's intention is the meaning of the doctrine. There is no timeless kernel that can be identified apart from its husk. The basic meaning of the datum of revelation is to be found in our reinterpretation. It cannot be understood and named apart from such reception. (1997, 310; italics orig.)

Rather than leading toward a base relativism, however, what emerges is the space within which new theologies can make their case alongside other historically particular expressions of Christian faith. In terms of the intra-Christian situation, what emerges is similar to the "lively disagreements" (Brown 2000, 293–342) which sorts out competitive conflicts following the model of Paul's confrontation with Peter in Galatia. In terms of the inter-religious situation, this means a recognition of the ongoing debate and engagement of Christian faith with other faith claims and praxis—a "competition of the religions," one might say (cf. Pinnock 1992, 126)—whereby truth emerges historically in the give-and-take of interreligious engagement and eschatologically for all. In terms of the ongoing conversation of Jerusalem and Athens and Beijing, etc., theological reflection's task is to give continual account of Christian faith in a fully public manner—currently, in and to a postmodern world. Judgments have been, are being, and will still be made—they cannot and should not be avoided. Yet such judgments need to proceed as self-critically as possible. Further, as theological judgments, they must be set forth tentatively, subject to the processes of traditioning and therefore to assessment and scrutiny by the Church, the academy, and the world (and not necessarily in that order). Finally, theological ideas will continue to be received, even if some are modified in the process, and others are rejected. Sometimes reception of the same idea will occur in some communities and rejection in others. Oftentimes, their fate is decided long after their original introduction to the traditions of discourse. Eschatologically, of course, the truth will be revealed.

In the meanwhile, the tension between tradition as given and tradition as the process of traditioning remains at the heart of theological interpretation. In that sense, tradition functions normatively by laying claim on us, both because of the Christian conviction that underneath the vicissitudes of history the Spirit has been at work, and because tradition is the *memoria* that sustains Christian identity and Christian being-in-the-world by way of vivifying the Word of Christ in and through the ecclesia to the world. In the latter sense, as important as is tradition to Christian theology, and as inseparable as is tradition from Scripture itself, tradition is still only one aspect of the hermeneutical trialectic. To re-label it the "Great Tradition" (cf. McGrath 2000) is potentially deceiving since the result could be the hegemony of tradition analogous to the kind of bibliolatry that emerges from over-emphasizing *the* "Word of God"![6] Tradition shapes theological interpretation; theological interpretation shapes the tradition. The next chapter seeks to elucidate this tension by way of reflection on the third moment of the hermeneutical trialectic: Community.

---

[6] But, my citation of McGrath is not to imply that is what he does, since what he is after is precisely a fidelity to tradition without denying the necessity for submitting even the Great Tradition to the ongoing critique of Scripture. Except for the most diehard traditionalists, most hermeneuticians recognize at least a dialectical tension between tradition and Scripture. On this point, it is instructive to compare and contrast McGrath's theological method articulated in this essay with Kathryn Greene-McCreight's theological hermeneutics which she also claims to be from and within the "Great Tradition" (2000, esp. 249–52). My contribution in this book is to open up the dialectic to the trialogue between Spirit, Word, and community (a broader category than tradition).

9   The Contexts of Interpretation: Community

Beginning with the Spirit (as we did in this book) has enabled us to see that Word and Community are mediated, formed and transformed in the Spirit. Alternatively, the focus on particularity and alterity has also enabled us to affirm that the work of the Spirit in a community of faith is normed by the lived, spoken, written and traditioned Word. Yet according to the trinitarian pattern of this book, Community as cannot simply be subordinated to either Spirit or Word. Rather, Community is just as central to theology and the task of theological reflection (cf. Grenz 1994; Grenz and Franke 2001, esp. Part Three). In this chapter, then, we turn finally to explore how Community provides the context for the activity of the Spirit and the presence of the Word. To say that Spirit and Word come together in Community can be variously understood: the Spirit addresses, empowers, quickens or confirms a community of faith with the Word of God, or the Word proclaimed to a docile community of believers creates faith for the reception and experience of the Spirit. Alternatively, the coming together of the activity and the object of interpretation can be seen to occur, I suggest, when theological reflection is contextualized in its various communal arenas.

My intention here is to bring together the preceding discussions of the various notions of truth, the dimensions of normative engagement, and the foci of theological intentionality in order to explore theology's diverse publics. Here, I adopt as my starting point David Tracy's (1981) tripartite division of the theological task: fundamental theology as being directed to the academy; systematic theology as being directed to the ecclesial self-understanding; and practical theology as being directed to ecclesial praxis.[1] However, I proceed in inverse order from Tracy and expand on his categories in order to demonstrate

[1] Richard Lints (1993, ch. 9) proposes the three publics or audiences of theology as the Church, popular culture, and the academy. I should also mention the much more extensively developed notion of the contexts of theologizing within the framework of reception theory by Ormond Rush, who posits twelve *loci receptiones* or "sites of reception" signifying the various arenas of theological engagement, exchange, appropriation, and construction (1997, esp. 206–07 and 331–58).

how theological interpretation in each arena is semiotically, truthfully and normatively engaged. Whether theology is focused on praxis (ecclesial activity or subjectivity), on identity (ecclesial objectivity), or on the boundaries (ecclesial traditioning or contextualizing, engaged by the Church understood as in-but-not-of-the-world), I will attempt to show that theological method is itself shaped by these various contexts on the one hand, and yet works transformatively on the various disciplines associated with these contexts if accomplished in a manner that is faithful to the task of theology on the other. The method that emerges in what follows will therefore bring about a convergence of the various theological and non-theological disciplines in pursuit of a contextually sensitive theology that does not neglect questions of truth.

9.1 Ecclesial Praxis

My argument here is that theological interpretation proceeds, in part, by the Church and for the Church, and as such is directed toward discerning ecclesial praxis (cf. Johnson 1996). With regard to the theological interpretation of Scripture, for example, the reading of the Bible can be understood to be a type of "practical reasoning" that derives from and is driven by the convictions, concerns, habits, dispositions, virtues, practices and faithful living of the Christian community (cf. Fowl 1998, 196–206; Hütter 2000; Work 2001). This should not be a point of contention since the centrality of praxis flows out of the logic of trinitarian theology (cf. Cunningham 1998). Theology's role in this regard is liberative and normed in part by its ecclesially intended goals of right living and of carrying out the Christian mission in particular places and times. Truth is pragmatic, transformative, and, liberative. Theologically, truth is said to be salvific and sanctifying.

In what follows, I tease out the idea of theology as ecclesial praxis by brief engagements with the intuitions and central convictions of narrative theologies, liberation theologies, and Pentecostal theologies. In each case, attempt will be made to illuminate how the biblical and theological symbols have "worked" to transform the souls of believers within specific socio-historical and communal contexts on the one hand, even while the particular locatedness of the activity of theologizing has fueled the emergence and value of specific theological methods and symbols on the other.

9.1.1 Narrative theology is a fairly recent label for an ancient theological phenomenon: that of theologizing through the media of storytelling.[2] Clearly, Christian Scripture is itself full of narratives—the patriarchal, the histories of Israel, the gospels, etc.—all of which tell the story of God's interactions with the world. And, why would the Bible not be replete with narratives if in fact that is how personal and communal identities are formed? Our identities consist of our stories—where and when we were born and to whom, where we went to school and what we learned, who we married and why, the names and characteristics of our children, what we do vocationally and where, who our friends are and why they are friends, and so forth. Communal identities are embedded in the stories that are shared by community's members, as memories of where, when and how the community was first formed, its triumphs and victories as well as its trials and struggles, explanations for its values, convictions and virtues, and so on. Persons and communities tell stories in part because these stories witness to their identity, and testify to who they are.

The question of who we are, or what kind of people we are called to be, is a question that many narrativists are insisting Christians think about. Part of the debate on this question has been played out in the field of theological ethics. Historically, on the one side are those who have argued that Christian deliberations about ethics turn finally on deontological issues related to universally obligating moral laws, and on the other side are those who have insisted on utilitarian or teleological ethics focused on the consequences or results of moral actions. A more-or-less recent third party to this debate is the communitarians who want to reframe the ethical issue away from either

[2] The recent literature on narrative theology is immense. The following is a select list of proposals during the last generation, listed by date of publication: McClendon (1974) explores the possibility of an approach to theologizing through the biographies of twentieth century public figures; Navone (1977) emphasizes the travel and journey motifs central to the biblical narratives; Stroup (1981) focuses on the revelatory function of the biblical narrative for Christian identity, both communally and individually; Goldberg (1982) pursues the question concerning the justification of narrative theology; Tilley (1985) argues for narratives as the substance of Christian faith; Thiemann (1987) addresses the problems posed by foundationalist epistemology and reconstructs the Christian doctrine of revelation as God's identifiability within a narrative framework of divine promises and fulfillment; Hauerwas and Jones (1989) is a collection of previously published seminal essays on the emergence of narrative theology; Fasching (1992) charts a post-Holocaust theological ethics which takes the First Testament seriously as a Jewish text; Frei (1993) argues for the priority of the biblical narratives of Jesus Christ in all of their particularity over and against modern liberal theology's preference for an anthropological method based on a general theory of hermeneutics; Lodahl (1994) attempts a systematic theology guided by Wesleyan and narrativistic commitments; last, but certainly not least, Placher (1994) reconceives specific aspects of the traditional theological loci around the motif of God as love from the starting point of the biblical narratives.

278   Spirit-Word-Community

obligations or results, and focus instead on the question in terms of being rather than doing. With the help of narrative theology (among other instruments), communitarian ethicists see themselves as reminding Christians about what it means to be an ecclesial community (cf. Hauerwas 1974; 1975; 1981; 1983; etc.). What does it mean to be the people of God, or the body of Christ? Does not the question of what one is precede the question of what one should do or how one ought to act? Better, does not one's actions, ethical and otherwise, flow forth naturally from who one is? More widely put, does not the Christian community, formed and informed as it is by certain stories and not others, respond in just these ways and not others to contemporary ethical questions and concerns?

The socio-historical context of this particular contribution to this ethical debate should not be overlooked. Deontological versus teleological ethics has been an especially heated conversation in the Western world since Kant and the English utilitarian philosophers in the seventeenth century. In this arena, the debate has been carried out at a fairly high level of abstraction. Not surprisingly, the emergence of more and more sophisticated schools of historiography during this same period of time has supported this method of argumentation since it made it increasingly difficult to accepted historical narratives at face value. Since Lessing, of course, the chasm between historical facts and theological significance has been opened up. The former are particular truths, while the latter can only be universal principles or abstractions. Historical criticism in the Western has thus consistently demythologized the central narratives of the Western traditions even while attempting to get back to the facts—difficult as they are to determine through historical methods—as they really were.

It is in this broader intellectual climate that the call of communitarian ethicists should be understood. Theirs is a countercultural move aimed at the dominant paradigm of academic inquiry in the West, at least since the Enlightenment. And in the process of rejecting the framework of the discussion set by Kantians, utilitarians, and historians, communitarian ethicists have sought to retrieve the category of narrative for argumentative purposes. Now those attuned to the contemporary situation realize, of course, that this retrieval of narrative is going on across the academy in various other disciplines as well. One might describe this central focus on local stories, indigenous narratives, and communal traditions as representing the reaction of the postmodern mind against the hegemony of Enlightenment values such as universality, abstraction, and fact. Recognizing this wider context explains, at least in part, the influence of communitarian ethics on the cultural paradigm shift as a whole on the one hand, and the growing acceptance of the former since the 1970s on the other.

Clearly, if the communitarians are right and hold fort, then the central Judeo-Christian narratives regain a measure of prominence not only in Christian ethics and praxis, but also for Christian theology as a whole. The gospel accounts of Jesus' life and attitudes are no longer simply interesting historical and theological details, but actually serve to shape in an ongoing sense the identity and, correlatively, activity of the Church. The given datum of the gospel narratives are thereby transposed through the act of imagination such that they serve to symbolize just who it is we are and what it is we are about (or should be about). Thus, Jesus' teachings (especially the Sermon on the Mount), it could be argued, set forth a challenging Kingdom worldview and concomitant ethic, one that centralizes peacemaking, forgiveness, reconciliation, and the quest for *shalom*. How he responded to the aggression of Pilate and the Roman soldiers would then be understood to flow forth from the ethic that he embodied. On another matter, his treatment of women, while egalitarian only if read in an anachronistic sense, nevertheless remains remarkable for his time and place, and provides an account that can serve as a symbolic catalyst for shaping the contemporary Church's attitudes toward issues regarding gender relationships. And, of course, other scriptural narratives would also contribute to the Church's self-understanding and, in that way, shape her ethical character.

This character is therefore seen to emerge not from narratives in general but from these particular formative narratives at the heart of the Church's identity. The narratives give rise to symbols which, in turn, give rise to thought and (extending Ricoeur's insights) action. Insofar as the narratives do function centrally for the community of faith; insofar as they are identified with; insofar as they serve functionally and formationally, to that extent, the narratives are symbolically and actually lived out by the Church in the world. In this sense, the object of theological interpretation flows forth from the stories—narratives, traditions, myths—that are told, retold and embodied because they mediate a soteriological experience. Interpretation translates into being and action. The theological community is not only a thinking organism, but a living and acting one. Theological reflection serves the practical purpose of transforming the community of faith so that it lives rightly, according to its core convictions, in an alien world.

9.1.2 Liberation theology is also certainly concerned with the Church as an ethical community. More specifically, however, liberation theology is focused on the particular activities that nurture human freedom in a holistic sense. The dominant biblical symbol, of course, derives from the narrative of the people of Israel from the slavery and bondage—economic, social, political, physical, and otherwise—of Pharaoh's Egypt. Freedom and liberation in each of these dimensions, however, is to be understood not for its own sake, but in connection with Israel worshipping her God (cf. Exod. 7:16, 8:1, 20, 9:1, 13, 10:3ff., where the release of the people of Israel from Egypt is connected with worshipping God in the desert).

This exodus motif is also clearly present in the Christian Testament (e.g., Acts 7 and 13:17; Hebrews, passim; Jude 5), but extended in connection with the Christian celebration of freedom from slavery (e.g., John 8, esp. 34–36; Rom. 6–8, passim; Gal. 4:21ff.). The dominant thrust of the Judeo-Christian message is that while "the whole world lies under the power of the evil one" (1 John 5:19b), God's work through his Spirit and Word is "to bring good news to the poor,…to proclaim release to the captives and recovery of sight to the blind,…to let the oppressed go free, to proclaim the year of the Lord's favor" (Luke 4:18–19). Now in the cases preceding the final proclamation, the gospel accounts of the life of Christ seem to indicate that this work of God on behalf of the poor, the blind and the oppressed were understood literally rather than spiritually or figuratively (cf. Luke 7:22). Even in the case of the prisoners, it is arguable that while there is no record of Jesus visiting prisons, yet he certainly delivered those imprisoned, understood in socio-economic terms. The widow of Nain who had lost her only son (Luke 7:11–17) is but one case in point. Without her son, this widow would have been without social and political representation at the city gate, without any means of economic support, without hope in a patriarchal society. Jesus' raising the son from the dead was, in fact, an act for deliverance as much, if not more, for the mother as it was for the son.

His actions on this and other occasions served to signify the arrival of the year of the Lord's favor, also known as the Hebrew year of Jubilees (Lev. 25 and 27:17–24). This was the year of release whereby the means of redeeming life, land, and property are provided so that the Israelites in slavery, or without land or other means, could begin afresh and anew. Deliverance from the bondage of Egypt is thus sealed since Jubilee symbolizes God's ongoing oversight over Israel to ensure that the poor, the oppressed, and those in bondage as slaves do not always remain in their respective situations. The God of the Bible is therefore revealed as one who pronounced woes on the rich and those well off, but blesses the poor, the hungry, the marginalized, and the oppressed (Luke 6:20–25). The God of Jesus Christ "has brought down the powerful from their thrones, but lifted up the lowly; he has filled the hungry with good things, and sent the rich away empty" (Luke 1:52–53).

Liberation theology therefore sees in the scriptural narrative God's preferential option for the poor. This is a hermeneutic by the ecclesial poor and for the poor of the Church and the society it is located in. It derives from the margins and the undersides of history and society. It is not surprising, then, to observe that liberation theology emerged first from the barrios of Latin America, and has since been extended and given further explication and application by the marginalized Christian communities of Africa and Asia, including the Minjung of Korea and the Dalits of India. Arguably, liberation theology is symptomatic of the efforts of non-Western Christians to theologize for themselves, for their Churches, and for their situations, as opposed to simply repeating the formulaic theologies of Western missionaries. In this respect, liberation theology can also be understood as part of a larger historical movement taking place around the world: the reaction to Western, colonialist and modernist ideologies. The burden of liberation theology, therefore, is to articulate a more global view of God on the one hand—a God who wears a non-Western dress—even while recognizing the relevance of this God to the particularities of the histories, cultures, situations and struggles within which non-Western Christians find themselves on the other.

The questions motivating this project are thus intensely practical. What does Christian faith mean for a community which struggles on a daily basis just to ensure that each member has enough to eat? What does it mean to worship God amidst continuous strife and civil war in some instances, and being on the receiving end of an economic embargo of supplies, medicine, and even food in other instances? What does Christian witness entail in a situation where governments are corrupt, injustice prevails, and modernity encroaches on fragile eco-systems and environments? What does it mean to experience the Bible as a community of faith if one is socially, politically, and economically located on the margins of society and therefore perhaps even without sufficient reading ability? In short, how do Christians in such communities understand themselves and their relationship to God and their world?

Liberation theologians have therefore emphasized the importance of conscientization—analogous to what might be called conversion—for authentic Christian life, witness, and liberation. Such involves a process of catechism whereby individuals and whole communities come to understand Christian faith not only in individualistic terms, but as embracing, in a holistic sense, human embodiment within and responsibility for specific social, economic and political situations. The exodus motif of coming out of Egypt is re-read within the larger biblical context of the prophets engaging the peoples and socio-economic powers of their times, and of Jesus' mission to announce and do the works of the Kingdom of God over and against the agendas of the religious and political powers of his own day. Devotion to the cause of Christ and the Kingdom of God therefore entails prophetic denunciation of injustice and unrighteousness, and transformative action in the public sphere. The biblical symbol of "coming out"—liberation—is thereby understood not in terms of geographic migration but in terms of socio-political engagement, destruction, and reconstruction. The focus is, after all, on a theology that is done by and in the Church, and which enables socio-ethical activity—healing, liberation, transformation, salvation—as the Church in and for the world.

9.1.3 I have previously made brief mention of Pentecostalism [8.1.1] in the context of discussing the connection between experience (in that case, of glossolalia) and theological reflection (in that case, regarding the theological arguments for and against the cessation of the charismatic gifts). My focus here is on the context of Pentecostal theologizing and the transformative power of Pentecostal theological symbols, rather than on Pentecostal experiences as such. Clearly, the two are interconnected, but what I want to inquire about is the context that shapes how Pentecostals understand the relationship between their experience and their theology.

By way of historical influences, one must surely admit that a multitude of traditions converged at what we now call the Azusa Street revival. The African-American, Keswick Reformed, dispensationalist, and Wesleyan Holiness roots, among others, of modern Pentecostalism have been amply documented (e.g., Hollenweger 1997). Mention of these traditions confirms the general observation that the modern Pentecostal movement was initially centered largely among the lower social strata of early twentieth century North American society (e.g., Anderson 1979). The Wesleyan Holiness movement, it could be argued, was crucial to the development of early Pentecostal theology focused on encountering the Spirit. Nineteenth century Holiness efforts to understand the Spirit's second work of grace (second blessing) precipitated the intrigue with the biblical, theological and experiential sign that such had, indeed, occurred. Against this background, the connection between Pentecostal exegesis and central convictions can be made clear. I will highlight three aspects of this connectedness within the socio-historical context of modern Pentecostalism to show how the biblical and theological symbols of the Spirit have worked to transform the Pentecostal soul.[3]

The symbol of speaking in tongues is an obvious starting point. Early

---

[3] In what follows, I summarize previous work. For the details and supporting documentation, see Yong 1998 and 2000, ch. 5.

Pentecostals reared in the Wesleyan Holiness tradition were convinced, for example, that glossolalic tongues was that sign which clearly evidenced the Spirit's remarkable sanctifying and empowering work in the Christian life. The gift and reception of the Spirit of the day of Pentecost thus came to be understood as a normative Christian experience: "All of them were filled with the Holy Spirit and began to speak in other languages, as the Spirit gave them ability" (Acts 2:4). In another instance, mention of the phenomenon of tongues is connected with extolling and praising God (Acts 10:46). This, coupled with Paul's teachings on tongues as a language of prayer and praise (1 Cor. 14:13–14), led early Pentecostals to conceive of glossolalic utterances as a primary means of worshipping and adoring God. Tongues-speech symbolized therein the inexplicable and mysterious experience of the believer before the glorious and numinous God.

The language of tongues (considered by some as equivalent to the language of angels mentioned by Paul in 1 Cor. 13:1) also served an important social function for the marginalized and disenfranchised members of the early Pentecostal movement. Lacking in education and therefore in public influence, glossolalia performed a transformative role with regard the individual's self-identity. Otherwise an unimportant and insignificant person in society, this person now had clear evidence through the baptism of the Holy Spirit and the gift of other tongues that he or she does indeed have an audience in the presence of God. All in all, then, speaking in tongues was and remains central to the piety of Pentecostals precisely because it signifies a divinely given language through which the believer experiences and manifests the divine reality on his or her life. The Pentecostal is transformed through the glossolalic experience from being a "nobody" to being a "child of the king" who worships in the presence of God.

Pentecostal exegesis has since therefore focused on the Acts of the Apostles, or, the Acts of the Holy Spirit, as Pentecostals would remind us. Within the larger framework of the Lukan narrative, the infilling of the Spirit signifies the endowment of power so that the Church will be witnesses of the gospel in word, sign and deed from Jerusalem through Judea and Samaria to the ends of the earth (Acts 1:8). Two more aspects of the transformative power of theological symbols are connected to this Lukan motif. First, the empowerment of the Church on the day of Pentecost was followed by signs and wonders that confirmed to the early Church that they had indeed been commissioned to take the gospel to the ends of the earth. Thus, this infilling or baptism of the Spirit was understood as a gateway to experiencing the power of the Spirit as evidenced in the remainder of the Acts narrative as well as the charismatic or spiritual gifts of the Spirit discussed by Paul (1 Cor. 12:7–9). The power and gifts of the Spirit, however, are designed to accomplish specific objectives: to demonstrate the truth of the gospel to unbelievers on the one hand, and to edify the body of Christ on the other (see 1 Cor. 14:16–25 and 1 Cor. 12:14–26).

Spirit-filled Pentecostals therefore understood themselves as specially empowered and anointed vehicles through whom God would accomplish the bringing in of the Kingdom in the last days. Pentecostals were not only tongues-speakers; they were prophets, evangelists, apostles, and pastors-teachers, all through the power of the Spirit of God (as further testified in the book of Acts). Further, they would also be miracle workers since the same Spirit who worked in and through Jesus now worked in and through the Pentecostal believers. Thus it was that modern Pentecostals effectively took over the missionary enterprise of the nineteenth century such that the twentieth century has since come to be known as the century of Pentecostal missions. Correlatively, a theology of Spirit-baptism was developed to account for the Pentecostal experience of the Spirit, their empowerment for witness, and their missionary calling and vocation. Pneumatological symbols were central to these Pentecostal theologies, driven as they were by the transformative power of these experiences with and of the Spirit.

The other transformative aspect of the Lukan motif of empowerment for witness in Acts 1–2 is also connected to Pentecostal missionary expansion, but specifically in terms of the global horizons of the Pentecostal message and experience. Application of the Pentecostal hermeneutic to the Pentecost narrative in Acts 2 led to the recognition that the gift of tongues not only had missiological but also ecumenical implications. The former were certainly clear from the fact that those from every nation under heaven heard the gospel in their own languages (Acts 2:5–13). Early Pentecostal missionaries therefore set sail for India and Africa believing that glossolalic tongues was the divinely appointed means whereby the gospel would be expeditiously carried to those who had never heard. Needless to say, they returned from the mission field disappointed in their inability to communicate in other languages. Yet this disappointment pointed to a startling discovery: that it was through the outpouring of the Spirit that God was truly raising up a universal community of many nations, tribes, peoples, and languages.

Pentecost therefore represents the inverse of Babel. The present work of the Spirit of God transcended national, ethnic, social, and other barriers. It was such transcendence that took the gospel from its humble Palestinian beginnings to the ends of the empire (Rome, in Acts 28). For modern Pentecostals, however, this meant that the Pentecostal experience could not be denominationally copyrighted or manipulated. The mid-twentieth century charismatic renewal followed by the Third Wave in the late 1970s and 1980s were part of the evidence of the ecumenical breadth of this experience. The explosion of Pentecostal and charismatic churches around the world over the last century presents further food for thought regarding the universal dimensions of the Spirit's presence and activity. What has happened, then, is that Pentecostal theology has experienced the ecumenical potential of the Spirit's presence and activity, and has begun to theologize within the global Pentecostal context in such a way as to reflect that experience and awareness. The Pentecost narrative, in short, has come to be recognized as having spiritual, missiological, and ecumenical significance. Context, experience of transformation, and interpretation of biblical narrative are seen to be intertwined in Pentecostal theologizing. The hermeneutical trialectic of Spirit, Word and Community have, in effect, worked an outward spiral such that each has informed the other in an ever-widening (now global) sphere of significance.

In each brief case study presented here, it is arguable that the imagination has a future, pragmatic orientation. In this connection, Anthony Thiselton's "hermeneutics of promise" appears to be an appropriate overarching model for understanding the transformative power of theological interpretation. This model a) claims to avoid rigid objectivity and rank subjectivity; b) includes a temporally situated and teleologically directed responsibility; c) derives from the communicative acts of Scripture (e.g., declarations, proclamations, appointments, commands, worship, and promise); and d) seeks to criticize individualistic autonomy in the name of the other. Thiselton's emphasis is therefore on a hermeneutics of communicative action wherein intersubjective understanding mediates text and reader, understanding and action, relationality and obligation, description and performance. Scripture opens up communication between ourselves and others—communication characterized by "understanding, giving and receiving, loving and being loved" (Thiselton 1999, 151 and 222; cf. Thiselton 1992).

Certainly in both Thiselton's model and in those discussed in above, theological hermeneutics is ultimately concerned with praxis and the faithful living of the Church in and for the world. Theological interpretation therefore requires discerning the divine will—what the Spirit is saying and doing—precisely in order to imitate and follow after the Spirit, whether in worship, mission, or socio-ethical activity. Truth is the power that sets free, transforms, rights the wrongs, and brings about the Kingdom of God. As seen in the gospel narratives, truth is a way of life, Jesus' way of life, to be exact. And, insofar as theology is true to its object—the person of Christ—it brings about the appropriate transformation of soul in individuals and in the community of believers so that the body of Christ may live meaningfully and truthfully in the world.

Of course, however, truth as pragmatic and transformative is only part of the story, one aspect or moment of the hermeneutical trialectic. Further, theology considered only as by the Church and for the Church's life in the world is also only part of the story. Truth is pragmatic but not only pragmatic. Theology is by the Church, but not only by or for Christians. Theological reflection should translate into meaningful praxis, but the latter, if left to itself, can become nothing more than tool of legitimation or domination. Theology includes doxology, but can, in this mode, become ideology. What hinders theology as orthopraxis from being used to justify sectarianism or being captivated by the will to power? Pragmatics can neither dominate nor be made subservient to the theological task. Theology directed toward ecclesial praxis must therefore correct and be corrected by theology as ecclesial identification.

9.2 Ecclesial Identity

My overall argument is that theological hermeneutics involves the continual interplay of Spirit, Word and community, the latter including, but not limited to, tradition. Here, I suggest that theological interpretation proceeds, in part, by the Church and with the Church, including her tradition, and as such is directed toward dogmatic and systematic understanding of truth. Theology's role is this regard is didactic, strives for coherence, and is normed in part by its intended goals of right thinking about theological topics in continuity with the historic Christianity and relevant to contemporary Christian faith. Truth as coherence attempts to bring together into a meaningful framework the pluralism of Christian theological interpretation, including the biblical through later Christian traditions. I tease out the idea of theology as ecclesial tradition by way of probing further aspects of narrative, liberation, and Pentecostal theologies as related to the various types of theological endeavors: biblical, historical, and dogmatic. In each case, attempt will be made to illuminate how contextual and practical issues are confronted by the otherness of the theological tradition. Even here, however, theological interpretation is both shaped by the socio-historical contexts wherein it is being done on the one hand, even while the activity of theologizing itself transforms the tradition in a real way on the other.

9.2.1 Theology is done not only by the Church and for the Church, but also with the Church. Theological interpretation therefore aims at understanding how God's self-revelation has been grasped in previous generations, both by those within the biblical traditions, as well as those who have come later. For the moment, however, let us focus primarily on the theological context of the biblical traditions and how those may inform the contextual task of theology.

Even within the biblical traditions, one sees the ongoing activity of theological appropriation. The Hebrew Ketuvim (the Writings) are understood primarily as reflections of the post-exilic community to understand God's covenant promises. The Law and the Prophets are engaged in a deeply existential fashion. The outcome includes historical revisioning (Chronicles), biblical lament (in the Psalms, in Lamentations), imprecatory writings (also in the Psalms), and the sapiential tradition (Job, Ecclesiastes, etc.). Throughout these portions of the Hebrew Bible, the agony, confusion, and yet hope and faith of Israel is recorded for posterity. These texts have spoken and continue to speak to the human condition.

The Christian Testament itself reflects the efforts of some first century Jews to understand their experience of Christ. The Hebrew Bible is itself interpreted, rejected in certain respects, and reappropriated in others. Interpretive models are also evidenced, whether it is the use of allegory, citation of Scripture to substantiate a point, or fairly informal references as available through oral tradition. There are also quotations and allusions to other intertestamental literature which provide a window into how first century Jewish-Christians negotiated the issue of scriptural authority.

The process of canonization of the Christian Testament during the first few centuries cannot be understood apart from ecclesial developments as a whole. One aspect of this entire process was the issue of authority. Certain writings retained their capacity to speak to the needs of the Church over this period of time and were gradually recognized as authoritative, while others did not and were, in one sense, forgotten. Writings that seemed to make existential and ecclesial demands on those who followed the Christian way came to be canonized, while others that did not speak with power to the Christian life were excluded. Together, it was these texts that spoke most coherently to the truth of Christian faith, and not others. And, together, these texts still demand our attention. It is these interpretations of primordial experiences which have retained the capacity to speak across the ages. Christians have certainly developed sophisticated hermeneutical strategies to read the two Testaments as a unity, or the four gospels in harmony, or James alongside rather than against Paul, etc. These processes have had as their goal a coherent understanding of Christian faith beginning with the scriptural canon itself. Today, we might call this task biblical theology. Its goal is to understand the intentions and references of the biblical authors, and the reception of these messages by the original and later audiences of the biblical traditions, so far as both can be determined. In short, sense is made of each witness in the context of its of its own place and time, and of how the plurality of voices and texts fit together both diachronically in terms of the canonical shape of Scripture, and synchronically in terms of the systematic coherence of the biblical message.

The coherence that is sought after is, in some sense, an ideal or eschatological goal. Disruptions and dissonance emerges, oftentimes, from within the text itself. Communitarian ethics, for example, capitalizes on the scriptural narratives as telling a story about ecclesial being, and suggests that ecclesial doing emerges from the former account. This may connect well with Pauline images and metaphors of being "in Christ," for example, but is less successful in engaging the Hebraic priority of doing over being. On another front, how do the metaphors of royalty that permeate the biblical record fit within the framework of liberation theology's hermeneutical option for the poor? Or, does the Pentecostal canon of Luke-Acts within the broader canon show up both the strengths and weaknesses of a biblically based theology and hermeneutic?

My point is that while it is certainly legitimate to begin somewhere (one never starts nowhere or everywhere), the biblical traditions themselves demand more of us as we proceed forward with theological interpretation. However, should one insist on staying within the arena of biblical theology more or less strictly defined, then, it seems to me, only two options remain: either systematize the biblical materials through the adoption of a single motif or theme that is arbitrarily chosen, or insist, finally, on biblical theology as a pluralistic enterprise. The context of doing biblical theology does not seem to allow for alternative ways of proceeding. Thus one sees, on the one hand, the development of magnificently structured biblical theologies which attempt to be exhaustive but which critics claim to run roughshod over the particularities of individual biblical texts; or one sees, on the other, Johannine, Pauline, Lukan, etc., theologies which still struggle to hold the message of these authors together in a coherent manner. It is arguable that the biblical writers themselves set precedents for both moves. The initial reaction is usually the quest for coherence and harmonization. At some point in this process, however, there may come a realization that one's goal may only with difficulty be achieved, or perhaps even not at all using the here-to-fore devised hermeneutical tools and maneuvers.

Yet the move in the direction of accepting a thoroughgoing pluralism in biblical theology would be guided by at least two constraints. First, pluralism has limits, both at the level of authorial intention and at the level of shape of the received biblical canon. The former warns us against understanding the text in ways that the original author might never have intended and audience might never have conceived; together, both serve to mark the limits of interpretation on the one hand, and—because later biblical texts interpret former biblical texts—the continuity of the biblical message with what has preceded on the other. The canonical shape of scripture then calls us to account for the coherence of the biblical message as understood by the canonical communities. This leads to the second constraint against a radically pluralistic biblical theology. The canonical shape testifies at least to the fact that the canonical communities found a sufficient level of scriptural coherence to sustain Christian faith. Coherence is still required to unify the message, and cannot be stretched beyond the breaking point if that message is to retain its capacity to engage and nurture faith in the community. And, one sees this ongoing quest for coherence—at least at the core level of Christian confession—when one moves from the field of biblical theology to that of historical theology.

9.2.2 What is historical theology? I would suggest there are two distinct answers to this question, even if both, finally, operate together whatever we decide we are doing when we do historical theology. In the first place, historical theology could be understood as the effort to portray how post-biblical and post-canonical communities of faith have engaged and articulated their understanding of the biblical message regarding God, the self, and the world in and for their own places and times. How did the various patristic Fathers wrestle theologically with the emerging scriptural canon? What factors influenced and contributed to the Augustinian synthesis and why? What caused the Reformation to play itself out different in England, Holland, France, or Germany? What was the context, intentionality, and polemic motivating Warfield and the Princeton theologians on the one hand, and Barth and the Neo-Orthodox theologians on the other (cf. Gillingham 1998, 117–43; and McGlasson 1999)? In this sense, historical theology is primarily a historical enterprise focused on the development of theological thinking.

In the second place, however, historical theology may ask normative questions about the theological task by looking toward the history of Christian thought for guidance. While the motivating forces here could be exegetical or theological, they aim, finally, at coherence. The former may be driven by either the quest to resolve a problematic text, or the apparently contradictory message of two or more texts read together. The tradition then turns toward itself—in the sense of looking backward—to discern if previous interpreters can give guidance and hermeneutical discernment. This usually generates a tradition of commentary to which the current generation contributes by the process of traditioning. The goal throughout, however, is to hear the Word of God afresh. Yet this living word is mediated and conditioned by the historical tradition. Historical theology, in this vein, seeks to uncover the previous wisdom of Christian interpretation and self-understanding. What the Cappadocians believed informs Christian—especially Eastern Orthodox—belief today; what the Angelic Doctor accomplished remains helpful for Roman Catholic theology today; what the Reformers protested against continues to guide evangelical theologizing today, and so on.

I would argue, however, that those engaged in the task of historical theology are doing both even if their explicit goal may be either an historical account of theological development or a normative theological project utilizing historical resources. Now certainly if one's primary aim is the former, then the demands of coherence are less strenuous. Augustine could have said such and such in his place and time, and Arminius could have said the opposite in a different place and time, and neither would need, on the surface, to be reconciled to the other. However, for the task of theological interpretation as a whole, the continuity between the biblical and later theological traditions make indispensable historical theology alongside biblical theology. Theological interpretation runs tremendous risks in neglecting the former. In the same way as Christians insist that theological interpretation should always be normed by Scripture, so also should they insist on the norms of the Christian tradition. Again, my point is not to argue that both are equal in terms of weight since weightedness is a subjective matter anyway. My point is that unless theological interpretation is aware of previous reflection on whatever topic it is engaging, its claims will not have been completely contextualized vis-à-vis the tradition of theological conversation itself. The result of any incompletely uncontextualized theology is inevitably misunderstanding.

Take, for the moment, the emerging modern Pentecostal theology. We have already seen that in its nascent form, Pentecostal theology was an effort to exegete its experience and its mission. Understood in the context of the late nineteenth and early twentieth century Wesleyan Holiness movement, dispensationalism, and the fundamentalism-liberalism debates, this effort was the culmination of a trajectory in a theological tradition on the one hand, and a countercultural remonstration on the other. Throughout this early period and into the next generation or two, Pentecostals were consistently directed by their alliance first with fundamentalists and later including the evangelicals toward a primitivistic hermeneutic and, correlatively, strenuous insistence on the authority of Scripture. Along this vein, Pentecostal theology during this time was double-minded. On the one side, the genre of the testimony conveyed the theological ruminations of Pentecostals packaged for mass consumption and the edification of the laity. On the other side, Bible institutes and colleges training Pentecostal ministers required education in biblical doctrine (usually fundamentalist style), and theological manuals were written in the genre of scriptural citation (proof-texts).

The ongoing process of maturation of the movement, however, raised historical consciousness. The founding of the academic Society for Pentecostal Studies in 1972 was actually motivated primarily by trained historians concerned with proper documentation of Pentecostal history now that the generation that experienced Azusa Street was practically gone. It was this interest in history for its own sake that raised the questions of historical theology. How could Pentecostalism give a coherent account of itself amidst the theological conflicts and disputes its historians had now uncovered? How could the second-work of grace theology be reconciled with third-work of grace theology? What did it mean that practically from its inception, Pentecostals were divided into trinitarian and non-trinitarian movements and trajectories? What are the implications for soteriology, ecclesiology and the theology of the sacraments of early Pentecostal baptism in Jesus' name over and against baptism using the trinitarian formula? And in the forefront, what did Spirit-baptism now mean since its discussion within the Wesleyan Holiness tradition at the turn of the century was very different from the late twentieth century discussion between Pentecostal and mostly Reformed-type evangelicals?

Needless to say, Pentecostals have been driven beyond a naïve biblical theology toward historical theology as a multifaceted and multidimensional project. The early Pentecostal disdain for history has been transformed into the quest for roots in search of a theological identity for the twenty-first century. This project has sought to retrieve charismatic themes, emphases, and movements long buried in the history of Christianity. It has had to continuously reassess the role and importance of tradition vis-à-vis the biblical witness and the Pentecostal experience. It has joined in a the conversation with its sister Wesleyan Holiness movement about the works of grace. It has unearthed roots for a distinctively pneumatological paradigm for theology, both as a mode of and for theologizing and as a legitimate locus of theological reflection. In the process, of course, Pentecostals have wrestled with core Pentecostal experiential and doctrinal convictions—including the issue of the cessation of the charismata, the initial evidence doctrine, and the dispensationalist doctrine of imminent rapture of the saints, among others—with and against the history of Christian theology. On some of these issues—e.g., on the question of cessationism—they seem to have been able to generate some consensus, even to signal a turn in Christian theological reflection as a whole. On others—e.g., on initial evidence—the verdict so far seems to be against them. In the former case, the Pentecostal contribution has been central to the reformative dimension of theology. In the latter case, the tradition continues to demand Pentecostal accountability. Yet on the whole, definitive outcomes have not been decided, and, as with any process of traditioning, may not be decided in the foreseeable future especially given the youth of this tradition of interpretation. Yet the die has been cast. Pentecostals cannot return to a pre-critical mindset. Theological reflection has inevitably led to engaging historical theology.

This said, however, it is also clear that Pentecostal theologizing—as with all theologizing by any community of faith—cannot be understood if limited simply to its biblical and historical dimensions. After all, coherence may be achieved at both of these levels, at which point they become dogma. Yet while the resulting dogmatic theology may be coherent in and of itself with implications for Christian praxis, that does not necessarily mean it is right or true. To see how this is the case, a brief look at the role of dogmatic theology as it interfaces with the contemporary context of theological reflection is in order.

9.2.3 What is dogmatic theology? In the words of Vincent of Lérins, it is what has been believed everywhere, always, and by all (*quod ubique, quod semper, quod ab omnibus creditum est*). Arguably, this is, in itself, a biblical principle, appealed to by St. Paul in his correcting the Corinthians (e.g., 1 Cor. 11:2, 16). The implications are, then, that dogmatic theology builds on its biblical and traditional bases in order to prescribe the ongoing beliefs, habits and practices of the ecclesial community. It has always guided the course of Christian life and therefore should continue to be normative for life in the Christian way today. It is Christian truth by the Church, and for the Church, understood as a coherent set of beliefs and way of life in both the descriptive and the prescriptive sense. Dogmatic theology therefore lays claim to be the definitive form of articulating the Church's understanding of God, the self, and the world in her confessional, liturgical, catechetical, and practical mode. As such, like biblical and historical theology, dogmatic theology is both an inevitable and necessary moment of the overall task of theological reflection.

This said, dogmatic theology rides the tensions between being conservative, being reformative and being formative. The first case is certainly the one most familiar to us, and I will not belabor that point except by way of contrast with the other two. It could certainly be understood in terms of Luther's "here I stand!", signifying a return to the confession of the earlier Christian tradition. Yet the reformative aspect of dogmatics—*Ecclesia Reformata Semper Reformada*—emerged in this context as well, Luther himself growing in realization over the course of his later life and ministry that the tension between spirit and structure is unavoidable and should be engaged in a healthy manner (cf. Pelikan 1968). Dogmatic theology is, in different senses, both conservative and reformative.

The formative function of dogmatics, however, is much more difficult to define. Eastern Orthodoxy's dogmatic theology is, for example, clearly identified as conservative, implying that the patristic synthesis remains viable for all time. Yet its reality seems much more complicated than that. When one examines this "synthesis" with regard to dogmatic theology, rather than finding the doctrines of the Church at center stage, one finds a dynamic, complex and robust ecclesiology instead. Doctrinal beliefs certainly were most clearly depicted in the early rules of faith, and the later creedal efforts to understand the trinitarian and christological mysteries. Yet doctrines were also confessed in and through the sacramental, liturgical and devotional life of the early Christians, the emergent and always developing episcopate, the patristic oral and written traditions, iconography, and so on (cf. Abraham 1998). Dogmatic theology was therefore by no means limited to biblical theology and certainly did not come only in declarative and propositional forms. Rather, it took various forms and was expressed in the entirety of ecclesial life. Patristic dogmatics— what was believed everywhere, always and by all—both inhered in and was shaped materially and formally by ecclesial life and practice as a whole. In short, it functioned conservatively, reformatively, and formatively, all in different ways and with regard to different aspects of ecclesiality.

The result, in terms of dogmatic theology, needs to be distinguished with care. Under the narrower definition of dogma, Christian beliefs are those decided by the councils, expressed in the creeds, and extended by formal decisions of official ecclesial bodies. Dogmatic theology in this case becomes the property of ecclesial magisteriums, synods, and episcopates. In the case of the Roman Catholic Church, there exists a special relationship between the theological undertaking and the official teaching office of the Church which oversees the daily life of believers (cf. Thiel 1991, 201–20; Wicks 1994, 95–120).

Under the broader definition, however, dogmatics partakes of the pluralistic stream emergent from the scriptural and other canonical means of grace operative during the patristic period. Christian beliefs are expressed through a variety of media. Arguably, both definitions of dogmatic theology make their presence felt in the doctrinal pluralism that attends modern denominationalism in the West. Denominations are identified by statements of faith, lists of fundamental truths, confessional declarations, and the like. These are, usually, propounded as formal decisions of ecclesial bodies which are later ratified as official, if not already recognized as such at the time of doctrinal formulation. Yet the history of dogmatic pluralism in modern denominationalism suggests that various biblical and patristic emphases—what had previously been believed and expressed everywhere, always and by all—have found partial representation in these various canons of dogma.

If we keep in mind that theological and doctrinal formulations arise out of the continuous interplay of Spirit, Word and Community, dogmatic constructs are not exempt from this rule. This means that Trent, the Westminster and Augsburg Confessions, the Baptist General Conference Statement of Faith, and the Assemblies of God Sixteen Fundamental Truths, etc., all arise out of specific engagements at certain places and times with Scripture and tradition. It should therefore come as no surprise that even though similar in many respects, it is the differences from one dogmatic tradition to the next that catches our attention. These differences represent the vested interests, concerns, and convictions of legislative and doctrinal bodies in particular socio-historical locations. On the one hand, each is conservative in the sense that part of the biblical and dogmatic traditions are retrieved and reappropriated as conditioned by the accessibility of both, and by the needs and intentions of the retrieving community. Each act of retrieval and reappropriation is also reformative and formative in different respects since retrieval is not mere repetition, and reappropriation flows from and sets dogmatic and practical agendas.

This is certainly both the value and the Achilles' heel of communitarian forms of theology. Communitarians are right to call attention to the narrative features of Christian faith, but how these converge with particular socio-historical reflective engagements in order to produce Christian doctrine that is believed everywhere, always and by all is certainly another matter. This raises the issue of dogmatic statements by ecumenical bodies that also operate in similar ways. The Barmen Declaration could certainly be understood in terms of its declaring what has been believed everywhere, always, by all; at the same time, the force of the confession in that particular place and time gave new meaning to the notion of "dogmatics" (as Barth's use of the concept well illustrates). The World Council of Church's "Baptism, Eucharist, and Ministry," while engaging perennial themes and motifs of Christian faith and practice, is also both reformative in terms of spelling out an emerging dogmatic consensus among different ecclesial bodies, and formative in terms of the ecumenical challenge it lays out for the ecclesial praxis of these same bodies which remain painfully divided.

But what about ecclesial communities whose understanding of dogma is formative but not reformative in terms of later revisioning and envisioning of earlier pronouncements and declarations? Here, the Roman Catholic community comes to mind. Vatican II cannot undermine previous conciliar decisions even if it can clarify and provide guidance for the belief and praxis for late twentieth and early twenty-first century Roman Catholicism (cf. Ommen 1973). Such clarification does indeed recognize the normative claims of dogma. Yet, such normativeness is not entirely inflexible. As Ormond Rush puts it,

> Dogmas are like an open work that remains unfinalised until received by a reader. In this sense they are incomplete till lived out, and therefore are dependent on their reception. Their normativity is relative to their power to continue conveying the truth of the living tradition and empowering believers to live that truth. Therefore their normativity too must be received in a rejuvenating reception that is open to the provocation of the Gospel. Past doctrinal statements are classic and normative therefore when they (1) encapsulate in a true but partial way some content of Christian belief, (2) reveal the limits of present human horizons of understanding God as Mystery, (3) engender committed worship of God as Mystery, (4) illumine the perplexities of human existence and its questions, and (5) stimulate and empower committed Christian praxis. (1997, 309)

In one sense, then, dogmatic theology is somewhat inflexible, functioning normatively to constrain the excesses of the theological imagination (i.e., as represented by the ecclesial protectors of dogma itself during the late medieval period, and by the Nazi regime in Germany). On the other hand, dogmatic theology should also be understood contextually as the means through which the tradition asserts itself in order to speak authoritatively in every age. In this respect, Delwin Brown is correct to describe tradition as "a continuously reformed and formative milieu, as a dynamic stream of forces in which we live (or die), move (or stagnate), and gain (or lose) our being" (1994, 4). From this, it follows that we must move, as Brown suggests, from a precritical notion of tradition as *normative* to a postcritical understanding of tradition as *formative*, the latter more accurately representing how tradition actually functions for believing communities. Here, however, I would insist that embracing dogma's formative dimension does not mean discarding its normative function. On the contrary, dogmatic theology is what it is precisely because of its continuing capacity to hold together the tension between the past and the present, and to speak authoritatively, consistently, and coherently for Christian belief and practice at different times and places.

By way of summary so far, it should be noted that at the dogmatic level, the Church has to continually discern how the biblical and historical traditions affect ecclesial belief, confession, and praxis. The hermeneutics of dogma is the ecclesial task concerned with the ordering of truth about God-self-world that brings together canonical, traditional, and contemporary interpretations in a holistic act of traditioning for the edification of the Church. It thus requires discernment of the divine mind as revealed to the community of faith—the body of Christ—historically, contemporarily, and even futurally understood, especially in terms of the implications or working out of present decisions, beliefs and practices. This last notion of foresight or anticipation of how dogmatic truth needs to be considered is especially important also for understanding truth as correspondence since, as previously noted [5.2.2], theological truth is finally eschatological because it predicts that its claims about the transcendental character of the divine truly depicts the divine as it is.

Yet, truth as correspondence also requires an additional, even if not final, step of going beyond doing theology as ecclesial tradition. This is because historical and dogmatic theology cannot but uncover how theology continually expresses itself as ideology. Thus, theological and dogmatic claims have often been simply nothing more than human constructions emergent from the will to power. How then is the Church to be reformed and reforming if its objects of interpretation are simply nothing more than the biblical and theological traditions handed down and received dogmatically? Certainly in part by the work of the Spirit, as has been argued above. Also, however, in part through the influence of various communities, including those without the immediate community of faith. Reformation comes by precisely because Christian interpretation does not take place in isolation of Christian engagement with the world, both in terms of ecclesial praxis and in terms of the give-and-take in the public square. These are the ways in which reality corrects our interpretations. In short, ecclesial praxis and ecclesial theology cannot avoid engaging the other publics within which the Church is situated, and with whom the Church engages. As Francis Watson says, "to regard the church as a self-sufficient sphere closed off from the world is ecclesiological docetism, and it also makes impossible an adequate theological understanding of the world and its alleged secularity" (1994, 236). To the question of ecclesial boundaries we therefore now turn.

9.3 Ecclesial Boundaries

Spirit and Word come together in the communal context. I argue here for the notion of community in its broadest sense: the human community. Theological interpretation is, after all, not only by the Church and for the Church, but also in, to, and for the world. As such, theological interpretation is directed also toward discerning the world, and the Church's relationship to the world. Truth is not only transformative, pragmatic, and coherent vis-à-vis the Church's ministry and traditions, but also vis-à-vis the Church's situation in the world. Further, however, Christian claims to truth can never be only for Christians, but should be—if indeed all truth is God's truth—coherent within the universe of human understanding as the correspondence of their claims to reality as it is. In this arena, truth is subject to confirmation by other communities of inquiry, as well as by reality as it is or finally (eschatologically) unveils itself to be. Theology's role is this regard is thereby normed in part by its intended engagement with the totality of the real world—i.e., the carrying out of the Christian witness in various communities of faith and unbelief directed toward the end of time (Peirce's eschatological long-run). Other interpretive methods and academic disciplines are thereby brought into play in view of this larger public of engagement and eschatological vision. In what follows, I elaborate on the roles of a hermeneutics of nature, a hermeneutics of culture, and a foundational hermeneutics for theological interpretation. My goal is to illuminate how theological interpretation proceeds within the public square on the one hand even while it transforms it on the other.

9.3.1 By hermeneutics of nature, I mean the capacity to read, discern, and interpret the natural world. What does this have to do with theological interpretation? As briefly discussed above [6.2.1–2 and 7.2.1], a theology of nature can be understood as the dimension of theological reflection that attempts to comprehend God's relationship to the world. Nature, construed in its broadest terms, is the context of human engagement, including both Christian life and Christian theological reflection. Theology, as reflection on the relationship between God, the human self, and the world, cannot avoid nature. A theology of nature is at least assumed in order for theological discernment of the world to proceed. More explicitly, a theology of nature is committed to being measured or normed by reality as it is. Theological truth works and coheres because it corresponds—to put it crassly—with reality (nature) which is its measure (Neville 1989). I suggest that such a theology be made explicit for the purposes of cultivating and developing the capacity to discern theologically.

The question is how a theology of nature should be forged. The world is a large place with material, organic, and environmental dimensions. It has, within it, an innumerable variety of things, occasions, events, and so on. And, unsurprisingly, we cannot step outside of the world in order to theologize about it completely objectively. We cannot, in other words, elaborate a theology of nature except from within the natural world. Methodologically, at least, let me make the following suggestions.

First, a theology of nature cannot avoid being, at least in some senses, a theology from below. Whatever else may be claimed about our theological understanding of nature, our reflections on the world are inevitably shaped by our location, our being, and our moving in it. This does not mean that our theological understanding of the world is reductive of God as related only immanently within the world. It only means that theology cannot, finally, avoid the sense of God's immanence in the big picture of things. A theology of nature is one way that such immanence calls attention to itself.

Second, a theology from below raises the question of natural theology. Again, however, why would a theology of nature not be a natural theology, at least methodologically speaking, if not in other respects? If the incarnation and the Church are taken seriously, God meets humankind in and through the very stuff of the natural world. But, some might respond, does not embracing natural theology discount the reality and power of specific revelation? Only if one assumes either one operates apart from the other. The natural revelation-special revelation dualism is a specifically modern formulation of the problem. Such categories are both not productive nor especially sacrosanct within a trinitarian framework, especially not within a triadic, relational and social metaphysics. A theology of nature, I would argue, can and should be conceptualized which is able to transcend such dualisms even while it retains the important insights in those frameworks.

This leads, finally, to the method of inquiry that informs a theology of nature. After all, a theology from below requires a hermeneutics of engaging what is below: a hermeneutics of nature. This would include, certainly, the hermeneutics of the hard and soft sciences. It would be a method of inquiry—including the empirical method of the sciences—that takes the world seriously, that seeks to understand it both on its own terms (deferring, of course, to its singular and intrinsic values) and in terms of its relationship to us and to the creator, and that seeks to understand the reality of the creator from what is. Theological interpretation does not dominate nature, but rather submits to the truths it unveils. Theological interpretation, I would therefore argue, cannot disengage religion from the sciences. Religion can attempt to dominate the sciences, and vice versa. In either case, what emerges in the long run are ideological distortions fit to serve only the will-to-power of religious or scientific communities. Yet as the ancients and medievals acknowledge, there is one God who is revealed variously, including through the book of nature. At some points, advance in scientific knowledge clarifies and even corrects theological interpretation. At other times, the latter keeps the former aware of its limitations and its fallibility. Each is, in these senses, necessary for the other since, as Francis Watson suggests, "the exegesis of texts will at the same time be an exegesis of reality" (1994, 255).

That a theology of nature informs the theological task and vice-versa should be self-evident. At the risk of saying the obvious, only the briefest overview of an environmental theology should suffice to demonstrate this point. We are now close to the end of the first generation of what might be called "environmental consciousness." Historically, humankind has taken the creational mandate to subdue and exercise dominion over the earth (Gen. 1:28) literally. The result, of course, has been catastrophic for the environment. Awareness of such consequences has, since the late 1960s, led to theological rethinking about the relationship between human beings and the natural world. In the process, the following biblical and theological themes have been recovered in conjunction with the emergent environmental theology. First, creation, as the Genesis account shows, is good. The natural world is surely fallen, but yet retains its divinely ordered intentions and purposes in at least some respects. Natural laws and functions need not be ignored or discounted simply because they reflect the processes of the created order. Rather, such are theologically significant in ways that a pejorative understanding of the natural world will overlook. Second, albeit subjected to the fall, the created order also groans and longs, in and by the Spirit, for liberation by the triune God, a groaning most audible and visible in our own awaiting the redemption of our bodies (Rom. 8:19–23; cf. Prichard, ch. 2). Our concrete embodiment, as part of the created order and therefore good, is not just a temporal provision for our journey through the natural world. Rather, the Christian symbol of the resurrection of the body calls attention to the importance of the body in God's estimation. The same applies to the created order, which will be redeemed, renewed, and, in a sense, recreated, as the biblical symbols of new heavens and new earth point to. Finally, our increased understanding of the natural world has brought to awareness the radical interdependence and metaphysical interconnectedness of all creation. A holistic vision of humankind and the natural order is therefore required. What happens with human beings and the animal world is intrinsically connected with what happens with the environment, and vice-versa. More can be said, however, to include the togetherness not only of human beings, animals, and the environment, but also of God. This point was highlighted long ago by the Hebrew sages and prophets who understood shalom as the reign of God over the entire created order.

The result, of course, has been environmental consciousness, responsible living, and ethical consideration of human relationships to the natural world. Yet this has not been all. It is also arguable that theological reflection on the environment and natural world has brought forth a new doxology, one that sings the praises of the triune God. The metaphysical interdependence of things in the natural world has fired up the theological imagination of ancient trinitarian concepts and symbols like *perichoresis* and *circumincession*. I simply note that the reinvigoration of trinitarian theology has arisen also during the last generation. There has been crossover from both sides—environmentalists drawing from trinitarian theology and trinitarian theologians making environmental connections. I am not saying that these recent developments are necessarily related. Rather, I see the trinitarian hermeneutic informing environmental theology in powerful and transformative ways, even as I see the environment as providing a wonderful stimulus to theological reflection on the triune mystery.

My point is thus to emphasize the importance of a hermeneutics of nature to the theological task. At some point in theological interpretation, engagement of the world in all its complexity and profundity is required. Such interdisciplinary encounter can come up front, or later on. Either way, it certainly needs to be an ongoing and continuing relationship because a theology of nature relies on communities of inquiry whose work proceeds apace from theological reflection. Thus occasional, if not frequent, cross-consultation with those engaged in the empirical inquiry of the sciences is essential given the interdependence between attempts to discern the divine and attempts to discern divinity's creative work (cf. Van Huysteen 1997; 1999). Put another way, there is a mutuality between hermeneutics of nature and theological hermeneutics which we neglect at our own risk.

9.3.2 The same can be said of a hermeneutics of culture. By hermeneutics of culture, I mean the more specific science of reading, discerning and interpreting human life in all its complexity. Such would amount, in effect, to a theology of culture, which itself should be understood as an attempt to comprehend God's relationship to human life considered in its broadest social sense. Culture, construed in its broadest terms, is the context of human interrelationship, including both Christian life and Christian theological reflection. Theology, as reflection on the relationship between God and human beings, cannot avoid a theology of culture. A theology of culture is at least assumed in order for theological discernment of human habits, activities and thinking to proceed (cf. Niebuhr 1951; Tillich 1959; Jenson 1995; McClendon 1994, Part I).

This is why theology in general and Christian theology more specifically cannot be erected simply on communitarian lines. I will leave it to Buddhists to answer for Buddhism, Muslims to answer for Islam, secularists to answer for secularists, and so forth. As a Christian, I would certainly agree that Christian theology emerges from a complex of beliefs, practices, and experiences, all of which combine to make Christian faith distinctively itself and not Judaism, Buddhism, Islam, and the like. Along these same times, I would certainly agree that Christian theology therefore answers to Christian criteria, narratives, practices, dogmas, etc. And, it seems intuitively right to say that God's self-revelation in Jesus Christ, Scripture, and the ecclesial community is thereby normative for measuring Christian theological interpretation. Having agreed with all of this on the one hand, it is also important to qualify and perhaps take this all back on the other. Christian faith is distinctive from Judaism, Buddhism and Islam, but not absolutely so. Jesus' Jewishness, the acceptance of the Hebrew Bible as authoritative, and the fact that the earliest followers of Jesus were Jews are all counter points to the Christian claim to uniqueness, especially insofar as Judaism is concerned. More important, however, is that even this is not a special relationship that sets the Judeo-Christian tradition apart from other faiths in an absolutistic sense. How else should Judaism be understood apart from its situatedness in the ancient Near East? Is it the case that a clear-cut line can be drawn between the story of God's relationship with Israel and the story of God's relationship to ancient Near Eastern cultures? What about Melchizadek, Noah, Job, Namaan, Cyrus, and Ninevites of Jonah's time, and others? What about the collected wisdom of Israel's neighbors canonized in the Proverbs? What about the histories of Moab, Ammon, and Canaan of old, and of the Assyrians, the Chaldeans, the Medes and Persians? I would suggest that the story of Israel is incomprehensible apart from these other stories, and not only because of the divine intention of blessing all the nations of the world through Israel. More important, the identity of Israel is itself constituted by her relationships with those around her.

This is why Wittgenstein and Lindbeck are both so right and yet so wrong. Yes, cultures and theological traditions operate according to certain grammars, narratives, and assumptions. Yes, we initially encounter others in all of their strangeness and difference from ourselves. Yet such otherness is never completely other; otherness can be and is bridged through encounter. Further, cultural and religious grammars are never pure or homogeneous, but always exist as a complex togetherness of multiple histories, traditions, sources and experiences (cf. Sherry 1977). Beliefs and practices are therefore never purely religious. They are always already cultural, political, social, and economic, etc., as emergent from lived-experience, even as they in turn inform those various dimensions of human life (cf. Proudfoot 1985; Lash 1988; Davis 1989). As such, they are continuously encountered by others, sometimes rejected for sure, but also other times transferred and adopted, and thereby an emergent synchronic and diachronic synthesis of other grammars, beliefs, and practices. Religions are thereby complex phenomena that are also dynamic, fluid, syncretistic (in the non-pejorative sense). Cross-fertilization occurs here and there both in terms of shared beliefs and shared practices. This is what enables encounter, engagement, understanding and criticism across religious and cultural lines (not that any of these occur easily). And it is this ongoing process of engaging others that perspectives are obtained, falsehood is uncovered, and knowledge progresses toward its eschatological goal. This said, Christians should also acknowledge that deception, wrong turns, and misdirections occur. Human fallibility and fallenness undercuts any incessant or necessary movement toward the realization of utopian ideals like pure truth.

Thus the import of a hermeneutics of culture. To get at this requires the humanistic and anthropological sciences: the arts, literature, philosophy, rhetoric, languages, history, cultural anthropology, political science, economics, sociology, social-psychology, and even religious studies. All of this is required simply to situate the activity and language of human beings, much less the theological enterprise. And it is only by so situating theological discourse that one can even begin to discern its rhetoric, language and symbols, and more accurately identify its references, intentions, and purposes. In the process, theology is articulated and applied in specific cultural dress. At the same time, culture is itself transformed and transfigured by its encounter with theology. Of course, one never begins with either culture or theology in their purity, but enters the hermeneutical circle always already soaked in both. My argument, however, is that a specifically hermeneutics of culture must be engaged in earnest at some point in the process of theological interpretation.[4]

And this is all the more important given that individuals are never members solely of one culture or community. I grew up as a fusion of two Chinese traditions—the Hokkien (on my mother's side) and the Hakká (on my father's side)—in Malaysia. Insofar as the indigenous Malays have adopted Islam as the religion of the state, my religious roots are therefore multiple: Christian in terms of belief and practice, Confucian and Buddhist by means of silent socialization (my parents were first generation Christians who rejected their non-Christian roots consciously but passed them on unconsciously), and Islamic with regard to the school system and the public square. My teenage years were spent in negotiating the melting pot of Northern California. My education was completely in the West: a ministerial training program at a Pentecostal (Assemblies of God) institution in the Bible-college tradition on the Pacific coast; a graduate degree in the history of Christian thought from a Wesleyan Holiness seminary in the Pacific Northwest; a second graduate degree in Western intellectual history from a secular university in the same region; and a doctorate in the study of religion from a secular university in New England. I now teach in the Upper Midwest region amidst a tradition of pietist Swedes whose American roots are traced back only to the late nineteenth century (Baptist General Conference).

My point is to make explicit that in the context of the postmodern global village, insider-outsider distinctions with regard to communities of participation are no longer watertight. Each of us is an insider to one or more traditions to a greater or lesser extent, and an outsider to others in equally greater or lesser extents. Yet, being outsiders does not mean being cut off from those traditions. The case of theological interpretation, especially in the modern West, by academically trained individuals both exemplifies and yet complexifies this assertion. Academics are often members of a guild that now features radical diversity. Any particular academic could be a member of the Evangelical Theo-

---

[4] Thus, for example, Louis Dupré's *Passage to Modernity* (1993), while being intended as an interpretation of the phenomenon of modernity—specifically how modern culture has conceptually domesticated nature, the cosmos, and reality—is indispensable for understanding the worldview and paradigmatic presuppositions of modern theologies. Another approach is the dialectical method of Jacques Ellul whose theological reflections are imbued with sociological analyses (Clendenin 1987). To put it in the terms used by the early "Chicago School," biblical exegesis needs to proceed along with exegesis of the socio-historical reality of both the biblical and the interpreter's worlds (see the writings especially by Shailer Mathews, Gerald Birney Smith and Shirley Jackson Case in Peden and Stone 1996).

304 Spirit-Word-Community

logical Society on the one hand, the American Academy of Religion on the other, the Society for the Scientific Study of Religion on the third, and so on. This same person's heritage could be even more complex than my own. And so far, nothing has been said about the intellectual, political, social, economic, and other affiliations and allegiances which each person subsists in and through. The fact is undeniable: each theological interpreter negotiates membership in multiple intellectual, national, socio-political and cultural-religious communities, each of which have identities that are shaped by specific canons, narratives, rituals, and the like.

This means that a theology that intends its claims to be universally applicable needs to be a fully public theology, engaging any and all claims to ultimate truth. And, insofar as a Christian theology is intended to be valid not only for Christians but also for Jews, Muslims, Buddhists, Hindus, Neo-Confucianists, etc., to that extent it needs to engage the claims of these religious others seriously. And, such engagement is not only polemical, but genuinely dialogic. Interreligious theological encounter cannot remain at the surface or learning enough about the other religious tradition only for apologetic purposes. Rather, as previously discussed, the claims of religious others have to be taken seriously in all of their particularity and intended comprehensiveness. If one fears syncretism, it only needs to be pointed out that Christianity as a missionary religion cannot do otherwise, at least insofar as it has always risked translation, contextualization, and acculturation. At some level, serious Christian engagement with the religious other will lead to a fresh discovery of truth, goodness, and beauty; at another level, such engagement will lead to a deepened appreciation for one's own tradition. Of course, sincere engagement with others always results in transformation and conversion at various levels. Is it possible that the quest for truth will result in the religious conversion of the Christian? Theoretically yes, otherwise one's dialogue with the other would never have been a sincere dialogue but a disguised monologue. That, I would suggest, is the risk one embraces when one follows in the footsteps of Jesus and puts on the mind of Christ, "who, though he was in the form of God, did not regard equality with God as something to be exploited, but emptied himself, taking the form of a slave, being born in human likeness. And being found in human form, he humbled himself and became obedient to the point of death—even death on a cross" (Phil. 2:5–8).

The upshot of all this is that whether or not one explicitly engages in a hermeneutics of culture, theological interpretation inevitably emerges through the cultural and social matrix. Better to work consciously to discern the complex nexus of personal, social and divine trajectories from which all interpretation arises than to allow such factors to influence one's theologizing sub- or unconsciously. Better to be discerning about the contexts of interpretation rather than being held captive by the ideologies inherent in all human contexts and discourses. Better to include as a moment in the hermeneutical enterprise the task of theological anthropology which engages the full spectrum of the human psycho-social and cultural-religious situation. Better, in short, to interpret and discern one's social, cultural and religious contexts rather than allow only for the latter to interpret oneself (cf. Hall 1989, Part I). It is only by so doing that one can redeem culture through its transformation and transfiguration by theology, even as the latter is also shaped and formed through specific socio-cultural and religious contexts (cf. Gill 1975; 1977).

9.3.3 This leads, finally, to the issue of foundations where we began: foundational hermeneutics or fundamental theology [3.2.1]. Theological interpretation strives, after all, for truth: the reality of God and God's relationship to the self and to the world as it really is. This process of uncovering the truth treads its way, sometimes very slowly, through the self, through the Scriptures, the traditions, and the communities of Christian faith, through nature, and through culture, etc., oftentimes not in any particular order. The issue of foundational hermeneutics is also only arbitrarily placed either at the beginning, the middle, or the end. Theological interpretation nevertheless grapples at some point with foundational and fundamental issues during the hermeneutical process. These are the academic, philosophic, systematic, metaphysical, onto-logical, and speculative moments of theological inquiry. The goal of theological interpretation, after all, includes within its orbit not only truth as pragmatic and utilitarian, but also truth as systematic coherence and dyadic correspondence between propositional and doctrinal content with the diverse arenas of knowledge, including the sciences (God-self-world).

In the big picture, such truth will be fully known only eschatologically (Peirce's infinite long run). In the meanwhile, however, truth prevails through the process of inquiry, and theological understanding is one contribution to or perspective among the community of inquirers, broadly conceived. It is essential therefore that theological interpretation proceed via a pluralistic and dialogical hermeneutics that engages with any and all who are interested in the theological quest. Such an engagement requires an open-ended (i.e., eschatological) theological conversation that encounters others on their terms, their experiences, their traditions, their locations, and so on. It proceeds upon the conviction that all truth is God's truth, wherever it may be found, and that all persons are created in the image of God and therefore possibly reflect aspects of the truth in and through their lives and thinking. More important, truth itself will be compromised if we arbitrarily dismiss any perspective or understanding of the truth without critical apprehension. Thus the import of a foundational hermeneutics which not only assumes that truth is universal but also that it is universally available and fully public for engagement and corroboration.

A foundational hermeneutics that is pluralistic and dialogical is inevitably interdisciplinary (e.g., including a theology of nature), intercultural (e.g., including a theology of culture), and interreligious (cf. Lonergan 1972; Little 1988; Ebeling 1978). My point here is simply to say that the foundational element of the hermeneutical process requires that all theological interpretation—not only that of theology of nature or theology of culture, these being but moments of the hermeneutical process—be an ongoing process of engaging multiple voices, perspectives, and conversations with those within and beyond the borders of the Church. Theology, concerned as it is with the biggest picture, stretches across the diverse fields of knowledge and therefore engages the largest possible public(s). In this sense, theological interpretation is not only by the Church but also by those related to even if not committed to Christian faith. Theological interpretation is also not only for the world but also for the Church which lives in the world. A foundational hermeneutics is therefore a hermeneutics of the world understood as reality in its totality. Yet a foundational hermeneutics, as previously articulated, is not totalitarian. It simply strives to articulate the Christian vision as informed by Spirit, Word, and the communities of inquiry after truth. My argument throughout is that all intertwine to influence and correct the other precisely because, to use Jürgen Moltmann's conceptualization, the world itself has been taken up into the trinitarian life of God through incarnation and Pentecost (2000, 134–50).

The crucial role of foundational hermeneutics for the theological enterprise can be illustrated in various ways. Here, I want to tease out its implication with regard to a theology of gender relations. Certainly, theological interpretation on this topic will need to make connections at some point with the empirical (biology, neurology, physiology, and so on), humanistic and cultural sciences, the latter two insisting on global perspectives of what it means to be male and female. One will also need to grapple at various points with a theology of sexuality, a theology of the image of God, a theology of incarnation, a pneumatology, etc. The goal of a robust theological anthropology, one assumes, emerges out of prolonged encounter of all of these topics with the biblical, historical, and dogmatic traditions of Christian faith.

Clearly, the theological hermeneutic and methodology I have outlined in these pages is precisely what some who are concerned to develop a theology of gender relations are opposed to. Indeed, the fierce debates which characterize this area of theological reflection in some quarters of the Christian world can be said to arise precisely out of the disagreement over the norms and canons to be consulted. My argument, however, is that whatever limits one places with regard to theological method, an adequate theology of gender relations cannot be developed in any other way. The conservative evangelical Christian attempt to re-read the biblical narratives by utilizing a hermeneutics of suspicion focused on the patriarchal bias of the tradition is a case in point. This egalitarian strategy refocuses on the liberating features of the biblical text apart from the traditional bias. Jesus' relationships with women and Paul's working alongside women in ministry, it is proposed, neutralizes other texts which imply the subordination of the woman to the man. Rather than reading the former in light of the latter (the patriarchal hermeneutic), why not, evangelical egalitarians suggest, the other way around (the egalitarian hermeneutic)?

There are at least two major problems here. The first is endemic to the evangelical community itself. While this community is verbally committed to the Bible as authoritative and normative for theological reflection and doctrinal claims, both read Scripture through a variety of lenses. The egalitarians approach the biblical text through the fires of modernity, of women's suffrage, of democratic ideals, and so forth. The conservatives approach the same text through what might be called the patriarchal perspective of tradition which "sees the universe as having a masculine tilt."[5] Both wish to claim commitment to Scripture, yet both are unwilling to acknowledge that Word works alongside both Spirit and Community, rather than norming them, or alone.

But—and this is the second problem—no amount of sophisticated re-reading of the biblical texts can do away with the patriarchal bias of the biblical authors themselves (cf. Brown 2000, 11–61). First century Jewish men were men of their times, not men of the twentieth century. To read egalitarian principles back into the biblical texts themselves is anachronistic at best and violates the integrity of the biblical authors' self-understanding at worst. Paul Jewett's (1975) argument that the Christian Testament mistake was to follow the rabbis in understanding male-female relationships according to narrative of the fall in Genesis 3 rather than the narrative of creation in Genesis 1 shows that he recognizes this temptation. Now while Jewett should be commended as an

---

[5] I owe this phrase to the memory of my good friend, Stanley Spicer, Vancouver, Washington, who went home to be with the Lord in July of 1998.

evangelical scholar and thinker for critiquing Paul in light of the creation narratives—saying Paul had proper insight into the issue of gender (as when he declared both equal in Christ), but a mistaken notion of how to implement such insight into the practice of the Church (as when he subordinates women to men)—it is still also the case that the author(s) of neither the creation narratives nor the rest of Scripture had modernist or egalitarian notions of gender equality in mind (cf. Powell 2001, 128–30).

A contemporary theology of male-female relationships therefore appears to be caught on the horns of a dilemma. On the one side, to say the meaning of the biblical texts is constrained by the self-understanding and intentions of the biblical authors and canonical communities would be to affirm an essentialist understanding of gender that is non-egalitarian but androcentric and patriarchal. On the other, to insist on an egalitarian anthropology would seemingly require the commitment to a reader-oriented hermeneutic such that meaning emerges from the interpretations of texts. If the issue is framed in terms of women's liberation, then we would have to go beyond the intentions of the biblical authors and the canonical communities. David Brown puts it this way: "While not denying the right of Scripture to offer a critique of later elements in the tradition, there is also...an equal right of later tradition to critique Scripture, and this is what makes it inappropriate to speak of one always acting as the norm for the other. Instead, a dialogue must take place, with now one yielding, now the other" (1999, 111; cf. Dickinson 1999).[6]

A liberative theology of women and of gender relations, then, has to engage both in historical theology and in biblical theology. And besides these, there is also the dogmatic issue that plays itself out on this topic in various ways, most problematic of which is in regard to the doctrine of ministry and ministerial ordination. Here, biblical, historical, and dogmatic issues are intricately intertwined. No wonder theological progress of this issue is slow. It can only come piecemeal, and yet has to reach across the board if genuine advance is to be made. The work of biblical scholars is imperative to uncover a diversity of

[6] Brown's *Discipleship and Imagination* (2000) is the sequel to *Tradition and Imagination* (1999). Both are extensions of his reconceived notion of revelation as an ongoing process of divine-human dialogue sketched in an earlier work (Brown 1985, ch. 2). In this later two volumes, Brown fleshes out this thesis by presenting a variety of case studies on theodicy, the patriarchal narratives, mariology, etc., to argue for understanding Scripture and tradition along a continuum of revelation as ongoing, rather than as distinct categories. I would suggest that the evangelical call for a hermeneutic that reads beyond the original authorial or even canonical intention of the Scripture toward understanding it as the living Word of God as led by the Spirit for today is an alternative way of stating, albeit in conservative rather than liberal terms, Brown's argument (see DeYoung and Hurty 1995).

trajectories even in the biblical canon itself on this topic. Historians and dogmaticians have to wrestle with the tradition's (mis-) understandings. At the level of historical understanding, historical theology proceeds only descriptively. At the level of theological understanding, however, historical theology has to engage dogmatic theology, and normative questions arise. And, at the level of dogmatics, whether or not such remain status quo is the surest signal about whether or not progress on this particular question is being made. It is only when dogmatic theology makes adjustments that transition toward a fully egalitarian view of male-female relationships comes into view.

For David Brown, it is the various socio-historical contexts within which Christians find themselves which pressures imaginative engagements with the Bible such that the

> canon of interpretation continued to develop, even if this ceased to be by the simple creation of wholly new texts. Sometimes this involved creative mistranslation; sometimes a new grid being imposed upon an existing story; sometimes lacunae being filled and thus indirectly an almost wholly new story generated. Sometimes even what is constitutive of this real canon is not written text at all but a narrative controlled by visual image. (1999, 123)

What I wish to add to Brown's analysis is the notion of imagination as the medium of the Spirit's engaging and transforming the Church's historical and dogmatic self-understanding. New significations and applications of the divine self-communication can and should be understood as emergent from the Spirit's ongoing work in and through the community of faith, even as the original biblical texts themselves are by-products of human encounters with God through the same Spirit. This is the import of Stephen Fowl's argument that the theological reading and interpretation of Scripture emerges from the conjunction of experiences of the Spirit and the reading of Scripture in and with the Spirit (it being impossible to determine whether experience precedes reading or vice-versa), sometimes producing novel conclusions that reach beyond the warrant of Scripture itself. Commenting on John 12:16, Fowl notes that "the disciples only 'remember' in the light of the resurrection. The act of remembrance that the Spirit enables here is not so much an exercise in recollection as an understanding of things said and done in the past from the perspective of the death and resurrection of Jesus" (1998, 100). As important, however, is Brown's observation that neither the (Spirit-inspired) imagination nor the scriptural revelation operate in a vacuum. Rather, both are situated in historical and dogmatic traditions, even while they work conjointly to transform such traditions. And, as the Spirit moves and the Word is engaged, the payoff can be determined by how dogmaticians respond. At all of these levels, of course, socio-historical factors are intertwined with political, economic, and other intellectual factors of the cultural situation. In short, our life in and commitments to various religious, social, intellectual, and political communities brings about a theological interpretation that negotiates in a subtle and sophisticated manner the numerous claims, convictions, and values espoused in the public square.

The danger of a consciously and fully public theology is, of course, the triumph of Athens, Beijing, or Rio over Jerusalem. There is always the threat of theological reductionism, of theological immanentism, of theological syncretism. Discerning the totality of the world—the discernment of spirits, including the divine absence—always risks discerning only the world and not the divine. One could, perhaps, decide to disengage the world for fear of contamination. Partial success in disengaging (complete disengagement would be impossible) would result in theological parochialism, isolationism, and sectarianism—a monologue at worst, and an in-house dialogue between Word and a limited community resisting inquiry at best. Theological interpretation which embraces the task of engaging the divine mystery in all of its fullness cannot but pursue its task trialogically, moving and being moved according to the trialectical interplay of Spirit, Word and Community.

Provisional Conclusions

We have traveled a long way since the claim was submitted in the introductory chapter that the task of developing a theological hermeneutics cannot be separated from the question of a hermeneutical theology. For this reason, our journey begun in the Spirit has taken us through the technicalities of trinitarian theology—explored according to the two hands and the mutual love models—as correlated with a metaphysics and ontology—one that is triadic, relational, and social—and an epistemology—more specifically, the pneumatological imagination. The gains made during this pilgrimage were suggestive of a hermeneutical and methodological trialectic: all theological interpretation and reflection proceeds by way of Spirit and Word in Community. By way of concluding provisionally, one major and two minor points should be emphasized.

First, this trinitarian proposal undercuts once for all any hermeneutical claim based on a single principle. Such logocentrism needs to be exposed and pre-scriptively rejected not only because the complexity of the world and of human activity resists any totalizing metanarrative, but also because, at the descriptive level, interpretation cannot succeed if driven by a single engine. A brief look at each moment of the trialectic isolation will confirm this basic point.

What would *sola spiritus* look like? I propose that Paul Feyerabend's *Against Method* reflects *sola spiritus* applied to scientific method. Feyerabend's thesis is that:

> the events, procedures and results that constitute the sciences have no common structure; there are no elements that occur in every scientific investigation but are missing elsewhere. Concrete developments (such as the overthrow of steady state cosmologies and the discovery of the structure of DNA) have distinct features and we can often explain why and how these features led to success. But not every discovery can be accounted for in the same manner, and procedures that paid off in the past may create havoc when imposed on the future. Successful research does not obey general standards; it relies now on one trick, now on another; the moves that advance it and the standards that define what counts as an advance are not always known to the movers....A theory of science that devises standards and structural elements for *all* scientific activities and authorizes them by reference to 'Reason' or 'Rationality' may impress outsiders—but it is much too crude an

instrument for the people on the spot, that is, for scientists facing some concrete research problem. (1990, 1; emphasis orig.)

Feyerabend's claims that scientific advances are not the product of a homogeneous method, that they do not reflect a single type of rationality, that they do not proceed from within a common structural framework, etc., may have parallels in the theological sciences as well. A pneumatic and charismatic bias in theological reflection, for example, might reject any and all attempts at defining either a hermeneutic or a method as constricting the free leading of the Spirit (cf. Maier 1994, 320–26). Certainly, such a bias would reject the authority of the author and the text over the reader, apply the hermeneutics of suspicion toward exposing the ideological elements of interpretive communities, and favor either the authority of the (usually charismatic) individual to discern truth by the power of the Spirit, or a rank plurality of interpretive authorities. Fundamentalists, some kinds of Pentecostals, and contemporary reader-response theorists all espouse a kind of *sola spiritus* hermeneutic and methodology at least in practice if not in theory. The result is that *sola spiritus* inspires an "enthusiastic" or radically individualistic Christianity which has perennially fallen prey to a thoroughgoing subjectivism.

To be sure, our own argument began with the Spirit. However, the claim made in Part One is that the dynamic of the Spirit opens up and requires trinitarian theology since the divine Breath points not to herself but to the Son and the Father. The theologian's response to Feyerabend et al., is not to exempt either scientific or theological method from criticism, but to examine closely the hermeneutical and methodological structures and movements themselves. Spirit, Word, and Community in that case can be understood as heuristic categories which actually better express the insights of *sola spiritus*. Certainly, the community of scientists and of researchers follow inspired hypotheses and abductions, often unpredictable in terms both of their formulation and their outcomes, and as such, perhaps conceivable as the leading of the Spirit. Equally certain, both communities of inquiry deal with givens that, while subjectively accessed and dynamic, nonetheless make claims on the researchers. Scientific and theological inquiry is focused only on the self but on the world in all of its complexity. And, such inquiry is nourished by communities of researchers and scholars who are, in the long run, responsible to validate discoveries and advances in their respective disciplines. In short, *sola spiritus* does not work. A pneumatological method needs to be set within the triadic framework of Spirit, Word and Community.

As much has already been said about *sola scriptura* [chapter eight]. Negatively put, the emerging consensus today is that *sola scriptura* never did function strictly according to its claims (see, e.g., Lane 1994; Williams 1999, esp. 229–34, and Abraham 1998, ch. 6, esp. 148–55). In fact, *sola scriptura* provides its own defeater since it cannot be biblically defended. Appeal cannot be made to the Church Fathers since they understood Scripture as one soteriological means of grace alongside other elements of the apostolic tradition. Clearly, it is a historically emergent hermeneutical principle that developed during the early modern period *after* the collapse of ecclesial authority in order to serve the epistemic function of providing a criterion of justification for theology. As such, *sola scriptura* advocates have never been able to develop an ecclesiology (theology of tradition) or pneumatology sufficient to the epistemic demands of the gospel.

Put positively, however, *sola scriptura* points to the radical alterity of the scriptural texts which confront us with the Word of God. And, when set within a triadic framework, it enables us to hear that Word in a meaningful way. In fact, I would go so far as to argue that biblical hermeneuticians are implicitly recognizing that all interpretation of Scripture needs to take place by the Spirit and within a community of faith. Consider, for example, the following hermeneutical principles suggested by Gerald O'Collins and Daniel Kendall (1997):

1. The principle of faithful hearing: theologians need to be faithful and regular hearers of God's Word through the Scriptures.
2. The principle of active hearing: interpretation should be undertaken with prayer, study and action.
3. The principle of the community and its creeds: theological interpretation and appropriation are done within a living community of faith and in light of its classic creeds.
4. The principle of biblical convergence: the entirety of the biblical testimony should be brought to bear on theological issues and questions.
5. The principle of exegetical consensus: centrist exegesis should guide the theological interpretation of Scripture.
6. The principle of metathemes and metanarratives: theological interpretation of the Bible should observe and take account of metathemes and metanarratives.
7. The principle of continuity and discontinuity: all interpretation results in discontinuities within continuities.
8. The principle of eschatological provisionality: all theological interpretation is tentative vis-à-vis the eschatological horizon of Christian experience.
9. The principle of philosophical assistance: theological interpretation of Scripture occurs in dialogue with philosophy.

10. The principle of inculturation: inculturating Scripture in diverse social and historical contexts shapes theological appropriation.

There is no explicit reference to the Spirit, although pneumatology is discussed in the Appendix of this book, specifically with regard to the inspiration of Scripture, but also with regard to the theological task. Yet clearly, principles two, seven, and eight are all suggestive of the pneumatic moment of biblical interpretation, whether that be the activity of the pneumatological imagination, or the novelty, dynamism and provisionality of interpretation. Principles one, three, five, and ten require a faithful community and demand that attention be paid to contextual variables. In short, faithful and submissive reading and interpretation of the Bible—the intention of *sola scriptura*—cannot proceed apart from Spirit and Community.

Finally, claims for *sola traditus* or *sola communitas* (if there be any) inevitably struggle to make relevant the ancient stories, creeds, doctrines, and practices to vastly different places and times, and to those who are outside the community in question. This is the burden of Eastern Orthodoxy, regardless of its present attractiveness. But the reality is that all communities labor under constraints since the boundaries of communities, no matter how clearly defined, are constituted at least in part by those on the margins. Communitarian activities (and interpretations) are therefore checked by voices and actions that resist the hegemony of the center. Further, communities are not static entities. Rather, their dynamic and continuously shifting nature means that even communities are not immune to the movements of spirit. Finally, "majority rules" does not guarantee truth. False ideologies can capture the hearts and minds of communities, even communities of faith. Community needs to be transformed by the Spirit and checked by the Word.

But, if the *solas* which have laid claim to hermeneutical and methodological rule need to be rejected, so do the various dyadic combinations. Theological interpretation that functions either monologically or dialogically will always struggle to achieve clarity, coherence, and relevance. The absence of the Spirit from the hermeneutical spiral means a lifeless repetition of the Word by the tradition. The absence of the Word means the domination of either enthusiasm or anarchy (or both) in the tradition. The absence of tradition means a primitivistic, biblicistic, fundamentalistic, and enthusiastic orientation. Positively put, I am arguing here that Spirit in conjunction with Word and community means that the Spirit is the dynamic of interpretation on the one hand, and that Spirit is delivered from its ideological captivity by those who would claim to be solely spiritual on the other. The Word in conjunction with Spirit and Community means that Scripture is a heuristic norm on the one hand, and that it is delivered from its ideological captivity by those who would claim to be solely biblical on the other. Community in conjunction with Spirit and Word means that tradition provides the context of interpretation on the one hand, and that tradition is delivered from its own ideological captivity by those who would claim control over interpretation on the other. In short, two moments without the third still runs the hermeneutical risk of insufficient checks and balances.

Put succinctly, and this is my second major concluding point, I have argued for a theological hermeneutic that is triadic, trialectical and trialogical. It is *triadic* in that it includes three moments: that of Spirit (praxis, experience, act of interpretation), that of Word (thought, object, given of interpretation), and that of Community (context, tradition, public of interpretation). It should be clear by now that these concepts are heuristic and descriptive on the one hand, even while being normative in the sense of making claims on theological interpretation on the other. It is *trialectical* in that these three moments are inter-structurally given, interdependent, interconnected, interrelated, interpenetrating and inter-influential, and reciprocal (one hopes the point is made!). None operate apart from the other two; each informs and is shaped by the other two; each requires the other two in order for it to be itself. It is *trialogical* in that the methodological procedure of theological hermeneutics requires the ongoing demand by and submission of each moment to the other two. One can and does begin anywhere in the hermeneutical trialectic, but must at some point confront the implications for the question at hand raised by and for the other two moments of the triad. The corrections that follow can and do come from everywhere even as they are fallible and subject to correction from other perspectives of the triad as these are engaged in the hermeneutical process. The possibilities of theological knowledge are propelled by this trialectic of interpretation: Spirit and Word in Community means that object and subject, text and context, interpreter and community/communities of interpretation all coinhere and inform each other as pairs (dialectically) and across pairings (trialectically).

The primary rationale for the hermeneutical trialectic is the pneumatologically driven doctrine of trinitarian perichoresis. While pneumatology contributes the emphases on relationality, otherness, and dynamic, incessant activity, the triune subsistent relations are suggestive of mutuality, indwelling, and sociality. Applied hermeneutically and methodologically, the result is close to what Stephen Dunning (1997) calls "transactional interpretation," which endeavors to find reciprocal relations, and "transformational interpretation," which attempts to discern and resolve oppositional meanings through a paradoxical union that nevertheless retains the opposing poles. In terms of the primary categories employed in this study, theological interpretation is an activity that bridges Word and Community, that transforms Word and Community, and holds together in tension, Word and Community; theological interpretation is also emergent from the Spirit transforming Community, and holds in tension continuity and discontinuity; finally, theological interpretation is a communal enterprise to discern the Spirit, to understand the Word, and to be transformed by the Spirit and the Word.

My third and final (for the purposes of this book) remark can be put in the form of a question: is this hermeneutical trialectic a novel idea? Yes and no. It connects well with other models of theological hermeneutics including canonical hermeneutics (e.g., Brevard Childs, James Sanders, Charles Scalise), the Anglican Triad of Scripture, tradition and reason (cf. Bauckham and Drewery 1988; Abraham 1998, ch. 8), the Wesleyan quadrilateral of the Triad plus experience (cf. Thorsen 1990; Coppedge 1991; Gunter et al. 1997), and the hermeneutical circle or spiral (cf. Osborne 1991). It incorporates many, if not all, of the features of theological interpretation advocated by contemporary theological hermeneuticians. It has aesthetic, descriptive, and normative components reflecting the triune God Christians worship and serve. It recognizes the multi-dimensionality of truth, the limitations of epistemic conditionality, and the multifarious operations of canonical norms and measures. In these ways and more, the hermeneutical trialectic is simply re-stating old truths perhaps in a new way.

In what ways, then, Yes? Perhaps only in recognizing the thoroughgoing interplay of Spirit, Word and Community in the processes of theological interpretation. This would not be only a Pentecostal (with emphasis on Spirit), or Protestant (with emphasis on Word) or Roman Catholic/Orthodox (with emphasis on Community) hermeneutic. It strives to describe theological interpretation as it actually occurs, and prescribe a model of doing theology relevant to the Church catholic and directed toward the eschaton. As such, I present this as a consensual hermeneutic and methodology, perhaps already discernible to be operative in Christian theological interpretation and theological method wherever such may be occurring. And, in adhering to Peirce's fallibilism, I expect to be corrected on points of details and even of major scope by others inquiring into the persisting question of theological hermeneutics and theological method.

Bibliography

Abraham, William J. 1981. *The Divine Inspiration of Holy Scripture*. Oxford: Oxford University Press.
———. 1990. "The Epistemological Significance of the Inner Witness of the Holy Spirit." *Faith and Philosophy* 7:434–50.
———. 1998. *Canon and Criterion in Christian Theology: From the Fathers to Feminism*. Oxford: Clarendon Press.
Abram, David. 1996. *The Spell of the Sensuous: Perception and Language in a More-than-Human World*. New York: Pantheon Books.
Albrecht, Daniel E. 1999. *Rites in the Spirit: A Ritual Approach to Pentecostal/Charismatic Spirituality*. Journal of Pentecostal Theology Supplemental Series 17. Sheffield: Sheffield Academic Press.
Allison, Dale. 1995. *The Silence of Angels*. Valley Forge, Pa.: Trinity Press International.
Alston, William. 1989. *Epistemic Justification: Essays in the Theory of Knowledge*. Ithaca, N.Y.: Cornell University Press.
———. 1991. *Perceiving God: The Epistemology of Religious Experience*. Ithaca, N.Y.: Cornell University Press.
———. 1996. *A Realist Conception of Truth*. Ithaca, N.Y.: Cornell University Press.
Anderson, Robert Mapes. 1979. *Vision of the Disinherited: The Making of American Pentecostalism*. Oxford: Oxford University Press.
Apczynski, John V. 1977. *Doers of the Word: Toward a Foundational Theology Based on the Thought of Michael Polanyi*. American Academy of Religion Dissertation Series 18. Missoula, Mont.: Scholars Press.
Austin, J. L. 1964. "Truth." Pp. 18–31 in *Truth*, ed. George Pitcher. Englewood, N.J.: Prentice-Hall.
———. 1975. *How to Do Things with Words*. 2nd ed. Ed. J. O. Urmson and Marina Sbisà. Cambridge: Harvard University Press.
Avis, Paul. 1999. *God and the Creative Imagination: Metaphor, Symbol, and Myth in Religion and Theology*. London: Routledge.
Badcock, Gary D. 1997. *Light of Truth and Fire of Love: A Theology of the Holy Spirit*. Grand Rapids and Cambridge: Eerdmans.
Balchin, John F. 1982. "Paul, Wisdom and Christ." Pp. 204–19 in *Christ the Lord: Studies in Christology presented to Donald Guthrie*, ed. Harold H. Rowdon. Leicester, U.K.: InterVarsity Press.
Barbour, R. S. 1976. "Creation, Wisdom and Christ." Pp. 22–42 in *Creation, Christ and Culture: Studies in Honour of T. F. Torrance*, ed. Richard W. A. McKinney. Edinburgh: T & T Clark.
Bauckham, Richard, and Benjamin Drewery, eds. 1988. *Scripture, Tradition and Reason: A Study in the Criteria of Christian Doctrine*. Edinburgh: T & T Clark.
Bednar, Gerald J. 1996. *Faith as Imagination: The Contribution of William F. Lynch, SJ*. Kansas City: Sheed & Ward.
Beeby, Harry Daniel. 2000. "A Missional Approach to Renewed Interpretation." Pp. 268–83 in *Renewing Biblical Interpretation*, ed. Craig Bartholomew, Colin Greene, and Karl Möller. Carlisle, U.K.: Paternoster Press; Grand Rapids: Eerdmans.
Bell, Catherine. 1992. *Ritual Theory, Ritual Practice*. New York: Oxford University Press.
———. 1997. *Ritual: Perspectives and Dimensions*. Oxford: Oxford University Press.
Berkhof, Hendrikus. [1962] 1977. *Christ and the Powers*. Trans. John H. Yoder. Waterloo, Ontario: Mennonite Publishing House.

Beuken, Willem, Sean Freyne, and Anton Weiler, eds. 1988. *Truth and Its Victims*. Concilium 200. Edinburgh: T & T Clark.

Bloesch, Donald G. 1992. *A Theology of Word and Spirit: Authority and Method in Theology*. Downers Grove: InterVarsity Press.

———. 1994. *Holy Scripture: Revelation, Inspiration and Interpretation*. Downers Grove: InterVarsity Press.

———. 2000. *The Holy Spirit: Works and Gifts*. Downers Grove: InterVarsity Press.

Blondel, Maurice. 1964. *The Letter on Apologetics; and, History and Dogma*. Trans. A. Dru and I. Trethowan. London: Harvill.

Bobrinskoy, Boris. 1999. *The Mystery of the Trinity: Trinitarian Experience and Vision in the Biblical and Patristic Tradition*. Trans. Anthony P. Gythiel. Crestwood, N.Y.: St Vladimir's Seminary Press.

Bolt, John. 1989. "Spiritus Creator: The Use and Abuse of Calvin's Cosmic Pneumatology." Pp. 17–33 in *Calvin and the Holy Spirit*, ed. Peter De Clerk. Grand Rapids: Calvin Studies Society.

Bonner, Gerald. 1960. "St. Augustine's Doctrine of the Holy Spirit." *Sobornost* 4:51–66.

Boyd, Gregory A. 1992. *Trinity and Process: A Critical Evaluation and Reconstruction of Hartshorne's Di-Polar Theism towards a Trinitarian Metaphysic*. New York: Peter Lang.

Bracken, Joseph, SJ. 1979. *What are They Saying about the Trinity*. New York, Ramsey, Toronto: Paulist Press.

———. 1985. *The Triune Symbol: Persons, Process and Community*. College Theological Society Studies in Religion 1. Lanham, Md., and London: University Press of America.

———. 1986. "Spirit and Society: A Study in Two Concepts." *Process Studies* 15:244–55.

———. 1991. *Society and Spirit: A Trinitarian Cosmology*. London and Toronto: Associated University Presses; Selinsgrove, Pa.: Susquehanna University Press.

———. 1995. *The Divine Matrix: Creativity as Link Between East and West*. Maryknoll: Orbis Books.

———. 2001. *The One in the Many: A Contemporary Reconstruction of the God-World Relationship*. Grand Rapids and Cambridge: Eerdmans.

Bracken, Joseph A., and Marjorie Suchocki, eds. 1997. *Trinity in Process: A Rational Theology of God*. New York: Continuum.

Bradshaw, Timothy. 1988. *Trinity and Ontology: A Comparative Study of the Theologies of Karl Barth and Wolfhart Pannenberg*. Edinburgh: Rutherford House Books.

Breck, John. 1991. *Spirit of Truth: The Holy Spirit in Johannine Tradition*. Vol. 1, *The Origins of Johannine Pneumatology*. Crestwood, N.Y.: St Vladimir's Seminary Press.

Bronowski, Jacob. 1978. *The Origins of Knowledge and Imagination*. London: Yale University Press.

Brown, David. 1985. *The Divine Trinity*. La Salle, Ill.: Open Court.

———. 1999. *Tradition and Imagination: Revelation and Change*. Oxford: Oxford University Press.

———. 2000 *Discipleship and Imagination: Christian Tradition and Truth*. Oxford: Oxford University Press.

Brown, Delwin. 1994. *Boundaries of Our Habitations: Tradition and Theological Construction*. Albany: SUNY Press.

Brueggemann, Walter. 1978. *The Prophetic Imagination*. Philadelphia: Fortress Press.

Bryant, David J. 1989. *Faith and the Play of Imagination: On the Role of Imagination in Religion*. Studies in American Biblical Hermeneutics 5. Macon, Ga.: Mercer University Press.

Buckley, James J., and David S. Yeago, eds. 2001. *Knowing the Triune God: The Work of the Spirit in the Practices of the Church*. Grand Rapids and Cambridge: Eerdmans.

Bultmann, Rudolf. 1960. "Is Exegesis Without Presuppositions Possible?" Pp. 289–96 in *Existence and Faith: Shorter Writings of Rudolf Bultmann*, ed. Schubert M. Ogden. Cleveland and New York: World Publishing Company/Meridian Books.

Burton-Christie, Douglas. 1999. "The Place of the Heart: Geography and Spirituality in the *Life of Antony*." Pp. 45–65 in *Purity of Heart in Early Ascetic and Monastic Literature: Essays in*

Honor of Juana Raasch, OSB, ed. Harriet A. Luckman and Linda Kulzer, OSB. Collegeville, Minn.: Liturgical Press.

Butin, Philip Walker. 1995. *Revelation, Redemption, and Response: Calvin's Trinitarian Understanding of the Divine-Human Relationship*. New York and Oxford: Oxford University Press.

Caird, G. B. 1956. *Principalities and Powers: A Study in Pauline Theology*. Oxford: Clarendon Press.

Callahan, James. 2001. *The Clarity of Scripture: History, Theology and Contemporary Literary Studies*. Downers Grove: InterVarsity Press.

Casey, Edward S. [1976] 1979. *Imagining: A Phenomenological Study*. Bloomington and London: Indiana University Press and Midland Books.

Cassirer, Ernst. 1944. *An Essay on Man: An Introduction to a Philosophy of Human Culture*. New Haven: Yale University Press.

Chan, Simon. 1998. *Spiritual Theology: A Systematic Study of the Christian Life*. Downers Grove: InterVarsity Press.

Clayton, John P. 1980. *The Concept of Correlation: Paul Tillich and the Possibility of a Mediating Theology*. Theologische Bibliothek Töpelmann 37. New York: Walter de Gruyter.

Clayton, Philip. 1999. "Missiology between Monologue and Cacophony." Pp. 78–95 in *To Stake a Claim: Mission and the Western Crisis of Knowledge*, ed. J. Andrew Kirk and Kevin Vanhoozer. Maryknoll: Orbis Books.

Clements, Ronald E. 1990. *Wisdom for a Changing World: Wisdom in Old Testament Theology*. Berkeley Lectures 2. Berkeley, Calif.: BIBAL Press.

———. 1992. *Wisdom in Theology*. Carlisle, U.K.: Paternoster Press; Grand Rapids: Eerdmans.

Clendenin, Daniel B. 1987. *Theological Method in Jacques Ellul*. Lanham, Md., New York, and London: University Press of America.

Coady, C. A. J. 1992. *Testimony: A Philosophical Study*. Oxford: Clarendon Press.

Cocking, J. M. 1991. *Imagination: A Study in the History of Ideas*. Ed. Penelope Murray. London: Routledge.

Coffey, David. 1979. *Grace: The Gift of the Holy Spirit*. Manly, NSW, Australia: Catholic Institute of Sydney.

———. 1984. "The 'Incarnation' of the Holy Spirit in Christ." *Theological Studies* 45:466–80.

———. 1986. "A Proper Mission of the Holy Spirit." *Theological Studies* 47:227–50.

———. 1990. "The Holy Spirit as the Mutual Love of the Father and the Son." *Theological Studies* 51:193–229.

———. 1999. *Deus Trinitas: The Doctrine of the Triune God*. New York and Oxford: Oxford University Press.

Colapietro, Vincent Michael. 1989. *Peirce's Approach to the Self: A Semiotic Perspective on Human Subjectivity*. Albany: SUNY Press.

Cole, Susan, Marian Ronan, and Hal Taussig. 1996. *Wisdom's Feast: Sophia in Study and Celebration*. 2nd ed. Kansas City: Sheed & Ward.

Collins, John J. 1998. *The Apocalyptic Imagination: An Introduction to Jewish Apocalyptic Literature*. 2nd ed. Cambridge, U.K.: Eerdmans.

Congar, Yves. 1967. *Tradition and Traditions: An Historical and a Theological Essay*. Trans. Michael Naseby and Thomas Rainborough. New York: Macmillan Company.

———. 1983. *I Believe in the Holy Spirit*. 3 vols. Trans. David Smith. New York: Seabury Press.

———. 1986. *The Word and the Spirit*. Trans. David Smith. London: Geoffrey Chapman; San Francisco: Harper & Row Publishers.

Coppedge, Allan. 1991. "How Wesleyans Do Theology." Pp. 267–90 in *Doing Theology in Today's World: Essays in Honor of Kenneth Kantzer*, ed. John Woodbridge and Thomas McComiskey. Grand Rapids: Zondervan.

Corrington, Robert. 1992. *Nature and Spirit: An Essay in Ecstatic Naturalism*. New York: Fordham University Press.

Corrington, Robert. 1993. *An Introduction to C. S. Peirce: Philosopher, Semiotician, and Ecstatic Naturalist.* Lanham, Md.: Rowman & Littlefield Publishers.

———. 1994. *Ecstatic Naturalism: Signs of the World.* Bloomington: Indiana University Press.

———. 1995. *The Community of Interpreters: On the Hermeneutics of Nature and the Bible in the American Philosophical Tradition.* 2nd ed. Studies in American Biblical Hermeneutics 3. Macon, Ga.: Mercer University Press.

———. 1996. *Nature's Self: Our Journey from Origin to Spirit.* Lanham, Md.: Rowman & Littlefield Publishers.

———. 1997. *Nature's Religion.* Lanham, Md.: Rowman & Littlefield Publishers.

———. 2000. *A Semiotic Theory of Theology and Philosophy.* Cambridge: Cambridge University Press.

Coulson, John. 1981. *Religion and Imagination: "In Aid of a Grammar of Ascent."* Oxford: Oxford University Press; New York: Clarendon Press.

Coward, Harold G. 1988. *Sacred Word and Sacred Text: Scripture in World Religions.* Maryknoll: Orbis Books.

Cunningham, David. 1998. *These Three Are One: The Practice of Trinitarian Theology.* Malden, Mass., and Oxford: Blackwell.

Dabney, D. Lyle. 1996. "Otherwise Engaged in the Spirit: A First Theology for the Twenty-first Century." Pp. 154–63 in *The Future of Theology: Essays in Honor of Jürgen Moltmann,* ed. Miroslav Volf, Carmen Krieg, and Thomas Kucharz. Grand Rapids: Eerdmans.

———. 2000. "*Pneumatologia Crucis:* Reclaiming *Theologia Crucis* for a Theology of the Spirit Today." *Scottish Journal of Theology* 53:511–24.

———. 2001. "He Will Baptize You with the Holy Spirit: Retrieving a Metaphor for a Contemporary Pneumatological Soteriology." Paper presented to Annual Meeting of the Society for Pentecostal Studies. Tulsa, Okla.: Oral Roberts University.

Davids, Peter H. 2001. "Authority. Hermeneutics, and Criticism." Pp. 2–20 in *Interpreting the New Testament: Essays in Methods and Issues,* ed. David Alan Black and David S. Dockery. Nashville: Broadman & Holman.

Davidson, Donald. 1984. *Inquiries into Truth and Interpretation.* Oxford: Clarendon Press.

———. 1986. "A Coherence Theory of Truth and Knowledge." Pp. 307–19 in *Truth and Interpretation: Perspectives on the Philosophy of Donald Davidson,* ed. Ernest LePore. Oxford: Basil Blackwell.

Davis, Caroline Franks. 1989. *The Evidential Force of Religious Experience.* Oxford: Clarendon Press.

Davis, James A. 1984. *Wisdom and Spirit: An Investigation of 1 Corinthians 1.18–3.20 Against the Background of Jewish Sapiential Traditions in the Greco-Roman Period.* Lanham, Md.: University Press of America.

Deely, John. 1994. *The Human Use of Signs, or: Elements of Anthroposemiosis.* Lanham, Md.: Rowman & Littlefield Publishers.

Del Colle, Ralph. 1994. *Christ and the Spirit: Spirit-Christology in Trinitarian Perspective.* New York: Oxford University Press.

Den Bok, Nico. 1996. *Communicating the Most High: A Systematic Study of Person and Trinity in the Theology of Richard of St. Victor, †1173.* Bibliotheca Victorina VII. Paris: Brepols.

DeYoung, James, and Sarah Hurty. 1995. *Beyond the Obvious: Discover the Deeper Meaning of Scripture.* Gresham, Ore.: Vision House Publishing.

Dickinson, Charles. 1999. *The Dialectical Development of Doctrine: A Methodological Proposal.* Ann Arbor, Mich.: Pryor Pettingill; Dearborn, Mich.: Dove Booksellers.

Dilthey, Wilhelm. 1986. "The Types of World-View and Their Development in the Metaphysical Systems." Pp. 33–54 in *Hermeneutical Inquiry,* ed. David E. Klemm. Vol. 2, *The Interpretation of Existence.* American Academy of Religion Studies in Religion 44. Atlanta: Scholars Press.

Dulles, Avery. 1983. *Models of Revelation.* Garden City, N.Y.: Doubleday.

Dulles, Avery. 1992. *The Craft of Theology: From Symbol to System*. New York: Crossroad.

Dunn, James D. G. 1998. *The Christ and the Spirit*. Vol. 2, *Pneumatology*. Grand Rapids and Cambridge: Eerdmans.

Dunning, Stephen. 1997. *Dialectical Readings: Three Types of Interpretations*. University Park: Penn State University Press.

Dupré, Louis. 1993. *Passage to Modernity: An Essay on the Hermeneutics of Nature and Culture*. New Haven and London: Yale University Press.

Durrwell, François Xavier. 1986. *Holy Spirit of God: An Essay in Biblical Theology*. Trans. Sister Benedict Davies, OSU. London: Geoffrey Chapman.

Dych, William. 1982. "Theology and Imagination." *Thought* 57:116–27.

Dyck, Elmer, ed. 1996. *The Act of Bible Reading: A Multi-disciplinary Approach to Biblical Interpretation*. Downer's Grove, Ill.: InterVarsity Press.

Ebeling, Gerhard. 1978. *The Study of Theology*. Trans. Duane A. Priebe. Philadelphia: Fortress Press.

Edwards, Denis. 1995. *Jesus the Wisdom of God: An Ecological Theology*. Maryknoll: Orbis.

————. 1999. *The God of Evolution: A Trinitarian Theology*. New York and Mahwah, N.J.: Paulist Press.

Edwards, Jonathan. 1993. *The Works of Jonathan Edwards*. Vol. 11, *Typological Writings*, ed. Wallace E. Anderson and Mason I. Lowance, Jr., with David H. Watters. New Haven and London: Yale University Press.

Engnell, I. 1955. "'Knowledge' and 'Life' in the Creation Story." Pp. 103–19 in *Wisdom in Israel and in the Ancient Near East: Festschrift for Harold Henry Rowley*, ed. Martin Noth and D. Winton Thomas. Supplements to Vetus Testamentum 3. Leiden: E. J. Brill.

Entrevernes Group, The. 1978. *Signs and Parables: Semiotics and Gospel Texts*. Trans. Gary Phillips. Pittsburgh: Pickwick Press.

Evans, Jeanne. 1995. *Paul Ricoeur's Hermeneutics of the Imagination*. New York: Peter Lang.

Fackre, Gabriel. 1987. *The Christian Story: A Pastoral Systematics*. Vol. 2, *Authority: Scripture in the Church for the World*. Grand Rapids: Eerdmans.

————. 1997. *The Doctrine of Revelation: A Narrative Interpretation*. Grand Rapids: Eerdmans.

Faivre, Antoine. 1994. *Access to Western Esotericism*. Albany: SUNY Press.

Faivre, Antoine, and Jacob Needleman, eds. 1992. *Modern Esoteric Spirituality*. World Spirituality: An Encyclopedic History of the Religious Quest 21. New York: Crossroad.

Farley, Edward. 1982. *Ecclesial Reflection: An Anatomy of Theological Method*. Philadelphia: Fortress Press.

————. 1996. *Deep Symbols: Their Postmodern Effacement and Reclamation*. Valley Forge, Pa.: Trinity Press International.

————. 1996a. *Divine Empathy: A Theology of God*. Minneapolis: Fortress Press.

Farley, Edward, and Peter C. Hodgson. 1982. "Scripture and Tradition." Pp. 35–61 in *Christian Theology: An Introduction to its Traditions and Tasks*, ed. Peter C. Hodgson and Robert H. King. Philadelphia: Fortress Press.

Farmer, Ronald L. 1997. *Beyond the Impasse: The Promise of a Process Hermeneutic*. Studies in American Biblical Hermeneutics 13. Macon, Ga.: Mercer University Press.

Fasching, Darrell J. 1992. *Narrative Theology after Auschwitz: From Alienation to Ethics*. Minneapolis: Augsburg Fortress Press.

Fawcett, Thomas. 1971. *The Symbolic Language of Religion: An Introductory Study*. Minneapolis: Augsburg Publishing House.

Fee, Gordon D. 1994. *God's Empowering Presence: The Holy Spirit in the Letters of Paul*. Peabody, Mass.: Hendrickson.

Fee, Gordon D. 2000. "Wisdom Christology in Paul: A Dissenting View." Pp. 251–79 in *The Way of Wisdom: Essays in Honor of Bruce K. Waltke*, ed. J. I. Packer and Sven K. Soderlund. Grand Rapids: Zondervan.

Ferreira, M. Jamie. 1991. *Transforming Vision: Imagination and Will in Kierkegaardian Faith.* Oxford: Clarendon Press.

Feyerabend, Paul. 1990. *Against Method.* Rev. ed. London and New York: Verso.

Fields, Stephen M., SJ. 2000. *Being as Symbol: On the Origins and Development of Karl Rahner's Metaphysics.* Washington, D.C.: Georgetown University Press.

Finger, Thomas. 2000. "'Universal Truths': Should Anabaptist Theologians Seek to Articulate Them?" Pp. 75–88 in *Anabaptists and Postmodernity*, ed. Susan Biesecker-Mast and Gerald Biesecker-Mast. Telford, Pa.: Pandora Press.

Fiorenza, Francis Schüssler. 1984. *Foundational Theology: Jesus and the Church.* New York: Crossroad.

———. 1991. "Systematic Theology: Task and Methods." Pp. 1–89 in *Systematic Theology: Roman Catholic Perspectives*, ed. Francis Schüssler Fiorenza and John P. Galvin. Vol. 1. Minneapolis: Fortress Press.

Florovsky, Georges. 1972. *Bible, Church, Tradition: An Eastern Orthodox View.* Belmont, Mass.: Nordland Publishing Company.

Fodor, James. 1995. *Christian Hermeneutics: Paul Ricœur and the Refiguring of Theology.* Oxford: Clarendon Press.

Forbes, Cheryl. 1986. *Imagination: Embracing a Theology of Wonder.* Portland, Ore.: Multnomah Press.

Forstman, H. Jackson. 1962. *Word and Spirit: Calvin's Doctrine of Biblical Authority.* Stanford: Stanford University Press.

Fowl, Stephen E. 1998. *Engaging Scripture: A Model for Theological Interpretation.* Oxford: Blackwell.

Fox, Patricia. 2001. *God as Communion: John Zizioulas, Elizabeth Johnson and the Retrieval of the Symbol of the Triune God.* Collegeville, Minn.: Michael Glazier/Liturgical Press.

Franklin, Stephen T. 1990. *Speaking from the Depths: Alfred North Whitehead's Hermeneutical Metaphysics of Propositions, Experience, Symbolism, Language, and Religion.* Grand Rapids: Eerdmans.

Frei, Hans. 1986. "The 'Literal Reading' of Biblical Narrative in the Christian Tradition: Does It Stretch or Will It Break?" Pp. 36–77 in *The Bible and the Narrative Tradition*, ed. Frank McConnell. Oxford: Oxford University Press.

———. 1993. *Theology and Narrative: Selected Essays.* Ed. George Hunsinger and William C. Placher. New York and Oxford: Oxford University Press.

Freyer, Thomas. 1982. *Pneumatologie als Strukturprinzip der Dogmatik: Überlegungen im Anschluß an die Lehre von der "Geisttaufe" bei Karl Barth.* Paderborner Theologische Studien 12. Paderborn, München, Wien und Zürich: Ferdinand Schöningh.

Gadamer, Hans Georg. 1994. *Truth and Method.* 2nd ed. Trans. Joel Weinsheimer and Donald G. Marshall. New York: Continuum.

Gamble, Richard C. 1989. "Word and Spirit in Calvin." In *Calvin and the Holy Spirit*, ed. Peter De Clerk. Grand Rapids: Calvin Studies Society.

Gaybba, Brian P. 1987. *The Spirit of Love: Theology of the Holy Spirit.* London: Geoffrey Chapman.

Geffré, Claude. 1974. *A New Age in Theology.* Trans. Robert Shillenn, with Francis McDonagh and Theodore L. Westow. New York: Paulist Press.

———. 1987. *The Risk of Interpretation: On Being Faithful to the Christian Tradition in a Non-Christian Age.* Trans. David Smith. New York: Paulist Press.

Gelpi, Donald L. 1984. *The Divine Mother: A Trinitarian Theology of the Holy Spirit.* Lanham, Md.: University Press of America.

———. 1988. *Inculturating North American Theology: An Experiment in Foundational Method.* Atlanta: Scholars Press.

———. 1994. *The Turn to Experience in Contemporary Theology.* New York and Mahwah, N.J.: Paulist Press.

———. 1998. *The Conversion Experience: A Reflective Process for RCIA Participants and Others.* New York and Mahwah, N.J.: Paulist Press.

Gelpi, Donald L. 2000. *Varieties of Transcendental Experience: A Study in Constructive Postmodernism.* Collegeville, Minn.: Liturgical Press/Michael Glazier.

———. 2001. *The Gracing of Human Experience: Rethinking the Relationship between Nature and Grace.* Collegeville, Minn.: Liturgical Press/Michael Glazier.

———. 2001a. *The Firstborn of Many: A Christology for Converting Christians.* 3 vols. Marquette Studies in Theology 20–22. Milwaukee, Wisc.: Marquette University Press.

———. 2001b. *Peirce and Theology: Essays in the Authentication of Doctrine.* Lanham, New York, and Oxford: University Press of America.

Gilkey, Langdon. 1969. *Naming the Whirlwind: The Renewal of God-Language.* Indianapolis and New York: Bobbs-Merrill Company.

Gill, Jerry H. 1989. *Mediated Transcendence: A Postmodern Reflection.* Macon, Ga.: Mercer University Press.

Gill, Robin. 1975. *Social Context of Theology: A Methodological Inquiry.* London and Oxford: Mowbrays.

———. 1977. *Theology and Social Structure.* London and Oxford: Mowbrays.

Gillingham, Susan E. 1998. *One Bible, Many Voices: Different Approaches to Biblical Studies.* Grand Rapids: Eerdmans.

Gilovich, Thomas. 1991. *How We Know What Isn't So: The Fallibility of Human Reason in Everyday Life.* New York: Free Press.

Goldberg, Michael. 1982. *Theology and Narrative: A Critical Introduction.* Nashville: Abingdon.

Goldingay, John. 1994. *Models for Scripture.* Grand Rapids: Eerdmans.

Goodman, Nelson. 1978. *Ways of Worldmaking.* Indianapolis: Hackett Publishing Company.

Gore, Charles. 1889. "The Holy Spirit and Inspiration." Pp. 263–302 in *Lux Mundu: A Series of Studies in the Religion of the Incarnation,* ed. Charles Gore. 5th ed. New York: John W. Lovell.

Gorringe, Timothy J. 1990. *Discerning Spirit: A Theology of Revelation.* London: SCM Press; Philadelphia: Trinity Press International.

Graves, Charles Lee. 1972. *The Holy Spirit in the Theology of Sergius Bulgakov.* Geneva: World Council of Churches.

Green, Garrett. 1998. *Imagining God: Theology and the Religious Imagination.* 2nd ed. Grand Rapids and Cambridge: Eerdmans.

Green, Harold Johnson. 1980. *The Word and the Spiritual Realities: A Translation of and Critical Introduction to Ferdinand Ebner's Das Wort und die Geistigen Realitäten and a Comparison with Martin Buber's Ich und Du.* Ph.D. dissertation, Northwestern University.

Greene-McCreight, Kathryn. 2000. "The Logic of the Interpretation of Scripture and the Church's Debate over Sexual Ethics." Pp. 242–60 in *Homosexuality, Science, and the "Plain Sense" of Scripture,* ed. David L. Balch. Grand Rapids and Cambridge: Eerdmans.

Grenz, Stanley J. 1994. *Theology for the Community of God.* Nashville: Broadman & Holman.

———. 2000. "Articulating the Christian Belief-Mosaic: Theological Method after the Demise of Foundationalism." Pp. 107–38 in *Evangelical Futures: A Conversation on Theological Method,* ed. John G. Stackhouse, Jr. Grand Rapids: Baker.

Grenz, Stanley, and John Franke. 2001. *Beyond Foundationalism: Shaping Theology in a Postmodern Context.* Louisville, Ky.: Westminster John Knox Press.

Gresham, John L., Jr. 1993. "The Social Model of the Trinity and Its Critics." *Scottish Journal of Theology* 46:325–43.

Groothius, Douglas. 2000 *Truth Decay: Defending Christianity against the Challenges of Postmodernism.* Downers Grove: InterVarsity Press.

Guerrière, Daniel. 1990. "The Truth, the Nontruth, and the Untruth Proper to Salvation." Pp. 75–104 in *Phenomenology of the Truth Proper to Religion,* ed. Daniel Guerrière. Albany: SUNY Press.

Gunter, W. Stephen. 1999. *Resurrection Knowledge: Recovering the Gospel for a Postmodern Church.* Nashville: Abingdon Press.

Gunter, W. Stephen, et al. 1997. *Wesley and the Quadrilateral: Renewing the Conversation.* Nashville: Abingdon Press.

Gunton, Colin. 1993. *The One, the Three, and the Many: God, Creation and the Culture of Modernity.* Cambridge: Cambridge University Press.

———. 1995 "Relation and Relativity: The Trinity and the Created World." Pp. 92–112 in *Trinitarian Theology Today: Essays on Divine Being and Act*, ed. Christoph Schwöbel. Edinburgh: T & T Clark.

———. 1996. *Theology through the Theologians: Selected Essays, 1972–1995.* Edinburgh: T & T Clark.

———. 1997. *The Promise of Trinitarian Theology.* 2nd ed. Edinburgh: T & T Clark.

———. 1998. *The Triune Creator: A Historical and Systematic Study.* Edinburgh: Edinburgh University Press; Grand Rapids: Eerdmans.

Haack, Susan. 1993. *Evidence and Inquiry: Towards Reconstruction in Epistemology.* Oxford: Blackwell.

Haight, Roger, SJ. 1999. *Jesus Symbol of God.* Maryknoll: Orbis Books.

Hall, Douglas John. 1989. *Thinking the Faith.* Vol. 1, *Christian Theology in a North American Context.* Minneapolis: Augsburg Fortress Press.

Hamilton, Kenneth. 1966. "Created Soul—Eternal Spirit: A Continuing Theological Thorn." *Scottish Journal of Theology* 19:23–34.

Hart, Ray L. [1968] 1985. *Unfinished Man and the Imagination: Toward an Ontology and a Rhetoric of Revelation.* Atlanta: Scholars Press.

Hart, Trevor. 2000. "Imagining Evangelical Theology." Pp. 191–200 in *Evangelical Futures: A Conversation on Theological Method*, ed. John G. Stackhouse, Jr. Grand Rapids: Baker.

———. 2000a. "Imagination and Responsible Reading." Pp. 308–34 in *Renewing Biblical Interpretation*, ed. Craig Bartholomew, Colin Greene, and Karl Möller. Carlisle, U.K.: Paternoster Press; Grand Rapids: Eerdmans.

Hartt, Julian N. 1977. *Theological Method and Imagination.* New York: Seabury Press.

Hauerwas, Stanley. 1974. *Vision and Virtue: Essays in Christian Ethical Reflection.* Notre Dame: Fides Publishers.

———. 1975. *Character and the Christian Life: A Study in Theological Ethics.* San Antonio: Trinity University Press.

———. 1981. *A Community of Character: Toward a Constructive Christian Social Ethic.* Notre Dame: University of Notre Dame Press.

———. 1983. *The Peaceable Kingdom: A Primer in Christian Ethics.* London and Notre Dame: University of Notre Dame Press.

Hauerwas, Stanley, and L. Gregory Jones, eds. 1989. *Why Narrative? Readings in Narrative Theology.* Grand Rapids: Eerdmans.

Hauerwas, Stanley, Nancey Murphy, and Mark Nation, eds. 1994. *Theology without Foundations: Religious Practice and the Future of Theological Truth.* Nashville: Abingdon Press.

Hawthorne, Gerald F. 1991. *The Presence and the Power: The Significance of the Holy Spirit in the Life and Ministry of Jesus.* Dallas: Word Publishing.

Hendry, George. 1980. *Theology of Nature.* Philadelphia: Westminster Press.

Henn, William. 1987. *The Hierarchy of Truths according to Yves Congar.* Analecta Gregoriana, Series Facultatis Theologiae, Sectio B, 246:83. Rome: Editrice Pontificia Università Gregoriana.

Henry, Carl F. H. 1979. *Fifteen Theses, Part Three.* Vol. 4, *God, Revelation and Authority: The God Who Speaks and Shows.* Waco, Tex.: Word Books.

Heyward, Carter. 1982. *The Redemption of God: A Theology of Mutual Relation.* Lanham, New York, and London: University Press of America.

Hilkert, Mary Catherine. 1997. *Naming Grace: Preaching and the Sacramental Imagination.* New York: Continuum.

Hill, R. Charles. 1996. *Wisdom's Many Faces.* Collegeville, Minn.: Michael Glazier.

Hodgson, Peter C. 1995. "The Face and the Spirit." In *Theology and the Interhuman: Essays in Honor of Edward Farley*, ed. Robert R. Williams. Valley Forge, Pa.: Trinity Press International.

Hoedemaker, Bert. 1999. "Toward an Epistemologically Responsible Missiology." Pp. 217–33 in *To Stake a Claim: Mission and the Western Crisis of Knowledge*, ed. J. Andrew Kirk and Kevin Vanhoozer. Maryknoll: Orbis Books.

Hogan, John P. 1989. *Collingwood and Theological Hermeneutics*. College Theological Society Studies in Religion 3. Lanham, New York, London: University Press of America.

Holl, Adolf. 1998. *The Left Hand of God: A Biography of the Holy Spirit*. Trans. John Cullen. New York: Doubleday.

Hollenweger, Walter J. 1997. *Pentecostalism: Origins and Developments Worldwide*. Peabody, Mass.: Hendrickson Publishers.

Hordern, William, and Frederick Dale Bruner. 1984. *The Holy Spirit—Shy Member of the Trinity*. Minneapolis: Augsburg Fortress Press.

Hoskins, Richard. 2000. *The Doctrine of the Trinity in the Works of John Richardson Illingworth and William Temple, and the Implications for Contemporary Trinitarian Theology*. Toronto Studies in Theology 81. Lewiston, Queenstron, and Lampeter: Edwin Mellen Press.

Howard, Evan. 2000. *Affirming the Touch of God: A Psychological and Philosophical Investigation of Christian Discernment*. Lanham, New York, and Oxford: University Press of America.

Hütter, Reinhard. 2000. *Suffering Divine Things: Theology as Church Practice*. Trans. Doug Scott. Grand Rapids and Cambridge, U.K.: Eerdmans.

Irvin, Dale T. 1998. *Christian Histories, Christian Traditioning: Rendering Accounts*. Maryknoll: Orbis Books.

Iseminger, Gary, ed. 1992. *Intention and Interpretation*. Philadelphia: Temple University Press.

Jagger, Alison M. 1989. "Love and Knowledge: Emotion in Feminist Epistemology." Pp. 145–71 in *Gender/Body/Knowledge: Feminist Reconstructions of Being and Knowing*, ed. Alison M. Jagger and Susan R. Bordo. Brunswick, N.J.: Rutgers University Press.

James, Robison B., ed. 1994. *The Unfettered Word: Confronting the Authority-Inerrancy Question*. Macon, Ga.: Smyth & Helwys Publishing.

Jansen, Henry. 1995. *Relationality and the Concept of God*. Currents of Encounter 10. Grand Rapids: Eerdmans; Amsterdam: Editions Rodopi.

Jeanrond, Werner G. 1988. *Text and Interpretation as Categories of Theological Thinking*. Trans. Thomas J. Wilson. New York: Crossroad.

———. 1991. *Theological Hermeneutics: Development and Significance*. New York: Crossroad.

Jenson, Robert. 1984. "The Holy Spirit." Pp. 105–82 in *Christian Dogmatics*, Vol. 2, ed. Carl Braaten and Robert W. Jenson. Philadelphia: Fortress Press.

———. 1995. *Essays in Theology of Culture*. Grand Rapids: Eerdmans.

———. 1997. *The Triune God*. Vol. 1, *Systematic Theology*. New York and Oxford: Oxford University Press.

Jewett, Paul K. 1975. *Man as Male and Female*. Grand Rapids: Eerdmans.

John, Ottmar. 1988. "The Tradition of the Oppressed as the Main Topic of a Theological Hermeneutics." Pp. 143–55 in *Truth and Its Victims*, ed. Willem Beuken, Sean Freyne, and Anton Weiler. Concilium 200. Edinburgh: T & T Clark.

Johnson, Elizabeth A. 1993. *She Who Is: The Mystery of God in Feminist Theological Discourse*. New York: Crossroad.

———. 1993a. *Women, Earth, and Creator Spirit*. New York and Mahwah, N.J.: Paulist Press.

Johnson, Luke Timothy. 1996. *Scripture and Discernment: Decision-Making in the Church*. Nashville: Abingdon Press.

———. 1998. "Imagining the World Scripture Imagines." Pp. 3–18 in *Theology and Scriptural Imagination*, ed. L. Gregory Jones and James J. Buckley. Oxford and Malden, Mass.: Blackwell.

Johnson, Wayne G. 1981. *Theological Method in Luther and Tillich*. Washington, D.C.: University Press of America.

Jones, Gareth. 1995. *Critical Theology: Questions of Truth and Method*. New York: Paragon House; Cambridge, U.K.: Polity Press.

Jones, Rufus Matthew. [1941] 1963. *Spirit in Man*. Berkeley, Calif.: Peacock Press.

Jüngel, Eberhard. 1976. *The Doctrine of the Trinity: God's Being is in Becoming*. Grand Rapids: Eerdmans.

———. 1983. *God as the Mystery of the World*. Trans. Darrell L. Guder. Grand Rapids: Eerdmans.

Kärkkäinen, Veli-Matti. 2001. "David's Sling: The Promise and Problem of Pentecostal Theology—A Response to Lyle Dabney." *Pneuma: The Journal of the Society for Pentecostal Studies* 23:147–52.

Kaufman, Gordon. 1960. *Relativism, Knowledge and Faith*. Chicago and London: University of Chicago Press.

———. 1981. *The Theological Imagination: Constructing the Concept of God*. Philadelphia: Westminster Press.

———. 1995. *An Essay on Theological Method*. 3rd ed. Atlanta: Scholars Press.

Kearney, Richard. 1988. *The Wake of Imagination: Toward a Postmodern Culture*. Minneapolis: University of Minnesota Press.

Kelly, Anthony, CSSR. 1989. *The Trinity of Love: A Theology of the Christian God*. New Theology Series 4. Wilmington, Del.: Michael Glazier.

Kelly, J. N. D. 1978. *Early Christian Doctrines*. Rev. ed. San Francisco: HarperSanFrancisco.

Kelsey, David H. 1999. *Proving Doctrine: The Uses of Scripture in Modern Theology*. 2nd ed. Harrisburg, Pa.: Trinity Press International.

Kennard, Douglas Welker, ed. 1999. *The Relationship Between Epistemology, Hermeneutics, Biblical Theology and Contextualization: Understanding Truth*. Lewiston: Edwin Mellen Press.

Kilby, Clyde S. 1981. "Christian Imagination." Pp. 37–46 in *The Christian Imagination: Essays on Literature and the Arts*, ed. Leland Ryken. Grand Rapids: Baker.

Kirkham, R. L. 1992. *Theories of Truth: A Critical Introduction*. Cambridge: MIT Press.

Klooster, Fred H. 1984. "The Role of the Holy Spirit in the Hermeneutic Process." Pp. 451–72 in *Hermeneutics, Inerrancy, and the Bible*, ed. Earl D. Radmacher and Robert D. Preuss. Grand Rapids: Zondervan.

Knight, Henry H., III. 1997. *A Future for Truth: Evangelical Theology in a Postmodern World*. Nashville: Abingdon Press.

Koester, Helmut, and James M. Robinson. 1971. *Trajectories through Early Christianity*. Philadelphia: Fortress Press.

LaCugna, Catherine Mowry. 1982. *The Theological Methodology of Hans Küng*. American Academy of Religion Academy Series 39. Chica, Calif.: Scholars Press.

Lai, Pan-Chiu. 1994. *Towards a Trinitarian Theology of Religions: A Study in Paul Tillich's Thought*. Kampen, Netherlands: Kok.

Lamb, Matthew. 1992. "Communicative Praxis and Theology: Beyond Modern Nihilism and Dogmatism." Pp. 92–118 in *Habermas, Modernity, and Public Theology*, ed. Don S. Browning and Francis Schüssler Fiorenza. New York: Crossroad.

Lampe, G. W. H. 1977. *God as Spirit: The Bampton Lectures, 1976*. Oxford: Clarendon Press.

Lane, Anthony N. S. 1994. "Sola Scriptura? Making Sense of a Post-Reformation Slogan." Pp. 297–327 in *A Pathway into the Holy Scripture*, ed. Philip E. Satterthwaite and David F. Wright. Grand Rapids: Eerdmans.

Lash, Nicholas. 1981. *Easter in Ordinary: Reflections on Human Experience and the Knowledge of God*. Charlottesville: University of Virginia Press.

Lategan, Bernard C., and Willem S. Vorster. 1985. *Text and Reality: Aspects of Reference in Biblical Texts*. Atlanta: Scholars Press.

Lawrence, Frederick. 1981. "Method and Theology as Hermeneutical." Pp. 79–104 in *Creativity and Method: Essays in Honor of Bernard Lonergan, SJ*, ed. Matthew L. Lamb. Milwaukee, Wisc.: Marquette University Press.

Lawrence, Irene. 1980. *Linguistics and Theology: The Significance of Noam Chomsky for Theological Construction*. ATLA Monograph Series 16. Metuchen, N.J., and London: Scarecrow Press and American Theological Library Association.

Lawson, John. 1948. *The Biblical Theology of Saint Irenaeus*. London: Epworth Press.

Lee, Sang Hyun. 2000. *The Philosophical Theology of Jonathan Edwards*. Expanded ed. Princeton: Princeton University Press.

Leftow, Brian. 1999. "Anti Social Trinitarianism." Pp. 203–49 in *The Trinity: An Interdisciplinary Symposium on the Trinity*, ed. Stephen T. Davis, Daniel Kendall, SJ, and Gerald O'Collins, SJ. Oxford: Oxford University Press.

Lehrer, Keith, and Stewart Cohen. 1987 "Justification. Truth, and Coherence." Pp. 325–33 in *Human Knowledge: Classical and Contemporary Approaches*, ed. Paul K. Moser and Arnold Vander Nat. New York and Oxford: Oxford University Press.

Levinas, Emmanuel. 1969. *Totality and Infinity: An Essay on Exteriority*. Duquesne Studies Philosophical Series 24. Trans. Alphonso Lingis. Pittsburgh: Duquesne University Press; The Hague: Martinus Nijhoff.

———. 1985. *Ethics and Infinity: Conversations with Philippe Nemo*. Trans. Richard A. Cohen. Pittsburgh: Duquesne University Press.

———. 1987. *Collected Philosophical Papers*. Trans. Alphonso Lingis. Dordrecht, Boston, and Lancaster: Martinus Nijhoff Publishers.

———. 1991. *Otherwise than Being or Beyond Essence*. Trans. Alphonso Lingis. Dordrecht, Boston, and London: Kluwer Academic Publishers.

———. 1996. *Basic Philosophical Writings*. Ed. Adriaan T. Peperzak, Simon Critchley, and Robert Bernasconi. Bloomington and Indianapolis: Indiana University Press.

Lewis, Alan E. 2001. *Between Cross and Resurrection: A Theology of Holy Saturday*. Grand Rapids: Eerdmans.

Lindbeck, George. 1984. *The Nature of Doctrine: Religion and Theology in a Postliberal Age*. Philadelphia: Westminster.

Lints, Richard. 1993. *The Fabric of Theology: A Prolegomenon to Evangelical Theology*. Grand Rapids: Eerdmans.

Little, Joyce A. 1988. *Toward a Thomist Methodology*. Toronto Studies in Theology 34. Lewiston: Edwin Mellen Press.

Lodahl, Michael. 1994. *The Story of God: Wesleyan Theology and Biblical Narrative*. Kansas City: Beacon Hill.

———. 2001. "*Una Natura Divina. Tres Nescio Quid*: What Sorts of *Personae* are Divine *Personae*?" *Wesleyan Theological Journal* 36:218–30.

Loder, James E. 1989. *The Transforming Moment*. 2nd ed. Colorado Springs, Co.: Helmers & Howard.

———. 1998. *The Logic of Spirit: Human Development in Theological Perspective*. San Francisco: Jossey-Bass Publishers.

Loder, James E., and W. Jim Neidhardt. 1992. *The Knight's Move: The Relational Logic of the Spirit in Theology and Science*. Colorado Springs: Helmers & Howard.

Lonergan, Bernard. 1972. *Method in Theology*. New York: Herder & Herder.

Long, Charles H. 1986. *Significations: Signs, Symbols, and Images in the Interpretation of Religion*. Philadelphia: Fortress Press.

Lossky, Vladimir. 1976. *The Mystical Theology of the Eastern Church*. Crestwood, N.Y.: St. Vladimir's Seminary Press.

Lundin, Roger. 1993. *The Culture of Interpretation: Christian Faith and the Postmodern World*. Grand Rapids: Eerdmans.

Lundin, Roger, ed. 1997. *Discplining Hermeneutics: Interpretation in Christian Perspective.* Grand Rapids: Eerdmans; Leicester, U.K.: Apollos.

Lynch, William F., SJ. 1973. *Images of Faith: An Exploration of the Ironic Imagination.* Notre Dame: University of Notre Dame Press.

Macchia, Frank. 2000. "Justification and the Spirit: A Pentecostal Reflection on the Doctrine by which the Church Stands or Falls." *Pneuma: The Journal of the Society for Pentecostal Studies* 22:3–22.

MacDonald, A. J. 1944. *The Interpreter Spirit and Human Life.* London: SPCK.

Mackey, James P. 1983. *The Christian Experience of God as Trinity.* London: SCM Press.

———. 1995. "Social Models of the Trinity." Pp. 123–30 in *Readings in Modern Theology: Britain and America,* ed. Robin Gill. Nashville: Abingdon Press.

Maffie, James. 1990. "Recent Work on Naturalized Epistemology." *American Philosophical Quarterly* 27:281–93.

Maier, Gerhard. 1994. *Biblical Hermeneutics.* Trans. Robert W. Yarbrough. Wheaton. Ill.: Crossway Books.

Malcolm, Norman. 1977. "The Groundlessness of Belief." Pp. 199–216 in *Thought and Knowledge,* ed. Norman Malcolm. Ithaca, N.Y.: Cornell University Press.

Marshall, Bruce D. 2000. *Trinity and Truth.* Cambridge and New York: Cambridge University Press.

Marshall, Donald. 1997. "Truth, Universality, and Interpretation." Pp. 69–84 in *Discplining Hermeneutics: Interpretation in Christian Perspective,* ed. Roger Lundin. Grand Rapids: Eerdmans; Leicester, U.K.: Apollos.

Martin, Dale B. 1995. *The Corinthian Body.* New Haven and London: Yale University Press.

Martin, R. M. 1979. *Pragmatics, Truth, and Language.* Dordrecht, Holland, and Boston: D. Reidel Publishing.

McCallum, Dennis, ed. 1996 *The Death of Truth.* Minneapolis: Bethany House Publishers.

McClendon, James William, Jr. 1974. *Biography as Theology: How Life Stories Can Remake Today's Theology.* Nashville: Abingdon Press.

———. 1986. *Ethics.* Vol. 1, *Systematic Theology.* Nashville: Abingdon Press.

———. 1994. *Doctrine.* Vol. 2, *Systematic Theology.* Nashville: Abingdon Press.

———. 2000. *Witness.* Vol. 3, *Systematic Theology.* Nashville: Abingdon Press.

McCready, Wayne O. 2000. "The Nature and Function of Oral and Written Scripture for the Christian Devotee." Pp. 34–62 in *Experiencing Scripture in World Religions,* ed. Harold Coward. Maryknoll: Orbis Books.

McDonnell, Kilian. 1982. "The Determinative Doctrine of the Holy Spirit." *Theology Today* 39:142–61.

———. 1985. "A Trinitarian Theology of the Holy Spirit?" *Theological Studies* 46:191–227.

McFague TeSelle, Sallie. 1975. *Speaking in Parables: A Study in Metaphor and Theology.* Philadelphia: Fortress Press.

McFague, Sallie. 1982. *Metaphorical Theology: Models of God in Religious Language.* Philadelphia: Fortress Press.

McGiffert, Arthur Cushman. 1932. *Early and Eastern.* Vol. 1, *A History of Christian Thought.* New York and London: Charles Scribner's Sons.

McGlasson, Paul C. 1999. "The Significance of Context in Theology: A Canonical Approach." Pp. 52–72 in *Theological Exegesis: Essays in Honor of Brevard S. Childs,* ed. Christopher Seitz and Kathryn Greene-McCreight. Grand Rapids: Eerdmans.

McGrath, Alister E. 2000. "Engaging the Great Tradition: Evangelical Theology and the Role of Tradition." Pp. 139–58 in *Evangelical Futures: A Conversation on Theological Method,* ed. John G. Stackhouse, Jr. Grand Rapids: Baker.

McIntyre, John. 1976. "Theology and Method." Pp. 204–30 in *Creation, Christ and Culture: Studies in Honour of T. F. Torrance,* ed. Richard W. A. McKinney. Edinburgh: T & T Clark.

———. 1986. "New Help from Kant: Theology and Human Imagination." Pp. 102–24 in *Religious Imagination,* ed. James P. MacKey. Edinburgh: Edinburgh University Press.

McIntyre, John. 1987. *Faith, Theology and Imagination*. Edinburgh: Handsel Press.

———. 1997. *The Shape of Pneumatology: Studies in the Doctrine of the Holy Spirit*. Edinburgh: T & T Clark.

Michalson, Carl. 1963. *The Rationality of Faith: An Historical Critique of the Theological Reason*. New York: Charles Scribner's Sons and University of Virginia.

Middleton, J. Richard, and Brian J. Walsh. 1995. *Truth is Stranger than It Used to Be: Biblical Faith in a Postmodern Age*. Downers Grove: InterVarsity.

Milbank, John. 1986. "The Second Difference: For a Trinitarianism without Reserve." *Modern Theology* 2:213–34.

———. 1995. "Can a Gift be Given? Prolegomena to a Future Trinitarian Metaphysic." Pp. 119–61 in *Rethinking Metaphysics*, ed. L. Gregory Jones and Stephen E. Fowl. Oxford: Blackwell.

Miller, Keith B. 1993. "Theological Implications of an Evolving Creation." *Perspectives on Science and Christian Faith: Journal of the American Scientific Affiliation* 45:150–60.

Miller, Perry. 1948. "Introduction." Pp. 1–41 in *Images or Shadows of Divine Things by Jonathan Edwards*. New Haven: Yale University Press.

Minns, Denis, OP. 1994. *Irenaeus*. Washington, D.C.: Georgetown University Press.

Miyahira, Nozomu. 2000. *Towards a Theology of the Concord of God: A Japanese Perspective on the Trinity*. Carlisle, U.K.: Paternoster Press.

Moberly, R. W. L. 2000. *The Bible, Theology and Faith: A Study of Abraham and Jesus*. Cambridge: Cambridge University Press.

Moltmann, Jürgen. 1992. *The Spirit of Life: A Universal Affirmation*. Trans. Margaret Kohl. Minneapolis: Augsburg Fortress Press.

———. 1997. *The Source of Life: The Holy Spirit and the Theology of Life*. Trans. Margaret Kohl. Minneapolis: Augsburg Fortress Press.

———. 2000. *Experiences in Theology: Ways and Forms of Christian Theology*. Trans. Margaret Kohl. Minneapolis: Augsburg Fortress Press.

Montague, George. [1976] 1994. *Holy Spirit: Growth of a Biblical Tradition*. Peabody, Mass.: Hendrickson Publishers.

Morris, Charles. 1955. *Signs, Language and Behavior: An Original, Important Contribution to Semantics*. New York: George Braziller.

Moule, C. F. D. 1978. *The Holy Spirit*. Grand Rapids: Eerdmans.

Mueller, John J. 1984. *What are They Saying about Theological Method?* New York: Paulist Press.

Murphy, George L. 1993. "The Third Article in the Science-Theology Dialogue." *Perspectives on Science and Christian Faith* 45:162–99.

Murphy, Roland E. 1990. *The Tree of Life: An Exploration of Biblical Wisdom Literature*. 2nd ed. Grand Rapids and Cambridge: Eerdmans.

Navone, John J. 1977. *Towards a Theology of Story*. Slough, U.K.: St. Paul Publications.

Neville, Robert Cummings. 1981. *Reconstruction of Thinking*. Albany: SUNY Press.

———. 1987. "Sketch of a System." Pp. 253–74 in *New Essays in Metaphysics*, ed. Robert Cummings Neville. Albany: SUNY Press.

———. 1989. *Recovery of the Measure: Interpretation and Nature*. Albany: SUNY Press.

———. 1991. *A Theology Primer*. Albany: SUNY Press.

———. 1992. *The Highroad Around Modernism*. Albany: SUNY Press.

———. 1995. *Normative Cultures*. Albany: SUNY Press.

———. 1996. *The Truth of Broken Symbols*. Albany: SUNY Press.

Newell, William Lloyd. 1990. *Truth is Our Mask: An Essay on Theological Method*. Lanham, New York and London: University Press of America.

Newman, John Henry. 1989. *An Essay on the Development of Christian Doctrine*. 6th ed. Notre Dame: University of Notre Dame Press.

Newman, Paul W. 1987. *A Spirit Christology: Recovering the Biblical Paradigm of Christian Faith.* Lanham, Md.: University Press of America.

Niebuhr, H. Richard. 1951. *Christ and Culture.* New York: Harper & Brothers.

O'Collins, Gerald. 1982. "Criteria for Interpreting the Traditions." Pp. 327–39 in *Problems and Perspectives of Fundamental Theology,* ed. René Latourelle and Gerald O'Collins. Trans. Matthew J. O'Connell. Ramsey, N.J.: Paulist Press.

O'Collins, Gerald, SJ, and Daniel Kendall, SJ. 1997. *The Bible for Theology: Ten Principles for the Theological Use of Scripture.* New York and Mahwah, N.J.: Paulist Press.

O'Connor, D. J. 1975. *The Correspondence Theory of Truth.* London: Hutchinson.

Oden, Thomas C. 1994. *Life in the Spirit.* Vol. 3, *Systematic Theology.* San Francisco: HarperSanFrancisco.

O'Donnell, John J., SJ. 1983. *Trinity and Temporality: The Christian Doctrine of God in the Light of Process Theology and the Theology of Hope.* Oxford: Oxford University Press.

———. 1989. "In Him and Over Him: The Holy Spirit in the Life of Jesus." *Gregorianum* 70:23–45.

Oliver, Harold H. 1981. *A Relational Metaphysic.* The Hague, Boston, and London: Martinus Nijhoff Publishers.

Olson, Alan M. 1992. *Hegel and the Spirit: Philosophy as Pneumatology.* Princeton: Princeton University Press.

Ommen, Thomas B. 1973. *The Hermeneutic of Dogma.* American Academy of Religion Dissertation Series 11. Missoula, Mont.: Scholars Press.

Orange, Donna. 1984. *Peirce's Conception of God: A Developmental Study.* Lubbock, Tex.: Institute for Studies in Pragmatism.

Orr, William F., and James Arthur Walther. 1976. *I Corinthians, A New Translation: Introduction with a Study of the Life of Paul, Notes, and Commentary.* Anchor Bible 32. Garden City, N.Y.: Doubleday & Company.

Orsy, Ladislas. 1976. *Probing the Spirit: A Theological Evaluation of Communal Discernment.* Denville, N.J.: Dimension Books.

Osborne, Grant. 1991. *The Hermeneutical Spiral: A Comprehensive Introduction to Biblical Interpretation.* Downers Grove: InterVarsity Press.

Ottmar, John. 1988. "The Tradition of the Oppressed as the Main Topic of a Theological Hermeneutics." Pp. 143–55 in *Truth and Its Victims,* ed. Willem Beuken, Sean Freyne, and Anton Weiler. Concilium 200. Edinburgh: T & T Clark.

Pailin, David. 1990. *The Anthropological Character of Theology.* Cambridge: Cambridge University Press.

Palmer, G. E. H., Philip Sherrard and Kallistos Ware, eds. 1979– . *The Philokalia: The Complete Text Compiled by St Nikodimos of the Holy Mountain and St Makarios of Corinth.* 4 vols to date. London and Boston: Faber & Faber.

Palmer, Richard E. 1969. *Hermeneutics: Interpretation Theory in Schleiermacher, Dilthey, Heidegger, and Gadamer.* Evanston, Ill.: Northwestern University Press.

Pannenberg, Wolfhart. 1970. *What is Man? Contemporary Anthropology in Theological Perspective.* Trans. Duane A. Priebe. Philadelphia: Fortress Press.

———. 1985. *Anthropology in Theological Perspective.* Trans. Matthew J. O'Connell. Philadelphia: Westminster Press.

———. 1991. *Systematic Theology.* Vol. 1. Trans. Geoffrey Bromiley. Grand Rapids: Eerdmans.

———. 1997. "The Doctrine of the Spirit and the Task of a Theology of Nature." Pp. 65–79 in *Beginning with the End: God, Science, and Wolfhart Pannenberg,* ed. Carol Rausch Albright and Joel Haugen. Chicago and La Salle, Ill.: Open Court.

———. 1997a. "Spirit and Energy in the Phenomenology of Pierre Teilhard de Chardin." Pp. 80–89 in *Beginning with the End: God, Science, and Wolfhart Pannenberg,* ed. Carol Rausch Albright and Joel Haugen; trans. Donald W. Musser. Chicago and La Salle, Ill.: Open Court.

Parret, Herman. 1983. *Semiotics and Pragmatics: An Evaluative Comparison of Conceptual Frameworks*. Pragmatics & Beyond: An Interdisciplinary Series of Language Studies IV:7. Amsterdam and Philadelphia: John Benjamin's Publishing.

Patte, Daniel. 2000. "Critical Biblical Studies from a Semiotic Perspective." Pp. 3–26 in *Thinking in Signs: Semiotics and Biblical Studies…Thirty Years After*, ed. Daniel Patte. Semeia 81. Atlanta: Society of Biblical Literature and Scholars Press.

Patterson, Orlando. 1991. *Freedom in the Making of Western Culture*. New York: Basic Books.

Peden, W. Creighton, and Jerome A. Stone, eds. 1996. *The Early Chicago School, 1906–1959*. Vol. 1, *The Chicago School of Theology—Pioneers in Religious Inquiry*. Studies in American Religion 66a. Lewiston: Edwin Mellen Press.

Peirce, Charles Sanders. 1931–58. *The Collected Papers of Charles Sanders Peirce*. Vols. I–VI, Charles Hartshorne and Paul Weiss, eds.; Vols. VII–VIII, Arthur W. Burks, ed. Cambridge, Ma.: Belknap Press.

Pelikan, Jaroslav. 1968. *Spirit Versus Structure: Luther and the Institutions of the Church*. New York: Harper & Row.

Pepper, Stephen. 1942. *World Hypotheses*. Berkeley: University of California Press.

Perdue, Leo G. 1994. *Wisdom and Creation: The Theology of Wisdom Literature*. Nashville: Abingdon Press.

Peters, Ted. 1993. *God as Trinity: Relationality and Temporality in Divine Life*. Louisville, Ky.: Westminster John Knox Press.

Phillips, D. Z. 1988. *Faith After Foundationalism*. London and New York: Routledge.

———. 1997. "'In the Beginning Was the Proposition.' 'In the Beginning Was the Choice.' 'In the Beginning Was the Dance.'" Pp. 159–74 in *Philosophy of Religion*, ed. Peter A. French, Theodore E. Uehling, Jr., and Howard K. Wettstein. Vol. 21, *Midwest Studies in Philosophy*. Notre Dame: University of Notre Dame Press.

Pico della Mirandola. 1930. *On the Imagination*. Ed. and trans. Harry Caplan. Cornell Studies in English XVI. London: Oxford University Press; New Haven: Yale University Press.

Pinnock, Clark. 1992. *A Wideness in God's Mercy: The Finality of Jesus Christ in the World of Religions*. Grand Rapids: Zondervan.

———. 1993. "The Work of the Holy Spirit in Hermeneutics." *Journal of Pentecostal Theology* 2:3–23.

———. 1993a. "The Work of the Spirit in Interpretation." *Journal of the Evangelical Theological Society* 36:491–97.

———. 1996. *Flame of Love: A Theology of the Holy Spirit*. Downers Grove: InterVarsity Press.

Placher, William C. 1994. *Narratives of a Vulnerable God: Christ, Theology, and Scripture*. Louisville: Westminster John Knox Press.

Plantinga, Alvin. 1983. "Reason and Belief in God." Pp. 16–93 in *Faith and Rationality: Reason and Belief in God*, ed. Alvin Plantinga and Nicholas Wolsterstoff. Notre Dame: University of Notre Dame Press.

———. 1993 *Warrant: The Current Debate*. New York and Oxford: Oxford University Press.

———. 1993a. *Warrant and Proper Function*. New York: Oxford University Press.

———. 2000. *Warranted Christian Belief*. New York and Oxford: Oxford University Press.

Ponzio, Augusto. 1990. *Man as a Sign: Essays on the Philosophy of Language*. Trans. Susan Petrilli. Approaches to Semiotics 89. Berlin and New York: Mouton de Gruyter.

Powell, Mark Allan. 2001. *Chasing the Eastern Star: Adventures in Biblical Reader-Response Criticism*. Louisville: Westminster John Knox Press.

Power, William L. 1993. "Peircean Semiotics. Religion, and Theological Realism." Pp. 211–24 in *New Essays in Religious Naturalism*, ed. W. Creighton Peden and Larry E. Axel. Highlands Institute Series 2. Macon, Ga.: Mercer University Press.

Poythress, Vern S. 1987. *Symphonic Theology: The Validity of Multiple Perspectives in Theology*. Grand Rapids: Zondervan.

Prenter, Regin. 1953. *Spiritus Creator*. Trans. John M. Jensen. Philadelphia: Muhlenberg Press.

———. 1965. *The Word and the Spirit: Essays on Inspiration of the Scriptures*. Trans. Harris E. Kaasa. Minneapolis: Augsburg Fortress Press.

Prestige, G. L. [1952] 1985. *God in Patristic Thought*. 2nd ed. London: SPCK.

Prichard, Rebecca Button. 1999. *Sensing the Spirit: The Holy Spirit in Feminist Perspective*. St. Louis: Chalice Press.

Proudfoot, Wayne. 1985. *Religious Experience*. Berkeley: University of California Press.

Rahner, Karl. 1963. *The Church and the Sacraments*. Trans. W. J. O'Hara. New York: Herder & Herder.

———. 1966. "The Theology of the Symbol." Pp. 221–52 in *Theological Investigations* 4, trans. Kevin Smyth. London: Darton, Longman & Todd.

———. 1969. "Reflections on the Unity of the Love of Neighbor and the Love of God." Pp. 231–49 in *Theological Investigations* 6. London: Darton, Longman & Todd.

———. 1970. *The Trinity*. Trans. Joseph Donceel. New York: Herder & Herder.

———. 1982. *Foundations of Christian Faith: An Introduction to the Idea of Christianity*. Trans. William V. Dych. New York: Crossroad.

Raposa, Michael. 1989. *Peirce's Philosophy of Religion*. Peirce Studies 5. Bloomington: Indiana University Press.

Rappaport, Roy. 1999. *Ritual and Religion in the Making of Humanity*. Cambridge Studies in Social and Cultural Anthropology. Cambridge: Cambridge University Press.

Reid, Duncan. 1997. *Energies of the Spirit: Trinitarian Models in Eastern Orthodox and Western Theology*. American Academy of Religion Academy Series 96. Atlanta: Scholars Press.

Rescher, Nicholas. 1973. *The Coherence Theory of Truth*. Oxford: Clarendon Press.

Richard of St. Victor. 1979. *Book Three of the Trinity*. Trans. Grover A. Zinn. New York: Paulist Press.

Ricoeur, Paul. 1965. *Fallible Man*. Trans. Charles Kelbley. Chicago: Henry Regnery Company.

———. 1969. *The Symbolism of Evil*. Trans. Emerson Buchanon. Boston: Beacon Press.

———. 1995. *Figuring the Sacred: Religion, Narrative, and Imagination*. Ed. Mark I. Wallace and trans. David Pellauer. Minneapolis: Augsburg Fortress Press.

Robin, Richard. 1981. "Peirce on the Foundations of Knowledge." Pp. 293–99 in *Proceedings of the C. S. Peirce Bicentennial International Congress*, ed. Kenneth L. Ketner et al. Lubbock: Texas Tech Press.

Rorty, Richard. 1980. *Philosophy and the Mirror of Nature*. 2nd ed. Princeton: Princeton University Press.

———. 1990. "Pragmatism as Anti-Representationalism." Pp. 1–6 in *Pragmatism: From Peirce to Davidson*, ed. John P. Murphy. Boulder, Colo.: Westview Press.

———. 1991. *Objectivity, Relativism, and Truth*. Cambridge and New York: Cambridge University Press.

———. 1998. *Truth and Progress*. Cambridge and New York: Cambridge University Press.

Royce, Josiah. [1913] 1968. *The Problem of Christianity*. 2 vols. Chicago: Henry Regnery.

Rush, Ormond. 1997. *The Reception of Doctrine: An Appropriation of Hans Robert Jauss' Reception Aesthetics and Literary Hermeneutics*. Tesi Gregoriana Serie Teologia 19. Rome: Editrice Pontificia Università Gregoriana.

Russman, Thomas A. 1987. *A Prospectus for the Triumph of Realism*. Macon, Ga.: Mercer University Press.

Rust, Eric C. 1981. *Religion, Revelation and Reason*. Macon, Ga.: Mercer University Press.

Ruthven, Jon. 1993. *On the Cessation of the Charismata: The Protestant Polemic on Postbiblical Miracles*. Journal of Pentecostal Theology Supplemental series 3. Sheffield: Sheffield Academic Press.

Ryan, W. F. J. 1978. "Trinification and Phenomenology." Pp. 97–109 in *Trinification of the World: A Festschrift in Honour of Frederick E, Crowe in Celebration of His 60th Birthday*, ed. Thomas A. Dunne and Jean-Marc Laporte. Toronto: Regis College Press.

Sachs, John R. 1993. *"Deus Semper Major—Ad Majorem Dei Gloriam*: The Pneumatology and Spirituality of Hans Urs Von Balthasar." *Gregorianum* 74:631–57.

Sanders, James A. 1984. *Canon and Community: A Guide to Canonical Criticism.* Philadelphia: Fortress Press.

———. 1987. *From Sacred Story to Sacred Text.* Philadelphia: Fortress Press.

Sanneh, Lamin. 1989. *Translating the Message: The Missionary Impact on Culture.* Maryknoll: Orbis Books.

———. 1993. *Encountering the West: Christianity and the Global Cultural Process—The African Dimension.* Maryknoll: Orbis Books.

Savan, David. 1987. *An Introduction to C. S. Peirce's Full System of Semeiotic.* Monograph Series of the Toronto Semiotic Circle 1. Toronto: Victoria College of the University of Toronto.

Scalise. Charles J. 1994. *Hermeneutics as Theological Prolegomena: A Canonical Approach.* Studies in American Biblical Hermeneutics 8. Macon, Ga.: Mercer University Press.

———. 1996. *From Scripture to Theology: A Canonical Journey into Hermeneutics.* Downers Grove: InterVarsity Press.

Schillebeeckx, Edward, OP. 1963. *Christ the Sacrament of the Encounter with God.* Kansas City: Sheed, Andrews & McNeel.

Schlitt, Dale. 2001. *Theology and the Experience of God.* American Liberal Religious Thought 8. New York: Peter Lang.

Schrag, Calvin. 1961. *Existence and Freedom: Towards an Ontology of Human Finitude.* Evanston, Ill.: Northwestern University Press.

———. 1992. *The Resources of Rationality: A Response to the Postmodern Challenge.* Bloomington: Indiana University Press.

Schreiter, Robert J. 1985. *Constructing Local Theologies.* Maryknoll: Orbis Books.

Schroer, Silvia. 2000. *Wisdom Has Built Her House: Studies in the Figure of Sophia in the Bible.* Trans. Linda M. Maloney and William McDonough. Collegeville, Minn.: Michael Glazier.

Schwobel, Christoph, ed. 1995. *Trinitarian Theology Today: Essays on Divine Being and Act.* Edinburgh: T & T Clark.

Scott, Martin. 1992. *Sophia and the Johannine Jesus.* Journal for the Study of the New Testament Supplement Series 71. Sheffield: Sheffield Academic Press.

Searle, John. 1995. *The Construction of Social Reality.* New York: Free Press.

Seebok, Thomas A. 1991. *A Sign is Just a Sign.* Bloomington and Indianapolis: Indiana University Press.

———. 1994. *Signs: An Introduction to Semiotics.* Toronto and Buffalo: University of Toronto Press.

Segal, Alan F. 1999. "'Two Powers in Heaven' and Early Christian Trinitarian Thinking." Pp. 73–95 in *The Trinity: An Interdisciplinary Symposium*, ed. Steven T. Davis, Daniel Kendall and Gerald O'Collins, SJ. Oxford: Oxford University Press.

Segovia, Fernando. 1995. "Toward a Hermeneutics of the Diaspora: A Hermeneutics of Otherness and Engagement." Pp. 57–73 in *Social Location and Biblical Interpretation in the United States*, ed. Fernando F. Segovia and Mary Ann Tolbert. Vol. 1, *Reading from This Place.* Minneapolis: Augsburg Fortress Press.

———. 2000. *Decolonizing Biblical Studies: A View from the Margin.* Maryknoll: Orbis.

Seung, T. K. 1982. *Semiotics and Thematics in Hermeneutics.* New York: Columbia University Press.

Shapland, C. R. B., trans. 1951. *The Letters of Saint Athanasius Concerning the Holy Spirit.* New York: Philosophical Library.

Sheriff, John K. 1989. *The Fate of Meaning: Charles Peirce, Structuralism, and Literature.* Princeton: Princeton University Press.

Sherry, Patrick. 1977. *Religion, Truth, and Language-games.* New York: Barnes & Noble Books.

———. 1992. *Spirit and Beauty: An Introduction to Theological Aesthetics.* Oxford: Clarendon Press.

Shils, Edward. 1981. *Tradition.* Chicago: University of Chicago Press.

Shults, F. LeRon. 1999. *The Postfoundationalist Task of Theology: Wolfhart Pannenberg and the New Theological Rationality.* Grand Rapids: Eerdmans.

Smith, Huston. 2000. "Methodology, Comparisons, and Truth." In *A Magic Still Dwells: Comparative Religion in a Postmodern Age,* ed. Kimberly C. Patton and Benjamin C. Ray. Berkeley: University of California Press.

Smith, James K. A. 2000. *The Fall of Interpretation: Philosophical Foundations for a Creational Hermeneutic.* Downers Grove: InterVarsity Press.

Smith, Jonathan Z. 1982. *Imagining Religion: From Jonestown to Babylon.* Chicago: University of Chicago Press.

Smith, P. Christopher. 1991. *Hermeneutics and Human Finitude: Toward a Theory of Ethical Understanding.* New York: Fordham University Press.

Smith, Steven G. 1988. *The Concept of the Spiritual: An Essay in First Philosophy.* Philadelphia: Temple University Press.

Snook, Lee. 1999. *What in the World is God Doing? Re-Imagining Spirit and Power.* Minneapolis: Augsburg Fortress Press.

Stagg, Frank. 1973. *Polarities of Man's Existence in Biblical Perspective.* Philadelphia: Westminster Press.

Stein, Robert H. 1994. *Playing By the Rules: A Basic Guide to Interpreting the Bible.* Grand Rapids: Baker Books.

Stronstad, Roger. 1995. *Spirit, Scripture, and Theology: A Pentecostal Perspective.* Baguio City, Philippines: Asia Pacific Theological Seminary Press.

Stroup, George W. 1981. *The Promise of Narrative Theology: Recovering the Gospel in the Church.* Atlanta: John Knox Press.

Stuhlmacher, Peter. 1977. *Historical Criticism and Theological Interpretation of Scripture: Toward a Hermeneutics of Consent.* Trans. Roy A. Harrisville. Philadelphia: Fortress Press.

Stylianopolous, Theodore. 1997. *The New Testament: An Orthodox Perspective.* Vol. 1, *Scripture, Tradition, Hermeneutics.* Brookline, Mass.: Holy Cross Orthodox Press.

Sullivan, John Edward, OP. 1963. *The Image of God: The Doctrine of St. Augustine and Its Influence.* Dubuque, Iowa: Priory Press.

Suurmond, Jean Jacques. 1994. *Word and Spirit at Play: Toward a Charismatic Theology.* Trans. John Bowden. Grand Rapids: Eerdmans.

Swartley, William M., ed. 1984. *Essays on Biblical Interpretation: Anabaptist-Mennonite Perspectives.* Text-Reader Series 1. Elkhart, Ind.: Institute of Mennonite Studies.

Swartz, Ronald M., Henry J. Perkinson, and Stephenie G. Edgerton, eds. 1980. *Knowledge and Fallibilism: Essays on Improving Education.* New York and London: New York University Press.

Sykes, Stephen W. 1984. *The Identity of Christianity: Theologians and the Essence of Christianity from Schleiermacher to Barth.* Philadelphia: Fortress Press.

Taylor, John V. 1973. *The Go-between God: The Holy Spirit and the Christian Mission.* Philadelphia: Fortress Press.

Thiel, John E. 1991. *Imagination and Authority: Theological Authorship in the Modern Tradition.* Minneapolis: Augsburg Fortress Press.

Thiemann, Ronald F. 1987. *Revelation and Theology: The Gospel as Narrated Promise.* Notre Dame: University of Notre Dame Press.

Thiselton, Anthony. 1992. *New Horizons in Biblical Hermeneutics: The Theory and Practice of Transforming Biblical Reading.* Grand Rapids: Zondervan.

———. 1995. *Interpreting God and the Postmodern Self: On Meaning, Manipulation and Promise.* Grand Rapids: Eerdmans; Edinburgh: T & T Clark.

Thiselton, Anthony, Roger Lundin, and Clarence Walhout. 1999. "Communicative Action and Promise in Interdisciplinary Biblical and Theological Hermeneutics." Pp. 133–239 in *The Promise of Hermeneutics.* Grand Rapids: Eerdmans; Cambridge, U.K.: Paternoster Press.

Thomas, John Christopher. 2000. "Reading the Bible from within Our Traditions: A Pentecostal Hermeneutic as Test Case." Pp. 108–22 in *Between Two Horizons: Spanning New Testament Studies and Systematic Theology*, ed. Joel B. Green and Max Turner. Grand Rapids: Eerdmans.

Thorsen, Donald A. D. 1990. *The Wesleyan Quadrilateral: Scripture, Tradition, Reason and Experience as a Model for Evangelical Theology*. Grand Rapids: Zondervan.

Tilley, Terrence W. 1985. *Story Theology*. Wilmington, Del.: Michael Glazier.

Tillich, Paul. 1957. *Dynamics of Faith*. New York: Harper Colophon Books.

———. 1959. *Theology of Culture*. Ed. Robert C. Kimball. London, Oxford, and New York: Oxford University Press.

———. 1960. "The Religious Symbol." Pp. 75–98 in *Symbolism in Religion and Literature*, ed. Rollo May. New York: Braziller.

———. 1961. "The Meaning and Justification of Religious Symbols." Pp. 3–11 in *Religious Experience and Truth: A Symposium*, ed. Sidney Hook. New York: New York University Press.

Tompkins, Jane P., ed. 1980. *Reader-Response Criticism: From Formalism to Post-Structuralism*. Baltimore and London: Johns Hopkins University Press.

Torrance, Thomas F. 1971. *God and Rationality*. London, New York, and Toronto: Oxford University Press.

———. 1994. *Trinitarian Perspectives: Toward Doctrinal Agreement*. Edinburgh: T & T Clark.

———. 1988. *The Trinitarian Faith: The Evangelical Theology of the Ancient Catholic Church*. Edinburgh: T & T Clark.

Tracy, David. 1975. *Blessed Rage for Order: The New Pluralism in Theology*. New York: Seabury Press.

———. 1981. *The Analogical Imagination: Christian Theology and the Culture of Pluralism*. New York: Crossroad.

Trevett, Christine. 1996. *Montanism: Gender, Authority and the New Prophecy*. Cambridge: Cambridge University Press.

Tuveson, Ernest Lee. 1960. *The Imagination as a Means of Grace*. Berkeley: University of California Press.

Van Beeck, Franz Jozef. 1999. "Trinitarian Theology as Participation." Pp. 295–325 in *The Trinity: An Interdisciplinary Symposium*, ed. Steven T. Davis, Daniel Kendall and Gerald O'Collins, SJ. Oxford: Oxford University Press.

Van Dusen, Henry Pitt. 1958. *Spirit, Son and Father: Christian Faith in the Light of the Holy Spirit*. New York: Charles Scribner's Sons.

Van Huyssteen, J. Wentzel. 1989. *Theology and the Justification of Faith: Constructing Theories in Systematic Theology*. Trans. H. F. Snijders. Grand Rapids: Eerdmans.

———. 1997. *Essays in Postfoundationalist Theology*. Grand Rapids: Eerdmans.

———. 1999. *The Shaping of Rationality: Toward Interdisciplinarity in Theology and Science*. Grand Rapids: Eerdmans.

Vanhoozer, Kevin. 1997. "The Spirit of Understanding: Special Revelation and General Hermeneutics." Pp. 131–65 in *Discplining Hermeneutics: Interpretation in Christian Perspective*, ed. Roger Lundin. Grand Rapids: Eerdmans; Leicester, England: Apollos.

———. 1998. *Is There a Meaning in This Text? The Bible, the Reader, and the Morality of Literary Knowledge*. Grand Rapids: Zondervan.

———. 2000. "The Voice and the Actor: A Dramatic Proposal about the Ministry and Minstrelsy of Theology." Pp. 61–106 in *Evangelical Futures: A Conversation on Theological Method*, ed. John G. Stackhouse, Jr. Grand Rapids: Baker.

Vattimo, Gianni. 1993. "The Truth of Hermeneutics." Pp. 11–28 in *Questioning Foundations: Truth/Subjectivity/Culture*, ed. Hugh J. Silverman. Continental Philosophy 5. New York: Routledge.

Victorin-Vangerud, Nancy M. 2000. *The Raging Hearth: Spirit in the Household of God*. St. Louis: Chalice Press.

Von Balthasar, Hans Urs. 1982. *Seeing the Form.* Vol. 1, *The Glory of the Lord: A Theological Aesthetics.* Trans. Erasmo Leiva-Merikakis, ed. Joseph Fessio, SJ, and John Riches. San Francisco: Ignatius Press; New York: Crossroad.

———. 1990. *Mysterium Paschale: The Mystery of Easter.* Trans. Aidan Nichols, OP. Edinburgh: T & T Clark.

———. 1993. *Creator Spirit.* Vol. 3, *Explorations in Theology.* Trans. Brian McNeil, CRV. San Francisco: Ignatius Press.

Wainwright, William J. 1995. *Reason and the Heart: A Prolegomenon to a Critique of Passional Reason.* Ithaca, N.Y.: Cornell University Press.

Walhout, Clarence, Roger Lundin, and Anthony Thiselton. 1999. "Narrative Hermeneutics." Pp. 65–131 in *The Promise of Hermeneutics.* Grand Rapids: Eerdmans; Cambridge, U.K.: Paternoster Press.

Walker, Ralph C. S. 1989. *The Coherence Theory of Truth: Realism, Anti-realism, Idealism.* London and New York: Routledge.

Wallace, Mark I. 1995. *The Second Naiveté: Barth, Ricoeur, and the New Yale Theology.* 2nd ed. Studies in American Biblical Hermeneutics 6. Macon, Ga.: Mercer University Press.

———. 1996. *Fragments of the Spirit: Nature, Violence, and the Renewal of Creation.* New York: Continuum.

Warner, Sharon. 2000 *Experiencing the Knowing of Faith: An Epistemology of Religious Formation.* Lanham, New York, and Oxford: University Press of America.

Warnock, Mary. 1976. *Imagination.* Berkeley: University of California Press.

Watson, Francis. 1994. *Text, Church and World: Biblical Interpretation in Theological Perspective.* Grand Rapids: Eerdmans.

———. 1997. *Text and Truth: Redefining Biblical Theology.* Grand Rapids: Eerdmans.

Watson, Francis, ed. 1993. *The Open Text: New Directions for Biblical Studies?* London: SCM Press.

Weaver, J. Denny. 2000. *Anabaptist Theology in Face of Postmodernity: A Proposal for the Third Millennium.* Telford, Pa.: Pandora Press.

Weinandy, Thomas G., OFM. 1995. *The Father's Spirit of Sonship: Reconceiving the Trinity.* Edinburgh: T & T Clark.

Weinberg, Julius R. 1965. *Abstraction, Relation, and Induction: Three Essays in the History of Thought.* Madison and Milwaukee: University of Wisconsin Press.

Welch, Claude. 1952. *In This Name: The Doctrine of the Trinity in Contemporary Theology.* New York: Charles Scribner's Sons.

Welker, Michael. 1994. *God the Spirit.* Trans. John F. Hoffmeyer. Minneapolis: Fortress Press.

Wenk, Matthias. 2000. *Community-Forming Power: The Socio-Ethical Role of the Spirit in Luke-Acts.* Journal of Pentecostal Theology Supplemental Series 19. Sheffield: Sheffield Academic Press.

Westphal, Kenneth R., ed. 1998. *Pragmatism, Reason, and Norms.* American Philosophy Series 10. New York: Fordham University Press.

White, Alan R. 1971. *Truth.* London: Macmillan.

White, James Emery. 1994. *What Is Truth? A Comparative Study of the Positions of Cornelis van Til, Francis Schaeffer, Carl F. H. Henry, Donald Bloesch, Millard Erickson.* Nashville: Broadman & Holman.

Whitehead, Alfred North. 1964. *Religion in the Making.* Cleveland and New York: World Publishing Company/Meridian Books.

———. 1978. *Process and Reality: An Essay in Cosmology.* Corrected ed. Ed. David Ray Griffin and Donald W. Sherburne. New York: Free Press.

Wicks, Jared. 1994. *Introduction to the Theological Method.* Casale Monferrato: Edizioni Piemme.

Wilken, Robert Louis. 2000. "Is Pentecost a Peer of Easter? Scripture, Liturgy, and the *Proprium* of the Holy Spirit." Pp. 158–77 in *Trinity, Time, and Church: A Response to the Theology of Robert W. Jenson,* ed. Colin E. Gunton. Grand Rapids and Cambridge: Eerdmans.

Williams, D. H. 1999. *Retrieving the Tradition and Renewing Evangelicalism: A Primer for Suspicious Protestants*. Grand Rapids and Cambridge: Eerdmans.

Wink, Walter. 1984. *Naming the Powers: The Language of Power in the New Testament*. Philadelphia: Fortress Press.

———. 1986. *Unmasking the Powers: The Invisible Forces that Determine Human Existence*. Philadelphia: Fortress Press.

———. 1992. *Engaging the Powers: Discernment and Resistance in a World of Domination*. Philadelphia: Fortress Press.

Winston, David. 1976. *The Wisdom of Solomon: A New Translation with Introduction and Commentary*. Anchor Bible 43. Garden City, N.Y.: Doubleday.

Witherington, Ben, III. 1995. *The Jesus Quest: The Third Search for the Jew of Nazareth*. Downer's Grove, Ill.: InterVarsity Press.

———. 1998. *The Paul Quest: The Renewed Search for the Jew of Tarsus*. Downers Grove: InterVarsity Press.

Wolterstorff, Nicholas. 1995. *Divine Discourse: Philosophical Reflections on the Claim that God Speaks*. Cambridge: Cambridge University Press.

Wong, Joseph H. P. 1984. *Logos-Symbol in the Christology of Karl Rahner*. Biblioteca di Scienze Religiose 61. Rome: Libreria Ateneo Salesiano.

———. 1992. "The Holy Spirit in the Life of Jesus and of the Christian." *Gregorianum* 73:57–95.

Wood, Charles. 1993. *The Formation of Christian Understanding: Theological Hermeneutics*. 2nd ed. Valley Forge, Pa.: Trinity Press International.

Work, Telford. 2001. *Living and Active: Scripture in the Economy of Salvation*. Grand Rapids: Eerdmans.

Worthing, Mark William. 1996. *Foundations and Functions of Theology as Universal Science: Theological Method and Apologetic Praxis in Wolfhart Pannenberg and Karl Rahner*. European University Studies, Series 23, Theology Vol. 576. Frankfurt am Main: Peter Lang.

Wright, Stephen I. 2000. "An Experiment in Biblical Criticism: Aesthetic Encounter in Reading and Preaching Scripture." Pp. 240–67 in *Renewing Biblical Interpretation*, ed. Craig Bartholomew, Colin Greene, and Karl Möller. Carlisle, U.K.: Paternoster Press; Grand Rapids: Eerdmans.

Yong, Amos. 1997. "Oneness and the Trinity: The Theological and Ecumenical Implications of 'Creation *ex nihilo*' for an Intra-Pentecostal Dispute." *Pneuma: The Journal of the Society for Pentecostal Studies* 19:81–107.

———. 1998. "Tongues of Fire in the Pentecostal Imagination: The Truth of Glossolalia in Light of R. C. Neville's Theory of Religious Symbolism." *Journal of Pentecostal Theology* 12:39–65.

———. 2000. *Discerning the Spirit(s): A Pentecostal-Charismatic Contribution to Christian Theology of Religions*. Journal of Pentecostal Theology Supplemental Series 20. Sheffield: Sheffield Academic Press.

———. 2000a. "The Demise of Foundationalism and the Retention of Truth: What Evangelicals Can Learn from C. S. Peirce." *Christian Scholar's Review* 29:563–89.

———. 2000b. "On Divine Presence and Divine Agency: Toward a Foundational Pneumatology." *Asian Journal of Pentecostal Studies* 3:163–84.

———. 2002. "In Search of Foundations: The *Oeuvre* of Donald L. Gelpi, SJ, and Its Significance for Pentecostal Theology, Philosophy, and Spirituality." *Journal of Pentecostal Theology* 11,1: 3–26.

———. 2003. "Spiritual Discernment: A Biblical and Theological Reconsideration." In *The Spirit and Spirituality: Essays in Honor of Russell P, Spittler*, ed. Wonsuk Ma and Robert P. Menzies. New York: Continuum.

Yu, Carver T. 1987. *Being and Relation: A Theological Critique of Western Dualism and Individualism*. Theology and Science at the Frontiers of Knowledge 8. Edinburgh: Scottish Academic Press.

Zizioulas, John D. 1985. *Being as Communion: Studies in Personhood and the Church*. Crestwood, N.Y.: St Vladimir's Seminary Press.

Scripture Index

Genesis
1:2 35, 43
1:3 254
1:28 299
2:7 40, 45, 257
6:5 125
8:21 125
42:16 170

Exodus
3:6 239
3:14 239
7:18 280
8:1 280
8:20 280
9:1 280
9:13 280
10:3ff 280
13:21 44
14:19–20 44
14:21 134
16:4 44
16:10 44
31:3–5 37
33:20 210, 240

Leviticus
25 280
27:17–24 280

Numbers
24:2 47

Deuteronomy
6:5 125
17:4 170
22:20 170
23:1 34
29:19 125, 240
31:21 125

1 Samuel
13:14 125

1 Chronicles
29:18 125

Job
5:7 45
7:7 212
33:4 45

Psalms
8:5 44
19:1 51, 199
19:9 166
22:1 242
33:6 44, 45
34:8 242
42:7 242
51:10–11 46
78:39 212
86:8 176
102:25 51
103:15–16 212
104:29–30 44, 134
119 40
119:160 166
139 112
139:6 43
139:7–15 112, 228

Proverbs
1–9 36
6:18 125
8:22–31 35, 38
18:21 45

Isaiah
6:8 193
11:1 37
11:2 43
28:11–12 208
32:15 43
38:1 255
40:1–2 254
40:3 256

40:12 51
45:1 47
45–47 176
55:11 255
56:3–8 34
61:1 29

Jerermiah
3:17 125
7:24 125
9:14 125
11:8 125
13:10 125
16:12 125
18:12 125
23:17 125

Ezekiel
13:2 125
13:17 125
36:25–27 46
37:1–14 45, 134

Daniel
4:25 254
4:33 254
4:34–37 255

Amos
9:11–12 270

Joel
2:28 208

Habakkuk
2:4 248

Matthew
1:18 257
1:20 29
3:11 30, 257
11:19 37
15:19 125

Matthew, cont.
   16:17 206
   25:31–46 193, 207
   27:46 257

Mark
   1:8 30, 257
   1:15 258

Luke
   1–2 255
   1:25 257
   1:35 28
   1:41–44 29
   1:51 125
   1:51–52 34
   1:52–53 280
   1:67–79 29
   1:80 29
   2:47 37
   2:49 29
   2:52 29, 37
   3:1–14 255
   3:4 256
   3:16 30, 46, 257
   3:22 29
   4:1 29, 257
   4:14 29, 257
   4:18–19 29, 255, 257, 280
   6:20–26 34, 280
   7:11–17 280
   7:22 280
   8:1–3 33
   10:38–42 33
   11:2–4 255
   11:13 255
   11:49 37
   22:42 29
   23:46 30
   24:49 30, 136, 257
   28:25–28 256

John
   1:9 103
   1:14 41, 102, 170, 254
   1:17 41
   1:18 54
   1:33 30
   1:34 257

3:6–8 166
3:8 46, 139, 212, 229
3:34 68
4 57
4:7–14 63
4:24 44, 139, 239
5:19 170
5:23 170
5:36 170
6:63 40, 166, 256
7:37–39 63
7:39 206
8:19 170
8:28 170
8:32 41, 165, 166, 225
8:34–36 280
10:30 30, 54, 170
10:38 54
12:16 309
12:24 46
12:49–50 170
14:6 41, 166
14:7–11 170
14:9 170
14:10–11 54
14:12 32, 257
14:15–21 174
14:17 41, 166, 225
14:26 41, 64, 72, 223
14:31 170
15:15 170
15:23–24 170
15:26 41, 63, 64, 72, 166,
     225, 257
16:8–11 166
16:13 41, 136, 166, 174, 223,
     225, 227
16:14 54, 136, 174
16:15 174
17 57
17:5 170
17:11 170
19:30 30, 68, 71
20:22 63, 64, 68, 257

Acts
   1:5 63, 257
   1:8 30, 33, 136, 257, 283
   1:14 33

2:1–4 134
2:4 103, 248, 283
2:5–11 33, 103
2:5–13 284
2:16 208
2:17 31, 208
2:17–18 33
2:19–21 47
2:22 29
2:33 30, 50
2:38 63
2:38–39 31
2:41–47 46, 255
2:44–45 33
2:46 250
3:19–21 31
4:7–12 257
4:13 33
4:36–37 33
5:1–2 33
6:1–2 33
6:7 33
7 280
7:55 50, 228
8 34
8:20 63
9:36 33
10 270
10:34–35 34
10:38 29, 230
10:45 63
10:46 283
11:27–30 33
13:17 280
15:4 270
15:7 270
15:12 270
15:14 270
15:16–17 270
15:20–21 270
15:28 37, 270
16:1 33
16:7 64
16:14–15 33
16:25 252
17:4 33
17:11 242
17:28 112, 228
17:34 33

Acts, cont.
  18:8 33
  18:18–26 33
  21:8–9 33
  21:13 252
  28 284

Romans
  1:4 30, 134, 257
  1:17 248
  1:19 199
  1:21 125
  12:11 41
  5:1 31
  5:5 31, 63, 251
  6–8 31, 226, 280
  6:1–14 46
  8:9 67, 227
  8:15–16 70
  8:18–28 48
  8:19–23 299
  8:23 31
  8:34 50
  11:33–36 42, 242
  13:11 247
  15:8 166

1 Corinthians
  1:10–13 39
  1:17 38, 39
  1:18 39
  1:18–20 39
  1:19–22 38
  1:20 38
  1:24 37
  1:25 39
  1:25–28 39
  1:30 37, 39
  2:1 38
  2:2 39
  2:4 38
  2:6 38
  2:7 39
  2:8 39
  2:9 178, 222, 229,
  2:9–10 240
  2:10–11 39, 43
  2:10–16 38, 39, 222
  2:11–12 257

  2:16 257
  3:3–9 39
  3:13–15 46
  3:19 39
  7:40 37
  11:2 292
  11:16 292
  11:20–22 250
  12–14 39
  12:7–9 284
  12:13 30, 32
  12:14–26 284
  13:1 283
  13:12 178, 210, 224
  14:13–14 283
  14:16–25 284
  14:21 208
  14:29 257
  15:24–28 258
  15:54 46

2 Corinthians
  1:22 32
  3:1–6 138
  3:6 40, 223
  3:7–18 224
  3:12–18 40
  3:18 238
  4:7–12 252
  5:17 46
  6:6 41
  10:5 125, 148
  11:14 252
  11:23–33 252
  12:1–6 252
  12:4 211
  12:9–10 252
  13:13 16, 46, 67, 115

Galatians
  2:5 166
  2:14 166
  2:19 251, 252
  2:20 252
  3:28 34
  4:6 64
  4:6–7 70
  4:21 280
  5 251

  5:3–26 226
  5:13–26 46

Ephesians
  1:3 31
  1:20 50
  2:18 57
  3:20 178
  4:3–12 103
  4:4–6 57
  4:14 139
  4:15 32
  4:21 166
  4:30 31

Philippians
  1:9 64
  2:1–4 46
  2:5–8 304
  3:3–14 252
  4:11–13 252

Colossians
  1:15 103, 170
  1:17 205
  1:19 170
  2:9 170, 258
  2:12 46
  3:1 50
  3:11 34
  3:23 125

2 Thessalonians
  1:7 46

1 Timothy
  1:5 125
  2:5 30
  3:15 175

2 Timothy
  2:15 40
  3:16 234, 236, 240
  4:6–8 252

Hebrews 280
  1:1 254
  1:3 102, 103, 170, 258
  4:12 256

Hebrews, cont.
9:14 30
10:29 31
11:13 41
12:1 238
12:22–24 239
12:28–29 239
12:29 46

James
1:6 139
2:14–17 206

1 Peter
1:7 46
1:11 64
3:18 30
3:20–21 46
4:14 44

2 Peter
1:3–4 175
1:21 40, 235

3:7–12 46
3:22 50

1 John
1:8 166
2:20 41
2:22–23 170
2:26 166, 223
2:27 41, 166
3:2 178, 210, 223
3:17 206
4:7–21 46
4:6 41, 225
4:8 44
4:13 62
4:16 44
4:20–21 206
5:6 41, 166, 174
5:19 280

Jude
5 280

Revelation
1:18 240n
3:18 46
4:2 240
5:9 103
7:9 103
14:9 240n
21:22 240n
21:24–25 103
22:4 240n
22:17 48

Ecclusiasticus
39:6 37

Wisdom
1:7 43
7:22–28 36
7:27 58
9:1–2 36, 45
9:17 36, 43

Name Index

Abraham, William J. 19n, 235, 242, 254, 293, 313, 316
Abram, David 260
Albrecht, Daniel E. 250
Allison, Dale 142
Alston, William 97, 167
Anderson, Robert Mapes 282
Apczynski, John V. 165
Aristotle 85, 124
Aquinas 86, 201n
Athanasius 53–54, 61n, 73, 241
Augustine 40, 55, 59–69, 70n, 76–77, 85, 94, 110, 115, 117, 159, 227, 242, 247, 290
Austin, J. L. 167, 254
Avicenna 85–86
Avis, Paul 168, 209n

Badcock, Gary D. 45, 74, 80
Balchin, John F. 39n
Barbour, R. S. 39n
Barth, Karl 57, 86, 108, 143, 261, 289, 295
Basil of Ceasarea 55n
Bauckham, Richard 316
Bednar, Gerald J. 137
Beeby, Harry Daniel 262
Bell, Catherine 249n
Berkhof, Hendrikus 135
Bloesch, Donald G. 7, 14n, 40, 172, 271
Blondel, Maurice 265n
Bobrinskoy, Boris 47, 74
Boehme, Jacob 200, 203
Boethius 85
Bolt, John 42n
Bonner, Gerald 64
Boyd, Gregory A. 19n, 135, 205
Bracken, Joseph 19n, 79–80, 89, 112–14
Bradshaw, Timothy 108
Breck, John 166
Bronowski, Jacob 126
Brown, David 143, 146, 272, 307–9
Brown, Delwin 104, 295
Brueggemann, Walter 121
Bruner, Frederick Dale 33

Brunner, Emil 143
Bruno, Giordarno 126, 200
Bryant, David J. 127, 143
Buber, Martin 86, 117, 137
Buckley, James J. 9
Bulgakov, Sergius 72
Bultmann, Rudolf 261, 269
Burton-Christie, Douglas 231
Butin, Philip Walker 245n

Caird, G. B. 135
Callahan, James 10
Calvin, John 42n, 138, 245n
Casey, Edward S. 128
Cassirer, Ernst 185
Chan, Simon 4
Childs, Brevard 316
Chomsky, Noam 145
Clayton, John P. 12
Clayton, Philip 183
Clements, Ronald E. 35n
Clendenin, Daniel B. 303n
Coady, C. A. J. 265
Cocking, J. M. 123n
Coffey, David 28n, 59, 60, 63, 65–72, 74–76, 79
Colapietro, Vincent Michael 191
Coleridge, Samuel 127
Collingwood, R. G. 5n
Collins, John J. 121
Congar, Yves 59, 63n, 65, 265n
Coppedge, Allan 316
Corrington, Robert 154, 163, 212
Coulson, John 130n
Coward, Harold G. 260
Cunningham, David 56, 103, 108, 276

Dabney, D. Lyle 8, 30, 31, 228, 247
Davids, Peter H. 234n
Davidson, Donald 168–69, 173
Davis, Caroline Franks 38, 40n, 302
Davis, James A. 38, 40n
Deely, John 156n
Del Colle, Ralph 28n

Den Bok, Nico 81n
Derrida, Jacques 167n
Descartes, Rene 90, 92, 158, 191, 220
Dewey, John 94, 131, 158, 164, 168, 212
DeYoung, James 308n
Dickinson, Charles 9, 308
Dilthey, Wilhelm 236
Dulles, Avery 208, 259
Dunn, James D. G. 36
Dunning, Stephen 315
Dupré, Louis 303n
Durrwell, François Xavier 29, 53, 70
Dych, William 141
Dyck, Elmer 233

Ebeling, Gerhard 306
Edwards, Denis 43, 103
Edwards, Jonathan 129, 130, 181, 194, 203–7, 214
Einstein, Albert 154n
Emerson, R. W. 204n
Engnell, I. 45
Evans, Jeanne 128

Fackre, Gabriel 172, 219n, 259
Faivre, Antoine 200
Fawcett, Thomas 209n
Farley, Edward 8, 109, 225, 247, 261–63, 267
Farmer, Ronald L. 177
Fasching, Darrell J. 277n
Fee, Gordon D. 39n, 44
Ferreira, M. Jamie 127
Feyerabend, Paul 173, 311, 312
Fields, Stephen M. 201n
Finger, Thomas 171
Fiorenza, Francis Schüssler 10, 97
Florovsky, Georges 265n
Fodor, James 158n
Forbes, Cheryl 146n
Ford, Lewis 107
Forstman, H. Jackson 138
Fowl, Stephen E. 270, 276, 309
Fox, Patricia 74, 111
Franke, John 10, 11, 98, 178, 275
Franklin, Stephen T. 156n, 177
Frei, Hans 3, 98, 277n
Freyer, Thomas 8

Gadamer, Hans Georg 4, 19, 143, 237, 266
Gamble, Richard C. 138

Gaybba, Brian P. 35, 70n
Geertz, Clifford 267
Geffré, Claude 13n, 20, 236
Gelpi, Donald L. 32, 39, 90–95, 101, 158, 159, 161, 174, 181, 182, 222, 246, 263
Gilkey, Langdon 236
Gill, Jerry H. 59
Gill, Robin 305
Gillingham, Susan E. 259, 289
Gilovich, Thomas 176
Goldberg, Michael 172, 174, 277n
Goldingay, John 259
Goodman, Nelson 143, 144
Gore, Charles 256n
Gorringe, Timothy J. 243
Graves, Charles Lee 72
Green, Garrett 143, 144, 209
Green, Harold Johnson 137
Greene-McCreight, Kathryn 273n
Gregory Nazianzus 55n, 239, 252
Gregory of Nyssa 55n, 64, 252
Grenz, Stanley J. 10, 11, 98, 172, 178, 275
Gresham, John L., Jr. 80
Groothius, Douglas 167
Guerrière, Daniel 165
Gunter, W. Stephen 176, 177n, 316
Gunton, Colin 19n, 58, 63, 79, 80, 103, 227

Haack, Susan 97
Haight, Roger 170
Hall, Douglas John 305
Hamilton, Kenneth 227
Hart, Ray L. 142, 270
Hart, Trevor 142, 260
Hartt, Julian N. 142
Hauerwas, Stanley 98, 172, 277n, 278
Hartshorne, Charles 88, 89, 94n, 112, 114n
Hawthorne, Gerald F. 28n
Hegel, G. W. F. 104, 105, 113, 117, 118n
Heidegger, Martin 4, 19, 127, 165, 182, 188, 201n
Hendry, George 103
Henn, William 171
Henry, Carl F. H. 256
Heyward, Carter 193
Hilary of Poitiers 55, 64, 85
Hilkert, Mary Catherine 121
Hill, R. Charles 35n
Hodgson, Peter C. 192, 261
Hoedemaker, Bert 106

Hogan, John P. 5n
Holl, Adolf 50
Hollenweger, Walter J. 282
Hordern, William 33
Hoskins, Richard 73
Howard, Evan 173, 181
Hume, David 90, 126, 129, 152, 206n
Husserl, Edmund 95n, 165
Hütter, Reinhard 111, 276

Ignatius of Antioch 254
Irenaeus 50–54, 56, 58, 60–65, 68
Irvin, Dale T. 269
Iseminger, Gary 10

Jagger, Alison M. 130
James, William 130, 152, 164
Jansen, Henry 86, 87
Jeanrond, Werner G. 5, 6, 13n, 229
Jenson, Robert 64, 65, 84, 106, 301
Jewett, Paul K. 307
John of Damascus 55
Johnson, Elizabeth A. 47, 58, 79
Johnson, Luke Timothy 138, 276
Johnson, Wayne G. 13n
Jones, Gareth 210
Jones, L. Gregory 277n
Jones, Rufus Matthew 42
Jüngel, Eberhard 79, 210

Kant, Immanuel 49n, 77, 85, 90, 92, 100, 118,
    126–27, 143–44, 152, 278
Kärkkäinen. Veli-Matti 1
Kaufman, Gordon 7, 12, 142, 143, 265
Kearney, Richard 123n, 124, 127
Kelly, Anthony 67, 80
Kelly, J. N. D. 62
Kelsey, David H. 142, 261
Kendall, Daniel 313
Kennard, Douglas Welker 164
Kierkegaard, Søren 127, 177n, 182, 227
Kilby, Clyde S. 142
Kirkham, R. L. 164
Klooster, Fred H. 256n
Knight, Henry H., III 172
Koester, Helmut 259
Kuhn, Thomas 173, 241

LaCugna, Catherine Mowry 264

Lai, Pan-Chiu 12
Lamb, Matthew 158
Lampe, G. W. H. 7
Lane, Anthony N. S. 313
Lash, Nicholas 302
Lategan, Bernard C. 158n
Lawrence, Frederick 20
Lawrence, Irene 145
Lawson, John 52
Lee, Sang Hyun 135, 205, 206n
Leftow, Brian 80
Lehrer, Keith 171
Levinas, Emmanuel 117, 118, 186–93, 207, 214, 227
Lewis, Alan E. 210
Lindbeck, George 98, 173, 208, 302
Lints, Richard 275n
Little, Joyce A. 306
Locke, John 90, 130n, 152, 206n
Lodahl, Michael 56, 277
Loder, James E. 13, 57, 84, 154n, 160, 199
Lonergan, Bernard 94, 220, 306
Long, Charles H. 209n
Lossky, Vladimir 65
Lundin, Roger 99
Luther, Martin 13n, 99, 247–48, 293
Lynch, William F. 136–37, 177n

Macchia, Frank 31
MacDonald, A. J. 39
Mackey, James P. 73n, 80
Maier, Gerhard 256n, 312
Maffie, James 199
Malcolm, Norman 99, 171
Marcion 260
Marion, Jean-Luc 167n
Marshall, Bruce D. 169, 170, 174
Marshall, Donald 175
Martin, Dale B. 166n
Martin, R. M. 164
McCallum, Dennis 164
McClendon, James William, Jr. 96, 98, 228, 236,
    277n, 301
McCready, Wayne O. 260
McDonnell, Kilian 19n, 228n
McFague, Sallie 209n
McGiffert, Arthur Cushman 60
McGlasson, Paul C. 289
McGrath, Alister E. 172, 273
McIntyre, John 7, 123, 125, 127, 264

Michalson, Carl 266
Middleton, J. Richard 100
Milbank, John 19, 73, 78
Miller, Keith B. 199
Miller, Perry 204n
Minns, Denis 51
Miyahira, Nozomu 75
Moberly, R. W. L. 9
Moltmann, Jürgen 20, 43, 73, 80n, 86, 90, 107, 306
Montague, George 35
Morris, Charles 155n
Moule, C. F. D. 41
Mueller, John J. 13n
Mühlen, Heribert 67, 117
Murphy, George L. 43
Murphy, Nancey 98
Murphy, Roland E. 35n

Navone, John J. 277n
Needleman, Jacob 200
Neville, Robert Cummings ix, 93, 131–32, 144–46, 158n, 165–66, 169, 179, 188, 194–98, 298
Newell, William Lloyd 237
Newman, John Henry 96, 130, 268
Newman, Paul W. 28n
Niebuhr, H. Richard 11, 301
Nietszche, Friedrich 127–28

O'Collins, Gerald 268, 313
O'Connor, D. J. 167
Oden, Thomas C. 211
O'Donnell, John J. 30, 79
Oliver, Harold H. 86
Olson, Alan M. 117n
Ommen, Thomas B. 295
Orange, Donna 159
Origen 142
Orr, William F. 39
Orsy, Ladislas 270
Osborne, Grant 316
Ottmar John 226

Pailin, David 173
Palmer, Richard E. 4, 236
Pannenberg, Wolfhart 12–13, 45, 86, 90–91, 101n, 107–8, 227, 232
Paracelsus 126, 200, 203
Parret, Herman 157

Patte, Daniel 161
Patterson, Orlando 225
Peden, W. Creighton 303n
Peirce, Charles Sanders 24, 86, 91–96, 100–104, 117–18, 151–165, 169, 175–78, 183, 185, 188, 191, 193, 199, 202–8, 212, 215, 265, 297, 305
Pelagius 99
Pelikan, Jaroslav 293
Perdue, Leo G. 37
Peters, Ted 58, 107
Phillips, D. Z. 98–99, 175n, 211
Philo of Alexandria 38, 40n
Philoxenes of Mabboug 125
Pico della Mirandola 126
Pinnock, Clark 8, 80n, 172, 256n, 272
Placher, William C. 277n
Plantinga, Alvin 97, 130, 133, 152, 179, 183, 242
Plato ix, 124, 130
Ponzio, Augusto 156n
Powell, Mark Allan 233, 308
Power, William L. 159
Prenter, Regin 52, 71
Prestige, G. L. 54
Prichard, Rebecca Button 299
Proudfoot, Wayne 302
Pseudo-Dionysius 252

Rahner, Karl 12, 41, 68, 73n, 78, 101n, 194, 200–5, 207, 212, 214
Raposa, Michael 91, 159
Rappaport, Roy 249
Reid, Duncan 72
Reid, Thomas 152
Rescher, Nicholas 171
Richard of St. Victor 59, 60, 66–67, 73, 75, 80–81, 94, 110, 117
Ricoeur, Paul 128, 143, 156, 165, 182, 261, 279
Robin, Richard 152
Robinson, James M. 259
Rorty, Richard 168–69, 173
Royce, Josiah 94, 100, 117–18, 163, 204n
Rush, Ormond 10, 143, 225n, 259, 272, 275n, 295
Russman, Thomas A. 167n
Rust, Eric C. 229
Ruthven, Jon 249
Ryan, W. F. J. 95n

Sachs, John R. 227
Sanders, James A. 9, 235, 316

Sanneh, Lamin 262
Sartre, Jean-Paul 127–28, 131
Saussure, Ferdinand 157
Savan, David 156
Scalise. Charles J. 3, 316
Schelling, Friedrich 113
Schillebeeckx, Edward 170
Schleiermacher, F. D. E. 118n, 129, 220
Schlitt, Dale 237
Schrag, Calvin 101, 182
Schreiter, Robert J. 268
Schroer, Silvia 46
Schwobel, Christoph 19n
Scott, Martin 41
Scotus, Duns 93, 156n
Searle, John 167
Seebok, Thomas A. 158n
Segal, Alan F. 73
Segovia, Fernando 233
Seung, T. K. 105
Sheriff, John K. 157
Sherry, Patrick 223, 302
Shils, Edward 265
Shults, F. LeRon 13, 98
Smith, Huston 21
Smith, James K. A. 182
Smith, Jonathan Z. 271n
Smith, P. Christopher 266
Smith, Steven G. 15, 135
Smith, Wilfred Cantwell 177n
Snook, Lee 90
Spencer, Herbert 199
Stagg, Frank 106
Stein, Robert H. 256
Stone, Jerome A. 303
Stronstad, Roger 249
Stroup, George W. 277n
Stuhlmacher, Peter 263, 266
Stylianopolous, Theodore 238, 271
Suchocki, Marjorie 19n
Sullivan, John Edward 61
Suurmond, Jean Jacques 40
Swartley, William M. 40
Sykes, Stephen W. 1, 272

Taylor, John V. 28
Tertullian 64
Thiel, John E. 120n, 224, 293
Thiemann, Ronald F. 98, 277n

Thiselton, Anthony 10, 237, 285
Thomas, John Christopher 270
Thorsen, Donald A. D. 316
Tilley, Terrence W. 172, 277n
Tillich, Paul 11–13, 145, 168, 213, 301
Tompkins, Jane P. 233
Torrance, Thomas F. 54, 61, 102, 105, 172
Tracy, David 13, 121, 275
Trevett, Christine 248
Tuveson, Ernest Lee 130n

Vanhoozer, Kevin 4, 10, 11, 169, 254
Van Beeck, Franz Jozef 19n
Van Dusen, Henry Pitt 8, 18
Van Huysteen, J. Wentzel 13, 98, 210n, 300
Vattimo, Gianni 171
Victorin-Vangerud, Nancy M. 74
Vincent of Lérins 292
Von Balthasar, Hans Urs 20, 210, 227–30, 239

Wainwright, William J. 129–30
Walhout, Clarence 259
Walker, Ralph C. S. 171
Wallace, Mark I. 211, 264
Walsh, Brian J. 100
Ware, Kallistos 4
Warfield, Benjamin B. 248–49, 289
Warner, Sharon 211
Warnock, Mary 126–27, 129–30
Watson, Francis 3, 9, 256, 296, 299
Weaver, J. Denny 266
Weinandy, Thomas G. 70, 71, 75
Weinberg, Julius R. 85
Welch, Claude 80n
Welker, Michael 90
Wenk, Matthias 255–56
Westphal, Kenneth R. 164
White, Alan R. 164n, 169
White, James Emery 170
Whitehead, Alfred North ix, 88–91, 93–95, 112–14, 124, 177
Wicks, Jared 238, 293
Wilken, Robert Louis 27n
Williams, D. H. 265n, 313
Wink, Walter 88, 90, 91, 95–96, 113, 147
Winston, David 36
Witherington, Ben, III 39n, 166n
Wittgenstein, Ludwig 168, 175n, 208n, 302
Wolterstorff, Nicholas 254

Wong, Joseph H. P. 41–42, 205n
Wood, Charles 5, 242–43
Worthing, Mark William 101n
Wright, Stephen I.

Yeago, David S. 9
Yong, Amos 73n, 83n, 92n, 148, 166, 222n, 282
Yu, Carver T. 59, 114

Zizioulas, John D. 110–12, 114

Subject Index

abduction 152–56, 199
absolute idealism 104
actuality and actualities 93, 114n, 144
adoptionism 28n
aesthetics 37, 92, 127, 131, 171, 185, 197, 198
affections and affectivity 31, 67, 92, 96, 125, 129, 130, 144, 145, 162, 195, 239, 249
agnosticism 92
allegory 200, 203, 287
alterity 189, 191, 192, 194, 197, 224, 230, 252, 263, 313
ambiguity 43, 44, 87, 124, 139, 191, 211, 212
analogy and analogical language 168, 209, 210
analytic philosophy 167n
anthropology, theological 106, 306–10
apophatic theology 106, 168, 170, 171, 210, 211, 252
authority 219n, 224, 226, 262, 263, 287
axiology 131, 132, 140, 145, 148, 162, 165, 178, 186–88, 194–98

binitarianism 73, 75, 115
biology 113, 114, 179, 230–32
body of Christ; see Church
Buddhism 301, 303, 304
theory of the self 176

Cabalism 203
canon 225, 234, 235, 260, 261, 287–89
categories 27, 28
certainty 159, 162, 181, 211
charismatic movements 33, 208, 248, 249, 285
christology 28–30, 37–40, 170, 257, 258
Church (see also ecclesiology) 32, 39, 46, 103, 149, 201, 208
coinherence 18, 23, 53–55, 70, 72, 75, 76, 91, 93, 104, 215, 220, 300, 315
community 16, 17, 79, 80, 110–15, 162, 163
concreteness (see also actuality and actualities) 92, 103, 104, 117, 138
consciousness 45, 127, 246
conservativism 141, 307, 308
conversion 94, 101, 161, 222, 223, 304

cosmology 112–14, 132, 194–98
creation 35, 36, 43–45, 112, 135, 205, 299
creativity (see also imagination, as creative) 89, 90, 93, 95, 113, 127, 136, 143, 222–24
creed 208, 266, 267, 293, 294
critical realism 79, 83, 92, 101–105, 118, 149, 161, 167, 168, 216
culture 11–13, 233, 301–305

deconstruction 10, 94, 98, 100, 127, 128, 157
deduction 153–56
deism 203, 248
demonic 48, 140, 141, 146, 148, 149, 163, 183, 214, 244, 245, 253, 258
dialectic 12–14, 105–109, 133
discernment 9, 11, 41, 96, 120, 132, 147–49, 178, 183, 197, 214, 226, 233, 236–38, 243, 244, 257, 263, 264, 271, 285, 309
dispensationalism 248, 249, 282, 290, 292
dispositions; see habits
docetism 102
doubt 92, 152, 159, 169, 240–42
dualism 12, 13, 93, 107, 108, 140, 227, 228

Eastern Orthodoxy ix, 64, 65, 72, 73n, 77, 80n, 110–12, 233, 235, 290, 293, 314, 316
ecclesiology (see also Church) 110–12, 234, 235, 278, 293, 313
ecumenical theology 110–12, 284, 285
environment 44, 45, 88, 93, 114, 187, 196, 299, 300
epistemology 6, 8, 18, 19, 22, 79, 96, 97, 120
    finite character 182, 183, 229
    indwelling; see epistemology, participatory
    intersubjective 185
    justification 97, 98, 169n, 171–74
    naturalistic 199n
    partiality 176–78, 197, 229
    participatory 101, 147, 177, 227
    perspectival 178–81, 229
error 176, 178, 181, 182, 226, 227
eschatology (see also truth, as eschatological) 47, 48, 111, 137, 171, 178, 211, 227, 258, 284

ethics 92, 118, 127, 128, 166, 185, 187, 188–94, 196,
    207, 277–79, 288, 300
Evangelicalism and evangelical ix, 172, 238, 290,
    291, 307, 308n
evolution 93, 199
experience 7, 92, 93, 94, 95n, 133, 144, 152, 159,
    208, 246–49, 253

faith 3, 6, 12, 177n
fallibilism and fallibilistic 100, 104, 120, 133, 138,
    152–54, 159, 160, 176–83, 210, 226, 302
falsification 100, 133, 158
feeling; see affections
fideism 99
filioque 55, 63, 64, 69, 71, 72, 94
finitude 182, 183
force fields or fields of force; see law; see Holy
    Spirit, as field of force
foundationalism 97–101, 152
    nonfoundationalism 97, 98, 171
foundational pneumatology 21, 83, 95, 101, 112,
    116, 117, 135, 216
foundational theology 94, 100, 101
freedom 127, 128, 191, 224–26
fundamentalism 141, 232, 249, 290, 291, 312

generals and generality 93, 104, 153, 154, 157, 177,
    206
glossolalia 208, 248–50, 282, 283, 284
Gnosticism and gnosticism 52, 102, 260
grace 12, 70, 130n, 136, 143, 229

habits (see also law) 93, 95, 116, 132, 135, 140,
    144, 147, 155–57, 159, 165, 166, 180, 181, 183,
    205, 206, 212, 214, 224, 233
healing, bodily 250, 282
heart; see affections
heresies 266, 268
hermeneutical circle or spiral 23–25, 27n, 69,
    77, 115, 118, 219, 220, 238, 267, 302, 316
hermeneutics
    biblical 3, 161, 162
    canonical 3–4, 9, 10, 234n, 235, 288, 316
    consensual 1, 219, 316
    eschatological 204
    foundational 10, 305–10
    of culture 301–305
    of life and experience 236, 245–53, 301–305
    of nature 297–300

of suspicion 267, 307, 312
patristic 200
pluralising and pluralistic 259, 271, 305, 306
primitivism 291
spiritual 4, 312
trialectic or trialectical 7, 14, 20, 22, 76, 81,
    109, 217, 219, 220, 264, 269–71, 273, 285,
    286, 311–16
hermeticism 200
historical consciousness 263, 265, 266, 271, 291
history 12, 88, 115, 199, 200, 204, 206, 214
holism 60, 98, 106, 129, 131, 137, 144, 147, 151,
    161, 171
Holy Spirit
    and christology 28–30, 39, 68, 136–39
    and history 47
    and human spirit 41, 45, 46, 192, 227, 230
    and incarnation; see Holy Spirit, and
        christology
    and inspiration 234, 242, 243, 245
    and interpretation 222–30
    and Jesus; see Holy Spirit, and christology
    and meaning 42, 220
    and power 43–46, 134–36, 136
    and rationality 35–43, 83, 84, 115, 228n
    and relationality 28–34, 78, 79, 87, 115, 192,
        193, 315
    and Scripture (see also Scripture, inspira-
        tion) 226
    and transcendence 224, 227–30, 233
    and truth 41, 42, 174, 175
    as field of force 90, 113, 114
    as divine mind 35, 93, 123, 174
    as "mutual love" between Father and
        Son 59–72
    as power of the future 106, 107
    baptism of, and baptism in 30, 46, 71, 249,
        283, 284, 291
    gifts of 32, 222, 224
    life in 43–49, 77, 160, 234, 239, 315
    logic of 50, 54, 76–78, 96, 105–109, 120
    mission of 67–69, 71–74
    unpredictability of 46, 47, 224, 229, 242
idolatry 48, 183, 213, 214, 244
image of God 45, 106, 125, 160, 161, 199
imagination 12, 285, 309
    and fantasy 129
    and liberation 224–26

and religion 144, 145
and theology 141–43, 145, 146
and worldmaking 129, 134, 143–47
as active, constructive; see imagination, as
   creative
as affective 126, 129, 130, 222
as creative (see also creativity) 126–29, 136,
   141, 200, 222–24
as ethical 125, 127, 131
as integrative 129, 130, 136, 137, 144
as normative 129–32, 139
as passive 124, 129, 143
as productive; see imagination, as creative
as reproductive 124, 128, 129, 138
as spiritual 137, 222
as valuational 131, 222
christic or christomorphic 137, 148, 162,
   202, 212
pneumatological; see pneumatological
   imagination
incarnation 16, 28–30, 52, 102, 103
induction 153–56, 158, 164, 178
inference 152, 154, 155, 158, 160, 176, 178, 179, 199
injustice; see justice
intention and intentionality 15, 17, 62, 135, 139,
   140, 145, 148, 163, 165, 180, 221, 243
interpretation 2–7, 19–24, 40, 108, 121, 131, 157,
   180, 225, 229, 238, 247, 264, 313
intuitionism 92, 152
Islam 301, 303, 304

Jesus Christ 28–30, 170, 182, 207, 208, 257, 258
Judaism 16, 36, 193, 262, 301
judgment 166, 190
justice, and injustice 183, 186, 188, 190, 191, 282

language and linguistics 145, 153, 177, 179, 180
law and legality (see also habits) 93, 135, 139,
   140, 147, 153–54, 157, 206
   law of excluded middle 153, 183
   law of non-contradiction 153, 183
liberalism 141, 242
liberation and liberation theology 225, 226,
   266, 279–82, 288, 308
liturgy 208, 213, 266
Logos (see also Word) 11, 15, 16, 102, 103, 137,
   146n, 163, 205, 258

materialism (see also naturalism) 93, 142, 199, 206

metaphor 133, 139, 146, 168, 209, 210n
metaphysics 6, 8, 18, 19, 78–80, 107, 116, 117, 184, 215
   axiological 131, 144
   relational 79, 91, 105, 148, 298, 300
   social 83, 94, 112–14, 148
   substance 16, 56, 79, 85, 86, 89, 93
   triadic 91–96, 101, 116, 148, 215
method in theology 2–7
   apriori and aposteriori 12
   from above 12
   from below 12, 298
   transcendental 12
   trinitarian or triadic 14, 217, 219, 220
miracles 248, 249, 284
modalism 65
modern and modernity 126, 127, 131, 142, 303
monarchianism 52
monism 93
Montanism 248
myth and mythology 168, 172, 180, 209, 279
mystery 106, 210–12, 228, 283, 295
mysticism 200, 204n, 208, 251–53

narrative 128, 133, 171, 172, 180, 209, 247
   metanarratives 100
narrative theology 98, 172, 173, 276–79
natural theology 97, 298
naturalism 139, 140, 212
nature 12, 88, 143, 194–200, 230–32
   hermeneutics of 297–300
   theology of 203–206, 232
neopragmatism 168
nihilism 127, 130, 159
nominalism and anti-nominalism 89–91, 93,
   113, 134, 135, 185, 206n
norms and normative thinking 92, 120, 131–
   33, 139, 140, 149, 162, 163, 186–88, 246, 253,
   263, 264, 295, 296
   ethical 189–94

objectivity 11, 13, 22, 88, 137, 165, 167, 181, 195, 228
oppression 103, 109
orthodoxy 238–40
orthopraxis; see praxis
others and otherness (see also alterity) 102–
   104, 189–94, 198, 215
ontology 21, 67, 78–80, 91, 184, 200
   of personhood 110–12
   pneumatological 112

panentheism 114
pantheism 93, 204n, 205
parables 209
particularity (see also concreteness) 102, 103, 117
patriarchalism 307, 308
Pentecost, and Pentecost, Day of 30, 47, 52, 69, 103
Pentecostalism and Pentecostal theology ix, 208, 248–51, 282–85, 290–92, 312, 316
perception 92, 127, 129, 130, 144, 152–56, 158, 159, 177, 199
perichoresis; see coinherence
phenomenology 92, 95n
    of the face 189–94
physics 90, 113, 199
pneumatological imagination 22, 43, 76, 78, 120, 133–41, 147, 160–63, 183, 184, 192, 194, 197, 198, 202, 206–208, 212–14, 216, 223
pneumatological rationality; see Holy Spirit, logic of
pneumatology; see Holy Spirit
pneumatology of quest 8, 21–23, 95, 115, 121
poetry 128, 209
possibility 89, 92, 93, 114n, 125, 144
postfoundationalism 13, 97, 98
postmodernism and postmodernity 11, 42, 99, 101, 128, 130, 142, 171, 278
pragmatism 91, 94–96, 132, 155, 158, 160, 162
praxis 237, 238
predestination 99, 106
process philosophy 88–91, 112–14, 177
process theology 90, 114
prophecy and the prophetic 209, 233, 248, 282

rationalism 35, 77, 141, 203
realism; see critical realism
recapitulation 60–62, 68, 69
reception 10, 259, 269, 272, 273, 295
reconciliation 31–34
reference 157, 158, 243
Reformed epistemology 97, 152
relationality 15, 58, 59, 79, 80, 84–96, 192, 194, 196
relations 85–87
relativism 94, 158, 159, 173, 184
religion 12, 13, 143, 301, 302
religious language 209
repentance 62, 251, 258
resurrection 30, 32, 134, 135, 168, 230, 246, 299
revelation 12, 13, 102, 199, 203, 204, 210, 214, 232, 240, 245, 248, 298, 308n

ritual 213, 249–51
Romanticism 127
Roman Catholicism 200, 232, 235, 249, 250, 290, 293, 295, 316
root metaphors 133

sacraments 201, 202, 248, 249, 291, 295
salvation 31, 32, 45–47, 60, 61, 71, 166, 201, 279
sanctification 31, 160, 237, 238, 240, 283
science 12, 13, 162, 200, 298, 299, 302, 311, 312
Scripture 11, 40, 199, 200, 203, 204, 208, 226, 233–36, 247, 253–65
    inspiration of 242, 243, 314
self and selfhood 10, 42, 56, 62, 126, 128, 191
semantics 153, 155n, 209
semiotics 6, 91, 156–59, 161, 180, 185, 188, 202, 247
    theological; see symbols, theology of
sin and sinfulness 31, 32, 48, 62, 125, 160, 166, 182, 183, 226, 233. 237
skepticism 158, 159, 184
sociality; see community
sola scriptura 52, 248, 313, 314
sola spiritus 311, 312
sola scriptura 314, 315
song and singing 209, 250
soteriology; see salvation
speaking in tongues; see glossolalia
speech-act theory 254–56, 259
spirit and spiritual reality 15, 90, 96, 135, 138–41, 183, 185, 206
Spirit Christology; see Holy Spirit, and incarnation
spirit, Holy; see Holy Spirit
structuralism and poststructuralism 6, 10, 16, 84
subjectivism and subjectivity 11, 13, 22, 88, 92, 94, 129, 130, 137, 139, 149, 195, 221, 228, 230–36, 312
subordinationism 52, 55, 74, 138, 215
symbols 93, 157, 158, 168, 200–202
    cosmological 203–205, 212
    religious 146, 279
    theology of 91, 185, 204, 207–14
syncretism 262, 302, 304, 309

telos and teleology; see intention and intentionality
testimony 247, 291
texts and textuality 4–6, 8, 10, 11, 128
theological method; see method in theology

theological semiotics; see symbols, theology of
theology
    apophatic 72, 73n
    biblical 287–89
    dogmatic 20, 292–96
    Eastern Orthodox; see Eastern Orthodoxy
    fundamental 20, 97, 275, 305–10
    historical 289–92
    mediating 1, 13
    practical 275–86
    public of 304, 306
    systematic 288
theosis 228
Torah 260
totalism, totalizationism, and totalitarianism 84, 98, 100, 104, 117
tradition 11, 224, 233–36, 264–73, 289–92, 313
transversal rationality 101
Trinity
    and psychology 62, 66
    and relationality 56–59
    classical understanding, 18, 53–56
    constructive trinitarianism 21
    economic and immanent 67, 69, 72, 78, 115
    eschatological 106, 115
    mutual love theory 78, 91, 94, 101, 115, 215, 220, 226

social doctrine of 80
trinitarian structure 9, 14–18
tri-theism 80
two hands model 16, 50–60, 64, 65, 71, 78, 87, 101, 115, 138, 215, 220, 258
truth 22, 41, 120, 130, 216, 217
    and Jesus Christ 170, 286
    as coherence 169, 171–75, 286, 288, 289
    as correspondence 167–71, 296, 305
    as disclosure 165
    as eschatological 171, 175, 184, 273, 288, 296, 297, 305
    as performative 165
    as pragmatic 155, 164–67, 169, 276, 285, 286

universals (see also habits) 93, 127, 154, 177

vague and vagueness 104, 144, 152–55, 183, 211, 264
value and valuational (see axiology)
verification 100, 158

Wesleyan Holiness movement 282, 283, 290, 291
Wesleyan quadrilateral 14, 316
Wisdom 35–40
Word; see Logos
worship 239, 240, 242, 250, 280, 283